Globalizing Management

Globalizing Management

Creating and Leading the Competitive Organization

Edited by

Vladimir Pucik

Noel M. Tichy

Carole K. Barnett

John Wiley & Sons, Inc.

New York • Chichester • Brisbane • Toronto • Singapore

In recognition of the importance of preserving what has been written, it is a policy of John Wiley & Sons, Inc. to have books of enduring value published in the United States printed on acid-free paper, and we exert our best efforts to that end.

Copyright © 1992 by John Wiley & Sons, Inc.

All rights reserved. Published simultaneously in Canada.

Reproduction or translation of any part of this work beyond that permitted by Section 107 or 108 of the 1976 United States Copyright Act without the permission of the copyright owner is unlawful. Requests for permission or further information should be addressed to the Permissions Department, John Wiley & Sons, Inc.

This publication is designed to provide accurate and authoritative information in regard to the subject matter covered. It is sold with the understanding that the publisher is not engaged in rendering legal, accounting, or other professional services. If legal advice or other expert assistance is required, the services of a competent professional person should be sought. *From a Declaration of Principles jointly adopted by a Committee of the American Bar Association and a Committee of Publishers.*

Library of Congress Cataloging-in-Publication Data

Globalizing management : Creating and Leading the Competitive Organization /
   edited by Vladimir Pucik, Noel M. Tichy, Carole K. Barnett.
     p. cm.
  Includes index.
  ISBN 0-471-50821-7 (cloth)
  1. International business enterprises—Personnel management.
I. Pucik, Vladimir. II. Tichy, Noel M. III. Barnett, Carole K.
HF5549.5.E45G63 1992
658—dc20   92-1084

Printed in the United States of America.
10 9 8 7 6 5 4 3 2 1

Printed and bound by Malloy Lithographing, Inc.

To the next generation of global citizens, our children:

David and Mai
Michelle, Nicole, and Danielle
Elizabeth and Andrew

who inspire our inquiry
and searching

Preface

The objective of our book is to present a new synthesis of knowledge about globalization and organizational life. A central theme is how human resource management practices in global firms respond to ever-increasing change in world politics, economics, technology, and culture. We believe that the unrelenting demand for continuous improvement in global human resource management practices makes this collection of chapters a timely addition to the many streams of research on managing for global competitiveness.

We hope our work will lend insight in two realms by dealing realistically with today's competitive problems as well as tomorrow's challenges. To that end, this book strives to organize some of the latest reflections about global human resource management practices and strategies in a way that may be useful to business leaders and academics alike. We strongly believe that advancement in a complex, new age demands ongoing partnership between these interdependent communities both in research and practice. And we maintain that the time is long past due for progressive, collaborative approaches to meeting the human resources challenges created by the globalization trend.

Following our philosophy as advocates of team work, this volume draws on an interdisciplinary world forum for the most promising concepts and methods of managing and developing people in global organizations. Leading scholars from Europe, Asia, and North America offer a variety of ideas that contribute to a new vision of the global firm in a contemporary competitive environment.

Our dialogue with this consortium of scholars and researchers originated in 1983 when we first conceived our plans for an international human resource management conference. Many of the contributors to this book joined us in France during the summer of 1985 to begin sharing ideas about global organizing and to establish an agenda for research and practice. The forum was informal, highly interactive, and yielded many ideas that were subsequently transformed into a special issue of the *Human Resource Management* journal.

Far from being the culmination of the 1985 symposium, the papers from the gathering in France animated further inquiry, and a second symposium was held in Japan in 1987 to continue our search for innovative ideas about managing human resources in an increasingly complex global era. Many of the original participants from 1985 were joined in the 1987 symposium by other members of the academic and business circles, most notably from the Asia-Pacific area. A second special issue of the *Human Resource Management* journal was successfully published, spurring us on to further research.

When we decided to organize this volume, it became our vehicle for generating yet a new set of papers by some of the most highly regarded scholars in the field of organizational studies. Thus *Globalizing Management: Creating and Leading the Competitive Organization* comprises a core group of previously published articles, along with a large number of original chapters expressly developed to complete our intellectual and managerial agenda.

The scope of this book is intentionally broad in order to provide relevance for practitioners and academics in diverse industries, disciplines, and nations. We hope that our approach will allow members of one domain to inform the others with fresh insights, thereby strengthening the potential for theoretical and practical advances.

Many individuals have influenced and supported the development of this volume—executives, graduate students, and faculty colleagues. The range and quality of the work presented in *Globalizing Management: Creating and Leading the Competitive Organization* are a measure of the kind of collaborative commitment that can be generated when individuals are brought together in a common endeavor to learn. Every contributor to this book was instrumental in its development, giving unwaveringly of time for writing and/or conferencing, energy to keep the project going in spite of competing demands, and ingenuity in the face of stubborn old theoretical assumptions. The work has often been difficult and the progress toward publication slow. Thus, finally, we are indebted to our editor, John Mahaney, whose patience, steady support, and fidelity to our vision of this book made it a reality.

May 1992

Vladimir Pucik
Tokyo, Japan and Ithaca, New York, U.S.A.

Noel M. Tichy
Ann Arbor, Michigan, U.S.A.

Carole K. Barnett
Ann Arbor, Michigan, U.S.A.

Contributors

Carole K. Barnett
The University of Michigan
Department of Organizational
  Psychology
Ann Arbor, Michigan

Christopher A. Bartlett
Harvard Business School
Boston, Massachusetts

Michael I. Brimm
INSEAD/European Institute of
  Business Administration
Fontainebleau, France

Ram Charan
Independent Consultant
Dallas, Texas

Yves Doz
INSEAD/European Institute of
  Business Administration
Fountainebleau, France

Paul A. L. Evans
INSEAD/European Institute of
  Business Administration
Fontainebleau, France

Charles J. Fombrun
New York University
Stern School of Business
New York, New York

Sumantra Ghoshal
INSEAD/European Institute of
  Business Administration
Fontainebleau, France

Geert Hofstede
University of Limburg at
  Maastricht
The Netherlands

Manfred F. R. Kets de Vries
INSEAD/European Institute of
  Business Administration
Fontainebleau, France

Stephen J. Kobrin
University of Pennsylvania
The Wharton School
Philadelphia, Pennsylvania

André Laurent
INSEAD/European Institute of
  Business Administration
Fontainebleau, France

Peter Lorange
University of Pennsylvania
The Wharton School
Philadelphia, Pennsylvania

Christine Mead
INSEAD/European Institute of
  Business Administration
Fontainebleau, France

Ikujiro Nonaka
Hitotsubashi University
School of Commerce
Tokyo, Japan

C. K. Prahalad
The University of Michigan
School of Business Administration
Ann Arbor, Michigan

Vladimir Pucik
Cornell University
School of Industrial and Labor
  Relations
Ithaca, New York

Susan C. Schneider
INSEAD/European Institute of
  Business Administration
Fontainebleau, France

Hirotaka Takeuchi
Hitotsubashi University
School of Commerce
Tokyo, Japan

Noel M. Tichy
The University of Michigan
School of Business Administration
Ann Arbor, Michigan

Stefan Wally
New York University
Stern School of Business
New York, New York

Hideki Yoshihara
Kobe University
Research Institute for Economics
  and Business Administration
Kobe, Japan

Contents

Introduction

Vladimir Pucik

As the world economy moves into the 1990s, new environmental trends are exerting a profound impact on the patterns of global competition. Some of these trends are long-term and their competitive implications are well understood—for example, the ever-increasing investments across national boundaries spearheaded by large U.S., European, and Japanese multinational firms and improvements in communication and transportation that facilitate international exchange of goods, people, and information. Other developments happened quickly, creating uncertainty and demanding a swift strategic response, such as the breaking down of the market barriers within the European Community and the reunification of Germany together with democratization and perestroika in Eastern Europe and the former Soviet Union.

While all these events are making headlines, other more subtle trends are influencing the effectiveness of global competitive strategies. Rapid technological changes have transformed the time dimension of competition. Where in the past new entrants had years of monopoly to exploit their technological advantages, such windows of opportunities have shrunk to mere months today (contrast the worldwide expansion of Xerox with that of Apple, or consider Japanese and Korean entry into the electronics field). Speed and quality in addressing the needs of worldwide customers will greatly influence who the next winning firms are going to be.

However, not only is the technology-driven competitive advantage more and more temporary, but the diffusion of technological know-how around the world is also much quicker than at any time in the past. New powerful global competitors are emerging in countries previously on the periphery of global economic activities, such as Korea and Taiwan. Global competitive conditions are also affected by a rapid internationalization of service businesses, from advertising and data processing to investment and consumer banking, much of it again driven by the emergence of new boundary-crossing technologies.

The globalization of competitive capabilities is also accompanied by a globalization of market opportunities. In a number of product lines, basic customer requirements are similar, if not identical, in many of the major markets. Although, in spite of earlier high hopes, sizeable income differentials between "rich" and "poor" countries remain, large pools of "world-class" consumers have emerged in areas other than the traditional triad of North America, Western Europe, and Japan. In order to reach all prospective customers with "global" products adapted to the local needs, global firms are relying on strategic alliances of various kinds, from simple technological and marketing agreements to complex multi–joint venture arrangements. In this sense, globalization demands are transforming the boundaries of the firm.

All this means an intensification of global competition in most areas of manufacturing and services. The old rules and prescriptions are not valid any more. For any firm to succeed in the new global competition, a long-term, forward-looking dynamism, operational flexibility, and continuous improvement in all facets of its business activities are more important than its current size and short-term performance. Only through a sustained effort to do its very best can a global firm maintain the high level of internal energy required for success. Market leadership and superior financial performance cannot be upheld without a relentless drive to continuously renew the firm's competitive edge. However, there is no trade-off between long-term and short-term business objectives; rather, the two sets of goals are complementary.

One of the key characteristics of the best global competitors is an emphasis on the long-term accumulation of competitive capabilities. These firms' strategic intent is clear: long-term product/market leadership in the areas in which they have chosen to compete. However, a single competitive advantage, be it low production cost, high quality, or fast delivery, is not sufficient to provide lasting superiority in the global market; some competitors will always be able to bridge the gap in a relatively short period of time. To be effective players in the global competitive environment, firms have to master a wide variety of skills. The strategic objective of a globally competitive firm is therefore the creation of continuously evolving and interdependent layers of organizational capabilities that reinforce and enhance each other across all core businesses, functions, and markets.

While each capability (high quality, low cost, rapid design change, precise delivery) can perhaps be duplicated by a determined competitor, a globally interdependent organizational infrastructure is hard to build or copy. Managing the various forms of interdependence that involve extensive coordination and integration across countries, products, and business functions becomes one of the most important tasks for the firm to master. Its ability to do so effectively becomes a competitive advantage in itself.

The various dimensions of competitive advantage in global firms have one thing in common. They are all embedded in organizational systems, processes, and cultures and they reflect the capacity of a collective of people to think and act in a fashion that transcends the traditional limitations of an ethnocentric framework. To develop and manage a global organization implies developing and managing people who can think, lead, and act from a global perspective, who possess a "global mind" as well as "global skills." Not one, two, or a dozen "international" specialists, but a multitude of executives, managers, and professionals are needed to form the core of a global firm.

We believe that the process of globalization requires a radical transformation of our thinking about the role and tools of human resource management in multinational firms. This is what our book is all about. The idea that human resource management can and should make a contribution to the competitive strategy of a global firm is a concept that unites all the contributors to this volume. Some may differ on how this may be accomplished, as we have deliberately chosen to maximize the variety of viewpoints presented. We all, however, share a firm conviction that the secret to success in global competition lies in managing people.

Human Resource Management in Global Companies

The idea of editing a book on human resource management in the global environment began to crystallize in 1985, when the *Human Resource Management Journal* co-sponsored a symposium on international issues in human resource management at INSEAD in Fontainebleau. We were at that point disheartened with the state of knowledge in this area, since much of what had been written on international human resource management covered only specific, narrow topics, such as expatriate selection, training, repatriation, or technical aspects of expatriate compensation. Instead, we wanted to look at the key competitive and environmental challenges facing global corporations and define major strategic tasks facing the human resource management area over the next decade.

Approximately fifty academics and executives from Europe, Japan, and the United States spent several days in informal discussions on the state of international human resource management and its agenda for the future. We focused on the issues of global leadership, cultural diversity in management, and new organizational forms necessary for global competitiveness. Two years later, a second symposium with a similar format and agenda was held in Japan. This time, the discussion emphasized strategic alliances, global coordination and integration, and staffing and development processes. A number of chapters presented here are based on contributions made originally at these two workshops. Meanwhile, we began to pursue several major research and executive development projects related to human resource management in global firms, the results and experiences of which are also reflected in this book.

Our objective is to answer some of the most critical questions regarding human resources in global firms. What is the contribution of human resources activities to competitive strategies of a global firm? What is the value of cultural diversity, and what are its costs? How can executives strike a proper balance between the needs of global businesses, those of the country affiliates, and those of the whole corporation? How can they develop a multicultural top management group? What role should human resources play in the management of strategic alliances?

In contrast, we have not spent much time building typologies of global strategies or abstract conceptual frameworks. For example, we are not concerned with the classification of firms operating outside of their national boundaries as international, multinational, global, or transnational. (We use these terms freely, as long as it is clear what kind of a firm we have in mind.) Nor are we concerned with what human resource practices are related to what type of MNC. Our focus is on the globalization process through which firms achieve regional and global market differentiation while pushing forward with a rationalization of operations, selective geographical diversification, and far-reaching alliances that involve them in cooperative transnational networks and strategic groupings.

Two key ideas permeate our understanding of global competitive strategies: diversity and complementarity. We believe that globalization implies accepting that cultural diversity in management composition and management style contribute to the competitive advantage of the global firm. We also believe that effective globalization calls for the pursuit of a number of management approaches that on paper may seem contradictory, but that can be truly effective only through their simultaneous and balanced application. Global human resource management can then provide an organizing framework for developing and managing people who are comfortable with the strategic and operational paradoxes embedded in global firms and who are capable of harnessing the resulting cultural diversity.

The first part of the book, therefore, deals with the environment of global human resource management. We look at its competitive context by examining the role of human resource management in global competition; its strategic context by focusing on the linkage of human resource management with global corporate strategies; and its cultural context by relating human resource management to national cultures.

The second part of the book is devoted to specific functional aspects of human resource management that have a unique dimension in a global firm: organizational design issues focused on structural and process requirements of a global organization; the development of global managers and executives addressed from several conceptual viewpoints; and the role of human resource management in strategic alliances and other collaborative ventures.

The third part of the book, applying a comparative perspective, centers on specific human resource issues facing, in particular, American and Japanese multinational firms. The final chapters then review the action agendas for top management in global firms and for their human resources executives, as well as for management scholars involved in research and teaching on this topic.

The Competitive Context

Changes in the contemporary global economy are in the background of many of the emerging challenges facing human resource management. Vast macrosocietal changes increasingly bind countries into interdependent communities of nations in which goods, capital, and people move freely; but between these there remains a patchwork of regulatory and cultural barriers. Fombrun and Wally argue that to remain profitable in this new global age requires firms to commit themselves to transnationalism and to internalize strategies likely to lead to success in global competition. Implementing successful global strategies then requires careful attention to the paradoxes created in the design of corporate structures, the management of human resources, and the maintenance of multifaceted company cultures.

Tichy, Brimm, Charan, and Takeuchi examine the concept of global competition from the perspective of transformational leadership and "global mindset" essential for survival in global competition in the 1990s. They see the key competitive advantage of the global firm as the ability to continuously transform itself. They argue that corporations and their leaders must learn to engineer and manage such transformations or they will inevitably lose in the competition ahead. In their view, global leaders must have the capacity to turn threats into opportunities; to motivate people to excel, not just to survive; to drive innovations to the market place at an increasingly faster rate; and to operate globally through cross-cultural problem solving and team building.

Pucik reviews the linkages of human resource management in global firms to competitive advantage. He identifies three principal organizational capabilities as sources of sustainable competitive edge: the creation of a competitive culture inside the global firm, the existence of organizational learning systems based on the accumulation of invisible assets, and a strong organizational emphasis on continuous improvement. These three capabilities are then linked with specific human resource strategies, from staffing and development to organizational design. Pucik also discusses the main obstacles confronting global firms in the implemention of competitive human resource strategies and suggests concrete steps to enact the necessary changes.

The Strategic Context

The second part of the book deals primarily with the requirements of organization and human resource management systems driven by global strategies.

First, Evans and Doz discuss the human resource management problems in global firms in terms of dualities—organizational properties that seem contradictory or paradoxical, but that are in fact complementary. Evans and Doz point to the emerging consensus that the competitive advantage of the transnational firm lies in its organizational ability to cope with the multidimensional and complex demands of the global business environment. Using the concept of cultural layering (building new capabilities into the organization's culture while reinforcing its past cultural strengths) as an example, they show how management governance in a transnational enterprise becomes a matter of balancing opposite forces and using those forces as the motor of organizational development and change, with human resource management as the critical and essential tool.

The concern with the limitations of a structural solution to current strategic problems forms the core of Bartlett and Ghoshal's chapter. They argue that in many of the world's multinationals, strategic thinking has outdistanced organizational capability. Many have adopted elaborate organizational matrices that actually impair their ability to implement sophisticated business strategies. Bartlett and Ghoshal propose three techniques to improve strategic coordination across the various units of a global firm: development of a clear, consistent corporate vision internalized by managers worldwide; use of training and career-path management to broaden individual perspectives and increase identification with corporate goals; and co-opting all managers and organizational groups by inviting them to contribute to the corporate agenda and giving them direct responsibility for implementation.

From a complementary perspective, Doz and Prahalad analyze the contribution of human resource management in helping diversified MNCs meet the challenge of combining the strategic control driven by the imperatives of global competition and the strategic variety demanded by local market needs. As they see it, global firms need to develop "balanced" managers who have multifocal vision and who are sensitive to the demands for local responsiveness and opportunities for global integration. Doz and Prahalad explore the specific agenda that both HR professionals and top management must work through in order to build up quality and effectiveness in the MNC's human resource management process.

The Cultural Context

Hofstede's chapter provides the basic framework for the discussion of cultural influence on human resource management in global firms. Building on a variety of cross-cultural studies, Hofstede identifies the ability to cope with cultural relativity as the key requirement for tomorrow's global managers. Such familiar aspects of organizational life as organization structure, leadership styles, motivation patterns, training and development models, and indeed the very concept of "human resource" management are, according to

Hofstede, culturally relative and therefore need to be reconsidered when national boundaries are crossed. To facilitate such cross-cultural adaptation, he argues for more recruitment of top managers from different nationalities, acculturation through carefully planned career moves, and cultural awareness training.

In contrast to national cultures, corporate culture has often been described as the glue that holds global organizations together by providing cohesiveness and coherence among its parts. Multinational companies are increasingly interested in promoting corporate culture to improve the control, coordination, and integration of their subsidiaries. Yet these subsidiaries are embedded in local national cultures whose basic assumptions about people and the world may differ from the national and corporate culture of the multinational's home office. These differences may hinder the acceptance and implementation of human resource practices, in particular on questions of selection and socialization, career planning, appraisal, and compensation. Schneider discusses the cultural assumptions underlying these HRM practices as they may differ from those of the national culture of the subsidiary. She also reviews the issues concerning the use of corporate culture as a mechanism for globalization.

Finally, Laurent perceives the challenge faced by the field of international human resource management as a multidimensional puzzle located at the crossroad of national and organizational cultures. His research findings conclude that deep-seated managerial assumptions are strongly shaped by national cultures and appear quite insensitive to the more transient culture of organizations. However, how many headquarter executives genuinely believe they can learn from their foreign subsidiaries? How many multinationals implement such a rare belief by internationalizing headquarters staff and top management? Therefore, Laurent advocates that efforts should be directed toward the development of forward-looking international corporate cultures that could provide the framework for solving these vital issues in international HRM.

The Developmental Context

A number of authors identify the development of executives with a "global mindset" as one of the key strategic tasks facing human resource management in multinational firms. Kets de Vries and Mead then review the factors that enhance or hinder the process of developing such leaders. Among various desirable traits and skills, they emphasize cultural empathy and adaptability and consider a number of approaches to selection, management development, and organizational structure that promote the necessary cross-cultural capabilities. Apart from predispositions which stem from early childhood development and socialization, the authors identify a number of career development factors that may have an impact on the creation of a "global mindset" among high potential executives. In particular, they advocate that future top executives in global firms should have the opportunity for early cross-cultural experience through assignments in different countries.

The theme of global leadership development is expanded by Tichy. He argues that the successful development of future leaders of global corporations requires a radical transformation of thinking about basic premises of human resource development techniques. He defines five characteristics of global leaders: a global mindset, global leadership skills, an ability to lead cross-cultural teams, energy and talent to participate in global networking, and skills as global change agent. He contends that traditional training and development approaches fall far short of the mark in what is required for globalization. In contrast, the chapter discusses practical approaches to making management development an integral part of a global transformation process by linking compressed action learning with a firm's competitive strategies.

The Collaborative Context

Joint ventures, licensing agreements, project-based cooperative networks, and franchises are becoming commonplace arrangements for implementing strategy in global markets. Lorange considers six critical human resource management issues as they apply to each of these four types of cooperative ventures: assignment of managers to cooperative ventures; the human resource transferability issues; managers' concentration on operating versus strategic issues; the human resource competency issues (avoiding biases); loyalty issues; and career planning issues. He proposes that the cooperative venture must be seen as a vehicle to produce not only financial rewards, but also managerial capabilities that can be used later in other strategic settings.

Such capabilities are particularly important when firms are engaged in alliances that involve competitive collaboration—cooperative relationships with their existing or potential competitors. Pucik, in his chapter, argues that unless MNCs that are involved in competitive collaboration can build the capability to accumulate invisible assets through a carefully planned and executed process of organizational learning, they will jeopardize both their competitive advantage and control over the strategic direction of their cooperative ventures. His chapter defines organizational learning as the critical strategic task for human resource managers in MNCs, lists the key obstacles to organizational learning in international strategic alliances, and discusses the agenda for transforming the specific components of the HR system, from selection and development to appraisal and compensation practices, to support the organizational learning process.

The Comparative Context

In spite of the trend toward globalization, the concept of a globalized firm still reflects only an ideal organizational form, since nearly all multinational firms remain embedded in their respective cultural spheres, in particular those in the United States and Japan. It is therefore important to assess specific globalization issues in their distinct comparative framework. From this perspective, Kobrin examines the well-known fact that over the last two decades the number of U.S. managers working abroad as expatriates has decreased relative to the size of the international business activities conducted by U.S.–based multinationals. Is this decrease simply a positive indication of the globalization of U.S.–based multinational firms? Or are local (or third-country) nationals proliferating primarily because of cost reductions or to minimize conflict with host governments and other local interest groups? Kobrin looks beyond these valid—but surface—factors that contribute to expatriate phase-out and argues instead that deeper reasons dominate, in particular Americans' difficulty in adapting to overseas assignments. As international experience is becoming a condition for ascent to top executive jobs, would that mean that many Americans will be eliminated from the competition?

In the following chapter Bartlett and Yoshihara focus on the challenges facing Japanese multinationals. They argue that Japanese MNCs need a massive reorientation of their management structures and processes in order to redefine the basic role and responsibilities of their foreign operations and to restructure the relationship with the parent company. A three-stage program of development of the multinational organization is recommended: (1) resources should be transferred; (2) local knowledge, skills, and expertise must be developed, so that (3) responsibilities delegated to local subsidiaries can be expanded.

Finally, the dilemma facing Japanese multinationals is also addressed by Nonaka. He foresees the necessity for a new style of human resource management—creative HRM—to foster the self-renewal of Japanese firms whose production-oriented paradigms and traditional personnel systems may be incongruent with today's fiercely competitive global environment. The new style of management is based on three principal thrusts: (1) creation of a strategic vision in the firm with active employee participation and commitment, (2) emphasis on the role of middle managers in the self-renewal process through a new "middle-up-down" management style, and (3) transformation of the career development, appraisal, reward, and staffing systems to support a multidimensional personnel management program that recognizes the individual as a source of creativity and self-renewal for the multinational firm. This is, of course, a prescription with an appeal not limited to global firms originating in Japan.

Global Research and Teaching in the 1990s

The need to reassess traditional models for institutional administration, research, and teaching has never been more urgent. Whatever innovations we conceive today must be embraced and advanced by the next generation of managers and academics. The challenge of educating and enlightening tomorrow's global citizens thus falls to today's teachers and managers. Now is the time for us to develop an intellectual and managerial agenda that will satisfy the needs of global organizations and their members in the year 2000.

Barnett's chapter describes an innovative program for teaching, research, and managerial practice on a new, interdisciplinary scale in U.S. business schools. Based on an industry/academia conference, she presents a novel and fluid paradigm of MBA education in a global environment. The new mandate is to redesign the entire MBA experience, not just the curriculum. Industry/academia alliances in classroom teaching and real-world training are the mechanisms by which executives, faculty, and students can become part of an ongoing laboratory experiment on globalization. Only interdisciplinary faculty collaboration, blending functional concentrations into the total business process, can produce students who are problem-driven, team-oriented, and appropriately sensitized to the realities of managing global businesses.

Prahalad argues that although many senior managers are experimenting with approaches designed to cope with the competitive demands of the new order, the academic community in leading U.S. business schools seems less willing to experiment and innovate. His basic thesis is that the need for active collaboration between practitioners (managers) and researchers (academics) has never been more pronounced. But the two groups are running the risk of drifting apart, thereby sacrificing an opportunity for building a mutually beneficial symbiotic relationship. Against the backdrop of the diversified multinational corporation, Prahalad outlines many of the competitive challenges in today's global environment, examines the mismatch between managerial and academic agendas, and outlines an approach for developing a single agenda with utility to both communities.

Global Human Resource Management for the 1990s

Over the last 10 to 15 years, the rules of global competition have changed dramatically. No doubt, they will change again in the future. In fact, changing the rules is part of the new game. For better or worse, the global market has no other referee than the customer, and there is no penalty for introducing a new set of rules into the competition, unpleasant as this may be to other competitors. The playing field for global competition is not even and never will be. It handicaps those who are parochial in their outlook, who are committed to globalization in words, but not in action, who lack flexibility, who are uneasy about uncertainty, and who suspect diversity.

This book rests on the premise that effective global human resource management is a powerful competitive weapon. Removing the competitive handicap of parochialism is therefore a strategic task facing not only human resource specialists, but line managers and executives as well, from the CEO down. We hope in this respect that our book highlights not only the most critical challenges regarding the management of people in global firms, but also provides some ideas for specific programmatic actions aimed at speeding up and deepening the globalization process. Relevance is the key test of our ideas.

We also hope that our book stimulates other scholars and human resource professionals to review our contributions, rethink our questions, and propose additional solutions. Most importantly, we look forward to many of our colleagues extending our inquiry, as the global field of human resource management is of course broader than what is presented here. We had to make some hard choices on what topics to include and what issues we would like to leave for later exploration. We are biased toward strategic over operational issues, toward issues linked with global strategies over technical human resource problems, and toward issues cutting across countries and industries over specific agendas.

Finally, we anticipate that the very dynamism of the globalization process will continue to recast the spectrum of critical issues that may influence how people are managed in global firms. As champions of continuous revitalization, we would not be dismayed that some of our priorities will turn out to be only temporary, that some of our solutions will have only limited application. Our concern is with the way of thinking about human resources, about the world, about competition. We advocate an open, critical, and proactive approach. We are therefore looking forward to the time when our current frameworks will become obsolete so that our energies could be applied to yet unknown opportunities.

The Competitive Context

1

Global Entanglements
The Structure of Corporate Transnationalism

Charles J. Fombrun
Stefan Wally

Every man takes the limits of his own field of vision for the limits of the world.
ARTHUR SCHOPENHAUER

Corporations increasingly struggle with technological and political changes that affect the transnational mobility of capital, information, and people. Where national boundaries once provided a safe haven for the orderly unfolding of domestic competition, a new world order born of the collapse of communist regimes in Eastern Europe now offers the tantalizing possibility that large but traditionally insulated markets will soon open up to foreign trade. It has also stimulated a worldwide deregulation of domestic markets that pits local firms ever more directly against seasoned rivals based abroad. Such permeable national boundaries demand that firms have an ability to sustain their competitive advantage on a global scale.

Swept aside in this vortex of change are the old fears about multinationals that legislators and social critics voiced throughout the 1960s.[1] Replacing them is a clarion call for a liberalization of markets—an easing of legislative, regulatory, and economic constraints on the international op-

15

erations of firms. Where foreign direct investment (FDI) once signalled a loss of national hegemony, it is now understood as a sign of international confidence in the local economy. Where corporate behemoths were once feared for the power they were thought to wield, size and flexibility now constitute the *sine qua non* of efficiency and competitiveness.

And transnational companies are taking full advantage of the welcome. At the business level, firms have learned to locate operations where factor costs are lowest be they in production, distribution, or research. In the financially unstable world of the 1980s, managers learned to juggle local taxes and exchange rate imbalances by transferring revenues denominated in local currencies to maximize global profitability. They also learned to better hedge against political risk by forming partnerships with local governments and businesses.

Perhaps most important, however, in the last decade firms have extended their global operations through an aggressive strategy that combined corporate-level mergers with collective-level networking. The wave of global mergers that began in the late 1970s and peaked in the mid-1980s consolidated horizontal competitors from different countries and created pyramids of capital that today dwarf in size the firms produced by the three previous merger waves of 1900, 1920, and 1970. At the same time, managers initiated a plethora of contractual arrangements and joint ventures that now fuse them into strategic constellations, shifting the basis of competition from the traditional industry level to that of the alliance network.[2]

Difficult questions are raised by the pattern of global development that these corporate strategies present to us. Left behind in this scenario, for instance, are the net-oil importing developing nations whose plight appears progressively more serious as the industrialized nations cross the second industrial divide into the information age.[3] Shackled by the prodigious levels of debt accumulated in the 1970s, disfavored by transnational firms whose activities require an increasingly sophisticated supporting infrastructure, outdone by automated technologies requiring little unskilled labor input, these countries, which represent over 50 percent of the world's population, find themselves rapidly spiralling toward the world's outer periphery of development. Can the industrialized world—and the corporations responsible for industrialization—afford to ignore them?

As firms' tentacles involve them in ever more distant locations and businesses, their activities have become difficult to trace, let alone monitor, and the lack of an institutional superstructure to oversee their growth is starkly evident. No world government exists, and we have all too few global norms. Moreover, none of our admittedly limited international institutions have been empowered with the necessary resources or authority to sanction corporate activities that span the globe. Promising beginnings are evident in the regionalization of economic activity in Western Europe, North America, and Asia-Pacific and in the sudden return to prominence of the United Nations. These constitute tentative first steps in shaping a coherent global superstructure capable of displacing the anarchical and anachronistic nation-state system under which corporations still operate.

Not surprisingly, corporate strategies, lacking a normative framework to guide their actions, fail to incorporate many socially relevant externalities into their cost-benefit calculations. So corporate catastrophes abound: Consider the thousands of lives lost in Union Carbide's debacle in Bhopal, India; the ecological disaster wrought by Exxon's oil spill in Alaska; the Three Mile Island and Chernobyl nuclear reactor malfunctions. These industrial crises present many quandaries: When catastrophic accidents occur, who has jurisdiction? How should damage be gauged? What does "fair" compensation to victims mean? Who are the actual victims when public goods are irreversibly damaged? Such questions are likely to proliferate as firms' activities rely on ever more complex technologies, capable of doing enormous ecological damage and placing larger aggregates of humankind in life-threatening situations.[4] Industrial accidents also become more likely as firms, confronted by competitive pressures to rationalize global activities, cut costs while they simultaneously defend and pursue profitability and market share. In all too many countries, externalities are readily overlooked.

The influence of globalization extends inward, as well, to the employees of these leviathan firms. Managing globally is fraught with paradox. For instance, information technologies can potentially increase employee participation in decisions by increasing direct access. However, they also augment managers' ability to involve themselves in lower-level decisions, which centralizes decision making and *reduces* employee autonomy. Similarly, operating globally increases employee diversity within firms, enhancing a firm's ability to respond to local conditions. Paradoxically, it also dilutes corporate norms and values, reducing firms' global coherence and their capacity to coordinate transnationally. Such tradeoffs, central to the managerial task of implementing viable competitive strategies as firms globalize, require remarkably adroit leadership able to spearhead the design of flexible corporate configurations and mobilize the commitment of highly diverse employees.

This chapter invites us to consider the role that firms play in both fostering and resolving global interdependence. Transnationalism is here to stay. As the principal agents of transnationalism, global firms need leaders with the vision to chart a strategic course through the political complexities of a fragmented world and the resolve to implement that vision, not only by supporting the parochial profitability objectives of shareholders, but also, by recognizing the institutional mission that their firms fulfill in a world sorely devoid of effective global normative structures. Vision, however, also requires heeding Chekhov's sage advice: "If you cry 'forward!' you must without fail make plain in what direction to go."

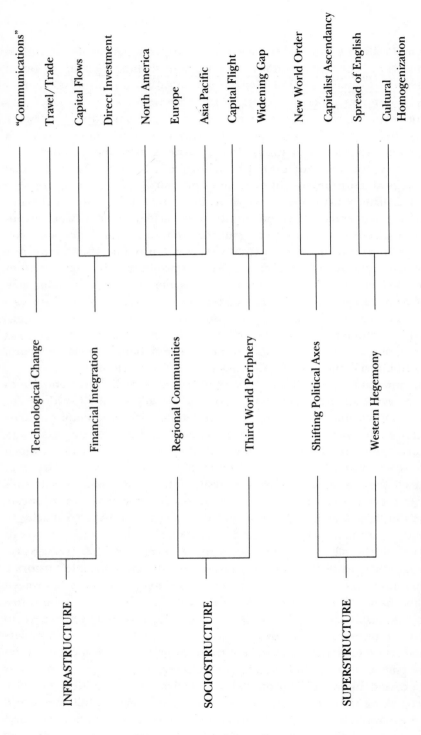

Figure 1.1 Mapping Global Interdependence.

INFRASTRUCTURE

Technological Change
- "Communications"
- Travel/Trade

Financial Integration
- Capital Flows
- Direct Investment

SOCIOSTRUCTURE

Regional Communities
- North America
- Europe
- Asia Pacific

Third World Periphery
- Capital Flight
- Widening Gap

SUPERSTRUCTURE

Shifting Political Axes
- New World Order
- Capitalist Ascendancy

Western Hegemony
- Spread of English
- Cultural Homogenization

18

The Global Web of Interdependence

The revolutions in transportation and communication create, inevitably, national societies and now, on the threshold, a world society.

DANIEL BELL

The global environment of firms has become more clearly structured in the postwar era, despite a lack of centralized direction setting. Structures emerge as individuals, corporations, and nation-states recognize their interdependence and form relationships from which behavioral norms evolve. These norms, in turn, constrain their subsequent actions.[5]

More specifically, Figure 1.1 describes how our global structure today results from developments in transportation, information technologies, and telecommunications that have shaped growing levels of interdependence in the world's infrastructure. Recognition of mutuality between nations fostered comparative specialization by nation-states, visible today in the proliferation of social exchanges linking specialized countries through trade and transportation. But communication and exchange also reduce social distance between disparate cultures. Today, heightened proximity brings us face to face with the possibility of—and resistance to—cultural homogenization within regions, and perhaps a sharing of world views between traditionally polarized East–West and North–South nations. A progressive convergence towards global norms has been made evident recently by the ever more frequent summit meetings among leaders of the seven largest industrialized nations of the West,[6] by the proliferation of regional associations devoted to coordinating economic and political activities, and also perhaps by the *de facto* adoption of English as the language of international business. Increasingly, global managers find themselves formulating and implementing transnational strategies for their firms against the evolving backdrop of these macro-societal changes.

Technological Developments Promote Global Exchange

Arguably, the most profound developments of the postwar era have been (1) dramatic improvements in transportation systems facilitating the movement of people and goods and (2) the incremental convergence of computer and communications technologies brought about by improvements in signal transmission and increasingly powerful microprocessors that made the conversion of analog to digital signals cost-effective. Just as the steam engine and the factory system made possible the Industrial Revolution, so too have transportation and communications technologies sparked a revolution, one that has brought us to the threshold of the information age.[7]

In transportation, development of the first commercial jet aircraft, the Boeing 707 in 1958 and the widebody Boeing 747 in 1969, ushered in a new age in airplane capacity and changed the economics of air travel.[8] Figure 1.2

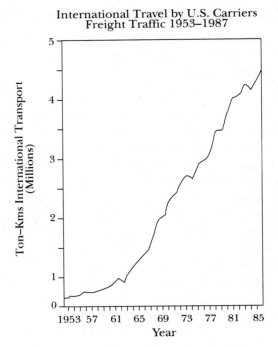

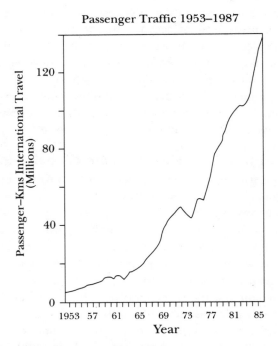

Figure 1.2   International Travel by U.S. Carriers
Source: United Nations Statistical Yearbook, various years.

charts the evolution of international air travel since 1950 and demonstrates the impetus that technological innovation provided to both passenger travel and freight transport in the postwar era.

Over the last two decades, advances in so-called *compunications* have had an even more visible influence on firms' shop floors and in their back offices.[9] In manufacturing, computer-aided design (CAD), computer-aided manufacturing (CAM), and robotics have made possible a dramatic restructuring of plants, reduced dependency on labor, and increased production efficiency while simultaneously enhancing marketing flexibility by reducing the economic order quantity. In banking, imaging technologies alleviate the traditionally cumbersome task of check processing and other back-office operations. In turn, they offer banks the ability to quickly move funds electronically to capitalize on profit opportunities; to centralize operations in a single geographical location to capture scale economies; and to build huge databases detailing customer consumption patterns that enhance marketing ability.[10]

The proliferation of computerized systems is creating unprecedented increases in the demand for knowledge-workers—people capable, for instance, of developing and implementing useful software, and entirely new economic sectors have emerged to provide such ancillary services. Again, partly because they cannot provide these support services, developing nations find themselves increasingly behind in the race to attract foreign investment capital.

Most profoundly, improved communication alters the relationship between people, the companies for which they work, and their governments. By connecting geographically remote locations, the microelectronic revolution is changing the kind and character of social distance. People now share information instantaneously through computer networks and teleconferencing. They order goods and services via home shopping networks and do their banking from home and office terminals. Satellites transmit special editions of national dailies like the *Wall Street Journal*, *USA Today*, and *The New York Times* for printing on local presses; facsimile transmissions have become indispensable adjuncts to every automated office.[11]

Linkages to government also are changing. In democratic societies, for instance, media politicians now readily bypass established political structures of representation to appeal directly to voters. Historically, communist states relied heavily on their ability to control information. Now the pervasiveness and intrusiveness of electronic communications and the mass media render increasingly difficult the obscurantism of governments inclined to totalitarian control.[12] The Chinese government's recent frustration at blocking Western radio and fax transmissions after the crackdown on students in Tiananmen Square provided a vivid example of how difficult it can be to maintain a totalitarian propaganda apparatus in an information-rich world.

The threat of public exposure also changes democratic governments' ability and inclination to conduct covert operations. In the United States, the surreptitious funding of Nicaraguan contraforces brought scandal, and, having finally won the release of long-held hostages from terrorist groups in Lebanon, caution and lack of media spectacle may have been the better of their governments' valor. Such developments portend important challenges to the sovereignty of both Eastern and Western governments, constrained as they are to act under the televised glare and critical scrutiny of their citizens and the world.[13]

Ultimately, the convergence of computer and communications technologies joins with improvements in air transportation to form the heart of a dramatic mutation in the global infrastructure of the last two decades that has fostered an increased recognition of interdependence between nation-states, and hence closer financial, social, and political ties. In turn, global interdependence has encouraged countries to specialize in the pursuit of comparative advantage. By increasing the size of the total market for goods and services, globalization has coaxed a differentiation of countries based on their relative natural resources, skills, and competitive strength—a worldwide division of labor.[14] Specialization, in turn, has induced more international exchange of goods and services, binding countries into mutualistic, organic communities.

Nowhere is this more apparent than in the increasing mobility of capital. Today stocks and bonds change hands around the clock as traders leapfrog from New York to London to Tokyo. Their unencumbered trades virtually tie local exchanges into a single global auction market that fosters a convergence of rates of return on similar financial assets from different countries. As Walter Wriston, the former Chairman of Citicorp, put it recently, "It is doubtful that the men and women who interconnected the planet with telecommunications and computers realized that they were assembling a global financial marketplace that would replace the Bretton Woods agreements and, over time, alter political structures."[15]

Interdependence Encourages Financial Integration

Capital mobility refers to the movement of assets between countries in response to actual or expected rates of return. From all accounts, capital mobility has increased significantly in the last two decades, partly as a result of declining transactions costs involved in using international financial markets and partly because of reduced exchange and interest rate controls. At present, no obstacles to long-term capital mobility exist in the United States, Canada, and the United Kingdom, while Germany, Japan, the Netherlands, and Switzerland have extensively liberalized their markets.

Various studies point to the increasing substitutability of assets held in those industrialized nations that face minimal political risk.[16] They demonstrate financial integration by either (1) correlating changes in return on assets trading in different national markets or (2) testing for evidence of interest rate parity between countries. Although much of the evidence derives from studies of short-term financial asset flows, there seems to be growing consensus that both long-term and short-term capital flows behave in ways consistent with a globalization of financial markets. As a result, assets become substitutable across countries.[17]

Three general measures of financial integration offer a sense of heightened global interdependence: (1) the total volume of world trade, (2) the stock of outward direct investment abroad, and (3) the degree of international banking activity.

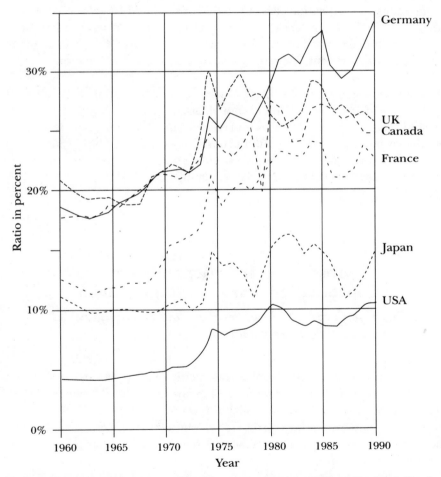

Figure 1.3   Trade in Goods and Services as a Proportion of Gross Domestic Product, Major Industrial Countries 1960–90[a].

Source: International Monetary Fund, *International Financial Statistics,* Yearbooks and Supplements.
[a]Trade is measured as the average of exports and imports.

World Trade. Figure 1.3 diagrams the growth of world trade as a proportion of gross domestic product for the major industrial countries and the world between 1960 and 1990. The rapid upturn in trade's importance to the economies of these countries since 1965 is striking. Also remarkable is the degree to which world trade has outpaced domestic production, confirming the increased importance of international exchanges in the world economy, especially since 1974.

Direct Investment Abroad. In the last 30 years, outward direct investment has grown at an average rate of 9.5 percent, a near ninefold increase since 1960.[18] The lion's share (97 percent) of outward investment flows from the seven leading industrialized nations (the United States, United Kingdom, West Germany, Japan, the Netherlands, France, and Canada) and into each other's economies. Indeed, the industrialized nations host over 60 percent of all inward direct investment, increasingly outpacing third world nations.

International Banking Activity. An estimate of the international character of banking is provided by the international holdings of banks, that is, assets representing cross-border or cross-currency claims. U.S. and Japanese banks hold the largest shares of international business, with some 25 percent each.[19] Most of these international assets involve claims on other banks, demonstrating how the infrastructure of the financial community itself has grown more tightly linked.

Absorbing Interdependence:
Coordinating Through Regionalism

Eager for access to large markets, the entire industrial world is getting more clubby.

FORTUNE, 5/22/89

As interdependence in the global infrastructure has grown, so have social relationships developed to absorb it. They are particularly evident in the heightened level of nation-state collaboration within regional communities. These social relationships have progressively shifted the axis of global dialogue away from the traditional East–West and North–South descriptions of the post–World War II era.

The Logic of Regionalism

Three regional communities seem likely to dominate global trade in the 1990s: North America, Europe, and Asia-Pacific.

North America. Canada and the United States generate the world's largest volume of bilateral trade, over $150 billion in 1988. Seventy-eight percent of Canada's exports and 69 percent of its imports in 1986 were with the U.S. In contrast, Canada absorbs only 22 percent of U.S. exports. Moreover, direct investment by the United States in 1986 amounted to $50.2 billion, making the U.S. Canada's principal foreign investor. Canada's investment in the U.S., however, totals a mere $18.3 billion, far behind Japan and Britain. Given the strong ties between them, the U.S. and Canada signed a Free Trade Agreement in 1989 that essentially created a North American Community, paving the way for the unencumbered flow of goods and capital between the two countries. As a result, Canadian investment in the U.S. is expected to top $41 billion in the early 1990s, and trade is expected to double by mid-decade.[20]

Efforts of Mexican leaders to open their economy to foreign trade also offer the possibility that a low-wage partner could enhance the competitiveness of the North American community. The Maquila program begun in 1965 (and renamed the Mexican Industrialization Program in 1986) created export processing zones for U.S. firms throughout Mexico. Some 1,100 firms now participate in the program, 67 percent of which are U.S. majority-owned, employing over 280,000 workers.[21]

Europe 1992. Since the mid-1980s, the leaders of the 12 member nations of the European Community have repeatedly committed to eliminating the regulatory patchwork inhibiting free trade in Europe by 1992, at which point a single market of 320 million consumers should emerge. Each country has also demonstrated a commitment to initiating free-market policies within its domestic economies, deregulating government-controlled industries, and privatizing numerous government-held monopolies. Jointly, these initiatives virtually guarantee that Europe 1992 will become a reality.

The implications of a united Europe are vast. Many sectors still controlled by government will be deregulated, including telecommunications, financial services, and advertising. For instance, sales of communications equipment are expected to increase at double the U.S. rate, expanding from $70 billion in 1988 to $105 billion in 1992. Where government once tightly rationed ad time and licensing to private broadcasters, European advertising billings are already increasing at 12 percent a year, double the U.S. rate. Grey Advertising has doubled European billings in the last two years to $1.4 billion. As one observer puts it: "In the decade of the 1990s Europe will become more and more a U.S.-style consumer society. Countries will retain their own tastes, cultures, languages, and almost certainly their own currencies. But for the first time, Europe won't be severely handicapped by its divisions. Economically, 320 million consumers will be speaking with one voice. Catering to Europe's finicky new consumers will take companies that are big, agile, and pan-European."[22] Today, a Volkswagen Golf costs 55 percent more (before taxes) in Britain than in Denmark. By 1992, such variations will disappear.[23]

Asia-Pacific. The diverse nations of Southeast Asia constituted the world's fastest growing economic region in 1988; growth rates have exceeded eight percent over the past two years, reaching double-digits in China, Thailand, South Korea, and Singapore. Led by Japan, trade tigers Korea and Taiwan have also formed into a community of sorts: Japan buys 21 percent of all Asian nations' exports, provides 64 percent of all nonmilitary aid, and accounts for between 20 percent and 50 percent of all foreign investment in all Asia-Pacific nations, with the exception of oil-rich Brunei and the Philippines.[24] As Masao Fujioka, president of the Manila-based Asian Development Bank, put it, "a full-grown economic sphere is evolving naturally among the countries around Japan." Japan is also now the largest aid donor in the region, doling out some $7 billion in Asia alone. Even Australia increasingly trades with Asia-Pacific nations, and has liberalized restriction on foreign direct investment. Interestingly, "the Japanese use a poetic but self-serving metaphor to describe their emerging role in Asia: Japan is the lead bird in a formation of wild geese. All are flying forward as each picks up the industries sloughed off by the countries ahead of it."[25]

Altogether, the three regions of North America, Europe, and Asia-Pacific constitute the new building blocks of transnational activity, raising the competitive struggle among industrialized nation-states to the level of regional communities. They leave in their wake a third, unorganized community of developing nations at the periphery of global development.

Third World Periphery

In 1988, total assets held overseas by citizens of the 15 largest Third World debtor countries amounted to $340 billion, up from $80 billion in 1980. Total Third World debt to industrialized nations topped $1.2 trillion. Mexico, Brazil, Argentina, and the Philippines suffer from the crushing burden of high debt servicing brought on by the careless export of petrodollars to the Third World by the Western banking system.[26] Given rapidly growing populations, the standard of living in the Third World is therefore declining rapidly.

At the same time, rapidly changing technologies erode the key comparative advantage of many developing nations, that is, their low labor costs, reducing the incentives for offshore production and sub-contracting. Where factory automation and advanced manufacturing techniques stand to dramatically improve capital productivity, they make labor a less and less important component of total productivity and thereby reduce an important source of foreign exchange for developing economies. Moreover, Third World countries increasingly find themselves unable to provide the supporting communication and computing infrastructure businesses need to link up with their global operations. As some observers have put it, "The awareness has grown that the critical resource of contemporary development is information—along with the organizational capabilities for gathering, retrieving, processing, generating, and disseminating information that is technically and economically relevant. Without a way of tapping into the dense information systems organized largely by multinational corporate networks, the potential for resource misallocation in the less-developed countries is vastly increased and the social opportunity costs of resource misuse are substantial."[27]

So developing countries naturally find themselves moving toward the periphery of global development, outside the large affluent communities of North America, Europe, and Asia-Pacific. They struggle to attract investors whose outlook is dominated by the need to maintain competitive party, and hence minimize costs. In this environment, Third World nations compete frantically with one another to attract foreign capital, further cutting domestic margins, eroding whatever common bonds might have united them as a community. Insofar as in coming years firms' productivity gains come principally from the development of advanced manufacturing technologies and automation, it seems likely that Third World nations will be spun further out to the periphery, relying ever more on handouts and castaways from the rapidly growing regional communities.

Forecasting Western Hegemony

It is useless to close the gates against ideas; they overleap them.

PRINCE KELMENS VON METTERNICH

Not only has the intensification of interdependence in the world's infrastructure fused nations into regional communities in the global sociostructure, it also has prompted dramatic changes in the global superstructure, the world's ideological and cultural coherence. Two indicators suggest that macro-social change is stimulating increasing homogeneity of ideas and thought structures worldwide: the capitulation of socialist ideals in Eastern Europe and in many developing nations and the rise of English as the international language of politics and business. In the global competition for ideas, the West appears to be settling into a position of hegemonic dominance over world affairs.

The Triumph of Market Capitalism?

The dramatic events of the past few years suggest that we are witnessing the dawn of a new world order no longer dominated by traditional East–West polarization. Developments emanating from Eastern Europe have substantiated the early conclusion among observers of the world scene that "ideologically, the foundation of the East European Alliance is sinking, the edifice of its socialism is cracked."[28] In the early 1990s, the winds of change blow from the East in two directions: (a) politically, they portend ever greater autonomy for the former Soviet republics and the Union's former satellite nations, and (b) economically, they concede the defeat of central planning and welcome market and price reform, particularly in agriculture and manufacturing.[29] They amount to a reordering of some time-honored beliefs. As Robert Legvold argues, "From Lenin's day it has been an article of Soviet faith that the struggle between two social systems, capitalism and socialism, creates the core dynamic of international politics. . . . No longer, say Gorbachev and the many who take their cue from him. Not the struggle between classes but the common plight of man forms the central imperative. Not a Manichaean contest between good and evil, but the entangling effect of interdependence, holds the upper hand."[30]

Early on the ascendancy of market-based philosophies could be adduced from the increasing number of joint ventures between Western businesses and socialist enterprises in Eastern Europe throughout the 1980s. Prior to 1980, only 43 joint ventures with equity participation from market economies were registered in the socialist countries of Eastern Europe. By 1987, some 831 joint ventures were registered in Bulgaria, Czechoslovakia, East Germany, Hungary, Poland, Romania, and the Soviet Union. They were clearly a first step in the stimulation of the private sectors of these countries, a harbinger of things to come.

Shaping Homogeneity Through Language and Culture

The global convergence toward market philosophies, however, constitutes only one aspect of what Figure 1.1 describes as the growing homogenization of the global superstructure. In a world fragmented into multiple religions, tribes, and local cultures, language provides one vehicle for developing greater levels of integration. The early excitement over the design and use of Esperanto as a universal language reflects this acknowledgment of the need for a medium of communication and shared experience to manage the increased levels of global interdependence. English appears to have taken on the role of medium in the conduct of world affairs.

In 1938, Otto Jespersen documented the increasing use of the English language between 1500 and 1930, estimating that by 1936 there would be some 191 million first-language speakers of English and 20 million second-language speakers. He attributed the spread of English to the political ascendancy of the English-speaking world, one aspect of its growing hegemony over world affairs.[31] Today, estimates put native speakers of English in the world at over 300 million; and more than another 450 million have a command of English as a second language. Although Chinese has more native speakers, none of its many dialects have diffused significantly outside China. Whereas with one of every seven people in the world conversant, English is clearly the dominant medium of international communication for both advanced study and the conduct of business. English is the native language of 12 countries and an official or semi-official language in 33 other countries. Furthermore, it is a required subject or widely studied in the schools of at least 56 other countries.[32]

A recent study confirmed the global pervasiveness of English by highlighting the growth of English in non-English mother-tongue countries.[33] Its principal findings were that:

1. English mother-tongue countries host more than 40 percent of the non–English speaking world's foreign students;

2. Developing countries of Asia and Africa account for more than 65 percent of foreign students in English mother-tongue countries;

3. English book production is more than double that of French in all non-native countries, making English the most viable medium through which ideas are presented worldwide;

4. Some 16 percent of all primary school students, 77 percent of secondary students, and over 98 percent of tertiary students receive significant exposure to English as a second language.

Additionally, newspapers like the *International Herald Tribune* and magazines like *Newsweek* and *Time* contribute to further diffusion of English into non–mother-tongue countries. Some 47 countries of Asia and Africa also publish English-language dailies, indicating a significant degree of local familiarity with English as a second language. As the study's authors conclude, "English is clearly the major-link language in the world today and that it alone shows signs of continuing as such, at least in the short run, while the use of local languages for official literacy/education related purposes is also likely to increase."[34]

These numbers suggest that as worldwide interdependence increases and firms seek global opportunities, English could well become the medium for sharing information internationally, which is not to say it will take over as a cultural beacon. Most probably it will not: customs and practices are more likely to be transmitted in the idioms of local cultures. It is simply that globetrotting executives are likely to find distant operations less foreign than ever before.

The dissemination of English also facilitates the transfer of Western culture and American lifestyles through exports of films, books, television programs, theater, and music. Statistics documenting the growing export of U.S. films abroad, for instance, provide indicative evidence of the ascendancy of

U.S. cultural products in global consumption. In 1988, the United States generated some 60 percent of worldwide theatrical showings of films, with U.S. films accounting for 45 to 65 percent of the local box office. Moreover, between 1984 and 1988, the fastest growing markets for theatrical films have been outside the U.S., in the following order: United Kingdom, Sweden, West Germany, and Spain, each with a greater than 100 percent increase; Japan and Italy, with over 80 percent growth in imports. However, the principal foreign markets for U.S. distributors remain Japan (14%), Canada (12%), West Germany (10%), France (10%), United Kingdom (9%), Italy (7%), Spain (7%), and Australia (5%).

If the growth pattern of film exports also applies to the export of other cultural goods, the ascendance of American values and life concepts may be on the rise. Nonetheless, for transnational films, American hegemony is unlikely to mean the irrelevance of local customs and native languages; it does indicate, however, that the ideational basis of the global mutuality of interests is probably going to be American in origin.

Global Strategic Competition

Over the past century, international trade has been increasingly carried on by manufacturing enterprises that marketed their goods through their own salaried sales force operating from their own office in foreign lands. . . . As the technologies of production and distribution and the markets for products became more homogeneous . . . competition forced the multinationals to acquire a broader, more global perspective.

ALFRED CHANDLER

Firms meet environmental challenges through strategic responses at the business level, the corporate level, and the collective level.[35] The forces shaping globalization are provoking a dramatic realignment of competitive processes within many industries, forcing firms to abandon their nationalistic postures and implement transnational strategies.

Business-Level Strategy: Stalking Global Consumers

Globalization significantly increases the market reach of firms. However, it also pits firms against strong rivals, many of whom are more closely attuned to the characteristics of local markets. A significant challenge of transnational marketing therefore involves defining and more carefully targeting consumer markets. Gone, then, are the mass markets of yesteryear for which manufacturers produced standard, single–brand name, homogeneous products. Developments in the speed and quality of information fortunately enables a more sophisticated identification of markets than ever before. Consider traditional mass marketers of consumer products like Procter & Gamble. In recent years, they have revolutionized their own operations by:

1. More carefully linking consumer data to product characteristics and point of purchase advertisements.

2. Introducing product line extensions to capitalize on brand names and customize products to individual tastes.

3. Advertising in new media, like schools or cable TV, to reach target populations.

4. Building stronger ties with retail clients, for example, through computer linkages and store-based promotional campaigns.

In the large, increasingly intertwined, but culturally disparate economies of the world, such a strategy of differentiated production and marketing should be key to achieving competitive advantage in consumer products. P&G has already shown how applying these techniques globally can pay off: between 1985 and 1989, P&G's earnings from foreign operations grew from 14 percent to 33 percent, on $8.4 billion in foreign sales.[36]

Customized marketing, however, presents firms with a significant quandary: the prospect of scale economies has encouraged firms to go global, yet achieving these economies requires firms to produce standardized goods. In many industries, these scale economies have failed to materialize, partly because of the pressure to customize, partly because of logistical barriers and costs of transporting goods from centrally located plants to remote consumers, and partly because efficient plant size may preclude capturing additional economies of scale. In the apparel industry, for example, competitive pressures make speed of delivery a key success factor, encouraging production closer to end markets. Similarly, the washing machine industry in Europe has demonstrated that local producers generally outdo competitors engaging in cross-border specialization because the transport costs and management costs of larger factories seriously dampen the gains from the scale they produce.

Within most industries' factories, a significant trend toward inducing labor cost savings has become evident, usually obtained by jointly emphasizing managerial efficiency and adapting new technologies to operations. CAD-CAM and robotics technologies have enabled U.S. auto manufacturers, for instance, to dramatically reduce the average cost of producing a car domestically. Simultaneously, Ford, GM, and Chrysler have worked to improve relations with the powerful United Auto Workers, negotiating contracts that provide for automation, participation in quality circles, cooperative conflict resolution, flexible allocation of tasks, and a stronger voice for workers in corporate decision.[37] In tandem, mimicking of Japanese practices has forced closer attention to relations not only with employees but with suppliers, sharing information with vendors, helping them improve quality, and jointly solving production problems[38] Similar process interventions have been documented at plants owned by Kodak, Timken, and Corning, among others. Through selective plant closures, layoffs, cost cutting, and quality control, entire industries have made over their manufacturing operations in an attempt to compete with low-cost foreign producers in globalizing markets.[39] Although the specifics vary, nationally the results seem good: according to the Bureau of Labor Statistics, U.S. labor productivity has increased from 1.4 percent (1974–79) to 3.1 percent (1980–84) to 3.6 percent (1985–88), while multifactor productivity (both labor and capital) increased from 0.5 percent to 2.2 percent to 3.3 percent.[40]

In preparation for the integration of Europe in 1992, U.S. companies spent some $20.9 billion in 1987 to obtain or build plants in Europe. Like appliance manufacturer Whirlpool and paper producer International Paper, some are moving into Europe for the first time. Similarly, European companies at home outside the common market, such as the Swedish paper firms, have used acquisitions to establish beachheads in anticipation of 1992. Also, East Asian companies often are ready acquirers of production or distribution facilities within the European Community.

Finally, firms facing global competition find themselves forced to allocate more funds to R&D than ever before. In order to spread risks, companies introducing products with short life cycles and relying on rapidly changing technologies lobbied U.S. government officials to overcome traditional antitrust laws that prevented cooperative R&D, both with domestic competitors and across borders. One result: in the early 1980s, a group of U.S. Silicon Valley companies formed an R&D consortium, Sematech, funded half by industry and half by government to reduce growing dependence on Japanese chip manufacturing—a top-down approach to technological development hotly debated in academic circles.[41]

Many similar cooperative R&D programs have been established in Europe. "[They] reflect a conviction that technological advances and the improvement of Europe's technological base can be better promoted through arrangements involving the cooperation of Governments and private firms rather than through structural changes in European industry."[42] At the same time, many U.S. and European companies are spending aggressively to develop products tailored to the European market.

While research results suggest that centralized R&D costs less and is easier to coordinate, we also know that the gains from commercialization are more difficult to capture if R&D is removed from ultimate markets.[43] The familiar business-level tension between marketing, R&D, and manufacturing is therefore exacerbated as firms struggle to compete in global markets by trying, on the one hand, to produce scale economies within functional areas while responding, on the other hand, to the customized requirements of differentiated markets.

Corporate-Level Strategy: Growth by Takeover

The close ties between nations fostered by increased travel, capital flows, trade, and the homogenization of global tastes, encourage firms to quickly find ways of penetrating foreign markets and claiming a beachhead against later entrants. Since internal growth takes time and frequently taxes the know-how and managerial talent of the expanding firm, mergers offer a quick route to achieving competitive positions abroad.

Throughout the 1970s, the isolationist policies of many nation-states were manifest in their antagonism to foreign direct investment and their willingness to expropriate foreign assets. Figure 1.4 charts the time pattern of expropriation acts between 1961 and 1985 and suggests that increasingly penetration by transnational firms now is welcomed rather than feared.[44]

Interpenetration of transnational corporations and nation-states through mergers has also been facilitated by government attempts to raise foreign equity investment in both developed and developing economies. Leading examples are France's privatization drive since the new government of 1986; privatization of NTT and Japan Tobacco in Japan in 1985; the Tory govern-

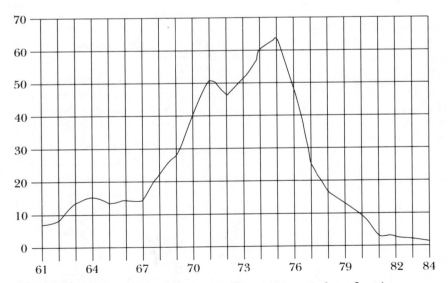

Figure 1.4   Expropriation acts (3-year moving average, number of acts).
Source: Data for 1960–1979 are from Kobrin (1984, p. 333) (unpublished); For the data for 1980–1985, see Michael Minor, *The Expropriation of Foreign Direct Investment in Developing Countries, Trends from 1980–1985* (unpublished).

ment's privatizations of prominent U.K. firms that included British Aerospace, British Telecom, Cable and Wireless, Enterprise Oil, British Gas, and Jaguar; and the aggressive privatization of public firms in Argentina, Brazil, Chile, Mexico, Malaysia, Pakistan, Philippines, Thailand, Guinea, Niger, Nigeria, Senegal, and Togo.

Figure 1.5 shows that between 1982 and 1990, U.S. companies spent over $54 billion to acquire some 1,758 foreign companies. In those same years, foreign firms consummated over 3,109 acquisitions of U.S. firms valued at $265 billion.[45] These numbers suggest how corporate transnationalism is progressing through mergers that cross national boundaries.[46] Throughout the 1980s, the U.S. was clearly a prime target of foreign acquisitions. As the regional communities of Europe and Asia-Pacific materialize, however, we expect to see a changing pattern of takeovers directed more heavily at these markets.

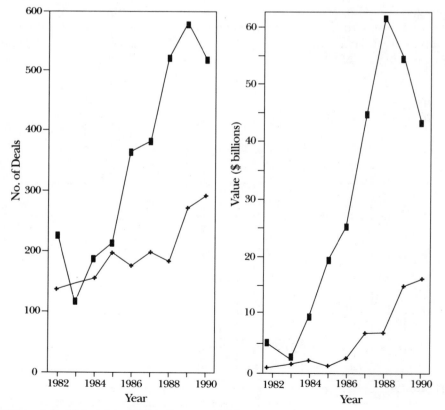

Figure 1.5   Gobal Acquisition Patterns 1982–1990.
Source: Mergers & Acquisitions (May/June 1991).

Of the 1,000 most highly valued firms in the world in 1989, U.S. firms number 353, 345 are Japanese, and 214 are European, accounting respectively for 33 percent, 47 percent, and 17 percent of total equity. Much of the increases in market value for U.S.and European firms throughout 1989 resulted from takeovers, such as British whiskey and food producer Grand Met's acquisition of U.S. food giant Pillsbury for $5.8 billion; Nestlé's $3.9 billion acquisition of British chocolate maker Rowntree PLC; French aluminum maker Pechiney's $1.2 billion purchase of American Can Co. from Triangle Industries; and French cement company Lafarge Coppee's $770 million purchase of Swiss holding company Cementia. Many of these cross-border mergers were spurred heavily by the prospect of Europe 1992 and are changing competitive dynamics in many industries. Some examples include:

- Telecommunications: France's Campagnie Generale d'Electricite purchased ITT Corporation's telecommunications division to become No. 1 in Europe and No. 2 in the world after AT&T; in 1987, France's Thomson purchased GE/RCA's TV operations in the U.S.for $800 million; Sweden's Asea and Switzerland's Brown Boveri have formed a global giant in power-generating equipment; Siemens of West Germany spent $2 billion in acquisitions of Britain's Plessey PLC, the Electronics division of Bendix, and France's IN2 computer manufacturer.

- Banking: In 1986, West Germany's Deutsche Bank, Europe's fifth largest bank, purchased Bank of America's Italian operations for $603 million and by 1989 had taken control of leading banks in Italy, Spain, Portugal, the Netherlands, and Austria.

- Public Relations: British agency Shandwick's buying spree of smaller PR firms in Europe; equity positions taken in foreign agencies by MSL Worldwide, PR subsidiary of D'Arcy Benton & Bowles; aggressive global growth from within by U.S. agencies Hill & Knowlton and Burson-Marsteller.

Taken together, these trends suggest that the search for global competitive positioning in response to the increasing coherence of the large regional markets of North America and Europe encourages firms to speed up their entry into multiple national markets through takeovers and mergers with local firms.

Collective-Level Strategy:
Managing Transnational Alliances

Firms are also responding to global market consolidations by forming collaborative agreements and joint ventures with multiple partners. The collective

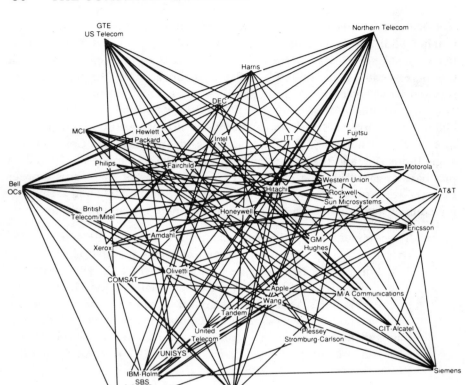

Figure 1.6   MultiDimensional Scaling Plot of the Telecommunications Community.

strategy of networking presents firms with a viable alternative to the takeover. Its principle strength lies in the speed with which it can be implemented and the limited resources required of firms to form global networks. Logically, then, smaller firms seeking competitive positioning in globalizing markets find it particularly attractive because of its affordability. Larger firms find networking attractive because it is simpler to manage and reduces complexity. Increasingly, competition has shifted from the level of the firm to that of the network.

The telecommunications industry provides a useful example of networking. Between 1980 and 1987, spurred by the growing convergence of computer and communications technologies, leading firms in the global telecommunications industry formed 1,134 alliances (nonequity agreements, joint ventures, or partial equity investments).[47] Figure 1.6 presents a multidimensional scaling plot of the network that binds the 38 leading firms into a dense community. Subgroup analyses suggest that the network further breaks down into dense regions, representing constellations of firms with identifiable strengths in the development, production, and marketing of particular communications products and services. It appears, therefore, that the network level of analysis provides a useful vehicle for identifying a new locus of competition, away from the traditional industry level, one that pits constellations strategically against one another.

Interfirm agreements binding firms into global communities of this sort have become the norm in many industries. Table 1.1 identifies the number of such interfirm agreements occurring around information technology in a selected set of countries between 1984 and 1986. Other nonequity interfirm agreements have also become popular, including:[48]

- Licensing arrangements: technology exporting from Korea's Lucky Group and Taiwan's Formosa Plastics Corporation to Saudi Arabia's Basic Industries Corporation.

- Exchange agreements: between the U.S.'s Micron Technology and Korea's Samsung; between Korea's Hyundai and the U.S.'s Amtel and U.K.'s Inmos; between the U.S.'s RCA and Taiwan's state enterprise ERSO.

- Sub-contracting: throughout the apparel industry with leading textile and clothing manufacturers providing designs and distribution and firms in developing countries providing labor-intensive production.

In many industries, the net effect of these strategies has been to shift competition away from its traditional locus at the level of the firm to competition between large networks of cooperating firms. For instance, IBM, long a stalwart rival intent on carrying out a solitary fortress strategy, has in recent years forged an active and aggressive network of allies with former competitors, none more prominent than archrival Apple.[49] As globalization progresses, and as the pace of change accelerates, more and more companies are finding themselves forging similar strategic networks. Their competitiveness will depend largely on their ability to carve out stronger cooperative networks than their competitors.

Globalization: Challenges to Implementation

Changes which run with the mores are easily brought about, but . . . changes which are opposed to the mores require long and patient effort, if they are possible at all.
W. GRAHAM SUMNER

Historical strategies—collective, corporate, and competitive—define firms' relationships with rivals and circumscribe their future options. Firms competing

Table 1.1 Interfirm Agreements in Information Technology,
Selected Developed Market Economy Countries, 1984–1986

COUNTRY	FIRM	NUMBER OF AGREEMENTS
Benelux	Philips	26
	All firms (5)	32
France	GGE	34
	Bull	27
	Thomson	21
	MATRA	19
	All firms (70)	210
Germany,	Siemens	24
Federal Republic of	All firms (17)	48
Italy	Olivetti	36
	All firms (10)	64
Japan	Fujitsu	8
	Toshiba	5
	NEC	3
	All firms (16)	32
United Kingdom	JCL	16
	Plessey	9
	British Telecom	8
	All firms (27)	75
United States	AT&T	14
	Control Data	12
	IBM	9
	All firms (91)	157

Source: United Nations Centre on Transnational Corporations.

in globalizing industries, therefore, experience historical and contextual constraints as they struggle to pursue, in varying degrees, strategies designed to achieve:

1. Differentiation and cost-control at the business-level.

2. Aggressive growth at the corporate-level, internally for some, through takeovers for others.

$\times$ 3. Cooperative arrangements and networking with competitors at the collective-level, to maintain parity in technology, marketing, production, and distribution.

Many contextual variables will affect the particular choice of growth strategy to pursue. Particularly important variables likely to influence the firm's strategic direction are its current slack and industry capacity.

Slack. Over time, firms develop excess or slack resources unnecessary for immediate operations. These cushioning resources not only serve firms in times of crisis, but also provide flexibility for creative initiatives. Depending on their particular histories, firms possess unabsorbed slack resources (evident in their uncommitted liquid assets), and absorbed slack resources (evident in unnecessary administrative overhead and other costs) in varying degrees. Firms with high levels of absorbed and unabsorbed slack should have a greater capacity to take on the challenges of globalizing single-handedly. The more readily excess resources can be mobilized, the faster a firm's ability to move into the global arena. Unfortunately, high levels of slack often signal managerial complacency, an inertial drag that inhibits change. Despite abundant resources, large firms in particular frequently find themselves unable to effect change as quickly as smaller competitors with fewer resources.[50] Global competition for large firms and firms with excess slack might therefore involve a sequencing of commitments, for instance, by rationalizing existing operations while preparing the internal culture of the firm for subsequent growth through either internal expansion or takeover of established competitors abroad. Lacking excess resources, smaller firms might elect to pursue alliances as a vehicle for global expansion.

Competitive Posture. Existing global overcapacity and a firm's strategic posture within its industry centrally influence the course of industry evolution. The consolidation of markets occurring within regional communities promises scale economies in many industries and segments within industries. Many nationally supported firms, operating in insular markets, now operate at low levels of capacity. Regional markets are likely to support fewer firms operating at peak capacity. Similarly, globalization is likely to benefit most competitors who are able to overcome inertia and quickly deploy assets to rationalize production, automate operations, and increase efficiency. Firms already occupying dominant positions in local markets are in a stronger position to capture regional markets by rapid expansion. Firms in secondary positions in the industry, lacking capacity or resources, need to consider corporate takeovers and collective strategies as means of moving quickly into globalized markets.

Barriers to Change: The Case of Citicorp

To implement a global strategy is far from simple. Asset redeployments call for dramatic changes in the internal configurations of their firms, whether in their structures, decision-making processes, cultures, or human resource management systems. Consider the U.S. leader in banking, Citicorp. With $207 billion in assets, Citicorp's $10.1 billion market value places it 140th in *Business Week*'s listing of the Global 1,000, well below Japanese leaders Sumitomo Bank, Fuji Bank, Dai-Ichi Kangyo Bank, and Mitsubishi Bank, but comparable to West Germany's Deutsche Bank, ranked 143rd with a market value of $10 billion and $152 billion in assets.

Today, Citicorp and Deutsche Bank seem poised for head-to-head combat in both the North American and European markets. Where Alfred Herrhausen has made aggressive acquisitions in the last few years to better position the Deutsche Bank in Europe, however, Citicorp's John Reed has found it more difficult to implement his global vision. "To fulfill Citi's potential requires not more vision, but boring old nuts-and-bolts implementation. And so far, the Citi team's record on 'execution' . . . is spotty."[51]

If a firm's success at implementing a global strategy can be measured in terms of its ability to generate profits outside its home market, then Citicorp is failing: the proportion of Citicorp's earnings from outside North America has fallen from a high of 70 percent in 1976 to 37 percent in 1987. Its strength in the domestic North American market may inhibit its ability to metamorphose into a truly global bank, capable of moving into the top tier and meeting head on the largest Japanese institutions. As for many other firms, significant strategic, structural, and cultural barriers must be overcome in implementing a global strategy.[52]

Strategic Barriers. Globalizing will require rapid growth through acquisition. Yet, unlike Deutsche Bank and the Japanese gains, Citicorp's financial resources are limited by regulatory constraints on capital and by set-asides for Third World loans. Moreover, Citicorp's record with past acquisitions has not been good: purchases of savings and loans institutions in Illinois, Florida, and California and of four banks in Europe, all bought on the cheap, have proven difficult to turn around and integrate into Citibank's operations. Acquisitions of investment banking subsidiaries have floundered. Despite some successes, mobility barriers into investment banking have proven difficult to overcome.

Structural Barriers. Citicorp operates within a highly decentralized market structure; its consumer, corporate, and investment banks run as autonomous fiefdoms. Yet the imminent collapse of the Glass-Steagall Act in the United States and the rise of nationwide banking makes dialogue across groups increasingly important to delivery of comprehensive financial services to clients. The regionalization of Europe also presents prospects calling for greater cooperation between divisions. One benefit banks can expect to gain from market consolidation in Europe, North America, and the Pacific is the ability to fuse all back-office operations and capture scale economies from costly check manipulating and record-keeping activities. Unfortunately, compared to the Deutsche Bank, Citicorp has, to date, been slow to centralize operations in Europe.

Cultural Barriers. Citicorp maintains its gung-ho culture through reward systems that encourage individual performance and promote careerism. In such an environment, decision making invariably becomes politicized and overconfidence is a natural outcome of competitive internal dynamics. Moreover, acquisitions prove difficult to integrate: they frequently involve dismissal of local staff and their replacement by Citi-trained management teams, weakening the managerial strength of the parent firm. Achieving global reach, however, will require capitalizing on the strengths of local firms, without necessarily seeking to homogenize acquisitions to the Citicorp way. Citi's internal culture may rebel.

Adapting to the interdependent transnational world of the 1990s will require overcoming significant organizational barriers to change. Particular configurations of structures, cultures, and human resource systems should prove especially helpful to firms seeking to implement global strategies.

Strategic Profiles for the Year 2000

Figure 1.7 summarizes four strategic profiles of firms struggling to maneuver into viable competitive postures over the coming decade. These profiles suggest what the dominant concerns might be for firms facing either high or low slack and attempting to compete from a dominant or secondary position in the regional markets of North America or Europe.

Dominant Position—Low Slack. Under these conditions, firms first should seek efficiencies to establish a bulwark against potential foreign rivals. At the business level, rationalization of production, centralization of operations, and investments in achieving business-level efficiency should prevail. At the corporate level, firms should narrow their corporate portfolios to pursue greater relatedness in their product/market activities. While at the collective level, marketing alliances should ensure distribution of their production volume. Japanese giant Matsushita's rationalized production, for instance, enables it to pursue centralized R&D aimed at developing global innovations. More efficient competitors with better price-quality products form the principal threat to such firms. To deal with this threat, visionary leaders capable of mobilizing employees toward the pursuit of a common goal working with strong, nuts-and-bolts managers capable of securing solid individual contributions to company performance become essential. To develop such leaders

STRATEGIC POSTURE

AVAILABLE RESOURCES		DOMINANT IN INDUSTRY	SECONDARY IN INDUSTRY
LOW SLACK	Business Strategy	Rationalization	Liquidation
	Corporate Strategy	Related Diversification	Asset Restructuring
	Collective Strategy	Joint Marketing	Nonequity Alliances
HIGH SLACK	Business Strategy	Differentiation	Automation
	Corporate Strategy	Unrelated Diversification	Leveraged Buyout
	Collective Strategy	Joint R&D	Equity Alliances

Figure 1.7 Strategic Profiles.

and managers, Matsushita rotates personnel in five-year periods, from central function to product divisions and back again.

Dominant Position—High Slack. Firms with high slack in dominant domestic positions need not pursue narrow mass markets. They possess the resources necessary to differentiate their products and services for consumption in regionalized and local markets. Heavy investment in new product development and advertising can capture the benefits of brand names and established reputations in local markets while still maintaining sufficient scale economies to preempt competitors. Dutch giant Philips is a past master of this global strategy. At the corporate level, this implies a willingness to broaden the corporate portfolio into related domains of activity, and at the collective level, a willingness to engage in R&D shared equity alliances to facilitate penetration of more remote markets. These firms can expect to devote considerable time and effort in articulating management systems for dealing with the diversity of their operations in different countries: human resource systems must conform to local and regional norms, yet instill identification with the firm as a whole. To develop multinational leaders, select individuals should be promoted across regions, while other employees may flourish within local systems. Balancing transnational and local criteria become the managerial challenge.

High Slack—Secondary Position. Lacking a solid foundation on which to build a global niche strategy, firms with high slack but in secondary domestic positions need to begin by shoring up positions in the regional markets. At the business level, this means improving efficiency of operations through investments in improved manufacturing techniques and automation of production. At the corporate level, takeovers are the medium of choice: they use firms' financial and managerial slack to quickly deliver national competitiveness and pave the way for subsequent global differentiation. Collectively, shared equity arrangements provide a natural basis for broadening exposure to differentiated markets and more quickly acquiring needed strength from locally superior businesses. The managerial challenge involves integrating acquisitions into the corporate culture without squandering the strong points of the internal cultures of acquired companies.

Low Slack—Secondary Position. The weakest global competitors are those firms lacking excess resources to expend on either acquisitions or differentiation. Liquidation of secondary positions in rapidly globalizing markets can help them return needed resources to core business and reinvest them in their home markets. In secondary markets, they should form multiple nonequity alliances with established firms, preferably with those pursuing regional strategies of either differentiation or rationalization that have demonstrated complementary strength in either distribution or production. These firms critically require an ability to manage cooperative arrangements and deal with the tensions and conflicts that multiple alliance partners inevitably generate.

Conclusion

Firms face huge challenges as they struggle to respond to technological, political, and regulatory changes that have dramatically heightened interdependence in the global infrastructure. To manage these exchanges, the world itself has rapidly become more structured as formerly independent nation-states have become fused into regional communities. Increasing homogeneity is also evident in the retreat of centrally planned forms of socialism and in the gradual adoption of English as the *lingua franca* of business.

In this evolving environment, competition demands that firms pursue combinations of business, corporate, and collective strategies that move them into advantageous positions vis-à-vis their local, regional, and foreign rivals.

The world over, globally oriented firms are struggling to achieve strategic positioning through sharper market differentiation, regional rationalization of production, selective related diversification, and far-reaching alliances that involve them in cooperative transnational networks. In the years ahead, corporate leaders must continue to articulate the broad parameters of that global vision. The true test of their leadership, however, will reside in their ability to design structures, internal cultures, and human resource systems that can mobilize managers and employees to implement that vision.

Notes

1. For instance, see Jean Jacques Servan Schreiber, *The American Challenge* (New York: Atheneum, 1968); Raymond Vernon, *Storm Over Multinationals: The Real Issues* (Cambridge, Mass.: Harvard Press, 1977).
2. W. Graham Astley and Charles Fombrun, "Technological Innovation and Industrial Structure: The Case of Telecommunications." In R. Lamb, ed., *Advances in Strategic Management*, (Greenwich, Ct.: JAI Press, 1983).
3. Michael Piore and Charles Sabel, *The Second Industrial Divide*. (New York: Basic Books, 1984).
4. Charles Perrow makes a convincing case for the inevitability of catastrophic "accidents" for systems that rely on complex technologies and demand extraordinary levels of reliability, Charles Perrow, *Normal Accidents* (New York: Basic Books, 1984).
5. Charles J. Fombrun, "Structural Dynamics within and between Organizations," *Administrative Science Quarterly* 31 (1986): 403.
6. The recent bid by Mikhail Gorbachev for inclusion of the U.S.S.R. in these summit meetings suggests the distinct possibility that they will evolve into a new forum for broad international standard-setting and the propagation of institutional norms.
7. In *The Second Industrial Divide*, Piore and Sabel described how the world is poised on the edge of a transformation away from traditional manufacturing, creating significant internal disruptions for advanced nations making the leap. The dividing line also would leave behind those developing nations still struggling to cross the first industrial divide into industrialization. In *The Winding Passage*, (Cambridge, Mass.: Abt Books, 1980) Daniel Bell argued similarly that technology was ushering us into a post-industrial age in which the service sector would dominate the composition of the output of the leading industrialized nations.
8. See Michael Tushman and Phil Anderson, "Technological Discontinuities and Organizational Environments," *Administrative Science Quarterly* 31 (1986): 439.
9. See Benjamin M. Compaine, ed., *Understanding New Media: Trends and Issues in Electronic Distribution and Information* (Cambridge, Ma: Ballinger Press, 1984) and Frederick Williams, *The Communications Revolution* (Beverly Hills, Ca.: Sage Publications, 1982).
10. Through their aggressive investments in Project Genesis, for instance, American Express managers gamble on their ability to draw on the firm's enormous client list to achieve precise marketing of products and services for new clients.
11. Paradoxically, information technologies also distort the character and kind of human interaction by making it possible for individuals to have less interpersonal contact. Alvin Toffler discusses some of these implications in *The Third Wave* (New York: Basic Books, 1979).

12. See Jacques Ellul, *Propaganda: The Formation of Men's Attitudes* (New York: Vintage Books, 1965).

13. As the former chair of Citicorp points out, "Like all technological advances, the new Information Standard makes the world's power structures very nervous, and with good reason." See Walter B. Wriston, "Technology and Sovereignty," *Foreign Affairs* 67 (2) (1988): 63.

14. Paraphrasing Adam Smith, Nobel laureate George Stigler showed that "the division of labor is a function of market size. So free trade enables greater global specialization," See George Stigler, "The Division of Labor Is Limited by the Extent of the Market," *Journal of Political Economy*, 59 (1951):185.

15. Walter B. Wriston, "Technology and Sovereignty," *Foreign Affairs* 67 (2)(1988): 63.

16. Shelagh A. Hefferman, *Sovereign Risk Analysis* (London: Allen & Unwin, 1986).

17. See M. A. Akhtar and K. Weiller, "Developments in International Capital Mobility: A Perspective on the Underlying Forces and the Empirical Literature" and V. Reinhart and K. Weiller, "Increasing Capital Mobility: Evidence from Short and Long-Term Markets," *International Integration of Financial Markets and U.S. Monetary Policy* (New York: Federal Reserve Bank of New York, 1987) 13–70, 71.

18. Foreign direct investment was quantified in Special Drawing Rights, a measure that mitigates exchange rate imbalances. See *International Direct Investment: Global Trends and the U.S. Role* (U.S. Dept. of Commerce, International Trade Administration, 1988) 8.

19. Based on a breakdown of international assets held in the banking offices of countries reporting to the Bank for International Settlements. See Ralph Bryant, *International Financial Intermediation* (Washington, D.C.: Brookings Institution, 1987).

20. As *Business Week* (7/17/89, p.77) concludes, "one thing is for sure. Free trade already is spawning much deeper economic ties along north-south corridors. Washington's ties with Vancouver are expanding, as are Minnesota's with Canada's prairie states, New York's with Ontario and Quebec, and New England's with the maritime provinces."

21. "Mexico: A New Economic Era," *Business Week*, 12 November 1990: 102.

22. Shawn Tully, "The Coming Boom in Europe," *Fortune*, 10 April 1989, 114.

23. Eric Friberg, "1992: Moves Europeans Are Making," *Harvard Business Review*, May–June 1989, 85.

24. Steven Erlanger, "In Southeast Asia, Japan Dominates in Aid, Trade, and Old Resentments," *New York Times*, 2 July 1989, 2.

25. *Business Week*, 10 April 1989, 43.

26. Felix Rohatyn, "America's Economic Dependence," *Foreign Affairs* 68:1(1989):53.

27. Lee Tavis and William Glade, "Implications for Corporate Strategies." In Lee Tavis, ed., *Multinational Managers and Host Government Interactions* (Notre Dame, Ind.: University of Notre Dame Press, 1988) 290.

28. Charles Gati, "Eastern Europe on its Own," *Foreign Affairs* 68:1 (1989): 99.

29. Susan Linz and William Moskoff, eds., *Reorganization and Reform in the Soviet Economy* (New York: Sharpe, 1988).

30. Robert Legvold, "The Revolution in Soviet Foreign Policy," *Foreign Affairs* 68:1 (1989): 85.

31. Otto Jespersen, *Growth and Structure of the English Language* (Garden City, N.J.: Doubleday, 1938).

32. "English: Out to Conquer the World," *U.S. News & World Report*, 18 February 1985, 49.

33. Joshua A. Fishman, Robert L. Cooper, and Andrew W. Conrad, *The Spread of English: The Sociology of English as an Additional Language* (Rowley, Mass.: Newbury House Publishers, 1977).

34. Fishman, Cooper, and Conrad, *The Spread of English*, 56.

35. Charles Fombrun and W. Graham Astley, "Beyond Corporate Strategy: A Framework for Collective Action," *Journal of Business Strategy* 1983, 47.

36. *Business Week*, "Stalking the New Consumer," August 18, 1989, 58.

37. Robert H. Hayes and Steven C. Wheelwright, *Restoring Our Competitive Edge: Competing through Manufacturing* (New York: Wiley, 1984).

38. "Shaking Up Detroit," *Business Week*, 14 August 1989, 74.

39. See "The Push for Quality," *Business Week*, 6 August 1987, 130; "It's Time for a Tune-Up at GM," *Business Week*, 9 July 1987; "Winning Back the Work that Got Away," *Business Week Innovation*, Special Issue, 148.

40. "Beating Japan at Its Own Game," *New York Times*, 16 July 1989, 3:1.

41. See George Gilder, "The Revitalization of Everything: The Law of the Microcosm," *Harvard Business Review* (March–April 1988) and the reply by Charles Ferguson in the *Harvard Business Review* (May–June 1988).

42. See *Transnational Corporations in World Development: Trends and Prospects*. (United Nations Centre on Transnational Corporations 1988) 243.

43. See "The Pharmaceuticals Industry: Sending R&D Abroad," *Multinational Business*, No. 1 (1989), 10.

44. See Stephen J. Kobrin and Robert Hawkins, "An Analysis of Forced Divestments of Foreign Affiliates by Host Countries," summarized in *The CTC Reporter* 24 (Fall 1982): 13, 36–68; and *Transnational Corporations in World Development*, op.cit., 314.

45. Data are from *Mergers & Acquisitions*, various issues.

46. See *The Process of Transnationalization and Transnational Mergers* (United Nations Centre on Transnational Corporations February 1989).

47. Charles Fombrun and Arun Kumaraswamy, "Strategic Alliances in Corporate Communities: The Evolution of Global Telecommunications 1980–88," *Japan and the World Economy*, forthcoming, 1989.

48. See *Transnational Corporations in World Development*, op.cit., 68–69.

49. See *Business Week*, "IBM–Apple Could Be Fearsome," 7 October 1991, 28.

50. See Charles Fombrun and Ari Ginsberg, "Shifting Gears: Changing Corporate Aggressiveness," *Strategic Management Journal* 11 (1990): 297–308.

51. Sarah Bartlett, "John Reed Bumps into Reality," *New York Times*, 5 February 1989, 3:1.

52. Ari Ginsberg, "Measuring and Modelling Changes in Strategy: Theoretical Foundations and Empirical Directions," *Strategic Management Journal* 9(1988): 559.

2

Leadership Development as a Lever for Global Transformation

Noel M. Tichy

Michael I. Brimm

Ram Charan

Hiroraka Takeuchi

If there's anything we've learned it's to give equal time to both the program's project and the globalization experience. If you walk away from this with an excellent project completion, but don't know how a Frenchman lives, don't know why a Japanese businessman gets promoted, haven't tasted sushi, haven't ridden in the British subway, you've blown it.

QUOTE FROM A SENIOR EXECUTIVE PARTICIPATING IN
A GLOBAL DEVELOPMENT PROGRAM

Introduction

In the last decade, global development has become a fundamental challenge to the competitiveness of all corporations operating in the international environment. We contend that traditional training and development approaches fall dangerously short of the requirement for effective global operations. It is time to relinquish conventional wisdom and teaching technologies so that we can start transforming how we think about human resource development in the new age.

The 1990s are a time for action. The business playing field has been radically altered and the stage set for its global transformation. The key differentiator for the 21st century corporate winners will be the effectiveness of the human organization. Winning companies will be led by true globalists, individuals who have:

1. A global mindset—those who can conceptualize complex geopolitical and cultural forces as they impact business.

2. A well-honed set of global leadership skills and behaviors.

3. An ability to build effective cross-cultural teams.

4. The energy, skills, and talents to be global networkers.

5. Skills as global "change agents."

These global winners will be able to "glocalize,"[1] that is, they will be able to use both the muscle and scale of the global giant and act as a local supplier to customers. People development is their key investment during this decade. The human capital challenge is immense. At the core of this challenge is development of a sufficiently large global leadership cadre to lead these institutions into the 21st century. Leaders need to be able to successfully tap into and help create these networks. The remainder of this chapter details an American corporation's unique approach to using development as a lever for global leadership transformation. The change agenda involved a duality: both developing individuals and transforming the organization. The story provides us with insight into what it will take in the 1990s to rapidly create global leadership for the 21st century.

Globalizing High Tech, Inc.

This high-tech company is the world's leading producer in its field, with sales of more than $3 billion and a work force of approximately 17,000 employees. It has one mission: to become the undisputed, worldwide *leader* in its industry. This objective is being accomplished by maintaining its technological leadership while becoming a low-cost producer with high quality, responsiveness, and strong customer orientation. In the 1980s, High Tech sought rapid globalization through a strategic alliance with an Asian company and the acquisition of a European business. The most challenging aspect in this pursuit has been the development of people and the creation of a global organization.

It would have been a significant challenge to transform the business toward a marketing orientation with global cost competitiveness. This is because of the history of strong U.S. orientation where engineers provided state-of-the-art technology in a protected domestic industry.

Globalization became even more challenging with High Tech's acquisition of almost 6,000 Europeans. A year earlier several thousand Asians had their organization shift from a 50/50 joint venture to one that was 80 percent American-owned and, hence, managerially controlled. This massive integration of the highly diverse European, American, and Asian cultures along with the radical transformation of the business itself made the human story of the corporation's transformation a fascinating case that captures much of the global dynamics in recent business history.

A series of strategic decisions were made regarding the distribution of products among the design and manufacturing facilities.[2] Other operating issues also had to be settled: integration of the functions of sales, service, marketing, financial accounting and reporting, and employee relations. The corporations needed to develop ways of communicating these changes and the rationale behind them to employees, customers, and governments.

Reaching these critical, strategic decisions to develop a global business with three organizational poles (Europe, Americas, and Asia) was much easier than implementing the strategies. The new global organization required global leadership and dramatic changes in human dynamics.

The CEO established the concept of a global leadership system to help transform the business. He called in a core faculty team headed by the authors to work with some of his own senior management in designing what was to become the Global Leadership Development System. Its aim was simultaneously to help reshape the entire business and develop leaders.

The major planning for the Global Leadership Development System occurred in February 1988. The authors and the top management at the company determined the need to develop the participants' global leadership skills, integrate the necessary global networks, and create an ability to develop teams across the three poles. The new design made use of a temporary system, one in which teams of Asians, Americans, and Europeans worked together for almost a year. These tasks were in addition to ongoing responsibilities. These projects were designed to address the "soft" issues of global teamwork, global mindsets, and global leadership while delivering on the key "hard" strategic tasks given to the teams. Figure 2.1 provides the rationale for the Global Leadership Program.

Teamwork at the Top

At the core of the global leadership system is the top management team. Its executives need to lead and guide the process while also striving to be good role models for global managers. When we started, the top team was not prepared for this task. The team had new members; there was a great deal of provincialism; walls, barriers, and interpersonal conflicts abounded; the team itself had not functioned in an integrative fashion. It was not surprising

Figure 2.1   Global Leadership Development.

that a great deal of team building at the top level was a prerequisite for deeper organizational change.

The process started in a three day off-site meeting of the top team and the faculty. Prior to the session each executive was given extensive pre-work assignments. Each participant was asked to articulate a vision of the company in the 1990s by writing a journalistic scenario of the future organization. These scenarios were shared and the themes summarized ahead of time to prepare a discussion of their differing views. Also during this session, the top team looked at its own interpersonal processes. Each person received feedback from every one of his colleagues on the team about things they needed to do *more* of, *less* of, and how to *continue* to be effective global leaders. Contracts were negotiated among members and specific leadership goals were set for each one.

The top group had become deeply committed to the global leadership system. Members selected key projects necessary to globalize the business so that in June 1988, the top 55 people from Asia, the United States, and Europe could begin the process by participating in a temporary system designed to bring about faster global integration while developing global leaders. The first set of projects included:

1.   Improvement of competitive analysis

2.   Cycle time reduction

3. Global career issues

4. Product quality and customer satisfaction

5. Worldwide product planning system

6. Management of new technology

The Program participants were formed into multi-cultural teams of six to eight individuals. Each team had a specified set of objectives to be completed within nine months, which would have impact on the total business. They would work on these projects in addition to performing in their regular jobs. Each project team was coached by a member of senior management who was there to work on the "soft" issues of teamwork and leadership but not lead the harder tasks of global achievement.

The essence of the global leadership system is a belief that the best individual and organization development occur simultaneously. The core concept is "compressed action learning." The teams are given real problems to solve. They have coaches and structured assignments so that as they work on the real problems, they are also self-consciously working on their leadership skills, team skills, and global networking skills.

Figure 2.2 outlines this intense action learning process. It includes three workshops along with ongoing team and project work, although participants simultaneously carry on their regular jobs.

Figure 2.3 portrays the GLP experience as an emotional "frame breaking" experience. There are pressure points, highs, and lows throughout the life cycle of each GLP.

Workshop I:
The Launch of the Global Leadership Program

In June 1988, the first GLP was launched with 55 top-level managers from around the world meeting in Europe. The week was designed for group members to get familiar with the vision of the business, launch their strategic projects, begin building high-performing global teams, focus on personal leadership skills, and plan project schedules for the coming year.

The event was complex and emotionally charged with cross-national and cross-functional problems. Many of these people had never met before. It had been only months since the European business had been acquired. Resentment and resistance surfaced. The Asian business was further along in its integration, but residual resentment was still evident. Many American managers were feeling unsure of their own futures, facing difficult decisions about the location of "centers of product excellence." These decisions would result in downsizing of the headquarter's engineering and manufacturing capacity in the U.S. headquarters.

TIME
LINE
0

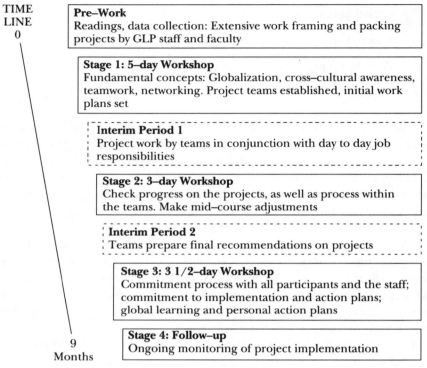

Pre–Work
Readings, data collection: Extensive work framing and packing projects by GLP staff and faculty

Stage 1: 5–day Workshop
Fundamental concepts: Globalization, cross–cultural awareness, teamwork, networking. Project teams established, initial work plans set

Interim Period 1
Project work by teams in conjunction with day to day job responsibilities

Stage 2: 3–day Workshop
Check progress on the projects, as well as process within the teams. Make mid–course adjustments

Interim Period 2
Teams prepare final recommendations on projects

Stage 3: 3 1/2–day Workshop
Commitment process with all participants and the staff; commitment to implementation and action plans; global learning and personal action plans

Stage 4: Follow–up
Ongoing monitoring of project implementation

9
Months

Figure 2.2   Program Overview.

At the start of the week, participants were confronted with multiple cross-cultural issues. The group included Americans, Japanese, and a number of Europeans. Divergent company cultures were brought together in the globalization effort. An additional emotional challenge at the European company was the feeling of just having been acquired. At the Asian company, managers were still unhappy with its American majority ownership. The group was being told that, in order to win globally, they were going to have to be team players. The complexity was heightened by language problems. Throughout the week simultaneous translation was used to facilitate communication.

During the second day, with attitudes quite negative and people still feeling anxious, an emotional breakthrough was precipitated by shifting the group into an outdoor setting for some "outward bound"–type activities. Such physical team activities are widely recognized as metaphors for communication, problem solving, and teamwork. Here the activities were additionally used as a carefully planned social technology for integrating the group. Ultimately, the group came together as it coped with the competitive challenge of people climbing over a fourteen-foot wall just by using their bodies to help each other in a race against time. By the end of the afternoon, there had been much

CRITICAL INCIDENTS FOR PARTICIPANTS

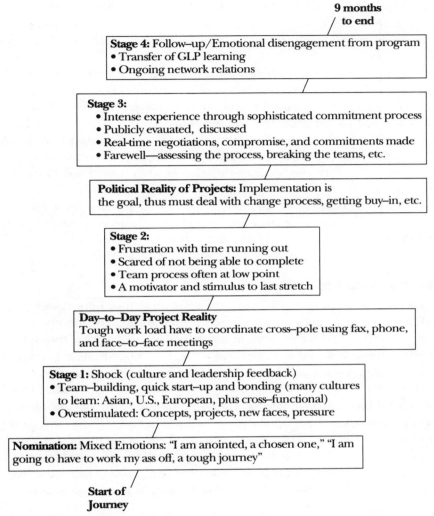

**9 months
to end**

Stage 4: Follow–up/Emotional disengagement from program
• Transfer of GLP learning
• Ongoing network relations

Stage 3:
• Intense experience through sophisticated commitment process
• Publicly evauated, discussed
• Real-time negotiations, compromise, and commitments made
• Farewell—assessing the process, breaking the teams, etc.

Political Reality of Projects: Implementation is
the goal, thus must deal with change process, getting buy–in, etc.

Stage 2:
• Frustration with time running out
• Scared of not being able to complete
• Team process often at low point
• A motivator and stimulus to last stretch

Day–to–Day Project Reality
Tough work load have to coordinate cross–pole using fax, phone,
and face–to–face meetings

Stage 1: Shock (culture and leadership feedback)
• Team–building, quick start–up and bonding (many cultures
to learn: Asian, U.S., European, plus cross–functional)
• Overstimulated: Concepts, projects, new faces, pressure

Nomination: Mixed Emotions: "I am anointed, a chosen one," "I am
going to have to work my ass off, a tough journey"

**Start of
Journey**

Figure 2.3 The GLP Journey: An Emotional Framebreaker.
The GLP is an intense, cross-cultural development experience. Learning is by doing
under pressure. It is akin to a "cultural outward-bound" experience. People and teams
are pushed beyond their perceived limits to achieve breakthroughs in performance.

laughter and fun and people were tired from being physically pushed. But it
was clear that they had for the first time broken through many of the national
and company cultural barriers. They were ready to move back into the workshop setting; struggle with engineering, manufacturing, and marketing problems; begin to build the teams; learn about issues of globalization; and link

up with their coaches who would be working with them for the following year on projects. When they returned to their regular jobs, they could continue to learn through working globally with their team, as project completion depends on coordinating, communicating and making decisions with people in Asia, Europe and the U.S.

The week ended with action plans. In addition, team members provided feedback to their team members in the following terms. In order to make you a better global leader, you need to do more of these behaviors, less of these behaviors, and continue doing these behaviors.

The goal was to help develop each person into a better global team member and leader. These feedback sessions (which occurred several times throughout the year) were some of the most powerful vehicles for individual development.

After approximately five months, the teams reconvened for a three-day event that turned out to be the most emotionally charged and difficult of the workshops.

Mid-Program Frustration

It was clear as we worked with the participants that they were reaching very high levels of stress both personally and professionally. For the first time in many of their careers, they were doing extensive international travel. Globalization had introduced individuals to jet lag and placed intense time pressures on them. Global activities were cutting into their local domestic teamwork, as they often had to make trade-offs between day-to-day activities and their global project commitments. They were having to re-examine the whole process by which they managed their personal time and the way they handled groups, teams, and the organization around them. Many of the participants resented having to meet in Tokyo because it would consume another week and weekend to deal with the global leadership program. On the other hand, many of them looked forward to visiting Japan and knew they needed help in managing the process.

All these emotions became evident in this meeting. As Figure 2.3 indicates, there was frustration and anxiety over the project, team process problems were emerging, and the predictable dynamics of mid-program frustration erupted.

In the following months, the pressure built. The final meeting was held in the United States. Here, each of the seven teams presented the results of their work. This event was not "show and tell" or a "pitch," but a "here's what we, as senior leaders in this business, are going to do and want you to do to resolve this problem." Therefore, it was designed as a *commitment event* at which the aim was to obtain the commitment of the top team as well as the other 55 people in the program. It was an event in "real time" where compromise, problem solving, and decision making took place. It represented a true global process where leader development interfaced with real-world problems.

Final Global Leadership Program Workshop

A very unique design was created for the final workshop. It was one which required the participants to behave as role models in a global organization. It was designed to model a fundamentally different global decision-making process. The 55 participants along with the 10 members of the Senior Management "top team" participated in a process of gaining commitment and advancing the implementations in the seven project areas. The design aimed to provide active dialogue, modification of recommendations, and a sign-on by all 55 participants plus the "top team." Each strategic area had a half-day session dedicated to the presentation with discussion and commitment. The process was radically different from the old way of doing things.

Table 2.1 contrasts the past "old way" with the global leadership "new way" process.

Impact of GLP

At the end of the first year, the participants in the Global Leadership Program (GLP I) were asked to write about the learnings that they hoped to carry

Table 2.1 Leadership Processes

OLD WAY	NEW WAY
No reports ahead of time	Written report prepared for everyone
No preparation by nonpresenting teams	Reading and preparation ahead of time
Formal presentation— a "pitch"	Minimal form presentation or "pitch"
Passive audience	Thorough discussion/ debate by all
	Real-time modification to improve recommendations
All energy focused on the boss	Total GLP commitment and buy-in to make change happen
No one has ownership	Continuous learning and development

forward from the program into their everyday work. Several themes emerged across these responses. One was a heightened awareness of their perceptions of the cultures and customs of people from other poles. Individuals had learned to respect and cooperate with those differences. The Asians and the Europeans found it was easy to let the Americans dominate team discussions, but that in doing so the interest and input of others was lost. It was observed that all participants really wanted to do a good job on the projects, though they varied in the ways they went about performing tasks. Many were surprised at the amount of time and effort necessary to really make the process work (e.g., team work, real two-way communication).

In the end, participants realized the long-term benefits of the program. They found that globalization would be a long journey and that patience was a key success factor. Quotes from several participants, each of whom wrote a "public" letter to the next group of GLP participants, offer insight:

> If there's anything we've learned about the process, it's to give equal time to both the project and the globalization experience. If you walk away from this with an excellent project completion, but don't know how a European lives, don't know why an Asian businessman gets promoted, haven't tasted kimchi, haven't ridden in the British subway, etc., you've blown it.

> Globalization or global brains is the ability to make global decisions— not domestic decisions that can be translated into the local language. To be global, you must know how the other poles think, what their customers want, and, bascially, what makes them "tick." To be successful at that, you must understand the basics for their being. This isn't as complex as it sounds. Just talk to them as colleagues, not aliens.

> Ensure that there is social time for your group. Force the group to do team activities (dinner, train ride, visit the fish market). Allow and demand that your colleagues from other poles use their native language. Never say "his English isn't very good" because, conversely, your Chinese probably sucks. Visit each other's homes as much as possible. Learn "how the other guy lives." Invite criticism during your team sessions and accept it well. Be honest in your assessment of others. Don't let "kindness" cloud your discussions. When you're in a crowd, look around. If your crowd consists of colleagues from your pole, change crowds. Most of all, don't look at this as a project assignment or you'll be wasting your time.

In addition to the Global Leadership Program, High Tech has established several other programs and actions to bring about globalization. One was to send ten of the corporation's "best and brightest" from each pole to another pole as part of an overall expatriate program. A Global Human Resource Programs Manager position was created. To fill this role, a manager from the European company was brought to the U.S. headquarters. The position of Manager of Human Resources was established in the European company and filled by an American from headquarters who was fluent in the local language. In addition, a Worldwide Planning Council was formed.

GLP I was followed in June of 1989 with the launch of Global Leadership Program II. The goal was to involve more and more managers in the globalization process. This time, 14 people from Asia, 20 from Europe and 23 from America were asked to participate. The presentation and commitment session for GLP II occurred in December 1989. GLP III was held in December 1990, and GLP IV in the same period in 1991. The GLP provided the foundation for continuous cultural learning and development along the globalization journey.

Through all these efforts, large numbers of people were learning to become personally sensitive to different cultures and to be willing to accept different approaches to problem solving. They were learning to deal with the paradox that it was culturally wrong to bend over backwards to accommodate differences and wrong to assume that one cultural way of doing things was best. It had become clear to those in the European and Asian corporations that learning about the American corporate philosophies and accepting them as their own was going to take time. Managers from all countries were understanding that globalization was truly a journey—a cultural journey—far more profound than traveling around the world.

Long-Term Impact of Global Leadership System

The process described above has some subtle and deep organizational development implications. On the surface, 50 to 60 senior executives were going through a six- to nine-month development experience with three workshops and projects on which they worked. At the end of that period, they had made progress on their projects and enhanced their global team and leadership capabilities. However, at a deeper level, their mindsets had been altered as they had been challenged to frame global issues and resolve them in an intense, cross-cultural experience.

Our research has shown that the social networks in the business have altered dramatically over time for people participating in a Global Leadership Program. Real changes have occurred regarding the network with which they interact to acquire the information that influences their global decisions. In addition, a cadre of leaders with global coaching skills is being developed. First, these skills are developed for the senior management group. Subsequently, each program selects an additional seven managers to become coaches

TOP MANAGEMENT
- *Provides a Global team–building process*—GLP forces teamwork through selection of projects, guidance of program, and commitment to take action
- *Provides a tool for developing global leadership skills*—group staff are tested and learn as leaders in a global contest
- *Provides global role models*—the group is on stage in the final workshop, making decisions publicly and demonstrating global leadership

ORGANIZATION
- *Provides an R&D lab* for new global behaviors; experimentation and learning are key to GLP
- *Global networks* are formed and reinforced
- *Global culture* and shared values are developed
- *Global information sharing*—best practices
- *Provides an assessment mechanism* for succession moves
- *Brings out external viewpoints/benchmarks* from global faculty

INDIVIDUAL PARTICIPANTS
- *Develops a global mindset*—new ways of framing business power
- *Global leadership skills* practiced and developed
- *Global team skills* practiced in program
- *Global networks* are formed among participants across the three poles

Figure 2.4   GLP "Soft" Impact on Management, Organization and Individual Participants.

in later programs. Coaching skills are increasingly important as the management mode for global organizations of the future.

The GLP has had both "hard" and "soft" impacts on the corporations's organization in terms of the implementation of changes coming from projects. New product development processes, technology transfer across the globe, marketing changes, and time-based telecommunication systems represent the hard issues. The other impact has been on a multidimensional set of "soft" people and cultural issues. Figure 2.4 provides a summary.

The global leadership process outlined here is transferable to other organizations. Several other companies, including some in Japan, have launched similar processes. *The core concept of a senior group simultaneously driving leadership development and organizational transformation is the key.* Other keys include the use of compressed action learning and intense cross-cultural team creation and problem solving. Figure 2.5 provides a summary of the building blocks and their effect on the goals of the GLP.

It is the careful blending and mixing of these building blocks that provides the high impact experience outlined in this chapter. Over time, through research and clinical practice, ways of improving existing elements and the invention of new building blocks will become clearer. In the interim, High Tech's results are exciting and encouraging in the context of a cross-cultural, individual, and organizational development effort in a global company.

IMPACT SCALE
○ = Little or no impact
◐ = Moderate Impact
● = Strong Impact

Building Blocks	Global Projects	Global Mind-set	Global Leadership	Global Team	Global Network
GEMS Top Team Leadership: Ownership of the projects, selection and sponsorship of participants and full involvement in the commitment process.	●	◐	◐	◐	●
Cross-Cultural Faculty: Multi-cultural, multi-lingual, multi-disciplinary faculty leading the process.	◐	●	◐	◐	◐
Coaching Role: Each team has a process consultant– someone selected and trained from the previous GLP–who coaches the team.	●	◐	◐	●	●
Process Learning: Team building activities including "outward bound," learning about high performing teams, systematic attention to feedback for each other.	●	◐	●	●	●
Learning Feedback Loops: Collection of data feedback to GLP participants. 1) Survey pre-GLP (self and others ratings of global leader behavior). 2) Team members provide feedback. 3) Coaches give feedback. 4) Another team analyzes and feeds back data. 5) Research team collects data and feeds back as part of program.	◐	◐	●	●	◐
Commitment Processes: Throughout GLP, individuals, teams, and the total group actively, publicly use processes for contracting and making "who, what, and when" commitments.	●	○	●	◐	◐
Concepts/Ideas: The GLP faculty present participants with new conceptual tools dealing with GEMS' global strategy, global operating mechanisms, time-based competitiveness, process loss, change process, and leadership.	◐	●	●	◐	◐

Figure 2.5

Notes

1. This is a term coined by such Japanese companies as Sony to emphasize the paradox of globalization: the need to be big and global while acting small and locally responsive.
2. Product line responsibilities were shifted, and the European, Asian, and American corporations each received R&D and product center responsibilities. This meant that product lines were discontinued and R&D centers restructured.

3

Globalization and Human Resource Management

Vladimir Pucik

In today's business environment, the traditional sources of competitive advantage cannot provide a sustainable edge. Low production cost, technology, or access to capital have become necessary, but not sufficient, conditions for success. Instead, contemporary approaches to global business strategies point to core competencies, invisible assets, and organizational capabilities as key factors influencing long-term success in global markets.[1] Thus, we are witnessing a renewed interest in human resource management as a major strategic tool that can uphold the competitive position of a global firm.[2]

The process of globalization not only brings the HR function closer to the strategic core of the business, it also changes the scope and content of human resource management. For example, in the past, international selection focused on testing managers for cross-cultural adaptability. Today's emphasis is on identifying managers capable of rapid learning across borders. Formerly, the international reward system stressed the coordination and equity of compensation policies; today's concern is the congruence of rewards with global business strategies. Traditional international training centered on cross-cultural knowledge; today's accent is on developing multicultural teams and networks.[3]

The shift of human resources activities from the top-down management of global rules and guidelines to a much broader focus on horizontal influence in managerial interactions is pushed forward by a set of inescapable contradictions that result from organizational challenges facing today's multinationals. With some simplification, these challenges can be aggregated along four principal dimensions linked to key facets of global organizations:

61

1. Strategic control (the challenge of reconciling the need for global centralization with local decentralization).

2. Integration (the challenge of leveraging diversified business strategies on a global scale).

3. Adaptation (the challenge of linking the global organizational forms to local environments).

4. Organizational boundaries (the challenge of accommodating organizational networks, alliances, and partnerships).

Each of these challenges requires that HRM activities adjust to seemingly contradictory perspectives.[4] This can be accomplished only if the past reliance on structural and administrative solutions to organizational issues is replaced with a focus on the quality of the management process.

For example, dealing with the centralization-decentralization dilemma requires moving away from the ideal, balanced structural configuration, which is too rigid to cope with frequent changes in the business environment, to one in which the benefits of both approaches can be applied simultaneously. In the truly global firm, managers must be equipped to decide in each situation how much autonomy or how much coordination will be necessary to implement the optimal strategy.

In this context, the essential role of the global HR function is to encourage maximum adaptability and maximum coordination, which allow the global firm to address market needs with the required mass and speed. Key HRM activities such as management development, evaluation, and compensation are the process levers through which this can be accomplished. The HRM system does not supplant a coherent global market strategy. It does, however, frame the organization charged with its implementation.

As global firms attempt to address key organizational paradoxes, it is becoming increasingly clear that the complexity of the task surpasses the traditional tool kits of "contingency" or "fit" approaches to management. Attempts to develop comprehensive operational guidelines for global managerial decision making framed around characteristics of the industry, competitive strategy, or political environment and reduced to a two-by-two matrix did not prove to be flexible enough to address the richness of management challenges facing a global firm. Similarly, efforts to develop global HRM policies from the conceptualization of stages of internationalization, while useful perhaps from an academic or pedagogical viewpoint, do not capture the essentials of the HR contribution to the execution of global business strategies.

We believe that to provide value to the business, HRM practices in a global firm should instead be constructed around, and focus on, specific organizational competencies critical for securing the competitive advantage in a global environment. The premise here is that three competencies are particularly important to a global firm. The first is organizational learning, the ability to acquire fast new technological or marketing skills across the whole organization. Second is continuous improvement, the ability of a firm to continuously improve the quality, cost, and delivery parameters of its products or services. Third is competitive culture, the ability to focus the energy of the people inside the firm on the task of winning in the marketplace. The need to master these three competencies is not unique to global firms. However, the linkages between HRM activities and these organizational competencies are very much influenced by the complexity and dynamism of global operations.

 ## Organizational Competencies in Global Firms

In a generic sense, the three organizational competencies are all centered on the accumulation of invisible assets: information-based organizational skills that are essential for the execution of flexible strategies in global markets. Examples are: a rapid development cycle, the just-in-time manufacturing process, a systematic cost reduction over time, and the ability to process fast customer feedback. All these assets provide value to the firm, yet they generally do not appear on the balance sheet—they are invisible.[5] They cannot be purchased; they are embedded in people and can be developed only through experience and training. It is because of the centrality of the human element that the HR practices play such an important role in acquiring and enhancing these competencies.

Organizational Learning

The core value of organizational learning is the enhancement of the long-term strategic capability of the organization. Its objective is to foster creativity, entrepreneurship, and autonomy, essential building elements supporting proactive and flexible global competitive strategies. However, an organization's capacity to learn is much greater than the collective capacity of all of its members to learn. It primarily reflects its collective capability to act and to implement what was learned. Individual knowledge that cannot be effectively applied in concert with the knowledge of others does not have much impact on how firms can compete.

The objective is to move beyond knowledge accumulation towards knowledge creation.[6] To develop an organizational capability to learn and to create new knowledge means to focus on the quality of interactions among organizational members and subunits. A number of factors may affect the quality of the interaction process: common language, shared experience, willingness to share information, mutual trust, opportunity to observe innovative behavior, etc. For global firms, this is a complex managerial task.

An example is the transfer of R&D capability from Japan to the United States by the leading Japanese automakers. At home, Japanese car makers are clearly at the leading edge of the "art" of car development in terms of cost, time, and quality. However, transferring this know-how to overseas locations turned out to be a task far more difficult than originally projected. Much of the domestic car R&D know-how is not codified or synthesized in easy-to-ship manuals; it is embodied in a complex set of tacit rules and behaviors that can only be mastered by direct observation and participation in the R&D activity. Under these circumstances, not surprisingly, the globalization of R&D is accomplished primarily by a large-scale transfer of domestic (Japanese) engineers to overseas locations, an effort that is not only costly, but also potentially disruptive to existing operations.

Continuous Improvement

Organizational learning is focused on the long-term survival and growth of the firm. At the same time, for a firm to maintain its competitiveness, long-term vision has to be balanced with constant attention to short-term tasks. Organizational learning requires slack resources, and only a continuous improvement in products and processes can allow the organization to accumulate sufficient means to learn. Organizational learning and continuous improvement are two sides of the same competitive strategy. One cannot be implemented without the other. There are no trade-offs here, only complementarity.

Nurturing an environment in which specific continuous improvement activities (*kaizen*), such as value-enhancing cost reduction, increase in product variety and customization, or rapid commercialization, may flourish again requires a focus on the quality of interactions within the organization. The interaction flow required is essentially horizontal, challenging the status quo in many global firms, which traditionally are organized in a fundamentally vertical fashion.

Effective continuous improvement programs are those that are integrated into the routine activities of the firm, including planning, accounting, and human resource management. From the HRM perspective, the selection, skill development, and recognition of global managers must take into account their accomplishment as champions of continuous improvement. However, dynamic global strategies cannot rest only on cost cutting. In this context, global HRM criteria must address the need for developing both bottom-line and top-line competence.

Competitive Culture

An organizational focus on learning and continuous improvement would be difficult, if not impossible, to sustain without a corporate culture dedicated to competition. Without a doubt, the pressure to cut cost and improve performance can be enormous. Nothing is permanent, and the cause of yesterday's success may be a cause of tomorrow's failure. The responsibility of management under such circumstances is to mobilize people's energy by providing the vision for a winning team. Managers strive to create a permanent sense of urgency for everyone in the organization, with top management setting the example.

In global companies with competitive culture, competition is not a threat but an opportunity to build on the creative energy of its people around the world, the glue that provides unity of purpose across countries, functions, and businesses. Companies with competitive culture, from Honda to Microsoft, see the global markets as "permanent Olympics." Every day, the company must prove that it belongs among the very best. However, perhaps in contrast to the traditional Olympic Games, it is not enough just to participate: the objective is to win, to be better, faster, stronger than any other competitor.

This focus on competition is not a blind obsession with winning; it emanates from recognizing that only through competition to provide the greatest possible value to the customer comes the excellence required for long-term organizational prosperity. Without striving constantly for the very best, even the mightiest global firms would atrophy and eventually decline. Examples abound. Development, support, and enhancement of a competitive culture is thus another key strategic task facing the human resource management function in a global firm.

Global Human Resource Activities

As pointed out earlier, the three core organizational competencies transcend the issue of globalization; they are linked as much to the competitive advantage of IBM or Toyota as to that of the local family store. However, the task of maintaining and expanding these competencies within global firms (given their cultural variety, complex structures, rapid environmental change, and multiplicity of customer requirements) presents the human resource function with obstacles and challenges far beyond those experienced in the past.

As HRM activities are becoming more and more an essential component of the strategy implementation process, traditional descriptions of HR activities in terms of operational or strategic direction become less relevant.[7] Operational and strategic issues are being merged. Together they determine the impact of the human resource function on the creation and enhancement of core organizational competencies. For that reason, the linkage of specific global HR activities with the respective competencies is thus probably a more productive conceptual base for our analysis.

This approach is presented in Table 3.1, which illustrates how specific HR roles are linked to the development of competitive advantage for the global firm. The strategic focus is reflected in the three organizational competencies,

Table 3.1 Direction and Criteria of Global Human Resource Activities

HR Roles	Core Competencies		
	Organizational Learning	Continuous Improvement	Competitive Culture
ORGANIZATION DESIGN	Integrated network	Task forces and teams Flexibility	Flat and lean Empowerment
STAFFING AND SELECTION	Slack resources Organizational competence	Implementation skills	Leadership Cross-cultural interactions
PERFORMANCE APPRAISAL	Teamwork Initiative	Customer focus Cost/Quality	Risk taking Values and behavior
REWARD SYSTEM	Cooperation Information sharing	Process improvement Recognition	Global sharing of rewards
MANAGEMENT DEVELOPMENT	Multifunction and multicountry careers	Operations Slower mobility	Socialization Global opportunities
COMMUNICATION	Cross-boundary linkages	Workshops and conferences	Shared mission and culture

each activity linked to a respective human resource management rule. The criterion of effective implementation is straightforward. Does the specific HR activity enhance organizational learning? Does it support continuous improvement? Does it contribute to maintenance of the competitive focus?

Organizational Design

Leading-edge global competitors, irrespective of their national origin, share one key organizational design characteristic. Their corporate structure is simple and flat, rather than tall and complex. The message is clear: the world outside is complicated enough, no need to add to the confusion with a complex internal structuring. Simple structures increase the speed and clarity of communication and allow the concentration of organizational energy and valuable resources on learning, rather than on controlling, monitoring, and reporting.

Responsibility for coordination between functions, markets, and businesses is delegated to line managers. They, as a team, should have all the information needed to make a decision that is best for the whole global organization. Management teams, organized in integrated networks, are charged with mapping the worldwide strategy for learning and its implementation. This involves setting learning priorities, making resource allocation decisions, and assigning people for specific learning tasks.

The need to rely on networks as an organizational mode to support learning extends beyond the core of the firm. With increasing global competition, network-like arrangements are often used to enable rapid entry into new markets and businesses. These arrangements can take a number of specific forms from simple supply/purchase agreements to complex joint-venture deals. However, strategic alliances are not a miracle cure that turn competitors into partners. Support in managing these collaborative networks, so the firm can maintain its learning focus, is again one of the key responsibilities of the HR function in a global firm.[8]

Task forces and ad hoc teams are also important features in the planning of global continuous improvement activities. However, the criteria for taking action are different. Learning teams strive to protect slack resources that are essential to support knowledge-creation. Improvement teams strive to identify resources that can be redeployed to a more efficient use. As pointed out, these two efforts are complementary, but from a team design perspective this duality of purpose must be recognized and explicitly managed.

Continuous improvement calls for a lean organizational structure and tight cost control. Corporate overhead can kill the company as surely as the cost of direct labor. In a typical global firm, coordination costs (staff, communication, and travel expense) are a significant element of the operating budget. However, the elimination of hierarchical layers, redundant meetings, and unnecessary reports (e.g., GE's "workout") not only improves the cost structure of the firm, it also promotes delegation—no one else but subordinates are around to do the job.

The advantage of task forces and teams is in their implied (or, even better, enforced) lack of permanence, enhancing the flexibility of the global organization. As customer needs are changing rapidly, the only type of organization with a chance to provide the customer with long-term value, and thus to survive, is one that is flexible and adaptable to changes in its environment. A lack of flexibility suggests unnecessary redundancies, waste, and decision-making "black holes." Structural flexibility is thus essential to continuous improvement.

Delivery of superior value to the customer (total customer satisfaction) is not possible without the involvement of all employees. Each activity counts, not only for those who interact directly with customers, but also for all others; employees are each other's customers. The final outcome will not be optimal unless maximum performance is achieved at all previous levels. Top management cannot control this process of "effort maximization;" it is far too dynamic, complex, and unpredictable. Attempts to control operations step-by-step only hinder the organization's flexibility and responsiveness.

In this sense, delegation of responsibility is not a "gift" to make employees feel comfortable, it is a necessary condition for winning in a global competition. To win, it is not enough to have involved spectators; it requires involved *players*. Full involvement and commitment to a chosen strategy is not sustainable without responsibility and sense of control over one's own destiny. "Flat and lean" means empowerment to make choices, not an overload of conflicting demands from multiple layers of bureaucracy.

Competitive culture rests on the premise of the acceptance of responsibility. This requires that hierarchy be flexible and the decisions made at lowest levels be dictated by common sense, rather than by organizational manuals or formal job descriptions. The aim is to create a climate in which everyone is encouraged to do what is necessary to succeed; to say "This is not my job" is not acceptable. In a global firm, this entails breaking down the barriers between the center and the affiliates, between those "inside" and those on the "outside." The increasingly popular corporate slogan "Think globally, act locally" is a succinct description of how a global firm should compete, provided that global thinking is not limited to the selected few.

Staffing and Selection

During the 1980s most global firms moved forward to implement major programs aimed at increasing the participation of local nationals in the management of overseas subsidiaries. While no comprehensive survey exists, the presence of local nationals in top subsidiary jobs is no longer exceptional—unless perhaps the subsidiary is Japanese-owned. Many U.S., and in particular European, firms are quite successful in staffing across borders, at least up to the upper middle management levels. At the very top of most global firms, however, executive teams are primarily dominated by nationals of the parent country. In that sense, having multinational executive teams is still more of an appealing goal than a reality.

Tapping into the potential of local managers is in line with the focus on global human resources. One of the driving forces behind this development is the sound belief that hiring local nationals may be a good strategy to limit the resentment of foreign managerial dominance in the subsidiary. The focus on developing a strong local management team may help to satisfy the rising ambitions and expectations of many local employees and also cuts immediate staffing costs by eliminating transfer-related expenses and adjustments.

At the same time, as pointed out by Kobrin later in this volume, reducing cross-national staffing ultimately leads to a reduction in the pool of managers with global rather than area-specific experience. Organizational competence at running a global business can thus be seriously jeopardized. This does not imply that a return to traditional ethnocentric staffing is desirable. Rather, building up global managerial competence means enlarging the pool of managers selected for global assignments to the point of ignoring the locale of entry into the corporation.

From the standpoint of creating an executive team capable of managing global competitive strategies, the issue is not how to resolve the dilemma between local and global competence. Rather, the issue is how to develop corporate human resources possessing both of the critical skills. Yet, while some short-term trade-offs are unavoidable, staffing decisions in many global firms are still being made primarily according to current needs without consideration of long-term strategic implications; even worse, decisions are based mainly on short term financial expediencies and tax considerations.

Effective organizational learning within a global firm, however, requires more than the ability to run a global business. Staffing and selection policies must also enable the fast transfer of technical or marketing know-how across subsidiaries in support of current business strategies, as well as enhance knowledge-creation, allowing the firm to pursue business opportunities in uncharted territory. For example, to push forward its research on superconductivity, NEC created a special multidisciplinary and multicultural task force. By combining their unique individual perspectives, its members were able to progress faster than the more homogeneous teams of their global competitors.

The cost of building a truly multinational team may be substantial. However, for the organization to learn, slack resources in terms of surplus staffing are essential. As a matter of policy, many Japanese multinationals dispatch their young staff for one-year internships to overseas locations, not to run the business, but to learn. Some, such as Sony, Honda, and Nissan, are now experimenting with reverse transfers, bringing young overseas staff to Japan for several years in order to increase the future receptivity of the overseas operations to the technology inflow from the parent firm.

As leading global firms strive to gain competitive advantage by emphasizing continuous improvement programs in their worldwide operations, their staffing and selection practices also reflect a shift in the strategic orientation. In the past, global assignments were initiated either in order to maintain control or to supplement specific skills that were not available locally. But in today's environment, managers seen as "on loan from Mecca," analytical and detached, do not engender much respect. The new emphasis is on implementation skills and the ability to make a contribution to the business.

To earn credibility, global managers have to be able to take initiative, not just judge what others have done. For this they need to know well how value is created in their operations, and they have to be seen as taking the lead in improving the competitive position of the organization. They also need to have a sufficient pull in other parts of the global business so that, if necessary, they can quickly mobilize the support from their peers elsewhere. "Has-beens" and "never-beens" do not travel well.

The staffing and selection criteria, especially for positions with substantial management responsibility, need also to consider the capability to demonstrate leadership, since leadership is one of the key factors that will spur the spirit of competition. However, to develop global leadership is far from simple.[9] How leadership is defined, what traits and behaviors are perceived as critical for a leader, may differ greatly according to the specific context embedded in country, company, and subunit cultures. On the other hand, a sensitivity to cross-cultural diversity, the ability to filter conflicting cultural messages, and the willingness to keep an open mind and listen are characteristics that most accomplished global leaders probably share.

Performance Appraisal

The proposition that an appraisal on the strategic level ought to be focused on the congruence of current performance with long-term corporate objectives is today accepted at least in theory, yet its practical application is often bogged down for lack of clarity about long-term goals and their measurement. In what form should long-term goals be expressed to be measurable against performance? What aspects of managerial performance should be evaluated from the long-term viewpoint? The long-term/short-term question is not the only one that a global appraisal process must deal with. In a global firm, there is also potential for conflict between global and local objectives.

The limitation of local profit-maximization strategies can be seen when competitive pressure requires a global firm to operate and compete in markets where, if isolated from other markets, it would choose not to compete. A typical case would be a firm's presence in a market that serves as a cash-flow base for a strong competitor, with the objective of limiting the competitor's advantage through an aggressive pricing policy. Obviously, traditional measurements do not capture this strategic intent.

In addition, many global firms use transfer prices and other financial tools to influence transactions between their subsidiaries worldwide in order to minimize their foreign-exchange risk exposure and tax liabilities. Therefore, the financial results recorded in the subsidiary often do not accurately reflect its contribution to the global business; such data should not be used as a primary input in the performance evaluation process.

In order to reconcile the contradictory perspectives, today's standard practice calls for key performance criteria to be customarily derived from negotiated budgetary targets. It is expected that during the internal negotiations, conflicting objectives can be, at least to some degree, harmonized. However, still being left out of the evaluation process are intangible aspects of performance linked to the development of core organizational competencies.

The fact of life in most organizations is that what is not being measured does not receive much attention from managers or executives. A commitment to learning, improvement, and competition will remain only a token expression in the company mission statement, unless backed up by well thought out criteria for measuring accomplishments. The mix of criteria is determined by business fundamentals; some are "soft," some are "hard," but they reflect the understanding that without assigning and evaluating responsibility—individual or team—the process of creating the core organizational competencies will be impossible to internalize and sustain.

Global organizational learning is driven by teamwork across boundaries, acceptance of risk, and the willingness to invest in new initiatives. Many of the learning criteria reflect attitudes and behaviors and thus may be seen as soft or ambiguous. However, while the learning process itself may be invisible, the results are not. Learning organizations are therefore "hard" about assigning responsibility for achieving learning objectives and for specific actions that enhance the quality of the learning process.

What competencies need to be mastered, who is responsible for this to happen, who will support the activity, and how and in what time frame will the results be measured? All this should be considered a part of the global appraisal process. In reality, too frequently, this is not the case. For example, in a recent survey, only 11 percent of large foreign firms operating in Japan indicated that their senior staff is evaluated on their contribution to the development of Japan-related business know-how in their worldwide operations.[10] It is no wonder, then, that Japan remains an enigma.

The appraisal of continuous improvement is linked to customer focus and the cost and quality improvement process. In this area, many companies achieve considerable success in developing methodology to monitor progress on the subsidiary level. However, the system often breaks down when improvement targets involve linkages across borders. A major quality problem in one part of the world may not seem of great significance to a manufacturing location on another continent. This makes it unlikely that managers will commit resources necessary to address the issue. Here, the appraisal process must ensure that the requirements of the most demanding global customers become the common standard of evaluation and measurement of progress. Also, as in the case of organizational learning, the sharing of know-how and resources with other units needs to be encouraged, for example, by entrusting some improvement teams with global responsibility and by appraising managers on their willingness to support such activities.

The appraisal system also has a major impact on the will to compete, which is often suppressed by strategic biases linked to traditional measurement criteria linked to earnings growth, margins, etc. Since competition generally reduces margins, at least in the short-term, the use of such criteria guides managers to pursue strategies that focus on those market niches that provide temporary earnings and margin shelter. Other markets and product lines may be abandoned and the overall competitive position may be weakened, although the performance is on target.

In contrast, global competitive culture rests on benchmarking against the best of the competition, risk-taking, and the drive to seek out new challenges. Effective performance goals linked to a competitive culture are externally oriented, based on customer-driven values and needs. They are usually simple to communicate, measure, and reward. Honda's obsession with winning U.S. customer satisfaction ratings in the late 1980s is a good example of such an approach.

Global Reward System

In principle, it is widely recognized that an effective global reward system should take into account differences in employees' appreciation of different reward alternatives. However, in reality, most global firms still consider rewards in purely monetary terms, not in terms of personal growth and challenge. While personnel systems in Japanese, European, and U.S. multinationals are often strikingly dissimilar, they often all share one common problem: an inability to reward promising locally hired employees with adequate global career opportunities.

In such an environment, it is not surprising that a local manager aware of the limitation of her career prospects is primarily concerned about the security and stability of only the local operation, disregarding or paying less attention to the broader goals of the global firm. It is naive to expect commitment to a long-term global strategy in which local executives have only a very limited input and from which they receive very limited benefits. Paradoxically, attempts to localize top management in the subsidiaries often merely serve to reinforce the gap in focus between local and global management.

The shift away from the short-term monetary focus of the reward system toward a longer-term career focus is also prompted by operational difficulties in administering a universal and fair spot reward package. First of all, such a system has to align the notion of equity within the organization to labor market conditions and differences in tax treatment between various countries. Globalization makes this a methodological nightmare. In addition, managers' expectations about what constitutes an equitable compensation and reward system do not always converge. These factors may create a fertile ground for frictions and conflicts that cannot be resolved by simply changing the salary or bonus formula. Finally, a cash-driven global reward system makes it very costly to develop and retain a population of global managers large enough to run the business effectively.

An emphasis on rewarding careers rather than short-term financial outcomes is also essential for the reward system to stimulate the enhancement of the critical organizational competencies. Since developing new competencies may require an increased use of multicountry teams and task forces, a frequent mixing of global and local managers in many international locations, and assignments of cross-border responsibilities to country executives, the traditional reward structure does not capture the impact of such organizational trends.

For global organizational learning to take place, for example, incentives must be present to diffuse and share critical information. In the past, key employees were often rewarded for their market value, that is, the gap between what they knew and what others did. The greater the gap, the bigger the reward. However, for an organization to learn, such a reward structure needs to be changed. Managers must be rewarded for sharing information, mentoring, and teaching others about what they themselves have learned.

Both organizational learning and continuous improvement processes also require at least a partial disassociation of rewards from rigid job descriptions, in order to foster behavior consistent with the notion of a borderless organization, teamwork, and reduction of waste. Traditionally, Japanese multinationals had an advantage in this respect because their reward systems were built around broad "pay-for-knowledge" salary bands.[11] Today, however, because of the home-country demographic issues, some Japanese multinationals are keen to adopt a Western system, more tightly linking the salary and bonus levels with current job responsibilities. How this will impact their capability to maintain *kaizen* globally remains to be seen.

Through the reward system, continuous improvement is linked with a growth-oriented competitive culture. Without growth, continuous improvement is difficult to sustain; cost reduction and similar programs are seen only as tools to reduce the ultimate reward: an employee's job. For example, a number of multinationals found it difficult to consolidate their operations in Europe in light of the EEC integration. Lacking growth, such a consolidation is viewed as a zero-sum game, fiercely resisted by managers and employees of affected subsidiaries.

In this sense, the distribution of rewards generated by success in global competition must be viewed as equitable by the employees. While the meaning of "equity" may vary in specific national cultures, a balance of risk, responsibility, and effort with reward is essential. Many winning firms today share two key characteristics in their reward systems: (1) some form of financial profit sharing extends deeply into the organization and across borders, and (2) concern with employment stability and employee development.

The emphasis on employment stability is important, otherwise the concept of rewarding careers lacks any credibility. The idea of winning is of no value to those no longer on the team. It should be pointed out, however, that effective employment policies do not provide a guarantee against lay-offs; employment stability must be earned by winning the global responsibility for making sure that the company strategy enhances opportunities for employees worldwide to pursue meaningful and challenging careers.

Global Management Development

The earlier discussion leads to one important conclusion. Probably the most formidable task in the human resource area facing many global firms is the development of a cadre of managers and executives who have a deep understanding of the global market environment, have the capability to transfer this knowledge into resolute action, and who expect to see their rewards and personal growth linked to opportunities for global careers.

As pointed out earlier, in the initial stages of international expansion, most global firms relied on a small but carefully selected group of managers who, after an initial exposure to domestic business, spent their careers in the company's international ventures. While this seemed to be a reasonable arrangement for a limited period of time, the reliance on expatriates limited the ability to develop, motivate, and retain capable local executives.

Over time, a thorough knowledge of local operations becomes more important than socialization into the culture of the home office, and the disadvantages of running the business through expatriates are greater than the benefits of easy control and smooth communication. Under such conditions, not to mention the pressure from the host governments, it was natural that many multinational firms refocused their management development on local resident managers, with expatriates shrinking in number and influence.

Today, many global firms are facing a dilemma. Because of the past and present investment in the development of local staff, they have no difficulties in finding competent managers well qualified to handle local operations in most of their principal markets. However, at the same time, they are short of seasoned executives with broader international skills who are also closely attuned to the global strategy of the firm.

These two conditions are linked. Because of the localization of developmental opportunities, there is a shortage of vacancies available to managers pursuing an international track. In some companies, such managers are indeed becoming an endangered species as a matter of deliberate corporate policy. In other words, too much localization resulted in insufficient globalization. To reverse this trend is far from easy, in terms of both the cost of developing a new breed of global executives and the challenge this provides to the established culture of international management development.

Why is it essential to change the direction of management development in multinational firms from a local to a global emphasis? First, because most businesses became global, not "multilocal." Second, because the firm's objective should be to develop organization-level competencies, not just the skills of individual managers. Coordinated on-the-job learning and the transfer of this know-how are in fact probably the only practical methods for absorbing and transmitting the tacit knowledge that encapsulates many of the critical competencies in today's global business (e.g., Japanese automotive R&D, mentioned earlier). Effective global learning is greatly enhanced through global careers, a well planned sequence of multicountry (and often multifunction) assignments.

To support the organizational commitment to learning, and especially to continuous improvement, will also require substantial adjustment in the optimal functional orientation and career timetable for international managers. The career focus will move away from the control and monitoring function to operations and implementation. On the one hand, some assignments will grow longer to provide sufficient time to learn about the environment and design strategies for improvement, as well as supervise their execution. In other instances, when the focus is primarily on management development, assignments will be short (sometimes even five- to six-month projects), but they will be strung together in a planned, coordinated sequence.

More emphasis should also be give to the socialization aspects of management development. A truly global competitive culture cannot emerge without a sense of common purpose and trust among employees and managers collaborating together on the execution of global strategies. Effective global managers need to share core values and learn both multidisciplinary and multifunction problem solving as well as a collegial style of leadership. All this can only emerge through frequent interaction, both on and off the job. Thus, socialization assignments, as well as socialization training, are quickly becoming an important management development tool.

The new "global" dimension of management development has two important consequences for the focus and timing of management development activities. First of all, global culture can only emerge when career opportunities are global and career distinctions between employees based on their country of origin are erased. This of course is a long-term challenge, as seen in the wide gap that exists today between the espoused culture of globalization and the reality of unicultural top executive teams in the vast majority of global firms.

To some extent, this gap may be reduced with time, as the multicultural profile of current middle managers will eventually be reflected at the top of the organization. However, to break through cultural "glass ceilings" will also require a sufficient commitment of developmental resources and the leadership necessary to break the traditional barriers. How global firms deal with this problem may even reorder the position of leadership in a number of industries. For example, as Bartlett and Yoshihara argue in this volume, the closed nature of Japanese society may put Japanese multinationals at a disadvantage in comparison to multinationals from countries in which cultural diversity is more the norm.

There is no doubt that the cost of developing a cadre of global executives is high. One way to reduce the cost, besides rethinking the logic of the reward system mentioned earlier, is to pursue various developmental alternatives to full-scale international assignments. The GE experience, described by Tichy, is a good example of a corporate-wide developmental effort to enhance the spirit of globalization.

A complementary strategy would be to put more emphasis on cross-border assignments during the early stages of an employee's career, when the cost of expatriation and the obstacles to international mobility (e.g., family constraints) are the lowest. This would contrast with the current trend of rationing global developmental opportunities to the few proven corporate "stars."

However, early globalization not only has cost advantages. There is also evidence that managers who experience cross-cultural exposure early in their careers assimilate better to other cultures, primarily because they develop closer social links with the local peer group. Obviously, the cross-border transfer of junior staff is acceptable to host entities only when the development programs operate two ways and similar opportunities are also available to the local staff.

Global Communications

Because the core global organizational competencies are all invisible assets based on information, their accumulation within the firm is driven by the acquisition and diffusion of information. Information becomes a valuable corporate resource: the more information available inside the organization, the richer the organization's asset base. The role of the global HR function is then to bolster the sharing of information, not by becoming an internal PR agent, but by assuring that communication processes, tools, and climate are aligned with corporate strategy, vision, and values.

The key mechanism for diffusing information in a global firm is usually the business decision-making process. The objective is for management to not only reach a decision, but to also clarify to all involved why such a decision was taken, what strategic parameters determine the outcome, and what the priorities of implementation are. Well-informed employees can take independent action, and a faster response time is thus built into the decision-making structure. Such information can also serve as a valuable input into learning loops and improvement activities.

Much of this obviously happens outside of the traditional domain of human resource management. Yet the contribution of the HR function, while indirect, is nevertheless critical. By recognizing that telecommunication technology can enhance information exchange only to the extent that its users are comfortable to interact at the personal level, it can sponsor activities that will support such a personal communication infrastructure.

The HR function can directly influence communication intensity within the global firm by creating opportunities for interaction among employees worldwide. For example, properly structured developmental assignments can help set up informal communication links between distant subunits that can benefit from joint learning. Workshops and conferences are very valuable tools for spreading continuous improvement know-how, in addition to providing the recognition of key contributors. In addition, the HR organization may serve as a corporate communication auditor, monitoring the climate for information sharing and suggesting corrective action when necessary.

Finally, the HR function is also responsible for setting up internal communication programs to support the firm's competitive culture centered around a shared vision of the strategic mission of the organization. The aim is simple: to win, to be the very best. Such an objective is easily understood by employees at all levels of the organization and it appeals to a desire common all over the globe: joining the winning team. This winning desire, together with a collective knowledge of competition and its capabilities and an appreciation of the value created by serving the customer, provides the essential cultural glue that helps to keep the far-flung global organization together.

However, no one in the corporation but the top management can articulate this competitive vision with the required strength and credibility. The role of the HR function then is to work with top management to create opportunities for them to interact and communicate directly to employees their vision, strategy, and competitive priorities. This cannot be done by simply shipping videotapes with New Year's messages around the world, but by ensuring that top executives find the time on their schedules to meet employees face-to-face and that top management is able to express the core corporate mission in a context understandable and acceptable to all.

The Global Role of HR Professionals

We have proposed that in order to enhance the competitive advantage of a global firm, its human resource activities should focus on developing the three essential core competencies: organizational learning, continuous improvement, and competitive culture. At the same time, the human resource function needs to shift from an administrative to a process orientation so that it can flexibly reconcile the organizational paradoxes inherent in the activities of global firms. This not only creates new demands on how specific HR activities are performed, but also sets a new agenda for HR professionals and their global role.

First of all, human resource executives need to learn about the fundamentals of global competition. They cannot assume a global strategic role without understanding global strategy. In order to become effective business partners, HR executives must develop an understanding of what drives global competition in their business, how this competition affects business conditions in specific markets, and what the social, political, and economic variables are that may have an impact on the firm's strategy in different parts of the world.

Second, a solid knowledge of strategy must be complemented by the globalization of the professional expertise. This rests primarily on the acceptance and understanding of the cultural relativity of many HR practices.[12] To what extent can company "home" HR systems be applied to other countries? Where and how should they be adapted? In what areas is diversity in customs, norms, and values acceptable, and where is it essential to promote and defend cultural synergy?

At the same time, the existence of "cultural distance" does not automatically imply that HR practices cannot be transferred. "This is a good idea, but it would never work in . . . " is an expression dreaded by many international HR executives. The critical test of cross-cultural skills is therefore the ability to distinguish between a legitimate cultural constraint and an attempt to avoid implementing difficult decisions. This also implies differentiating what needs to be done from how to go about doing it.

Another important competency expected from an international HR professional is the understanding of how the principal global competitors plan and execute their global HR strategy, what tools and methods they use to build their organizational competencies, and what implications may result from their actions. In most global firms, however, such competitive analyses of HR capabilities are not compiled, although periodic assessments of competitors' financial, market, and technological capabilities are now a common practice.

The understanding of the global strategy, cultural differences, and HR capabilities requires thorough globalization of the HR function by developing a cadre of HR professionals with an international perspective. Presently, however, many of the international HR skills are operationally oriented and deal mainly with the expatriate population and transfers of people across borders: compensation and benefits, tax, logistics. The number of HR executives with a multicountry experience or those on an international track is rather limited.

The lack of international experience among HR professionals is not surprising, since for most of them, there are relatively few opportunities to earn transfers to locations outside of their home country (excluding training assignments in the head office). The HR jobs are thought of as fundamentally local and culturally specific in terms of skills required, and many country and business executives have lingering doubts about the value-added of an expatriate HR professional. HR management positions are filled from abroad only if it is not possible to staff the HR function locally. In other words, in many global firms, the function in charge of globalizing management is itself still rather parochial.

This will have to change. However, structural solutions, such as setting up regional HR positions or assigning global responsibility to corporate HR functions, are not sufficient if the people in these positions lack critical international skills and experience, not because of a lack of potential to think and behave globally, but because of the lack of opportunities to develop their international competence. Thus, the education of a new breed of international HR professionals is one of the main internal challenges facing the global HR function today.

To address this issue, it is important to recognize that all factors discussed earlier with respect to selecting, developing, and motivating global executives apply equally to HR professionals. There is no great mystery in how to develop global HR skills: hire people with cross-cultural competence; provide them with opportunities to learn about HR in different parts of the world through assignments, projects, and interaction with their peers; and appraise and reward them for seeking out challenging international assignments and for contributing to the implementation of global strategies.

Companies that have successfully globalized their human resource activities share several important characteristics:

First of all, the global HR role has the strong support of top management, not in terms of "I believe in people" statements, but in terms of high expectations about the contributions the HR function can make to the formulation and implementation of effective global strategies and the readiness of the HR function to step up its responsibilities. A demanding global executive has a very powerful impact on the speed and direction of globalization.

The expectations and support of top management for the global HR role are usually derived from a longstanding commitment to dedicate management energy and resources to human resource issues as a reflection of a people-oriented corporate culture. In that sense, the global HR role is a natural extension of the positive orientation toward human resource management and the recognition of the strategic role that it can and should play.

Several other aspects of corporate culture also seem critical for successful globalization. Cultural diversity needs to be encouraged as a natural way of life, not just tolerated as a necessity brought about by the internationalization of business. This also implies accepting ambiguity as a way of dealing with the paradoxes embedded in many of the global HR issues. Not much is black or white, and it will never be otherwise.

The final condition for a successful implementation of global HR strategies is the competence and credibility of the HR staff. To earn that credibility, it is not enough for HR professionals just to wait around for service requests or until the line managers discover the value of human resources. It requires taking the risk and responsibility for putting forward policies and practices that can make a difference. No guts, no glory.

References

1. For a contemporary view on global business strategy, see the recent series of articles in *Harvard Business Review* (1989–1991) by G. Hamel and C. K. Prahalad, and Ch. A. Bartlett and S. Goshal, *Managing Across Borders* (Cambridge, Mass.: Harvard Business School Press, 1989).

2. This shift is well illustrated in Paul Evans, Yves Doz., and A. Laurent, eds., *Human Resource Management in International Firms* (London, Macmillan, 1989).

3. The recent actions of major global firms in this regard are described in K. Barnham and M. Devine, *The Quest for the International Manager: A Survey of Global Human Resource Strategies*, The Economist Intelligence Unit, London, 1991.

4. See Chapter 4, by Paul Evans and Yves Doz later in this volume.

5. For the definition of invisible assets, see H. Itami with T. W. Roehl, *Mobilizing Invisible Assets* (Cambridge, Mass.: Harvard University Press, 1987).

6. The importance of knowledge creation for the competitive strategy of a firm was pointed out first in various contributions of I. Nonaka (a concise summary of his views appears in *Harvard Business Review*, November–December 1991).

7. For a discussion of operational, managerial, and strategic approaches to human resource management see C. J. Fombrun, N. M. Tichy, and M. A. Devanna, eds., *Strategic Human Resource Management*, (New York, John Wiley & Sons, 1984).

8. On the human resource role in managing strategic alliances, see the chapter by V. Pucik later in this volume; also V. Pucik, "Strategic Alliances with the Japanese: Implications for Human Resource Management," in F. J. Contractor and P. Lorange, eds., *Cooperative Strategies in International Business* (Lexington Mass.: Lexington Books, 1988).

9. N. M. Tichy describes the leadership challenges of globalization in two chapters in this volume, drawing on specific examples of global leadership development.

10. "Developing and Managing Human Resources," Briefing Paper, Business International: Japan Business Group, Tokyo, October 24, 1991.

11. V. Pucik, "White-Collar Human Resource Management in Large Japanese Manufacturing Firms," *Human Resource Management* 3: 3, (1984).

12. For cross-cultural perspectives on the transferability of human resource practices, see chapters by G. Hofstade, S. Schneider, and Y. Laurent later in this volume.

PART TWO

The
Strategic
Context

4

Dualities
A Paradigm for Human Resource and Organizational Development in Complex Multinationals

Paul A. L. Evans and Yves Doz

In our studies of human resource management in complex multinational enterprises (summarized in Evans, Doz, and Laurent 1989), we find that dualities are a pervasive feature in the development of these organizations. Dualities reflect opposing forces that must be balanced—properties that seem contradictory or paradoxical, but which are in fact complementary. For example, complex multinational firms must typically provide integration to subsidiaries that need to be locally responsive—such enterprises must think globally but act locally. Top-down management processes must be combined with bottom-up processes. Adaptation, learning, and innovation require loose, organic properties, while efficiency and profitability require tight, mechanistic qualities. Balancing specialization with generalism and business logic with technical logic becomes more difficult and important in an era of changing technology. A partial list of some prevailing dualities is shown in Table 4.1.

Dualities were first captured in the concept of matrix. The problem with matrix is that it is usually thought of with yesterday's structural mind-set. In fact, matrix structures are no more than a structural response to this far wider management challenge. Davis and Lawrence (1977) saw a basic duality as being at the origin of the notion of matrix:

All forms of social organization have two simultaneous needs that are often at odds with each other: freedom and order. Freedom springs from intuition and leads to innovation. Order stems from intelligence and provides efficiency. Both are essential, but are they compatible-with each other? Within organizations, these requirements are translated into structural terms with which we are rather familiar. Freedom is translated as the specialized interests of different parts of an organization: the optimal goal of decentralization. Order is represented as the regulation and integration of all elements in harmonious and common action: the optimal goal of centralization. The problem with the centralization-decentralization debate, however, was that the more you realized the benefits of the one, the less you got the benefits of the other. The dilemma of organization was the dilemma of an either-or world, of being either a boss or a subordinate. The promise of a release from the dilemma of the flexibility of both centralization and decentralization, specialization and integration. (Davis and Lawrence 1977, xi)

Table 4.1   Some Common Dualities in Today's Complex Organizations

Competition — Partnership
Differentiation — Integration
Loose — Tight
Control — Entrepreneurship
Planned — Opportunistic
Formal — Informal
Vision — Reality
Dentralization — Centralization
Business Logic — Technical Logic
Analysis — Intuition
Delegation — Control
Individuality — Teamwork
Action — Reflection
Change — Continuity
Formal — Informal
Top-down — Bottom-up
Tolerance — Forthrightness
Flexibility — Focus

The purpose of this chapter is to explore the concept of duality, assessing the extent to which it provides a frame to guide organization development in complex organizations, notably multinational firms in competitive global environments. Organization development is a major challenge for such firms. Research on multinational enterprises suggests that their future competitive advantage may not reside in their strategy or structure, nor in their technologies or products, but in their organizational capabilities to cope with the multidimensional and complex demands of global business. As Prahalad and Doz (1987) put it, the quality of organization will increasingly become the prime competitive weapon.

As a component of organization, human resource management is a central element in this challenge of organization development. Dualities cannot be balanced with heavy, cumbersome management instruments—structure and basic systems—alone. Balancing opposite properties requires the parallel use of more subtle management mechanisms, notably those of human resource management.

The first part of this chapter outlines four principles of dualistic thinking, illustrated with examples from human resource management and international organization. In the second part, we suggest that dualities may constitute an emerging paradigm for management and organization in our increasingly complex and turbulent environment, contrasting this with the current "fit paradigm." And in the third section, we apply this theory to the development of the complex international organization, using a concept that we call "cultural layering." Not all of our examples are drawn from international firms; although we drew these lessons primarily from MNCs, they apply broadly to complex organizations.

Dualistic Principles

The concept of duality is not new. It can be found in philosophy (though it differs from other oppositional concepts such as dialectic, dilemma, or trade-off), in personality theory, and in the study of history (see Figure 4.1, "Dualities in Social Systems").

To explore this concept, let us focus on four principles of dualistic organization.

1. Most qualities of a social system have a complementary quality, which together constitute a duality.

Dualities reflect a mind-set, a way of thinking. So, although our focus is organizational, let us begin with an example at a personal level of analysis, namely personnel evaluation. In evaluating people, we make judgments based on categories or qualities—decisiveness, analytic ability, sensitivity, and so on.

The concept of complementary duality differs from other concerns with opposition in classical philosophy—from the Kantian philosophy of synthesis that underlies today's concept of synergy, or the Hegelian dialectic underlying Marxist economic theory. It is best described by the German philosopher Helweg (1951), while Gregory Bateson pointed out that without the tension that exists between simultaneous opposites in a social system, a cycle of "schismogenesis" occurs, a degenerative syndrome where an attribute perpetuates itself until it becomes extreme and thereby dysfunctional (Bateson 1936; Cameron 1986).

Carl Jung, whose work laid the foundations for personality theory, viewed dualities as the core of human existence. The tension between opposites is what gives life its meaning. All psychic energy is the result of the seesawing tension between dualities.

Jung saw the psyche as having four functions in a compass of oppositions: thinking and feeling, sensation and intuition (popularized in the widely known Myers-Briggs Personality Inventory). Because of these oppositions, each individual tends to specialize in a dominant function, and it is this specialization that gives rise to psychological types (Jung 1923).

Analogies can be drawn to organizations from many of Jung's insights. For instance, Jung saw the tension between functions as being less severe in primitive society, which would permit modest differentiation in all four functions. But as society becomes complex, so the individual is obliged to specialize in one function at the expense of others, thereby heightening the risk of personality disorders, that reflect extreme imbalance between functions. On the other hand, in the mid-life period (today's mid-life crisis) the person must come to grips with the opposite, "shadow" sides of personality in order to gain further maturity. By analogy, complexity and competition compel organizations to build distinctive capabilities, though this in turn forces attention to rebalancing.

Similar reasoning is found in Kets de Vries and Miller (1984), who show how the success formula of the entrepreneur becomes neurotic when there are no counterbalancing forces in the organization. Moreover, the basic thesis of the historian Arnold Toynbee in his monumental *Study of History* was that the decline of civilizations occurs when a society goes to extremes in what led it to be successful.

Figure 4.1   Dualities in Social Systems.

Each of these qualities has a complementary quality, which is most apparent in negative judgments. If someone has too much of a quality (e.g., decisive to the point of being impulsive), this implies that strength in that quality is not balanced by its complementary quality (in this case, reflectiveness). If someone has too little of a quality (e.g., "she is indecisive"), this means that the complementary quality overrides in an unbalanced way (i.e., the person is reflective but doesn't make decisions easily).

Most qualities have such complementary qualities, and some dualistic evaluation scales are shown in Figure 4.2. Thus the complementary quality to individualism is cooperation. If cooperation dominates and overrides individualism, the person will be negatively evaluated as a conformist (i.e., the op-

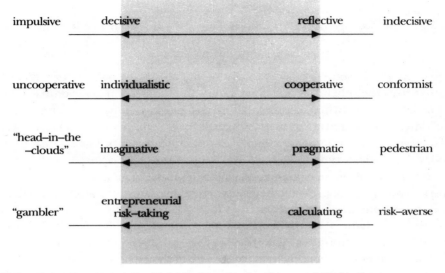

Zone of Complementarity

impulsive	decisive	reflective	indecisive
uncooperative	individualistic	cooperative	conformist
"head–in–the –clouds"	imaginative	pragmatic	pedestrian
"gambler"	entrepreneurial risk–taking	calculating	risk–averse

Figure 4.2   Four examples of dualistic scales for Personnel Evaluation.

posite of individualism). On the other hand, if individualism dominates cooperation, then the person will be negatively viewed as uncooperative (i.e.,
the opposite of cooperative). In Figure 4.2, the shaded zone between the two
complementary qualities is the *zone of complementarity*, that of desirable behavior. Where the person lies within that zone will have implications for the
specific job assignments.

We believe that the same principle of complementarity applies to the long-
term success of complex organizations. An empirical example is a study of
strategic decision-making processes in four firms in the volatile microcomputer
industry, an industry where the rate of technological and competitive change
is extreme and the cost of error is exit. Bourgeois and Eisenhardt (1988)
found that the distinguishing characteristic of the more successful enterprises
was that various dualities were balanced in the decision process. These firms
reached critical strategic decisions both more quickly *and* more carefully than
their competitors, following breathlessly paced and intensely focused analysis,
whereas less successful firms reached decisions either quickly or carefully, but
not both. Successful companies had a powerful, decisive chief executive officer, but they also had powerful management teams. And while seeking risk
in decision making, they executed safe and incremental implementation.
Ouchi (1989) argues that balancing the duality of individualism and teamwork
is the hallmark of firms with above average rates of return, while Prahalad

and Doz (1987) stress the importance of balancing the complementary qualities of corporate integration and local responsiveness.

2.   The balance between complementary dualities is dynamic rather than static.

Environmental events are likely to compel focus on one polarity of a duality rather than the other at a particular time—an organization is never in a state of balanced equilibrium. Thus global market expansion may have argued for decentralization and local responsiveness in the past, while technological change may dictate increased emphasis on strategic control and integration today. Similarly, a sudden competitive change or crisis may argue for strong leadership, while implementation may place a premium on management teamwork. Strategic management becomes the task of shifting attention, albeit within the zone of complementarity.

Since structures are difficult and costly to change (especially in large multinational organizations), it is important to be able to shift the balance within a duality with more flexible means. The organizational chart of a matrix organization may appear as one of straightforward reporting lines, but this masks the dotted-line relationships, the buy-in and consultation obligations, the informal relations that are the hallmark of the dualistically matrix firm. Management can influence these relationships without structural change. Other mechanisms for rebalancing are key appointments, changes in reward systems or communication channels, and what top management pays or does not pay attention to.

An example is the Royal Dutch/Shell, a group that has a complex matrix structure of shareholder, regional, and product interests that together with business and technical functions lead to the regulation of local operating companies. Recently, group management felt it necessary to reinforce the regional side of the matrix. Rather than restructuring operations, the balance of influence was shifted. It was decided that all contact with operating companies by product and functional departments would proceed via the regional coordinators and their small staffs. Group managers could no longer contact subsidiaries directly. The overloaded regional coordinators acted as a funnel, since they would screen out unimportant proposals and contacts and focus only on what was essential to regional interests. Yet, in the future, it will be possible to relax this norm, allowing more intervention on the part of other functions, and thereby boosting their influence.

The matrix allows the multinational firm to balance certain basic dualities: product logic and market logic, technical or functional logic and business logic. Indeed, in a changing competitive environment, the matrix is never static. Dynamic balance implies *selective asymmetry* in the matrix, not full symmetry (Prahalad and Doz 1980). Some companies have viewed matrix organization as providing full balance, issue by issue, between executives representing different interests. These organizations have usually failed (Davis and Lawrence 1977). The organization is maintained in a state of constant tension for no useful purpose; too much energy is devoted internally, rather than externally, and paralysis may result.

The concept of the asymmetric matrix and the changing patterns of influence behind it is essential lest dualities degenerate into single orientations. While single orientations (for example, global effectiveness or local responsiveness) are simpler to manage, they no longer allow companies to confront their competitive environments (Prahalad and Doz 1987; Ghoshal 1987). Altering the asymmetry, reinforcing one dimension of the matrix at the expense of others, is the steering task of top management.

3.   Minimal thresholds must be maintained in dualities.

Administrative and organizational theory has long debated whether organizations should be guided by principles of maximization or satisficing. Implicit in principle 2 above is a different conception—that of maintaining *minimal* threshold levels on salient dualities. In other words, an organization should not venture outside the zone of complementarity (the shaded zone in Figure 4.2).

Hedberg, Nystrom, and Starbuck (1976) were among the first researchers to recognize this, arguing that long-term survival of organizations depends on dynamically balanced management processes. Maximization, they argue, is an inappropriate concept for organizations. Instead of trying to maximize anything (e.g., decentralization, teamwork, formality, generalism), an organization should seek to ensure that it maintains at least a minimal threshold on desirable attributes. Organization requires a minimal degree of consensus, but not so much as to stifle the dissension that is the lifeblood of innovation, and a minimal degree of contentment and satisfaction sufficient to ensure that key actors wish to remain with the firm, but not so much as to allow arrogance or complacency. Minimal faith in plans is required, sufficient to ensure that the planning exercise leads its members to think through the future, but not so much that plans become road maps that blind attention to opportunity.

Adjustment in multinational organizations requires the organization to be in a state of constant readiness, sensitive even to weak signals from the environment. This means that asymmetry should never suppress other dimensions of the matrix. The dominant logic of the time should never suppress dissent.

The local responsiveness-global integration duality provides an example. Local subsidiary managers, concerned with serving their customers, are more sensitive to the need for differentiated responses to local conditions. Conversely, product executives, concerned with the efficiency of product development and manufacturing, are more sensitive to opportunities to standardize and rationalize. In the planning process, local managers develop plans for key accounts and customer segments, while product managers develop worldwide product plans. Whatever the current emphasis in the matrix, neither product nor country executives develop complete plans, but each develops elements of a plan from their different perspectives.

4. Unitary focus on a polarity leads ultimately to organizational degeneration and crisis.

The corollary to Principle 3 is that if dualistic tension disappears in an organization, if the seesaw of duality tilts so that one end touches the ground and stays there uncorrected, this may lead to the degeneration of the organization.

This appears to happen with firms that become trapped by the logic of their historical success factors. As Schein (1985) and others have pointed out, organizations tend to institutionalize dominant and simple logics, based on their explanations for their past successes and failures. In several MNCs that we analyzed, technological leadership was seen as the key to worldwide success, even though success factors were clearly shifting to customer service, political negotiation with host countries, project management skills, and cost control. Since technologists dominated the hierarchy with few countervailing matrix or dualistic forces, management looked for "solutions" to current problems by reinforcing the quest for technological leadership. This led to a few commercial successes, sufficient to reinforce the dominant technological drive. The opportunity cost of not responding to other competitive demands was ignored.

Changing Management Paradigms

The concept of duality appears to lead to an emerging paradigm for management and organization in a world of rapid change and high complexity, a world where global business requires multidimensional organizational capabilities. Current management paradigms no longer provide an adequate frame.

We can trace the postwar evolution of management in terms of three periods, characterized by successively more dynamic and complex environments, as illustrated in Table 4.2. Between the early 1950s and the early 1970s, the market, competitive, and social environments of most firms were relatively stable and favorable to growth. Products enjoyed such strong de-

Table 4.2 Three Paradigms of Management after 1950

	1950s–1960s	1970s–Early 1980s	Mid 1980s–1990s
Management metaphor:	**Structuring (providing order)**	**Fit, Matching, Consistency**	**Dynamic balance between dualities**
Nature of the environment:	Relatively orderly and stable	Incrementally changing with increasing competition	Turbulent, complex, highly competitive
Focus of management attention:	Structure and systems Planning systems Budgeting systems Organizational structure Information systems Job evaluation	Strategy and management processes Strategic management: *matching* environmental threats and opportunities to internal strengths and weaknesses Organization: ensuring *consistency* between the 7-S's Human resource management: *fitting* jobs to people Job design: *matching* technical and task specifications to social needs	Innovation, flexibility, and organizational capabilities Channeling entrepreneurship Focusing diversity Integrating decentralized subsidiaries/business units Creating teamwork among strong individuals Planning opportunism Partnerships between competitors

[handwritten annotation: that is a balance between]

mand and long lives that the notion of the product lifecycle had yet to be conceived; and markets tended to be local. The prevailing management paradigm was that of *structure*, and in a stable environment it indeed makes sense to search for the most effective structure to guide action. The underlying value was the rational value of order.

What is an appropriate supervisory span of control? Are there limits to size and economy of scale? Is a product organization superior to a functional organization? Where there was a concern for management processes, it was with orderly, rational models that today seem mechanical: management as the process of planning, organizing, deciding, and controlling; rational steps in the process of decision making. Job evaluation systems placed the emphasis on orderly structure. The prevailing metaphor in applied organizational theory was "organizational design," as if an organization could be rationalized architecturally, while problems of change focused on resistance to the rational. Even so, awareness of dualities was surfacing in the structural metaphor of matrix organization.

The theory and practice of management began to change slowly in the 1960s, gathering momentum in the 1970s. Growth slowed, the oil crisis triggered recession, and the environment became more competitive. Protected national markets were now open to international competition. Labor and legislative demands grew. Gone was the era of order and stability—change was now becoming a regular feature of organizational life.

Superimposed on the concern for efficient structure came a new paradigm, that of "fit" or matching (the initial insights are often ascribed to Leavitt (1965) and to Chandler's (1962) observations that structure follows strategy). The "one-best-way" search for the effective structure gave way to contingency theory, reflecting the notion that particular structures are only appropriate in particular environments. This led in turn to a heightened concern for management processes to match different aspects of the organization and its environment.

Strategic planning came into being, generally defined as a management process to match environmental opportunities and threats with organizational resources and capabilities. Within the organization, job design became the sociotechnical task of matching task imperatives and technological capacities with human and social needs. Performance motivation became the matching of people, with their distinct skills and needs, with tasks and goals—the human resource task of getting the right people into the right place at the right time. The underlying value shifted from order to short-term performance or effectiveness. During the 1980s, attention turned to culture change, the difficulties of realigning the so-called "soft S's" of style, skills, staff, and superordinate values to reorientations in the strategy, structure, and systems (Pascale and Athos 1981); or to the importance of developing congruence between task, formal and informal organization, and individual management in organizational design (Nadler and Tushman 1988; Galbraith and Nathanson 1979).

The Breakdown of the "Fit paradigm"

The paradox is that just as the "fit" paradigm has gained credence, so it is losing its usefulness. In a turbulent, competitive, and complex environment, the metaphor of fit breaks down. While a tight degree of fit, coherence, matching, or consistency is often viewed as ideal, the fact is that tight fit or consistency results in rigidity. Competitive demands outrun the slow pace of organizational change and adjustment. Top management starts to feel that the organization is constantly behind, that the organization itself is the biggest barrier to competitive and strategic development.

Viewed through the lens of fit, organizations go through extended periods of fine tuning the consistencies between strategy, structure, management processes, and people, with incremental adjustments to environmental change. However, these stages of stability alternate with traumatic periods of revolution, transformation, or frame-breaking change, leading to a new strategy, implemented progressively through structural and cultural changes and thus initiating a new period of incremental evolution (Chandler 1962; Greiner 1972; Tushman, Newman and Romanelli 1986).

Although largely substantiated by the empirical data of the past, this cycle of evolution and revolution is no longer a viable roadmap into the future. It takes a generation to realign people and management processes to strategic and structural changes, by which time strategy will have long since altered. This way of thinking locks us into a world of alternating complacency and panic, of crisis and "back to normal," of half-completed organizational shifts before the next strategic lurch. Thinking in terms of fit blocks the development of organizational capabilities that become necessary in a complex competitive environment—the stretching of the organization, building the tension into the firm that is vital for constant change and adjustment. We need a concept of organization that is dynamic rather than static, that has the tension of development processes built into it, rather than shunting those tensions aside until their force compels revolution.

Management scholars have sensed this breakdown, though they too were trapped by the absence of an alternative paradigm. For example, they are increasingly questioning the definition of strategic management as the matching of corporate resources with opportunities and threats, however plausible this may be with yesterday's logic. This conception may have unduly constrained the ambitions of companies by driving out goals where the means of achieving them are not yet obvious (Hamel and Prahalad 1989).

Flexibility, adaptation, learning, and responsiveness require the building of tension into the fabric of the organization in a managed way. An appropriate degree of tension needs to be built into its culture, neither so much as to interfere with operational performance and not so little as to induce complacency. The mechanism for doing this is built upon the dualities that are at the core of complex organization. Dualities should be viewed not as threats to consistency and coherence, but as opportunities for creative organization development, for gaining competitive advantage, for organizational learning and renewal.

Developing Dualistic Capabilities Through Cultural Layering

The key to developing dualistic capabilities in an organization is the use of *subtle* management processes rather than overt management tools. Overt management tools are the organizational girders: the choice of its structure and basic systems. Changing these girders is costly, time-consuming, and exacting in terms of its human price. Each time a complex international firm makes a significant modification in its structure so as to rebalance priorities in line with changing markets or technologies, a vast amount of energy is consumed by internal reorganization. Consequently, multinational firms such as IBM are now seeking to make frequent adjustments within their basic structure using subtle mechanisms rather than through periodic "reorganization."

Subtle management processes can be used to rebalance an organization, to provide complementary properties that its basic structure and systems lack. They can also be used to increase the self-balancing properties of an organization—to build a matrix culture that underlies a possible matrix structure. Doz and Prahalad (1981) have developed a three-fold category of subtle management processes: data management processes, conflict or tension management processes, and manager management processes. With our focus on human resource management, it is the latter that is of concern to us here. Human resource management is perhaps the most important tool for building dualistic properties into the firm.

Elsewhere, we have conceptualized how this happens through three mechanisms that we call layering, sequencing, and decision architecture (Evans and Doz 1989). Here we will focus on the former of these, namely *cultural layering*. It is through managed cultural layering that a company is able to build dualistic properties, a matrixed culture that is capable of handling multidimensional decision making.

Layering involves building new capabilities and qualities into the organization's culture while reinforcing its past cultural strengths. New and complementary capabilities are *layered* on top of the existing capabilities. Thus the enterprise becomes progressively more multidimensional and more capable of balancing dualities. Layering leads to a richer structure of shared meanings, mind-sets, relationships, and networks.[1]

A major tool of layering is management development—the recruitment, socialization, development, and career management of key position holders. It is the mind-sets of the key managers in the firm that shape the strategy of the firm, and management development influences such mind-sets. Through changes in recruitment profiles, new qualities are introduced into the firm, such as more entrepreneurship in the bureaucratic enterprise so as to balance renewal with efficiency. Through their experience in different jobs, potential executives become progressively more "layered," capable of bridging different perspectives. Through the choice of people for key positions, a company can manage dualistic interdependencies; for example, interdependencies between related product groups or between headquarters and subsidiaries.

An analogy can be drawn here to personality development. Each individual enters adulthood with a basic personality; adult development involves the refinement and extension of that personality. Skills, qualities, and attitudes are acquired and layered on top of that basic personality, leading to greater complexity of the individual. However, the outer veneers of personality (or organizational culture)—those most recently learned or layered—are stripped away under conditions of stress, as the person (or organization) falls back to more deeply ingrained behavioral and attitudinal responses.

Let us provide a number of examples of the way in which human resource management provides cultural layering, starting with a duality that is particularly characteristic of the multinational.

The Integration-Responsiveness Duality

An important application of layering is in balancing the dual forces of integration and responsiveness in the MNC. The important first step is to recognize that international integration and local responsiveness is an "and/and" requirement. This then leads to the "how" question: how can we integrate companies that also need their own local autonomy? How can we layer integration on top of local responsiveness? Careful attention to the management of managers is one of the most powerful mechanisms (Prahalad and Doz 1987).

For example, the basic principle behind Shell's organization is that its 250 operating companies are autonomous, with group management acting as a shareholder. Thus, there is considerable diversity of organization within the group, and local operating companies act as local citizens. Nevertheless, the group functions as a relatively integrated organization. According to one of its board members, the cohesion is provided by three elements—the common logo, some common business and financial principles, and above all the mobility of its managers. At Shell, as at other multinationals, the higher the potential of the manager, the more likely he or she is to change jobs (and for that matter location and function) every two to four years. The job itself forces the manager to take a local perspective; but personal career interests oblige the person also to take a wider group perspective, reinforced by the network of relationships and experiences that the person has acquired over the years.

Some firms are going further, layering dualities into key appointments in order to bridge the headquarter-subsidiary gap. Thus at Digital Equipment Corporation, with its European headquarters in Geneva, the responsibility for serving financial institutions in Europe has been attributed to the British subsidiary. Responsibility for international personnel at the Swedish group Alfa-Laval has been assigned to the British personnel manager, located in London.

Layering as a Means of Rooting Key Competencies and Providing Flexibility

For firms whose strength lies in a key strategic competence, layering can be used to balance the focus of managers on this core competence and complementary competencies. Core competencies are developed in the early part of the career before other qualities are developed. Thus merchandising is the basic business of Marks & Spencer, the successful British retailing company. The career norm at Marks & Spencer is that all executives, including those who will land in staff roles at headquarters, must have proved that they can run a store successfully before moving into career tracks that reflect their particular interests and competencies. Thus even the senior personnel executive should have run a store earlier in his or her career.

Similarly, the strength of many professional organizations lies in their professional expertise, though management and business expertise is needed to cope with their strategic and organizational challenges. In the accounting business of the "Big Eight" (soon to be Big Five?) audit firms no individual will be promoted into the partnership until he or she has demonstrated competence in audit work; thereafter, they may develop their professional skills along one of a number of competency tracks, including that of business leadership. The same pattern typically applies to academic universities and to the research departments of major firms.

Layering in Managing Strategic Development

Layering may be a successful tool for managing progressive strategic development. Davis (1984) has shown that reorientations or major culture changes will be rejected unless they are compatible with the existing culture of the firm. The enthusiasm of the 1980s for culture change led to delusions, now evaporating, about the extent to which we can significantly change corporate culture; firms are better advised to build upon (i.e., layer) their cultures (Schein 1989).

For example, Digital Equipment faces a strategic development problem that is typical of many firms. Its culture is strongly dominated by engineering values, but the need is to complement that strength with a marketing orientation. Task forces and training only serve to sensitize employees to the problem, not to bring about change. Injecting strong marketers recruited from the outside has been largely unsuccessful. Sometimes a conflictual, dialectic balance was created as the marketers fought with the engineers, or the marketing people wrestled to obtain power, which would have created a pendulum process. Sometimes the two groups worked separately and independently, avoiding contact.

The strategy today is one of layering, that is, finding within the ranks of the mainstream engineers those who have a nose for marketing and developing marketers out of these individuals. DEC believes that it may be easier to develop such engineers into marketing people (that is, layer new competencies on them) than to socialize outside marketing recruits into the mainstream engineering culture.

Marks & Spencer is also approaching strategic development through layering. The competence duality that they are striving to build is balancing a traditional culture of merchandising experimentation with new needs for analytic marketing skills. One of M&S's cultural values is a strong encouragement of experimentation, guided by merchandising experience. Store managers, for example, are encouraged to try out new lines on a small scale. The motto is, "If it sells, stock it up and tell the others; if it doesn't, drop it!" Thus success is built upon while failures are abandoned, largely accounting for their profitable expansion over the years into speciality foods, men's confection clothing, and other lines.

Yet by the mid 1980s it was becoming clear that new analytic and marketing skills would be needed within the company in order to internationalize into Europe and North America as well as to meet competition from speciality stores in the changing retailing industry. How should these new capabilities be developed? Although MBAs and marketers from other firms had the desirable skills, it was felt that their recruitment would lead to a destructive clash with the old culture, the strengths of which were still invaluable. The solution adopted was a careful graduate recruit program, taking people with the right skills and then socializing them through fast-tracking up the traditional entry path into store management that was mentioned earlier, a process to be monitored by a new management development function with board level attention. Over a generation, Marks & Spencer thus expects to layer a new business culture on its former strengths.

Layering in Organization Development

The focus of organization development should be on building organizational capabilities that complement the current strengths of the organization.[2] An example is the evolution of management practices in many Japanese multinationals, that are gradually introducing Western-style performance-based evaluation and rewards and speeding up the rapidity of decision processes—but without unduly compromising the principles of lifetime employment, company loyalty, and employee commitment. The changes in management practices are not intended to destroy the old system but to increase its flexibility (Mroczkowski and Hanaoka 1989).

However, in the face of accelerating globalization, another duality may be the Achilles heel of these Japanese multinationals, namely, the conflict between the ethnocentric orientation of their management development systems and the necessary internationalization of management development. Global business can no longer be managed with a cadre of mother country expatriates. However, the Japanese system is difficult to internationalize. After World War II, the allies removed the top layers of management in the large Japanese concerns; consequently, management development became a major priority long before it did in the West. This led to a finely tuned system of elite recruitment for long-term careers, intensive socialization, training, rotation, and competitive screening (see Pucik 1984). However, it is a system that is exceedingly difficult to open up to non-Japanese (Bartlett and Yoshihara 1988). Given the importance of management development in the multinational, the extreme ethnocentricity of the system risks creating degenerative problems. The more finely honed the system, the more difficult and traumatic modification will be.

Another example of organizational development through cultural layering is the balancing of hierarchic with network properties. Management development (especially rotation) leads to the development of a network of relationships within the organization, an informal nervous system that balances the formal organization, thereby enhancing the innovative properties of the enterprise. The relationship between management development and innovation processes in multinationals is shown by Ghoshal and Bartlett's (1988) empirical study of 66 North American and European multinationals. Firms that created, adopted, and diffused the greatest innovation were those with higher normative integration between headquarters and subsidiaries (measured by transfers and travel between them, as well as joint work in teams, task forces, and committees) and with more frequent intra- and intersubsidiary communication.

Network properties in organization are a current focus, although some firms are afraid of recognizing their importance for fear that this will legitimate covert behavior. However, networks will not replace hierarchies. They are not alternative forms of organization, but rather complementary forms—one layered on top of the other. Hierarchy and hierarchic mechanisms provide the formal business focus, the discipline and rigor, while networks provide the flexibility and innovation.

Here the direction of rebalancing may vary from one corporation to another. For example, the dominant cultural characteristic of most major

American multinationals is the tight, structured formalism of their hierarchic structure and systems. Thus the natural concern is with developing complementary properties—the loose, more informal network properties mentioned earlier and highlighted by many other American authors (e.g., Burns and Stalker 1961; Kanter 1983). However, the concern in Italy is precisely the opposite. The indigenous Italian culture is more loose, unstructured, informal. Behind the sometimes authoritarian structures of companies are informal networks of relationships that bewilder the American expatriate, who bemoans the "Latin" way of doing business. Yet these same cultural attributes are associated with the strong track record of Italian firms in creative innovation (many multinational companies have very successful research and development laboratories in Italy—IBM, Philips, CIBA-GEIGY, Digital Equipment). The cultural problem of the Italians is that they have less mastery of the structured, formalized systems that are necessary to effectively commercialize their innovations. Thus what sells today in the United States is communication, innovation, and flexibility. There is no market for this in Italy—what sells there is systems, implementation, and structure, namely what is needed there to layer complementary cultural capabilities into the organization.

Strategic Layering

The concept of layering can be extended into the domain of strategic management if one recognizes that tomorrow's focus of strategic attention is likely to be different and yet complementary to today's. A strategy can be viewed as a sequence of focused stages, where top management consciously anticipates that the capability in the foreground today will be in the background tomorrow. Strategic layering involves achieving a long-range goal by sequentially building and layering organizational capabilities.

The growth of Japanese multinationals is a good illustration—whether it is Honda taking on General Motors in the contest for the worldwide auto industry, Komatsu taking on the Caterpillar that ruled over the construction equipment business, or Matsushita faced with the RCAs and General Electrics of consumer electronics (Hamel and Prahalad 1986). Each of these Japanese firms was a minor league player in its world industry back in the 1960s. Their sole competitive advantages over their Western competitors were low labor costs and a protected domestic market. Driven by long-range strategic goals ("strategic intent"), the initial sequence in strategic layering was to use that cost advantage to gain volume in Western markets. Having secured that, the next sequence was to invest heavily in product and process technology while still reinforcing the earlier cost advantage. The third step was investment in order to create strong brand images in global markets and strength in distribution, adding another layer of competitive advantage. The products of these Japanese firms thus have the advantage of low cost, high quality, technological sophistication, and global marketing and distribution (Prahalad and Doz 1987).

Underlying Dilemmas in the Layered Firm

Dualistic enterprises experience in turn their own deeper underlying dilemmas, two of which merit comment here.

Balancing Mobility and Continuity

Layering is a relatively slow process since new competencies need to be developed, firmly rooted, and honed. If the firm tries to develop these competencies in individuals too fast, or tries to layer new and perhaps conflicting capabilities too quickly, then competency development will not take root firmly. American firms appear often to tackle layering with a naively short-term, "quick-fix" mentality. For example, management invests considerable time and resources in quality management—for one or two years. Then the focus of attention shifts, often following a change in leadership, to cost reduction through demanning. Two years later, the focus may be on innovation through enhanced communications. Instead of layered development, we have a pendulum swing from today's fashion to tomorrow's fad (see *Business Week*, January 20, 1986).

At the root of pendulum behavior may be an excessive attachment to mobility, which leads us to comment on a deeper duality—that of balancing mobility and continuity. Numerous considerations lead MNCs to rotate key managers once every two to four years: complementary layers of competence are developed in these individuals; local responsiveness is balanced with corporate cohesion; new executives are more likely to take strategic initiatives; and lateral relations are developed that complement the formal structure. However, frequent mobility leads to superficial organizational layering. The working through of a new initiative may take years to achieve: a critical mass of managers must be committed, and the change process must often be extended to workers throughout the organization. This is compromised by overly frequent mobility, since successors have little vested interest in continuing the paths of their predecessors if they are to earn the visibility that is seen as necessary for a successful career. It is often easy, gratifying, and rewarding to initiate a strategic shift, but difficult and time-consuming to stay the course.

Too frequent mobility leads to zig-zag management and the development of organizations that are long on initiatives but short on implementation and follow through. Indeed, we have observed that a major weakness in many Western multinationals is that depth of implementation is shallow, a view shared by Pehr Gyllenhammar, Volvo's president (speech at INSEAD, 1987). New capabilities rarely become solidly embedded in the organization, and the norms of personal career achievement are thereby undermining the potential for successful layering of organizational capabilities. In contrast, when a former European head of DEC was asked about the relative lack of mobility of their European country managers, he replied, "Just staying in the job was already a great achievement, given the pace of growth of the business!"

The Subtlety of the Layered Organization

As noted earlier, the notion of subtlety is essential to the process of layering. Organizations that are deeply layered, with dualities built into their matrixed cultures, are far from simple. There are rules, but these are more often than not guidelines where managers have a delicate sense of their freedoms and their constraints. There is a hierarchy, but much significant behavior cuts across the hierarchical lines. There are mangement processes, but underlying these management processes are complex attitudes and values. It is often difficult for the outsider, who has not been socialized into the nuances of the firm, to understand its culture, let alone operate within it.

Much layering occurs through managed long-term development of key managers and professionals who are recruited for careers rather than short-term jobs (though others who are neither key decision-makers nor being groomed for such roles may have shorter term employment with the firm). Human resource management is typically an important function in the dual-istic firm, since recruitment and selection, development, retention, and reward management are vital regulators of this process. It is likely to become more important in developed countries with increased labor market mobility and demographic decline.

Retention management is of corresponding importance. Yet on the other hand, this involves another balancing act, since one needs sufficient new blood and outside contact to avoid cloning and inbreeding. New blood can be pro-vided in a number of subtle ways: hiring consultants into senior positions on temporary assignments; rehiring people who left the firm to join another company; forming management training consortia with clubs of other enter-prises; building medium-term relationships with guest lecturers on manage-ment seminars who know enough about the system to challenge it realistically.

The subtlety and complexity of the dualistic firm creates further chal-lenges, notably the need to minimize politicization of the decision-making processes and the need to streamline decision making so that matrix processes do not lead to costly or paralyzing pseudo-bureaucracy.

Subtlety and complexity risk leading decision processes to be subverted by the vested interests of individuals and coalitions, leading to the blocking of decisions, negotiations for personal advantage, and various forms of sub-terfuge that can be camouflaged in the complexity of the firm. Consequently, norms of hard analysis are vital, as are respect for facts and well-argued views regardless of the position and status of the advocate. To avoid political be-havior, contention management systems need to be provided—open door pol-icies, ombudsmen, opinion surveys, committees of appeal, management by walking around. Such contention systems are not to be used regularly. Fre-quent recourse to arbitration is a signal to top management of the failure of dualism, and the need for deeper intervention. Similarly, clarity as to goals, targets, and visions minimizes politicization.

Complexity may lead to expensive and paralyzing pseudo-bureaucracy and large amounts of time devoted to management processes. To minimize this risk, clear goals are again of paramount importance. Values of lean organization, limiting staff and headcount, are also essential, and not just for cost reasons. The lean organization can afford to focus only on what is essential; it must focus on facts and well-prepared analysis, rather than on efforts to justify positions or vested interests. Structure is also a tool, leading to more differentiated structures. Some businesses are highly interdependent, while others manifest weaker relationships with other units. For example, in an effort to reduce its monolithic bureaucracy, IBM has reorganized its formerly integrated business. Some are integrated, governed by the disciplines of common reviews and shared planning. Other business units are quasi-independent, while still others are run as stand-alone business units. Conversely, Hewlett-Packard and Philips have recognized the need to integrate hitherto decentralized business units (Prahalad and Doz 1987).

Conclusion

The systems law of reguisite variety holds that the properties of an organization must reflect the complexity of its environment. With accelerating internationalization, economic change, tougher competition, and shorter product life cycles, the environment of most multinationals is becoming far more complex, to the point of challenging conventional thinking about organization.

Organization development as it faces the complex dualities confronting MNCs has been a theme running through this chapter in two senses: first, the challenge of developing new concepts of organization, and second, the challenge of constant actual innovation in organization. Organization, as Karl Weick has said, should be a verb, namely organizing; similarly, "matrix" is a verb and not a noun.

The traditional tools of top management, structure and systems, have become too cumbersome as instruments for organizing. They are not subtle and varied enough to provide the "requisite variety" that companies need to cope with the complexity of their environment. This is not to deny the importance of structure and systems, far from it—they provide the basic frame for organizing. But organizing involves constant balancing and rebalancing dualities, not just the static task of providing a structure. Top management governance of a multinational enterprise becomes one of balancing opposing forces and using those forces as the motor of organizational development. It is here that human resource management becomes an essential tool.

Human resource management is thus no longer a functional task, but an integral component of general management. Strategic, organizational, and human resource management become fused in the task of organizing, as is apparent from our discussion of cultural layering.

A quote from F. Scott Fitzgerald seems like a fitting conclusion:

The test of a first rate intelligence is the ability to hold two simultaneous ideas in mind and still keep the ability to function.

Notes

1. Given the current concern with structural "delayering," "layering" is a term with other connotations. Nevertheless, the metaphor is accurate in the sense that cultural layering should accompany structural delayering. Structural delayering involves pushing responsibility down the line by eliminating hierarchic levels of supervision and staff roles. But the corollary is that the sophistication of those in the "delayered" organization must be increased; the lean organization has fewer people but places greater demands on those people. Thus competency and cultural layering accompany structural delayering.

2. By "organization development," we refer to strengthening the capabilities of the organization, and not the more value-oriented domain of planned change known as "OD." Nevertheless, the objective of OD can be interpreted as that of building dualistic properties into organizations. American in its origin, the values of OD reflect latent polarities that are complementary to the dominant properties of U.S. organizations. OD interventions typically focus on properties that such organizations do not have—process skills as opposed to content skills, the social dimension of management rather than its instrumental aspects, collective teamwork rather than individualistic achievement. In this sense, the OD movement is a counterculture in the United States, and necessarily so. Its values are sufficiently compatible with the mainstream values of American culture to be tolerated (this is not true in other cultures such as Japan); yet they are sufficiently counter to that culture on salient dimensions to contribute to the development of desirable dualistic properties in organizations (see Evans 1989).

References

Bateson, G. 1936. *Naven.* Cambridge: Cambridge University Press.

Bartlett, C. A., and Yoshihara, H. 1988. "New Challenges for Japanese Multinationals: Is Organization Adaptation their Achilles Heel? *Human Resource Management,* 27(1): 19-44.

Bourgeois, L. J., and Eisenhardt, K. M. 1988. "Strategic Decision Processes in High Velocity Environments: Four cases in the Microcomputer Industry." *Management Science* 34(7): 816-35.

Burns, T., and Stalker, G. M. 1961. *The Management of Innovation.* London: Tavistock.

Business Week, 1986, Business Fads: What's in—and out. 20 January.

Cameron, K. S. 1986. Effectiveness as Paradox: Consensus and Conflict in Conceptions of Organizational Effectiveness. *Management Science* 32(5): 539-53.

Chandler, A. 1962. *Strategy and Structure.* Cambridge, Mass.: MIT Press.

Davis, S. M. 1984. *Managing Corporate Culture.* Cambridge, Mass.: Ballinger.

Davis, S. M., and Lawrence, P. R. 1977. *Matrix.* Reading, Mass.: Addison-Wesley.

Doz, Y., and Prahalad, C. K. 1981. Headquarters Influence and Strategic Control in MNCs. *Sloan Management Review* 23(1): 15-29.

Evans, P. A. L. 1988. "Organizational Development in the Transnational Enterprise."

In R. Woodman and W. Pasmore, eds., *Research in Organizational Change and Development, Volume 3*. New York: JAI Press.

Evans, P. A. L. and Doz, Y. 1989. "The Dualistic Organization." In P. A. L. Evans, Y. Doz, and A. Laurent, eds., *Human Resource Management in International Firms: Change, Globalization, Innovation*. London: Macmillan.

Evans, P. A. L., Doz, Y., and Laurent, A., eds. 1989. *Human Resource Management in International Firms: Change, Globalization, Innovation*. London: Macmillan.

Galbraith, J. R., and Nathanson, D. A. 1979. "The Role of Organizational Structure and Process in Strategy Implementation." In D. E. Schendel and C. W. Hofer, eds., *Strategic Management*. Boston: Little, Brown.

Ghoshal, S. 1987. "Global Strategy: An Organizing Framework." *Strategic Management Journal* 8: 425–40.

Ghoshal, S., and Bartlett, C. A. 1988. "Creation, Adoption, and Diffusion of Innovations by Subsidiaries of Multinational Corporations." INSEAD working paper, Fontainebleau.

Hamel, G., and Prahalad, C. K. 1989. "Strategic Intent." *Harvard Business Review* May–June.

Hedberg, B. L. T., Nystrom, P. C., and Starbuck, W. H. 1976. "Camping on Seesaws: Prescriptions for a Self-Designing Organization." *Administrative Science Quarterly* 21: 41–65.

Helweg, P. 1951. *Charakterologie*. Stuttgart: Ernst Klett Verlag.

Jung, C. G. 1933. *Personality Types*. New York: Harcourt, Brace & World.

Kanter, R. M. 1983. *The Change Masters: Innovation for Productivity in the American Corporation*. New York: Simon & Schuster.

Kets de Vries, M. F., and Miller, D. 1984. *The Neurotic Organization*. San Francisco: Jossey Bass.

Leavitt, H. J. 1965. "Applied Organizational Change in Industry." In J. G. March, ed. *Handbook of Organizations*. New York: Rand McNally.

Ouchi, W. G. 1989. "The Economics of Organization." In P. A. L. Evans, Y. Doz, and A. Laurent, eds., *Human Resource Management in International Firms: Change, Globalization, Innovation*. London: Macmillan.

Mroczkowski, T., and Hanaoka, M. 1989. "Continuity and Change in Japanese Management." *California Management Review*, 31(2): 39–53.

Nadler, D., and Tushman, M. 1988. *Strategic Organization Design*. Glenview, Ill.: Scott, Foresman.

Pascale, R. T., and Athos, A. G. 1981. *The Art of Japanese Management*. New York: Simon & Schuster.

Prahalad, C. K., and Doz, Y. 1987. *The Multinational Mission*. New York: Free Press.

Prahalad, C. K., and Doz, Y. 1980. "Strategic Management of Diversified Multinational Corporations." In A. R. Negandhi, ed., *Functioning of the Multinational Corporation: A Global Comparative Study*. New York: Pergammon Press.

Pucik, V. 1984b. "White-Collar Human Resource Management in Large Japanese Manufacturing Firms." *Human Resource Management* 23(3).

Schein, E. H. 1989. "Conversation with Edgar H. Schein by F. Luthans." *Organizational Dynamics* (Spring).

Schein, E. H. 1985. *Organization Culture and Leadership*. San Francisco: Jossey-Bass.

Tushman, M. L., Newman, W. H., and Romanelli, E. 1986. "Convergence and Upheaval: Managing the Unsteady Pace of Organizational Evolution." *California Management Review* XXIX(1).

5

Matrix Management*
Not a Structure,
a Frame of Mind

Christopher A. Bartlett
Sumantra Ghoshal

Top-level managers in many of today's leading corporations are losing control of their companies. The problem is not that they have misjudged the demands created by an increasingly complex environment and an accelerating rate of environmental change, nor even that they have failed to develop strategies appropriate to the new challenges. The problem is that their companies are organizationally incapable of carrying out the sophisticated strategies they have developed. Over the past 20 years, strategic thinking has far outdistanced organizational capabilities.

All through the 1980s, companies everywhere were redefining their strategies and reconfiguring their operations in response to such developments as the globalization of markets, the intensification of competition, the acceleration of product life cycles, and the growing complexity of relationships with suppliers, customers, employees, governments, even competitors. But as companies struggled with these changing environmental realities, many fell into one of two traps—one strategic, one structural.

The strategic trap was to implement simple, static solutions to complex and dynamic problems. The bait was often a consultant's siren song promising to simplify or at least minimize complexity and discontinuity. Despite the new

*Reprinted by permission of *Harvard Business Review* © 1990 by the President and Fellows of Harvard College, all rights reserved.

demands of overlapping industry boundaries and greatly altered value-added chains, managers were promised success if they would "stick to their knitting"; in a swiftly changing international political economy, they were urged to rein in dispersed overseas operations and focus on the "triad markets"; and in an increasingly intricate and sophisticated competitive environment, they were encouraged to choose between alternative "generic strategies"—low cost or differentiation.

Yet the strategic reality for most companies was that both their business and their environment really *were* more complex, while the proposed solutions were often simple, even simplistic. The traditional telephone company that stuck to its knitting was trampled by competitors who redefined their strategies in response to new technologies linking telecommunications, computers, and office equipment into a single integrated system. The packaged-goods company that concentrated on the triad markets quickly discovered that Europe, Japan, and the United States were the epicenters of global competitive activity, with higher risks and slimmer profits than more protected and less competitive markets like Australia, Turkey, and Brazil. The consumer electronics company that adopted an either-or generic strategy found itself facing competitors able to develop cost and differentiation capabilities at the same time.

In recent years, as more and more managers recognized oversimplification as a strategic trap, they began to accept the need to manage complexity rather than seek to minimize it. This realization, however, led many into an equally threatening organizational trap when they concluded that the best response to increasingly complex strategic requirements was increasingly complex organizational structures.

The obvious organizational solution to strategies that required multiple, simultaneous management capabilities was the matrix structure that became so fashionable in the late 1970s and the early 1980s. Its parallel reporting relationships acknowledged the diverse, conflicting needs of functional, product, and geographic management groups and provided a formal mechanism for resolving them. Its multiple information channels allowed the organization to capture and analyze external complexity. And its overlapping responsibilities were designed to combat parochialism and build flexibility into the company's response to change.

In practice, however, the matrix proved all but unmanageable—especially in an international context. Dual reporting led to conflict and confusion; the proliferation of channels created informational log-jams as a proliferation of committees and reports bogged down the organization; and overlapping responsibilities produced turf battles and a loss of accountability. Separated by barriers of distance, language, time, and culture, managers found it virtually impossible to clarify the confusion and resolve the conflicts.

In hindsight, the strategic and structural traps seem simple enough to avoid, so one has to wonder why so many experienced general managers have fallen into them. Much of the answer lies in the way we have traditionally thought about the general manager's role. For decades, we have seen the general manager as chief strategic guru and principal organizational architect. But as the competitive climate grows less stable and less predictable, it is harder for one person alone to succeed in that great visionary role. Similarly, as formal, hierarchical structure gives way to networks of personal relationships that work through informal, horizontal communication channels, the image of top management in an isolated corner office moving boxes and lines on an organization chart becomes increasingly anachronistic.

Paradoxically, as strategies and organizations become more complex and sophisticated, top-level general managers are beginning to replace their historical concentration on the grand issues of strategy and structure with a focus on the details of managing people and processes. The critical strategic requirement is not to devise the most ingenious and well coordinated plan but to build the most viable and flexible strategic process; the key organizational task is not to design the most elegant structure but to capture individual capabilities and motivate the entire organization to respond cooperatively to a complicated and dynamic environment.

Building an Organization

While business thinkers have written a great deal about strategic innovation, they have paid far less attention to the accompanying organizational challenges. Yet many companies remain caught in the structural-complexity trap that paralyzes their ability to respond quickly or flexibly to the new strategic imperatives.

For those companies that adopted matrix structures, the problem was not in the way they defined the goal. They correctly recognized the need for a multidimensional organization to respond to growing external complexity. The problem was that they defined their organizational objectives in purely structural terms. Yet formal structure describes only the organization's basic anatomy. Companies must also concern themselves with organizational physiology—the systems and relationships that allow the lifeblood of information to flow through the organization. And they need to develop a healthy organizational psychology—the shared norms, values, and beliefs that shape the way individual managers think and act.

The companies that fell into the organizational trap assumed that changing their formal structure (anatomy) would force changes in interpersonal relationships and decision processes (physiology), which in turn would reshape the individual attitudes and actions of managers (psychology).

But as many companies have discovered, reconfiguring the formal structure is a blunt and sometimes brutal instrument of change. A new structure creates new and presumably more useful managerial ties, but these can take months and often years to evolve into effective knowledge-generating and decision-making relationships. And since the new job requirements will frustrate, alienate, or simply overwhelm so many managers, changes in individual attitudes and behavior will likely take even longer.

As companies struggle to create organizational capabilities that reflect rather than diminish environmental complexity, good managers gradually stop searching for the ideal structural template to impose on the company from the top down. Instead, they focus on the challenge of building up an appropriate set of employee attitudes and skills and linking them together with carefully developed processes and relationships. In other words, they begin to focus on building the organization rather than simply on installing a new structure.

Indeed, the companies that are most successful at developing multidimensional organizations begin at the far end of the anatomy-physiology-psychology sequence. Their first objective is to alter the organizational psychology—the broad corporate beliefs and norms that shape managers' perceptions and actions. Then, by enriching and clarifying communication and decision processes, companies reinforce these psychological changes with improvements in organizational physiology. Only later do they consolidate and confirm their progress by realigning organizational anatomy through changes in the formal structure.

No company we know of has discovered a quick or easy way to change its organizational psychology to reshape the understanding, identification, and commitment of its employees. But we found three principal characteristics common to those that managed the task most effectively:

1. The development and communication of a clear and consistent corporate vision;

2. The effective management of human resource tools to broaden individual perspectives and develop identification with corporate goals;

3. The integration of individual thinking and activities into the broad corporate agenda by means of a process we call co-option.

Building a Shared Vision

Perhaps the main reason managers in large, complex companies cling to parochial attitudes is that their frame of reference is bounded by their specific responsibilities. The surest way to break down such insularity is to develop and communicate a clear sense of corporate purpose that extends into every corner of the company and gives context and meaning to each manager's particular roles and responsibilities. We are not talking about a slogan, however catchy and pointed. We are talking about a company vision, which must be crafted and articulated with clarity, continuity, and consistency: clarity of expression that makes company objectives understandable and meaningful; continuity of purpose that underscores their enduring importance; and consistency of application across business units and geographical boundaries that ensures uniformity throughout the organization.

Clarity. There are three keys to clarity in a corporate vision: simplicity, relevance, and reinforcement. NEC's integration of computers and communications—C&C—is probably the best single example of how simplicity can make a vision more powerful. Top management has applied the C&C concept so effectively that it describes the company's business focus, defines its distinctive source of competitive advantage over large companies like IBM and AT&T, and summarizes its strategic and organizational imperatives.

The second key, relevance, means linking broad objectives to concrete agendas. When Wisse Dekker became CEO at Philips, his principal strategic concern was the problem of competing with Japan. He stated this challenge in martial terms—the U.S. had abandoned the battlefield; Philips was now Europe's last defense against insurgent Japanese electronics companies. By focusing the company's attention not only on Philips's corporate survival but also on the protection of national and regional interests, Dekker heightened the sense of urgency and commitment in a way that legitimized cost-cutting efforts, drove an extensive rationalization of plant operations, and inspired a new level of sales achievements.

The third key to clarity is top management's continual reinforcement, elaboration, and interpretation of the core vision to keep it from becoming obsolete or abstract. Founder Konosuke Matsushita developed a grand, 250-year vision for his company, but he also managed to give it immediate relevance. He summed up its overall message in the "Seven Spirits of Matsushita," to which he referred constantly in his policy statements. Each January he wove the company's one-year operational objectives into his overarching concept to produce an annual theme that he then captured in a slogan. For all the loftiness of his concept of corporate purpose, he gave his managers immediate, concrete guidance in implementing Matsushita's goals.

Continuity. Despite shifts in leadership and continual adjustments in short-term business priorities, companies must remain committed to the same core set of strategic objectives and organizational values. Without such continuity, unifying vision might as well be expressed in terms of quarterly goals.

It was General Electric's lack of this kind of continuity that led to the erosion of its once formidable position in electrical appliances in many countries. Over a period of 20 years and under successive CEOs, the company's international consumer-product strategy never stayed the same for long. From building locally responsive and self-sufficient 'mini-GEs" in each market, the company turned to a policy of developing low-cost offshore sources, which eventually evolved into a de facto strategy of international outsourcing. Finally, following its acquisition of RCA, GE's consumer electronics strategy made another about-face and focused on building centralized scale to defend domestic share. Meanwhile, the product strategy within this shifting business emphasis was itself unstable. The Brazilian subsidiary, for example, built its TV business in the 1960s until it was told to stop; in the early 1970s, it emphasized large appliances until it was denied funding; then it focused on housewares until the parent company sold off that business. In two decades, GE utterly dissipated its dominant franchise in Brazil's electrical products market.

Unilever, by contrast, made an enduring commitment to its Brazilian subsidiary, despite volatile swings in Brazil's business climate. Company chairman Floris Maljers emphasized the importance of looking past the latest political crisis or economic downturn to the long-term business potential. "In those parts of the world," he remarked, "you take your management cues from the way they dance. The samba method of management is two steps forward then one step back." Unilever built—two steps forward and one step back—a profitable $300 million business in a rapidly growing economy with 130 million consumers, while its wallflower competitors never ventured out onto the floor.

Consistency. The third task for top management in communicating strategic purpose is to ensure that everyone in the company shares the same vision. The cost of inconsistency can be horrendous. It always produces confusion and, in extreme cases, can lead to total chaos, with different units of the organization pursuing agendas that are mutually debilitating.

Philips is a good example of a company that, for a time, lost its consistency of corporate purpose. As a legacy of its wartime decision to give some overseas units legal autonomy, management had long experienced difficulty persuading North American Philips (NAP) to play a supportive role in the parent company's global strategies. The problem came to a head with the introduction of Philips's technologically first-rate videocassette recording system, the V2000. Despite considerable pressure from world headquarters in the Netherlands, NAP refused to launch the system, arguing that Sony's Beta system and Matsushita's VHS format were too well established and had cost, feature, and system-support advantages Philips couldn't match. Relying on its legal independence and managerial autonomy, NAP management decided instead to source products from its Japanese competitors and market them under its Magnavox brand name. As a result, Philips was unable to build the efficiency and credibility it needed to challenge Japanese dominance of the VCR business.

Most inconsistencies involve differences between what managers of different operating units see as the company's key objectives. Sometimes, however, different corporate leaders transmit different views of overall priorities and purpose. When this stems from poor communication, it can be fixed.

When it's a result of fundamental disagreement, the problem is serious indeed, as illustrated by ITT's problems in developing its strategically vital System 12 switching equipment. Continuing differences between the head of the European organization and the company's chief technology officer over the location and philosophy of the development effort led to confusion and conflict throughout the company. The result was disastrous. ITT had difficulty transferring vital technology across its own unit boundaries and so was irreparably late introducing this key product to a rapidly changing global market. These problems eventually led the company to sell off its core telecommunications business to a competitor.

But formulating and communicating a vision—no matter how clear, enduring, and consistent—cannot succeed unless individual employees understand and accept the company's stated goals and objectives. Problems at this level are more often related to receptivity than to communication. The development of individual understanding and acceptance is a challenge for a company's human resource practices.

Developing Human Resources

While top managers universally recognize their responsibility for developing and allocating a company's scarce assets and resources, their focus on finance and technology often overshadows the task of developing the scarcest resource of all—capable managers. But if there is one key to regaining control of companies that operate in fast-changing environments, it is the ability of top management to turn the perceptions, capabilities, and relationships of individual managers into the building blocks of the organization.

One pervasive problem in companies whose leaders lack this ability—or fail to exercise it—is getting managers to see how their specific responsibilities relate to the broad corporate vision. Growing external complexity and strategic sophistication have accelerated the growth of a cadre of specialists who are physically and organizationally isolated from each other, and the task of dealing with their consequent parochialism should not be delegated to the clerical staff that administers salary structures and benefit programs. Top managers inside and outside the human resource function must be leaders in the recruitment, development, and assignment of the company's vital human talent.

Recruitment and Selection. The first step in successfully managing complexity is to tap the full range of available talent. It is a serious mistake to permit historical imbalances in the nationality or functional background of the management group to constrain hiring or subsequent promotion. In today's global marketplace, domestically oriented recruiting limits a company's ability to capitalize on its worldwide pool of management skill and biases its decision-making processes.

After decades of routinely appointing managers from its domestic operations to key positions in overseas subsidiaries, Procter & Gamble realized that the practice not only worked against sensitivity to local cultures—a lesson driven home by several marketing failures in Japan—but also greatly underutilized its pool of high-potential non-American managers. (Fortunately, our studies turned up few companies as shortsighted as one that made overseas assignments on the basis of *poor* performance, since foreign markets were assumed to be "not as tough as the domestic environment.")

Not only must companies enlarge the pool of people available for key positions, they must also develop new criteria for choosing those most likely to succeed. Because past success is no longer a sufficient qualification for increasingly subtle, sensitive, and unpredictable senior-level tasks, top management must become involved in a more discriminating selection process. At Matsushita, top management selects candidates for international assignment on the basis of a comprehensive set of personal characteristics, expressed for simplicity in the acronym SMILE: specialty (the needed skill, capability, or knowledge), management ability (particularly motivational ability), international flexibility (willingness to learn and ability to adapt), language facility, and endeavor (vitality, perseverance in the face of difficulty). These attributes are remarkably similar to those targeted by NEC and Philips, where top executives also are involved in the senior-level selection process.

Training and Development. Once the appropriate top-level candidates have been identified, the next challenge is to develop their potential. The most successful development efforts have three aims that take them well beyond the skill-building objectives of classic training programs: to inculcate a common vision and shared values; to broaden management perspectives and capabilities; and to develop contacts and shape management relationships.

To build common vision and values, white-collar employees at Matsushita spend a good part of their first six months in what the company calls "cultural and spiritual training." They study the company credo, the "Seven Spirits of Matsushita," and the philosophy of Konosuke Matsushita. Then they learn how to translate these internalized lessons into daily behavior and even operational decisions. Culture-building exercises as intensive as Matsushita's are sometimes dismissed as the kind of Japanese mumbo jumbo that would not work in other societies, but in fact, Philips has a similar entry-level training practice (called "organization cohesion training"), as does Unilever (called, straightforwardly, "indoctrination").

The second objective—broadening management perspectives—is essentially a matter of teaching people how to manage complexity instead of merely to make room for it. To reverse a long and unwieldy tradition of running its operations with two- and three-headed management teams of separate technical, commercial, and sometimes administrative specialists, Philips asked its training and development group to de-specialize top management trainees. By supplementing its traditional menu of specialist courses and functional programs with more intensive general management training, Philips was able to begin replacing the ubiquitous teams with single business heads who also appreciated and respected specialist points of view.

The final aim—developing contacts and relationships—is much more than an incidental by-product of good management development, as the comments of a senior personnel manager at Unilever suggest: "By bringing managers from different countries and businesses together at Four Aces (Unilever's international management training college), we build contacts and create bonds that we could never achieve by other means. The company spends as much on training as it does on R&D not only because of the direct effect it has on upgrading skills and knowledge but also because it plays a central role in indoctrinating managers into a Unilever club where personal relationships and informal contacts are much more powerful than the formal systems and structures."

Career-Path Management. Although recruitment and training are critically important, the most effective companies recognize that the best way to develop new perspectives and thwart parochialism in their managers is through personal experience. By moving selected managers across functions, businesses, and geographic units, a company encourages cross-fertilization of ideas as well as the flexibility and breadth of experience that enable managers to grapple with complexity and come out on top.

Unilever has long been committed to the development of its human resources as a means of attaining durable competitive advantage. As early as the 1930s, the company was recruiting and developing local employees to replace the parent-company managers who had been running most of its overseas subsidiaries. In a practice that came to be known as "-ization," the company committed itself to the Indianization of its Indian company, the Australization of its Australian company, and so on.

Although delighted with the new talent that began working its way up through the organization, management soon realized that by reducing the transfer of parent-company managers abroad, it had diluted the powerful glue that bound diverse organizational groups together and linked dispersed operations. The answer lay in formalizing a second phase of the -ization process. While continuing with Indianization, for example, Unilever added programs aimed at the Unileverization of its Indian managers.

In addition to bringing 300 to 400 managers to Four Acres each year, Unilever typically has 100 to 150 of its most promising overseas managers on short- and long-term job assignments at corporate headquarters. This policy not only brings fresh, close-to-the-market perspectives into corporate decision making but also gives the visiting managers a strong sense of Unilever's strategic vision and organizational values. In the words of one of the expatriates in the corporate offices, "The experience initiates you into the Unilever Club and the clear norms, values, and behaviors that distinguish our people—so much so that we really believe we can spot another Unilever manager anywhere in the world."

Furthermore, the company carefully transfers most of these high-potential individuals through a variety of different functional, product, and geographic positions, often rotating every two or three years. Most important, top management tracks about 1,000 of these people—some five percent of Unilever's total management group—who, as they move through the company, forge an informal network of contacts and relationships that is central to Unilever's decision-making and information-exchange processes.

Widening the perspectives and relationships of key managers as Unilever has done is a good way of developing identification with the broader corporate mission. But a broad sense of identity is not enough. To maintain control of its global strategies, Unilever must secure a strong and lasting individual commitment to corporate visions and objectives. In effect, it must co-opt individual energies and ambitions into the service of corporate goals.

Co-Opting Management Efforts

As organizational complexity grows, managers and management groups tend to become so specialized and isolated and to focus so intently on their own immediate operating responsibilities that they are apt to respond parochially to intrusions on their organizational turf, even when the overall corporate interest is at stake. A classic example, described earlier, was the decision by North American Philips's consumer electronics group to reject the parent company's VCR system.

At about the same time, Philips, like many other companies, began experimenting with ways to convert managers' intellectual understanding of the corporate vision—in Philips's case, an almost evangelical determination to defend Western electronics against the Japanese—into a binding personal commitment. Philips concluded that it could co-opt individuals and organizational groups into the broader vision by inviting them to contribute to the corporate agenda and then giving them direct responsibility for implementation.

In the face of intensifying Japanese competition, Philips knew it had to improve coordination in its consumer electronics among its fiercely independent national organizations. In strengthening the central product divisions, however, Philips did not want to deplete the enterprise or commitment of its capable multi-national management teams.

The company met these conflicting needs with two cross-border initiatives. First, it created a top-level World Policy Council for its video business that included key managers from strategic markets—Germany, France, the United Kingdom, the United States, and Japan. Philips knew that its national companies' long history of independence made local managers reluctant to take orders from Dutch headquarters in Eindhoven—often for good reason, since much of the company's best market knowledge and technological expertise resided in its offshore units. Through the council, Philips co-opted their support for company decisions about product policy and manufacturing location.

Second, and more powerful, Philips allocated global responsibilities to units that had previously been purely national in focus. Eindhoven gave NAP the leading role in the development of Philips's projection television and asked it to coordinate development and manufacture of all Philips television sets for North America and Asia. The change in the attitude of NAP managers was dramatic.

A senior manager in NAP's consumer electronics business summed up the feelings of U.S. managers: "At last, we are moving out of the dependency relationship with Eindhoven that was so frustrating to us." Co-option had transformed the defensive, territorial attitude of NAP managers into a more collaborative mind-set. They were making important contributions to global corporate strategy instead of looking for ways to subvert it.

In 1987, with much of its TV set production established in Mexico, the president of NAP's consumer electronics group told the press, "It is the commonality of design that makes it possible for us to move production globally. We have splendid cooperation with Philips in Eindhoven." It was a statement no NAP manager would have made a few years earlier, and it perfectly captured how effectively Philips had co-opted previously isolated, even adversarial, managers into the corporate agenda.

The Matrix in the Manager's Mind

Since the end of World War II, corporate strategy has survived several generations of painful transformation and has grown appropriately agile and athletic. Unfortunately, organizational development has not kept pace, and managerial attitudes lag even further behind. As a result, corporations now commonly design strategies that seem impossible to implement, for the simple reason that no one can effectively implement third-generation strategies through second-generation organizations run by first-generation managers.

Today the most successful companies are those where top executives recognize the need to manage the new environmental and competitive demands by focusing less on the quest for an ideal structure and more on developing the abilities, behavior, and performance of individual managers. Change succeeds only when those assigned to the new transnational and interdependent tasks understand the overall goals and are dedicated to achieving them.

One senior executive put it this way: "The challenge is not so much to build a matrix structure as it is to create a matrix in the minds of our managers." The inbuilt conflict in a matrix structure pulls managers in several directions at once. Developing a matrix of flexible perspectives and relationships within each manager's mind, however, achieves an entirely different result. It lets individuals make the judgments and negotiate the trade-offs that drive the organization toward a shared strategic objective.

6

Controlled Variety*
A Challenge for Human Resource Management in the MNC

Yves Doz
C. K. Prahalad

Introduction

Freer trade and freer investment, and the resulting intensification of global competition, now call for growing strategic control for multinational corporations (MNCs). All operations must contribute consistently to the firm's success in a coordinated fashion. Over the last decade, MNCs have had to come to terms with the process of strategic control—how the resource commitment decisions of multiple subsidiaries and headquarters are brought together into a consistent pattern that increases the competitive advantage of the firm over time. During the same period, the variety of conditions challenging MNCs has increased: product diversification has taken them to increasingly different businesses and geographic expansion to increasingly different countries (often to modes of market participation where strategic control is problematic, such as in joint ventures and consortia). Further, while industry globalization has called for centrally planned and coordinated strategic actions, intensified competition has demanded increased adaptation and responsiveness to local market, regulatory, and cultural conditions.

Thus, the challenge facing MNCs is one of controlled variety: internal variety needed to match the growing external variety calls for flexibility and adaptiveness; strategic control is needed for purposeful competitive actions

Human Resource Management, Vol. 25, Number 1, pp. 55–71, Yvez Doz and C.K. Prahalad, copyright © 1986 by John Wiley & Sons, Inc., reprinted by permission of John Wiley & Sons, Inc.

across markets and businesses, and over time, to maintain or enhance the competitive advantage of the multinational firm. Yet, combining strategic variety and strategic control is difficult at best.

In this chapter, we examine some of the issues facing human resource management and the contribution that it can make to help diversified MNCs meet the challenge of controlled variety. We start by analyzing the most critical dimensions along which strategic variety must be maintained in a diversified MNC, in order for it to remain responsive to environmental and competitive demands. We then briefly discuss the nature of the need for strategic control and the difficulties of maintaining such control in a complex, diversified MNC. In a second section we discuss what capabilities managers in these companies must develop in order to maintain both strategic variety and strategic control. In particular, we discuss the need for individual managers to be sensitive to both the local idiosyncracies and the global priorities in reaching strategic decisions. We then discuss several complementary approaches to developing such managers. Finally, we outline tentative implications for human resource management in diversified MNCs, both for human resource professionals and for top management.

Strategic Variety and Strategic Control

Strategic control in a diversified MNC does not have a single predetermined pattern: not all operations require equal strategic control, nor can strategic control be achieved in the same way for all of them. Strategic control must, therefore, be differentiated to match the variety of conditions faced in the various operations. While, in specifics, such variety can be endless, strategic variety can be captured along three main axes: between countries, between businesses, and between modes of market participation.

First, individual countries offer different strategic opportunities for MNCs, and the latters' subsidiaries are thus likely to be different. Differences in size, resource endowment, economic development, political regime, national development, and industrial policies, among others, play major roles in differentiating the opportunities offered to MNCs by individual countries. The roles of various countries in a global MNC strategy thus differ. Singapore, Germany, and India offer a very different mix of opportunities and constraints for MNCs. We can classify subsidiaries as:

1. Export platforms that are an integral part of a global manufacturing network for a business (e.g., Singapore for General Electric, Austria for Philips). Typically, these subsidiaries require extensive strategic control, and they need to be managed as part of a global business from a planning, budgeting, logistics, and even operating standpoint.

2. Large integrated subsidiaries, which contain significant research, product development, and manufacturing capabilities and which also constitute a large market for goods produced in other countries (Great Britain for Ford, Germany for IBM or Hewlett-Packard, the United States for CIBA-GEIGY). While such subsidiaries may require substantial strategic control, they may also be the locus of strategic initiatives. The corporate management issue, therefore, is not to exercise tight headquarters control over such operations—which might stifle their entrepreneurial and innovative capability and make them less responsive to the local market and policy conditions. Instead, the challenge is to ensure active and effective participation of these subsidiaries into the formulation of global strategies and the transfer and sharing of their information, knowledge, and expertise. For a company such as Philips, Germany constitutes a more vibrant, more advanced market for a number of "professional electronics" products and systems than the Dutch domestic market. Not sharing the experience gained in Germany would be a missed opportunity. Many European firms face a similar situation vis-à-vis the U.S. market: the most sophisticated users may be located there and their inputs may be key to successful product development.

3. Large self-contained subsidiaries which are prevented by protectionism from being fully part of a global network (e.g., Philips). For these subsidiaries strategic control may not be critical: so long as they remain protected and isolated they can hardly be part of a global strategy, nor are they usually exposed to severe competitive threats from other global competitors.

4. Small importing subsidiaries, many of which act as internal agents for the MNC. While their small size may make strategic control look unimportant, these subsidiaries may still be strategically critical if new global competitors nibble away market positions there* and they become part of a global defense perimeter. Conversely, although small, and even with small market share, they may allow competitive retaliation against competitors.

This classification highlights the differences in the need for and nature of strategic control between subsidiaries within the same business. It also suggests that the managerial competencies demanded from subsidiary management may differ considerably from subsidiary to subsidiary and that sim-

---

* The European automobile industry's overcapacity is partly the result of the Japanese competitors nibbling away at European manufacturers' export markets in South East Asia, Africa, and in smaller European markets with no local producers (Finland, Ireland, the Netherlands).

ple-minded criteria, like size or regional location, may not always capture these differences (Bartlett and Ghoshal, 1986). Consequently, the type of experience gained by managers varies a great deal from location to location. Having managed the Singaporian subsidiary (a key manufacturing location), or the Belgian one (often a hotly contested European "test" market for global competitors) may usefully prepare one to run a global business unit. By contrast, having run South Africa, or even India or Brazil—typically large complex operations—may develop the skills for managing a domestic business, but not a global one.

A second axis which creates variety between strategic control requirements is the rather obvious one of interbusiness differences. Some global businesses can be seen, for strategic management purposes, as a loose federation of nationally self-contained operations. This has, by and large, been the approach of numerous MNCs in the consumer goods industries (e.g., CPC in prepared food, Heineken in beer, Unilever in various non-durable goods). Some other businesses can be seen only as global, with the world as a single market (e.g., computer memory chips, civilian airliners). Most global businesses though, fall between these extremes. In these businesses forces of local responsiveness and forces of global integration are both at work, and they affect specific functions and decisions differently, as we analyze in detail elsewhere (Prahalad and Doz, 1986). For instance, in pharmaceutical companies, research and development may be best managed with very strong central strategic control, while marketing is best delegated to subsidiaries, the managers of which have a keen sense for local market and regulatory conditions.

These differences between businesses obviously call for a differentiated extent and nature of strategic control. While essentially global or local businesses can be submitted to much and to little strategic control respectively, in all key functions and decisions, multifocal businesses for which global and local concerns need to be traded off raise more difficult issues (Prahalad and Doz, 1984). Too tight control may lead to missed opportunities, while too little also creates difficulties. Let us look, for example, at when R&D expenditures increase, as for instance in the pharmaceutical business. Autonomy of subsidiaries in product choices (deciding to take on and sell or turn down products developed at headquarters) when heavy development costs have already been incurred, can be very costly and dysfunctional, as several European MNCs have discovered at their great expense. Conversely, forcing a relatively small subsidiary to carry a full corporate product range—almost as a matter of policy—may also be highly dysfunctional: the scarce marketing and sales resources of the subsidiary may be stretched thinly and wasted on too many products. Many similar trade-offs exist in all aspects of the business. Strategic control, under such conditions, cannot be a set of centrally edicted policies. Sensitivity to both local responsiveness demands and global integration opportunities is needed.

Despite the difficult trade-offs mentioned above, more and more multinational businesses are drawn into this middle ground where multifocal approaches are needed. Few multinational businesses can be run with a purely local orientation. Even when the product characteristics make the business local—as for instance for liquid oxygen, flatglass, or cement—global competitive rivalry may take place, forcing strategic decisions to be made in a global perspective. Once such a perspective is shared by several competitors, a number of decisions, such as pricing, can no longer be made locally, despite the business being essentially local in its customer base. Global competitors compete against each other across national markets. Conversely, few businesses can be run as purely global. When the economic conditions of an industry favor globally run businesses, political conditions often mitigate against such globalization. It follows that while differences across businesses remain significant, no simple "either or" choice can fit the requirements—elements of global integration and elements of local responsiveness need to be blended.

This suggests that the categories of expatriate vs. local managers, of ethnocentric vs. geocentric management, of international mobility vs. localism in career paths are probably too simple to answer the need to blend global and local priorities in running a business. We need a way to develop flexible individuals, who can successfully face ambiguous situations, where priorities are not clear and where complex trade-offs have to be considered.

A third dimension of variety is the differences in types of ownership and relationships. MNCs traditionally have engaged in joint ventures with local partners, and these already created difficulties: MNC employees seconded to the joint venture already felt tensions and divided loyalties. The more MNCs engage in more complex forms of collaboration among themselves (from North Sea oil development to joint product programs) and in collaboration with very different types of firms (e.g., large MNCs entering partnerships with small entrepreneurial ventures in new technological fields such as biotechnology, software development, and micro electronics), the greater the variety of strategic control they face. At the extreme, what is the meaning of strategic control in a large, multigovernment funded effort which receives a lot of public opinion and political attention, such as new breeder nuclear reactors or new combat planes (Horwitch, 1981)? Such new forms of partly collaborative, partly competitive relations raise difficult issues of loyalty, career path, respect for the interests of multiple parties, and integrity of project or venture management. When large MNCs cooperate with small ones, for instance, the MNC managers and scientists most closely associated with the small firms run the risk of being ostracised by their own peers (Doz, 1985). Managing such diversity of strategic control conditions probably requires MNCs to develop multiple modes of managing people and to be able to blend them according to the needs of the various operations. In some cases conventional hierarchical employment relationships still predominate, in others quasi-market ones may be more appropriate; in yet others, clan or network relationships may prevail. Even internally, within the MNC, such differentiation in relationships may be useful, to be adaptive, or to manage innovation (Lawrence and Dyer, 1983).

In conclusion, the concept of strategic control needs to be differentiated along at least three dimensions, as sketched below in Figure 6.1, with usually decreasing extents of strategic control as we move away from the origin.

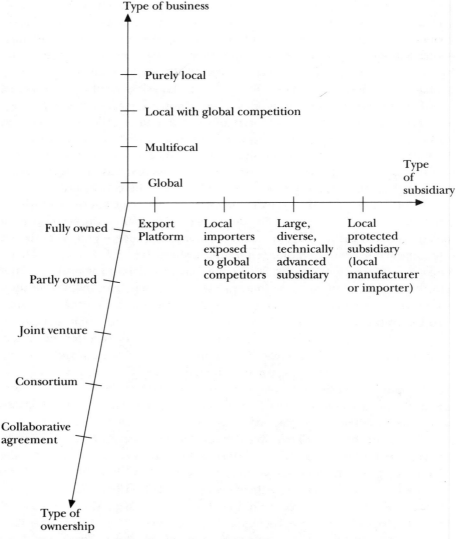

Figure 6.1 Required differentiation of strategic control by type of business, type of subsidiary, and type of ownership.

While a differentiated approach to strategic control is becoming increasingly important, traditional tools of control typically used by MNC headquarters over their subsidiaries are becoming less relevant. The most crude and widespread tool for strategic control is resource dependency. It is an obvious way for headquarters to secure power over subsidiaries (Pfeffer and Salancik, 1978). Yet, as the subsidiary matures and becomes bigger, the need for financial and technical resources to be provided from headquarters decreases. The subsidiary can afford a larger base of technical, manufacturing, and financial resources, and its success may depend more on how well it fits in its local environment than on how much support it needs from headquarters (Prahalad and Doz, 1981; Doz and Prahalad, 1981). Another usual tool for control, systems, and procedures such as planning, budgeting, measurement, and evaluation also become less useful as variety and complexity of the strategic control tasks increase. A single standard set of management systems and procedures can hardly cope with such diversity; either it becomes a straightjacket or it becomes irrelevant. Yet, modifying and differentiating the systems to fit specific requirements makes them less and less easy to use as a control tool for top management. Establishing a very rich standard set of systems, but selectively exempting operations from them (on grounds of size, local responsiveness, joint ownership, etc.) helps some, but also represents an admission of inability to deal with variety.

A third approach to strategic control, reliance on key individuals, in particular where resource dependency and systems and procedures fail, is not new. In fact, it predates the other two outlined above; eighteenth-century trading companies and colonial empires relied on such an approach (Brandel, in process). Our proposition is that as the required variety of strategic control configurations increases, MNCs will be less and less able to rely on resource dependence and standard systems and procedures to achieve the required level of strategic control over their operations. Consequently, human resource management has a key role to play in the continuation of the success of MNCs as institutions. While this is broadly recognized, the conflicts and difficulties of using human resource management as a strategic control method are often left implicit. The rest of this chapter will explore some of these issues and trade-offs, from the standpoint of strategic management, not from that of specialized human resource management function. We will review first typical orientations of individual managers and the pros and cons of having them develop a global or a local primary orientation. We will also discuss the need for developing balanced individuals, sensitive to both orientations. In particular, we will review what breeds balanced individuals, who can balance conflicting demands for local sensitivity and for loyalty to the headquarters, and at the same time be competent in their tasks. Finally, we will briefly discuss the issues faced by firms in creating an institutionalized system to identify, develop, and effectively use balanced individuals.

Key Orientations for MNC Managers: Sensitivity to Local Conditions and Loyalty to the Corporation

Sensitivity to Local Conditions

Sensitivity to local conditions and differences is required for various reasons. First, in order to be credible to local members of their organization, senior managers have to demonstrate such sensitivity to local differences as needed to convincingly defend local interests vis-à-vis headquarters. If they are not sufficiently sensitive to effectively represent a local point of view to headquarters when needed, they will lack credibility in the eyes of local employees and, therefore, will not be able to elicit their loyalty and commitment. This, ultimately, is detrimental to the efficiency of the MNC, no matter what its strategy may be.

Sensitivity to local conditions is also required for success in the external environment, not just for credibility within the subsidiary operations. It implies accepting the "rules of the game" as played in the local market; and understanding them well enough to be able to play successfully. This involves, first, an intellectual understanding of constraints and rules, such as the working of price controls in France and Italy, union participation in Germany and the Netherlands, the nature of distribution networks in Germany and the Netherlands, the nature of distribution networks in Japan, and so on. Compared to the home country of the MNC, these rules may translate into lost degrees of managerial freedom, particularly when the home country of the MNC is the U.S. Second, this involves sufficient empathy with the local environment to develop an emotional acceptance of these rules as a way to conduct business. The more peculiar and idiosyncratic the rules, the more important it is for executives to accept them, and to understand their rationale in the local environment. A lack of understanding of, or a neglect for local labor relation conditions and practices, for instance, may be a major disadvantage for MNCs.

Such sensitivity to local conditions has both advantages and disadvantages. The main advantages usually are:

1. *To provide a visible local face,* rather than a foreign one. This has been a critical strength of such companies as Brown Boveri or Philips in Europe, particularly when Europe was divided into rival (or ever warring) countries.

2. *To allow easier acceptance in the local community,* which involves not only providing a local face, but also behaving sufficiently like a domestic firm to allow its foreigners to be forgotten. Again, this has historically been a strength of such companies as Brown Boveri and Philips.

3. *To maximize the number of available options in the local environment.* The MNC can easily vary the level of strategic coordination between headquarters and subsidiaries. In some sense it can be "Janusfaced," leaving autonomy to the various subsidiaries to adjust to local conditions when appropriate, and to act in globally coordinated fashion when needed. This allows the use of multiple approaches to success in the local environment and yet to best leverage, in the context of that environment, the worldwide resources of the MNC.

4. *To be recognized as a legitimate participant to the local economy,* and be able to exercise an influence in the shaping of new policies and regulations, by participation in industry and trade associations, and to be eligible for government support (e.g., foreign export credit and insurance, preferential foreign exchange regulations, etc.)

5. *To effectively represent, in the decision-making processes within the MNC, local considerations and constraints,* so that local priorities and global demands can be balanced with due consideration given to the various relevant perspectives.

6. *To be enough of an insider,* locally, to be privy to local information and gain the opportunity to participate in local deals.

The benefits of genuine sensitivity to local conditions are therefore particularly important, no matter what the strategy of the MNC is. Yet, there are some potentially significant drawbacks to exercising local sensitivity as briefly summarized below.

1. *It makes balancing advocacy between local demands and global priorities more difficult.* Managers committed to the local environment may also see their knowledge of this environment, and the credibility it gives them with their own employees, as a power base to be protected and to be used to bargain with the local environment. They may easily shift from representing a point of view to becoming blind partisans of autonomy of the subsidiaries, in an undiscriminating way. Their credibility to local employees and others is rooted in their successfully defending local autonomy against headquarters.

2. *To put off difficult local decisions,* such as layoffs, until they are unavoidable in a crisis situation and are even more difficult, costly, and painful than if they had been implemented earlier. In our research, examples abound of difficult decisions being postponed rather than faced. Paradoxically, it may be easier for local national executives to carry out such decisions since they do not prove their commitment to local employees as much as expatriate managers, whose credibility

constantly has to be bolstered by tangible action which demonstrates commitment to local interest.

3. *To create delays in identifying and accepting a global role* for subsidiaries, when such a role entails compromising local interests for global priorities. First, global competitive threats may not be easily identified early, since they are perceived piecemeal, country by country, rather than globally. Second, accepting the reality of such threats requires that managers make a cognitive shift that is particularly slow and difficult since it implies an acceptance of more global consideration and a concurrent loss of strategic autonomy on the part of the subsidiaries.

Sensitivity to local conditions therefore needs to be counterbalanced by other demands and priorities. Loyalty to corporate interests is another critical dimension.

Loyalty to Corporate Interests

Loyalty to corporate interests can be defined as an understanding of corporate priorities and an acceptance of headquarter-determined rules, motivated by a commitment to corporate goals, not only to local subgoals. It assumes that, somehow, subsidiary managers see themselves as instruments of headquarters in managing subsidiaries, not as advocates of subsidiary interests bargaining with headquarters. This also implies that subsidiary managers see themselves as contributing to a global optimum, not to a local one, and are willing to make difficult trade-offs to the benefit of the whole corporation, even at the cost of their short-term personal interest. They are committed to overall corporate performance, rather than local results.

Strong loyalty to corporate interests, as sensitivity to local conditions, has both advantages and disadvantages. The advantages are clear:

*   *To allow strong implicit strategic control over strategic objectives,* since their managers will on their own, pursue courses of action most in line with corporate priorities and not favoring local interests to the detriment of overall corporate interests.

*   *To make subsidiaries pliable parts* of a global network which can easily be centrally managed.

*   *To speed up the responses from subsidiaries to headquarters,* and to be able to quickly mobilize the subsidiaries for globally coordinated competitive actions.

The disadvantages are clear:

*   *Too much visible loyalty to head office may make it difficult to elicit com-*

mitment from local employees. This may adversely affect local performance and alternatively result in a loss of strategic control by severing critical communications between the top management of the subsidiaries (who are often expatriates) and their subordinates (local employees).

- *Inability to articulate and represent effectively local needs*, opportunities, and threats to headquarters since management may not devote sufficient efforts to understanding local conditions and may be more preoccupied with successfully interfacing with headquarters than with dealing with the local environment.
- *Weakness in negotiating locally*, since the necessary credibility will be lacking.

The Dilemma

Sensitivity to local conditions and corporate loyalty represent complementary rather than mutually exclusive orientations. Each corresponds to important but fundamentally different strategic requirements in the running of various businesses. As we argued in the first section, most businesses require that their managers provide a blending of sensitivity to local interests and loyalty to overall corporate interests.

The adoption of matrix organizations by a significant number of American and European companies in the 1970s, and the subsequent disappointment of many managers with this organization form, witness the need for such blending and the difficulties in achieving it. Multinational matrix organizations are based on the premise that both managers sensitive to local interests (usually local subsidiary managers) and managers imbued with the overall corporate interest (usually in the form of central product division managers and corporate staffs) participate jointly in decision making on key aspects of business strategy. Yet, in many cases, the results have been disappointing. Part of the disappointment stems from undermanagement of the matrix: too often, top management adopted the matrix as if it were merely another organizational hierarchy, without recognizing its intrinsic instability, and, therefore, the need for active top management involvement in running it.

Part of the disappointment with matrix organizations also stems from the lack of preparation of middle and senior managers for an advocacy process— or as sometimes put by matrix managers for "constructive conflict"—that confronts sensitivity to local interests and loyalty to overall corporate interest. In our view, managers who can easily understand and relate to both sets of interests are much better prepared to deal with the complexity of managing varying levels of strategic control or strategic autonomy, whether in a formal matrix organization, or via informal matrixlike overlays in a global business. A critical issue, therefore, for human resource management in MNCs is to develop "balanced" individuals who are not only equally comfortable defending global corporate interests and local ones, but who can also transcend these conflicts to search for solutions that are better than weak compromises between both sets of interests. While we fully recognize that this is not an easy task, we turn in the next section to a few tentative propositions on how "balanced" individuals can be developed, based on our observation of several MNCs struggling with this issue.

Providing for Balance

Human resource management can make a major contribution to meeting the requirements outlined in the preceding section. As we argued, mere resource dependence, or the imposition of centrally designed systems and procedures, cannot cope with the variety of strategic control conditions faced by most diversified multinational companies. Diversified MNCs need individuals who are sensitive to the complexity of responsiveness—integration trade-offs, and to how these trade-offs contribute to or preclude the competitive advantage. "Balanced" individuals are needed.

The most usual response by MNCs to the need for balanced individuals is to provide career paths for high potential executives where globally oriented and locally oriented positions alternate. Someone may start as assistant product manager for a global product line at headquarters, move to a marketing management job in a small subsidiary, to a regional coordinator staff assistant position, to a larger subsidiary, to product division management, and so forth. While this approach is attractive, and often works, it has some potential drawbacks. First, it faces the usual problems of moving people from one hierarchical line to another: bosses are likely to be tempted to hide their best people for too long, because they are concerned with replacement. Second, speed of movement involves a difficult trade-off. Too many, too fast moves may encourage a short-term management orientation, deter from a strategic focus (particularly when new managers can freely change the strategies they inherit), and also make management evaluation difficult, for lack of continuity in responsibilities. Fast moves may lead to superficiality and to the local subsidiary managers or the lower level technical product executives (who see themselves as the repositories of in-depth market and product knowledge) not relying seriously on their (temporary) bosses. As a result, these highly mobile managers may be discouraged from making the in-depth investments needed to understand either industry and product or country environments and thus from developing a truly grounded balanced view. A veneer of internationalism may not be enough to make complex trade-offs sensibly. Yet, too few, too slow moves may delay the promotion of managers to senior levels to an age where they can only contemplate short tenures, particularly with mandatory retirement ages. This creates its own instability, often even more disruptive than instability at lower levels. A slow pace of moves also requires that each promotion involves a big step upward, a move that many firms see as too risky. Obviously, as observed by researchers, short-term job filling priorities often take precedence over the concern for longer-term development and socialization of individuals (Galbraith and Edstrom, 1977; Edstrom and Galbraith, 1977).

Further, as most companies start from a global integration focus (usually reflected in the organization by the primacy of product-oriented executive positions) or from one of national responsiveness (usually reflected by the primacy of country managers positions), initiating a process leading to a balance in career paths may be difficult unless top management, itself a product of the dominant orientation, takes steps which may be seen as turning against its own following—or its own basis of power. Thus, changes towards balanced career paths tend to lag, rather than lead, strategic redirection and organizational transitions. Career path management, as a tool to develop balanced individuals is thus fraught with difficulties, and is seldom sufficient.*

Some companies, while providing for the alternations mentioned above, make balanced career development easier. Some use regional headquarters deliberately as mixing grounds for home country expatriates and executives seconded from the subsidiaries in the region. It allows the local subsidiaries to be staffed almost totally by local nationals, providing for a sensitivity to local conditions and the corporate and divisional headquarters to be staffed mainly by home country nations. IBM, for example, used this approach (Salter, 1974). Some companies also create positions of "assistant-to" for very senior executives at headquarters which are staffed systematically by young promising executives from foreign subsidiaries, as a way to acquaint them with the workings of corporate headquarters. Such practices range from numerous young executives being provided to several corporate vice presidents (e.g., at IBM) to a very selective detachment of the already senior managers about to be promoted to head major subsidiaries as deputy to the company president or chairman (e.g., at EXXON).

Beyond this, diversified MNCs may also structure management systems and decision-making processes in such a way as to require a balanced perspective from executives who want to use them successfully. At CIBA-GEIGY for instance, the decision-making process for management appointments in the product-geography-function matrix structure requires key individuals such as subsidiary managers and functional managers of divisions to develop and

---

* We have not mentioned the well-known more operational, set of difficulties which active career path management faces, such as the added compensation costs for expatriates, the difficulties faced by dual-career couples, the problems faced by mothers raising children through multiple school systems, or the seemingly different propensity of national cultures for international moves.

evidence a balanced perspective to have an effective say in such decisions (Doz and Van den Poel, 1983). Subsidiary executives must know headquarters well and understand their concerns, and headquarter executives must be sensitive to the national idiosyncracies affecting the operations of their subsidiaries. In other words, exercising influence in favor of integration and responsiveness requires an understanding of, and empathy with, the other perspective—a homeostatic characteristic which means that the most successful executives are themselves balanced individuals.

Other companies institute "key country" teams to advise product and divisional management, or, in some cases, to run the business collegially. Yet, this works only if the "debating society" syndrome is overcome. This assumes that measurement and reward systems are based on contribution to the collective interest, not just on goodwill, or worse, individual subsidiary results. In other words, unless the measurement and reward systems are themselves balanced, balanced individuals are unlikely to develop. This was, for instance, the major problem faced by companies such as Brown Boveri in Europe or Corning in the U.S. when they tried to move away from national responsiveness and develop a concern for global competition and for integration requirements (Doz, 1983; Prahalad and Doz, 1981). Product teams, or key country teams in a business, can work only if participants in these teams are rewarded for contributing to their success, not for blocking or stalling their decisions.

Strongly held corporate beliefs, independent from specific configurations of strategic control and from positions in terms of responsiveness and integration, can also help develop a set of priorities that transcend parochial interests (Prahalad, 1983; 1986). The priorities may be set in a relatively concrete style, but leave room for much interpretation. "Service to customers" or being a "responsible partner in the provision of health care" (to host governments) can be interpreted in several ways, and leaves room for orientations that privilege responsiveness or integration, but are unlikely to be achieved by making one orientation so dominant as to exclude the other. Corporate ideology, itself, may thus contribute to nurture a balanced perspective that encourages management to consider complex trade-offs between integration and responsiveness and to be willing not only to accept differences in strategic control but also to actively seek to match strategic control with the requirements of businesses, subsidiaries, and varied ownership patterns.

Some Implications; Towards an Agenda for HRM and Top Management

A strong, well-established, institutionalized HRM and management development process is a key contribution to providing balance. Such a system faces limitations, however, particularly in dealing with the most senior executives. Let us review the contributions first.

The HRM system can ensure the planned development of a large enough pool of young potential executives to allow flexibility in staffing positions. This avoids "position-filling" being—perforce—the only consideration guiding executive appointments. A large enough pool allows to bring considerations of balanced development into the choice of executive appointments in various subsidiary and headquarter positions.

A well-structured system can also provide safeguards against idiosyncracies in appointments. It may prevent good potential managers from being "forgotten" in positions with low visibility to top management (such as product managers in the bowels of large divisions vs. managers in small subsidiaries who at least can draw the attention of visiting senior executives). It may also provide, through checks and balances, limits to the risks of nepotism or of informal "cliques" developing. Middle managers risk seeing their future better assured by attaching themselves to that of a particular senior executive or board member than by developing a sense of corporate, rather than personal, loyalty. In a company afflicted by such a process, this was described to us as the "wolfpack syndrome."

By providing structure and discipline to the management succession process, a well-developed HRM system may limit the risk of such syndromes. This is all the more important in the complex matrix structures often adopted by diversified MNCs as these structures no longer provide the hierarchical "one-person—one boss" simplicity but allow, or even encourage, political behavior and coalition games.

A strongly established system also allows an explicit linkage of strategic control configurations with executive appointments. Individuals, with their own varied personality characteristics and leadership skills, may function more or less effectively under this or that configuration of strategic control (as, for instance, structured in Figure 6.1). While this tends to be often overlooked it is, in fact, a leverage point to provide strategic directions for a business in a complex diversified MNC matrix structure (Prahalad and Doz, 1986).

An HRM system can only be strong, though, with extensive top management support and involvement. First, from a certain level up (usually that of the top few hundred managers in a large diversified MNC) only top management can credibly make appointment decisions. Second, to avoid the "wolfpack syndrome" such decisions must be made—and seen by the organization—as collective decisions of the top management team, not as a compromise resulting from power plays among top managers. The role of the HRM professionals may be to help prepare key decisions—and encourage discipline on the part of top management in making decisions—but in no way to be seen as favoring this or that outcome.

Top management faces several challenges. The first, already alluded to earlier, results from the long lead times involved in human resource management. Developing balanced individuals takes time, and may require top management to recognize early that the pattern of personal development that brought them to the top may no longer be functional. To draw top management from the ranks of subsidiary managers may have been perfectly appropriate to the 1960s when market fragmentation and protection made a nationally responsive approach mandatory, but such an approach may become totally dysfunctional in the 1980s with global markets and global competitors. Yet, unless steps have been taken early to develop balanced executives, there may not be much choice but to continue choosing top managers from the ranks of subsidiary managing directors. Early identification of needed changes and early implementation of changes requires vision and courage on the part of top management. One challenge for both HRM professionals and top management is to speed-up the development of individuals with balanced orientations, particularly in companies whose historical growth pattern has privileged one single orientation strongly.

Second, top management must blend multiple tools for strategic control, ranging from resource dependence in some situations where this is applicable, to management systems tailored to strategic control configurations, and to the selective matching of individuals' characteristics with strategic control configuration described above. Combining these various approaches is a critical challenge for top management.

Third, top managers must exercise personal and collective discipline in key appointments—probably the single most important decision they frequently make—and in interpreting patterns of key appointments for the members of the organization. In European firms with collegial decision-making bodies (management board, executive committees, and the like) this requires consistency and coherence in the group, a statesman's rather than an entrepreneur's attitude on the part of each member, and a sense for organizational interpretation processes. Again, this may be a major challenge, particularly for individual managers who have acceded to top management through individual success and visible prowess as subsidiary or division manager. This calls for senior managers making difficult role transitions that successful middle-aged individuals do not necessarily find easy to accomplish.

In conclusion, we see the implications outlined above as raising major challenges for the quality of the HRM process and for the responsibilities of top managers in making the HRM process effective in addressing the need for controlled variety faced by most diversified MNCs.

References

Bartlett, Christopher A., and Ghoshal, Sumantra. "The New Global Organization: Differentiated Roles and Dispersed Responsibilities," *Harvard Business Review*, 1986.

Bartlett, Christopher A., and Yoshino, M. Y. "Corning Glass Works: International (A)," Harvard Business School Case Services, 0-381-160, 1981.

Brandel, Fernand. *The Wheels of Commerce*. Volume 2.

Doz, Yves. "Brown Boveri & Cie," Harvard Business School Case Services, 4-378-115, 1983.

Doz, Yves, and Prahalad, C. K. "Headquarter Influence and Strategic Control Multinational Companies," *Sloan Management Review*, **23** (1), Fall 1981.

Doz, Yves. "Transcultural Partnerships between Large and Small Firms: Strategic Issues and Managerial Pitfalls" (presented at the European International Business Association Annual Conference, Glasgow, 15–17 December 1985).

Doz, Yves, and Van den Poel, Martine. "CIBA-GEIGY" (mimeographed case study available from INSEAD, 1983).

Edstrom, Anders, and Galbraith, Jay. "Transfer of Managers as a Coordination and Control Strategy in Multinational Organizations," *Administrative Science Quarterly*, June 1977, **22**, 248–263.

Galbraith, Jay, and Edstrom, Anders. "Alternative Policies for International Transfers of Managers," *Management International Review*, **17**,(2), 1977.

Horwitch, Mel. *Clipped Wings*. Cambridge, MA: MIT Press, 1981.

Lawrence, Paul R., and Dyer, G. *Renewing American Industry*. New York: The Free Press, 1983.

Pfeffer, Jeffrey, and Salancik, Gerald R. *The External Control of Organization*. New York: Harper & Rowe, 1978.

Prahalad, C. K. "Developing Strategic Capability: An Agenda for Top Management, *Human Resource Management*, Fall 1983, **22**(3), 237–255.

Prahalad, C. K., and Doz, Yves. "An Approach to Strategic Control in Multinational Companies," *Sloan Management Review*, **22**(4), Summer 1981.

Prahalad, C. K., and Doz, Yves. "Patterns of Strategic Control within MNCs," *Journal of International Business Studies*, Fall 1985, **15**(1).

Prahalad, C. K., and Doz, Yves. *The Work of Top Management*. New York: The Free Press, 1986.

Salter, Malcolm S. "Manpower Priorities in Emerging Multinationals." Paper presented at the Academy of International Business, 1974 Annual Meeting, San Francisco, 28–29 December 1974.

The Cultural Context

7

Cultural Dimensions in People Management
The Socialization Perspective

Geert Hofstede

Managing Multicultural Work Forces

The story of the Tower of Babel in the first book of the Old Testament is the oldest case study of what can go wrong in managing a multicultural work force. God confused the languages, so that people could no longer communicate and their construction project had to be stopped.

Today's international business and public organizations often resemble the Babel Construction Corporation. Not only the languages but also the cultures become confused, and the latter confusion is less obvious and therefore even more difficult to cope with. My preferred working definition of "culture" is: the collective programming of the mind that distinguishes the members of one group or category of people from another. The "group or category" may be a nation, but also an occupation, a type of business, or a corporation. Tower of Babel stories occur also after mergers of companies within one national environment, just on the basis of their different corporate cultures. The merger of two banks, one a former cooperative savings bank and the other a former merchant bank, provides a perfect example of a culture clash.

Increasing integration of organizations across business and national borders demands that the modern manager be able to operate multiculturally. This is more easily written down than practiced: it demands an insight in the extent to which familiar aspects of organizational life like organization structure, leadership styles, motivation patterns, training, and development models are culturally relative and need to be reconsidered when borders are crossed.

It also, therefore, demands self-insight on the part of the managers involved, who have to be able to compare their way of thinking, feeling, and acting to those of others, without immediately passing judgment. This ability to see the relativity of one's own cultural framework does not come naturally to most managers, who often got to their present positions precisely because they held strong convictions. Yet, coping with cultural relativity may become a survival skill in global organizations. In this chapter, research results will be used to demonstrate the extent to which culture affects our thinking, feeling, and acting.

This book concerns "human resources." A first culture shock for the reader may be that from a global cultural perspective, this term itself is culturally undesirable. It reflects an individualist cultural philosophy in which people can be considered "human resources" to be managed. As we shall see later in this chapter, the United States, where, according to some opinions, the term "human resource management" originated, has a pronouncedly individualistic culture. From a cross-cultural point of view, "people management" is a more neutral term, which is why it figures in the title of this chapter.

Coping with Cultural Differences: Understanding Socialization

Management, of course, is getting things done through (other) people. This is true the world over. In order to manage, one has to know the "things" that must be done and one has to know the people who have to do it. Understanding people means understanding their backgrounds, from which present and future behavior can be predicted.

A useful way to look at people in organizations is in terms of the *socialization* they received before joining the organization and the socialization they receive at work. Socialization is a term from sociology that refers to the way in which a person is conditioned by environment(s). Differences in socialization explain why equally gifted persons will act quite differently in a given situation.

In industrial societies, the family, the school, the workplace, and the community are the main centers of socialization. When a person starts participating in the formal work process, she or he has been presocialized by a family environment and, usually, by one or more schools. Family and school presocialization are beyond the influence of the employer. They will affect the selection and self-selection processes that precede the placement of a person in a first job, and they will influence the way a person works and his or her subsequent career. It is, therefore, very important that managers understand the ways their people have been socialized by their families and schools before they started working.

14

In the socialization process, four elements of culture are transferred (from superficial to deep): symbols, heroes, rituals, and values.

Symbols are words, objects, and gestures that derive their meaning from convention. On the level of national cultures, symbols include the entire area of language. At the level of organizational culture, symbols include abbreviations, slang, modes of address (formal or informal), signs, dress codes, and status symbols, all recognized by organizational insiders only.

Heroes are real or imaginary people, dead or alive, who serve as models for behavior within a culture. Countries have national heroes; generations have their own heroes. At the level of organizations, selection processes are often based on hero models of "the ideal employee" or "the ideal manager." Founders of organizations sometimes become mythical heroes to whom incredible deeds are ascribed.

Rituals are collective activities that are technically superfluous but, within a particular culture, socially essential. Countries and ethnic groups as well as religious groups have their rituals. The shaking of hands when two Frenchmen meet is a national ritual, as is its absence when two Englishmen meet. In organizations, rituals include not only celebrations, but also many formal activities defended on apparently rational grounds: meetings, the writing of memos, and planning systems, plus the informal ways in which formal activities are performed: who can afford to be late for what meeting, who speaks to whom, and so forth.

Values represent the deepest level of a culture. They are broad feelings, often unconscious and not discussable, about what is good and what is evil, beautiful or ugly, rational or irrational, normal or abnormal, natural or paradoxical, decent or indecent. These feelings are present in the majority of the members of the culture, or at least in those persons who occupy pivotal positions.

The various levels in a culture will interact, so that, for example, symbols, heroes, and rituals reflect some of the values, and the values are reinforced by rituals. The different nature of socialization in the family, at school, and in the work organization has been diagrammed in Figure 7.1.

Nationality (and sex as well) is an involuntary attribute—we are born within a family within a nation and are subject to the mental programming of its culture from birth. Here we acquire most of our basic *values*. Occupational choice is partly voluntary; (depending on the society and family); it leads to the choice of schools, where we are further socialized to the values *and* the practices of our chosen occupation. When we enter a work environment, we are usually young or not-so-young adults with most of our values firmly entrenched, but we will still become socialized to the *practices* of our new work environment.

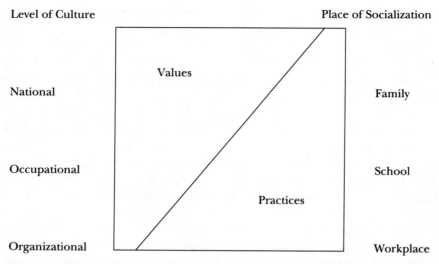

Figure 7.1 Elements Transferred in the Socialization Toward National, Occupational, and Organizational Cultures.

National Culture Differences

The following section uses the results of three research projects. As, according to Figure 7.1, national culture differences reside mainly at the level of values, all three projects focused on values.

1. The first project compared work-related values among matched groups of employees in subsidiaries of the multinational IBM in 40 countries (Hofstede 1980). Since the samples were so well matched, the national component in their values, based on presocialization in families and at school, could be isolated quite clearly. Later on the database was extended to include 64 countries, divided into 50 single countries and three multicountry regions (Hofstede 1991). The differences in values among the countries studied could be broken down into four factors, which will be described later.

2. The second project studied value differences among students in different countries. It reanalyzed data collected with a modified version of the Rokeach Value Survey (Rokeach 1968, 1973) among students in nine countries in the Asia-Pacific region (Ng et al. 1982). The reanalysis produced five factors, four of which were significantly correlated with the factors found earlier in the IBM data (Hofstede and Bond 1984).

3. The third project studied value differences among students in different countries; this study used a new values questionnaire, entirely designed by Chinese scholars in Chinese, which was translated and administered to students in 23 countries around the world. Analysis of the data produced four factors, three of them significantly correlated with the factors from the IBM

data, the fourth new and interpretable (The Chinese Culture Connection 1987; Hofstede and Bond 1988).

The three dimensions of national culture differences common to the IBM and Rokeach studies and the Chinese Value Survey are the following:

1. *Power distance*. This dimension is the extent to which the less powerful members of organizations and institutions (like the family) accept and expect that power is distributed unequally. This represents inequality (more versus less), but it is defined from below, not from above. It suggests that a society's level of inequality is endorsed by the followers as much as by the leaders. Power and inequality, of course, are extremely fundamental facts of any society, and anybody with some international experience will be aware that "all societies are unequal, but some are more unequal than others."

Table 7.1 lists some of the differences in socialization emphasis in the family, the school, and the work situation in small versus large power distance cultures. The statements refer to extremes; actual situations may be found anywhere in between the extremes.

2. *Individualism versus collectivism*. This dimension describes the degree to which individuals are integrated into groups. On the individualist side, we find societies in which the ties between individuals are loose: all members are expected to look after themselves and their immediate families. On the collectivist side, we find societies in which people from birth onward are integrated into strong, cohesive groups, often extended families (with uncles, aunts, and grandparents) that continue protecting them in exchange for unquestioning loyalty. The word "collectivism" in this sense has no political meaning: it refers to the group, not to the state. Again, the issue addressed by this dimension is an extremely fundamental one, regarding all societies in the world.

Table 7.2 lists some of the differences in socialization emphasis in collectivist versus individualist cultures; most real cultures will be somewhere in between those extremes.

3. *Masculinity versus Femininity*. The distribution of roles between the sexes is another fundamental issue for any society to which a range of solutions are found. The analysis of the IBM data revealed that (1) women's values differ less among societies than men's values; (2) if we restrict ourselves to men's values, (which vary more from one country to another), we find that they contain a dimension from very assertive and competitive and maximally different from women's values on the one side, to modest and caring and similar to women's values on the other. We have called the assertive pole "masculine" and the modest, caring pole "feminine." The women in the feminine countries have the same modest, caring values as the men; in the masculine countries, the women are somewhat assertive and competitive, but not as much as the men, so that these countries show a gap between men's and women's values.

Table 7.3 lists some of the different socialization emphases in the family,

Table 7.1 Different Socialization Emphases According to Power Distance

	SMALL POWER DISTANCE SOCIETIES	LARGE POWER DISTANCE SOCIETIES
In the family	Children encouraged to have a will of their own Parents treated as equals	Children educated towards obedience to parents Parents treated as superiors
At school	Student-centered education (initiative) Learning represents impersonal "truth"	Teacher-centered education (order) Learning represents personal "wisdom" from teacher (guru)
At the workplace	Hierarchy means an inequality of roles, established for convenience Subordinates expect to be consulted Ideal boss is resourceful democrat	Hierarchy means existential inequality Subordinates expect to be told what to do Ideal boss is benevolent autocrat (good father)

144

Table 7.2 Different Socialization Emphases According to Collectivism and Individualism

	COLLECTIVIST SOCIETIES	INDIVIDUALIST SOCIETIES
In the family	Education towards "we" consciousness	Education towards "I" consciousness
	Opinions predetermined by group	Private opinion expected
	Obligations to family or in-group: • harmony • respect • shame	Obligations to self: • self-interest • self-actualization • guilt
At school	Learning is for the young only	Permanent education
	Learn how to do	Learn how to learn
At the workplace	Value standards differ for in-groups and out-groups: *particularism*	Same value standards apply to all: *universalism*
	Other people are seen as members of some group	Other people seen as potential resources
	Relationship prevails over task	Task prevails over relationship
	Moral model of employer-employee relationship	Calculative model of employer-employee relationship

Table 7.3 Different Socialization Emphases According to Femininity and Masculinity

	FEMININE SOCIETIES	MASCULINE SOCIETIES
In the family	Stress on relationships Solidarity Resolution of conflicts by compromise and negotiation	Stress on achievement Competition Resolution of conflicts by fighting them out
At school	Average student is norm System rewards students' social adaptation Students' failure at school is relatively minor accident	Best students are norm System rewards students' academic performance Students' failure at school is disaster—may lead to suicide
At the workplace	Assertiveness ridiculed Undersell yourself Stress on life quality Intuition	Assertiveness appreciated Oversell yourself Stress on careers Decisiveness

the school, and the workplace, of the most feminine versus the most masculine cultures, in analogy to Tables 7.1 and 7.2.

The three dimensions described so far all refer to expected social behavior toward people higher or lower in rank (power distance), toward the group (individualism/collectivism), and according to one's sex (masculinity/femininity). It is obvious that the values corresponding to these cultural choices are bred in the family: power distance by the degree to which children are encouraged to have a will of their own; individualism/collectivism by the cohesion of the family with respect to other people, and masculinity/femininity by the role models that the parents and older children present to the younger child. These three dimensions deal with fundamental problems of any human society, but to which different societies have found different answers. This is shown by different scores on the dimensions.

The actual scores found in our research are listed in the first three columns of Table 7.4. The scores for power distance, individualism, and masculinity are based on the IBM data, and they are *relative:* we have chosen our scales so that the distance between the lowest and highest scoring country is about 100 points. The other columns in Table 7.4 will be discussed in the next section.

The Socialization of the Researcher: Western Minds versus Eastern Minds

As mentioned earlier, our research produced a fourth dimension of national culture differences, but this dimension differed between the "Western" IBM and Rokeach Value Survey studies, and the "Eastern" Chinese Value Survey. These dimensions do not refer directly to social relationships, but to basic questions of human existence.

The fourth dimension found in the IBM and Rokeach studies concerns a society's tolerance for uncertainty and ambiguity—we believe that it ultimately refers to man's search for Truth. We call it "uncertainty avoidance:" it indicates to what extent a culture programs its members to feel either uncomfortable or comfortable in unstructured situations. Unstructured situations are novel, unknown, surprising, different from usual. Cultures that avoid uncertainty try to minimize the possibility of unstructured situations with strict laws and rules and safety and security measures. On the philosophical and religious levels, there is a belief in absolute Truth; "there can be only one Truth and we have it." People in countries that avoid uncertainty are also more emotional and are motivated by inner nervous energy. The opposite type, cultures that accept uncertainty, are more tolerant of opinions that are different from what they used to be; they try to have as few rules as possible. On the philosophical and religious levels, they are relativist and allow

Table 7.4 Scores of 50 countries and 3 regions on 5 dimensions of national values

Country	Power Distance		Individualism		Masculinity		Uncertainty Avoidance		Long-Term Orientation	
	Index (PDI)	Rank	Index (IDV)	Rank	Index (MAS)	Rank	Index (UAI)	Rank	Index (CFD)	Rank
Argentina	49	35–36	46	22–23	56	20–21	86	10–15		
Australia	36	41	90	2	61	16	51	37	31	14–15
Austria	11	53	55	18	79	2	70	24–25		
Belgium	65	20	75	8	54	22	94	5–6		
Brazil	69	14	38	26–27	49	27	76	21–22	65	6
Canada	39	39	80	4–5	52	24	48	41–42	23	20
Chile	63	24–25	23	33	28	46	86	10–15		
Colombia	67	17	13	49	64	11–12	80	20		
Costa Rica	35	42–44	15	46	21	48–49	86	10–15		
Denmark	18	51	74	9	16	50	23	51		
Ecuador	78	8–9	8	52	63	13–14	67	28		
Finland	33	46	63	17	26	47	59	31–32		
France	68	15–16	71	10–11	43	35–36	86	10–15		
Germany (FR)	35	42–44	67	15	66	9–10	65	29	31	14–15
Great Britn	35	42–44	89	3	66	9–10	35	47–48	25	18–19
Greece	60	27–28	35	30	57	18–19	112	1		
Guatemala	95	2–3	6	53	37	43	101	3		
Hong Kong	68	15–16	25	37	57	18–19	29	49–50	96	2
Indonesia	78	8–9	14	47–48	46	30–31	48	41–42		
India	77	10–11	48	21	56	20–21	40	45	61	7
Iran	58	29–30	41	24	43	35–36	59	31–32		
Ireland	28	49	70	12	68	7–8	35	47–48		
Israel	13	52	54	19	47	29	81	19		
Italy	50	34	76	7	70	4–5	75	23		
Jamaica	45	37	39	25	68	7–8	13	52		
Japan	54	33	46	22–23	95	1	92	7	80	4
Korea (S)	60	27–28	18	43	39	41	85	16–17	75	5
Malaysia	104	1	26	36	50	25–26	36	46		

148

Country										
Mexico	81	5–6	30	32	69	6	82	18		
Netherlands	38	40	80	4–5	14	51	53	35	44	10
Norway	31	47–48	69	13	8	52	50	38		
New Zealand	22	50	79	6	58	17	49	39–40	30	16
Pakistan	55	32	14	47–48	50	25–26	70	24–25	0	23
Panama	95	2–3	11	51	44	34	86	10–15		
Peru	64	21–23	16	45	42	37–38	87	9		
Philippines	94	4	32	31	64	11–12	44	44	19	21
Portugal	63	24–25	27	33–35	31	45	104	2		
South Africa	49	35–36	65	16	63	13–14	49	39–40		
Salvador	66	18–19	19	42	40	40	94	5–6		
Singapore	74	13	20	39–41	48	28	8	53	48	9
Spain	57	31	51	20	42	37–38	86	10–15		
Sweden	31	47–48	71	10–11	5	52	29	49–50	33	12
Switzerland	34	45	68	14	70	4–5	58	33		
Taiwan	58	29–30	17	44	45	32–33	69	26	87	3
Thailand	64	21–23	20	39–41	34	44	64	30	56	8
Turkey	66	18–19	37	28	45	31–33	85	16–17		
Uruguay	61	26	36	29	38	42	100	4		
U.S.A.	40	38	91	1	62	15	46	43	29	17
Venezuela	81	5–6	12	50	73	3	76	21–22		
Yugoslavia	76	12	27	33–35	21	48–49	88	8		
Regions:										
Arab Ctrs	80	7	38	26–27	53	23	68	27		
East Africa	64	21–23	27	33–35	41	39	52	36	25	18–19
West Africa	77	10–11	20	39–41	46	30–31	54	34	16	22
Not in IBM study:										
Bangladesh									40	11
China									118	1
Poland									32	13

Ranks: 1 = highest, 53 = lowest (for L.T. Orientation, 23 = lowest) many currents to flow side by side. People within these cultures are more phlegmatic and contemplative and are not expected by their environment to express emotions.

Table 7.5 lists some of the different socialization emphases in the family, the school, and the workplace, related to either weak or strong uncertainty avoidance. The column entitled "Uncertainty Avoidance" in Table 7.4 lists the scores on this dimension by country, based on the IBM subsidiary data.

In the analysis of the Chinese Value Survey data from students in 23 countries around the world, no dimension was found resembling uncertainty avoidance. It seems that, to the Chinese minds who designed the questions, the search for Truth is not an essential issue. One of the basic differences between Eastern thinking (represented by, for example, Confucianism, Buddhism, and Hinduism) and Western thinking (dominant in the Judeo-Christian-Muslim intellectual tradition) is that in the East, a qualification does not exclude its opposite, which is an essential element of Western logic (e.g., Kapp 1983). Thus, in the East, the search for Truth is irrelevant because there is no need for a single and absolute Truth.

The fourth dimension in the Chinese Value Survey data is something we called "Confucian dynamism." It can be said to deal with Virtue regardless of Truth. Values positively rated in Confucian dynamism are thrift and perseverance; values negatively rated are respect for tradition and protecting one's "face." None of these values appeared in the values survey of Milton Rokeach, who, as an American, tried to compose a universal list of human values. These values simply did not occur to his Western mind. Both the positively and the negatively rated values of this dimension are directly present in the teachings of Confucius (e.g., King and Bond 1985). However, the values of thrift and perseverance, rated positively, are oriented more toward the future; tradition and "face" deal with the past and present. This is why we called this dimension "Confucian dynamism;" because it applies to countries without a Confucian heritage, we have chosen as an alternative and more neutral label "Long-Term Orientation" versus "Short-Term Orientation."

Which fourth dimension we find, uncertainty avoidance or Confucian dynamism, depends on what research instruments we used and ultimately on the cultural background of the minds that designed the questions. Cultural differences not only affect the socialization of ordinary people, but also affect researchers and scholars who study and explain the behavior of others.

Western instruments (the IBM and Rokeach questionnaires) identify a dimension related to Truth, on which even Eastern cultures can be scored (from high in Japan to very low in Singapore and Hong Kong). An instrument with a deliberate Eastern bias, the Chinese Values Survey, discovers another dimension, related to Virtue, on which again all countries can be scored, even Western ones. The column "Long-Term Orientation" in Table 7.4 lists the scores for Confucian dynamism by country, this time based on the student

Table 7.5 Different Socialization Emphases According to Uncertainty Avoidance

	WEAK UNCERTAINTY AVOIDING SOCIETIES	STRONG UNCERTAINTY AVOIDING SOCIETIES
In the family	What is different, is ridiculous or curious	What is different, is dangerous
	Ease, indolence, low stress	Higher anxiety and stress
	Aggression and emotions not shown	Showing of aggression and emotions accepted
At school	Students comfortable with • Unstructured learning situations • Vague objectives • Broad assignments • No timetables	Students comfortable with: • Structured learning situations • Precise objectives • Detailed assignments • Strict timetables
	Teachers may say "I don't know"	Teachers should have all the answers
At the workplace	Dislike of rules—written or unwritten	Emotional need for rules—written or unwritten
	Less formalization and standardization	More formalization and standardization

data collected by Bond et al.; these data have been transformed to a 0–100 scale in the same way as the IBM subsidiary data in the other columns of Table 7.4. From the table, one may notice that a long-term orientation is found most in Eastern countries: in particular, China, Hong Kong, Taiwan, Japan, and South Korea. As these are also the countries in the world with the fastest economic growth in the past 25 years, this means that the "Virture" scores are correlated with this economic growth (see Hofstede and Bond 1988). None of the IBM dimensions correlated with economic growth across all countries; it is remarkable that the values associated with the unparalleled economic success of a number of East Asian countries in the past 25 years can be identified only with a questionnaire designed by East Asian minds.

Basically these findings show that not only values and practices, but even theories, are products of culturally determined socialization. This should make us modest when we try to transfer, for example, Western types of education and management or training packages to people in a Third World country. Not only the tools but even the categories available for thinking may be unfit for the other environment.

Differences in Organizational Cultures

Research data on organizational cultures were collected in 1985 and 1986 in 20 work organizations or parts of organizations in Denmark and the Netherlands (Hofstede et al. 1990). The units studied varied from a toy company to a municipal police corps. In-depth interviews were held with a cross-cut of nine informants per unit of various levels and categories, but always including the top manager. Subsequently, a paper-and-pencil survey was administered to a sample of 20 managers, 20 professionals (non-managers with a job for which a higher education is usually required), and 20 nonprofessionals. The 150 questions in the survey were partly derived from earlier cross-national research (to be described later), but most questions were developed on the basis of the in-depth interviews within the units.

Some survey questions dealt with values, as did the cross-national studies, but most dealt with practices—the way people perceived their work environment, that is, its symbols, heroes, and rituals. Analyses of the survey data for the "practices" showed large differences among units; this was not surprising, because the questions had been formulated around issues for which the interviewers had noticed that units were different. The questions on values, the more profound feelings such as those concerning good and evil, which we discussed in the previous sections, produced responses that differed primarily according to demographic criteria of the respondents: nationality (Danish or Dutch), education level, sex, and age. After we had controlled for these demographic criteria, the remaining differences in respondent values among the various organizational units were relatively small. We concluded that different organizations can maintain very different practices on the basis of fairly similar employee values (compare Figure 7.1).

Workplace socialization, according to this research, is mainly a matter of practices that have to be learned by the newcomer. Employee values have been developed in the family and the school, but they play a role in the selection and self-selection process for the job. Workplace socialization, however, can change people's values only to a limited extent. In the recent popular management literature, organization cultures are often presented as a matter of values (e.g., Peters and Waterman 1982). The confusion arises because this literature does not distinguish between the values of the founders and leading elites and those of the bulk of employees. Founders and elites shape organizations according to their values; an organization can become "the lengthening shadow" of its founder (Belden and Belden 1962). Founders and elites create the symbols, heroes, and rituals that constitute the daily practices of the organization's members. However, members have to adapt their personal values to the organization's needs only to a limited extent. A work organization, as a rule, is not a total institution (Goffman 1961). Workplace socialization, according to our data, takes place at a more superficial level of mental programming than family and school socialization.

Dimensions of Organizational Cultures

Organizational cultures are usually quite specific—every organization, or even part of an organization, shows partly different symbols, heroes, and rituals. Nevertheless, our research across 20 units (organizations or parts thereof) in Denmark and the Netherlands identified six main dimensions of differences among the cultures studied. Although on the basis of this limited sample of units (in terms of types of organizations, countries, and moments in time) we obviously cannot claim that the same six dimensions will be found universally, we do believe that these dimensions provide a useful insight into the variety of socialization emphases to which people in organizations are subjected. Also, the dimensions found partly overlap with the reported results of other studies: from the United States by Litwin and Stringer (1968) and from Switzerland by Pümpin (1984).

The six dimensions were found through a factor analysis of the mean answer scores on 74 questions about practice for 20 organizational units. We labeled them:

1. Process-oriented versus results-oriented

2. Employee-oriented versus job-oriented

3. Parochial versus professional

4.   Open system versus closed system

5.   Tight control versus loose control

6.   Pragmatic versus normative emphasis towards clients

The first dimension opposes units which we called "process-oriented" to units which can be labeled "results-oriented." In process-oriented units, people think that their colleagues are concerned about means rather than ends, that they avoid taking risks, that they expend the least effort possible, and that they experience each day as pretty much the same as the previous day. On this side, we find production departments and large office operations in particular. The units at the opposite pole of this dimension, those with "results-orientations" units, have people who think that their colleagues are concerned about ends rather than means, seem comfortable in unfamiliar situations, always put in maximal effort, and feel that each day brings new challenges. On the results-oriented side, we find operations that have direct contact with customers and research and development units. However, not all production and office operations score equally low, and not all service and research operations score equally high. Apart from the nature of the task, the history and leadership of a unit also clearly play a role.

The process/results-oriented dimension appears to be related to the *strength* of the culture. The management literature often refers to cultures being "strong" or "weak," but rarely indicates how this strength can be measured. We have interpreted a "strong" culture as one with a strong and unambiguous socialization pressure; we assume that the strength of the culture can be measured through the *homogeneity* of employees' perceptions of their work situation. A unit in which all people surveyed described their practices in about the same terms is, to us, a strong cultural unit; a unit in which different people give widely different answers to the same questions is a weak culture (weak = heterogeneous). On the basis of the mean standard deviations of individuals' answers on 18 key questions, we could allocate to all 20 units a "culture strength" score. This score appears to be correlated with the units' position on the first dimension: process-oriented units tend to have weak, heterogeneous cultures (large standard deviations of individuals' answers); results-oriented units tend to have strong, homogeneous cultures (small standard deviations of individuals' answers).

The second dimension opposes "employee-oriented" to "job-oriented" units. In employee-oriented units, people feel that their personal problems are taken into account at work and that the organization takes a major responsibility for the welfare of employees and their families. Also, these units more often use groups or committees for decision making. In job-oriented units, people feel strong pressure to get the job done; they think that the organization is interested only in the work they do. Also, decisions in these units tend to be taken by individuals. The position of a unit on this dimension seems to be mainly a matter of style and tradition, often based on the philosophy of the founder or founders of the organization. However, units that in the not-too-distant past went through reorganizations involving collective lay-offs tend to have moved toward the job-oriented pole. Units managed by entrepreneur-type top leaders (who consider profits to be the first success indicator) tended to be perceived by their people as job-oriented; units led by "manager-type" leaders (who consider budget fulfillment to be their first success yardstick) tended to be perceived by their people as employee-oriented.

The third dimension opposes "parochial" and "professional" units. In "parochial units", identity is primarily determined by the employee's belonging to the organization. In the "professional" organization, the employee's profession—regardless of the organization—is the primary source of identity. If asked what he or she does, the "parochial" unit employee answers: "I work for X." The "professional" unit employee answers: "I am a computer engineer." "Parochial" unit employees feel that their employers prefer to hire people from the right family, social class, and school background, that the norms of the organization also cover their behavior at home, and that they are not supposed to think far ahead. "Professional" unit employees feel that they are hired on the basis of job competence only, that their private lives are their own business, and that they are supposed to think years ahead. There is an obvious relationship between the mean education level of a unit's employees and its degree of professionalism: parochial units tend to have employees with less formal education. Sociology has long known this dimension as "local" versus "cosmopolitan", the contrast between an internal and an external frame of reference, first suggested by Ferdinand Tönnies (1887).

The fourth dimension opposes "open-system" and "closed-system" units. People in open-system units feel that the organization and the people are open to newcomers and outsiders, that almost anyone would fit into the organization, and that new employees need only a few days to feel at home. People in closed-system units see their organizations and their colleagues as closed and secretive, even to insiders; only very special people fit into the organization, and new employees need more than a year to feel at home. This dimension is the only one of the six which in our research distinguishes most Danish from all Dutch organizations. It seems that organizational openness is a societal characteristic of Denmark, much more so than in the Netherlands. One Danish organization, however, scores very closed, which shows that organizational peculiarities can sometimes overrule national tendencies.

The fifth and sixth dimensions refer to the predictability of the organization's functioning. The fifth dimension, tight versus loose control, indicates to what extent the internal functioning is structured. The sixth dimension, pragmatic versus normative, indicates to what extent the external functioning is structured. Tight-control units (fifth dimension) report that everybody is cost-conscious, meeting times are kept punctually, and everybody speaks seriously about the organization and their job. Loose-control units report that nobody thinks of cost, meeting times are kept only approximately, and a lot of jokes are made about the organization and the job. On the "tight" side, we find units with precision-demanding or risky outputs—money transactions or pharmaceuticals. On the "loose" side, we find innovative or unprogrammable activities: surprisingly, police units are loosely controlled, because the daily work of a police officer can only very partly be planned.

Pragmatic units (sixth dimension) report that there is a major emphasis on meeting customer or client needs, and that results are more important than correct procedures. They also report a flexible attitude toward business ethics. Normative units, on the other hand, report a major emphasis on correctly following organizational procedures, which are more important than results. They also report high standards of business ethics and honesty, fostered by the feeling that their organization fulfills a useful task for the well-being of society—an issue about which the pragmatic units have considerably more modest feelings ("Our organization contributes little to the well-being of society"). This sixth dimension, obviously, deals with the fashionable topic of customer orientation. We found that units working under competition are found on the pragmatic side, whereas monopolistic units, and in particular units working at tasks defined by law, occupy the normative side. One of the police departments studied scored extremely normative; the other, which was organized into citizen-friendly neighborhood teams, scored considerably more pragmatic. In fact, it was more pragmatic than some of the units from business companies.

Consequences for Multicultural Personnel Management

This chapter has pictured the scope of cultural variety, across both national and organizational dividing lines, that may be found in a multicultural organization. Being multicultural puts a particular responsibility on personnel departments; not all personnel managers, nor their general management superiors, are aware of this.

Multicultural personnel departments are caught between the devil and the deep blue sea. "The devil" is the assumption that there is uniformity in people's mental programs where such uniformity is lacking. This assumption results in corporate-wide policies and programs being imposed on subsidiaries where they will not work or where they will receive only lip service from obedient but puzzled locals. "The deep blue sea" is the assumption that everybody is different and that people in subsidiaries, therefore, always should know best and be allowed to go their own ways. In this case an opportunity is lost to build a corporate culture with unique features that keep the organization together and provide it with a distinctive and competitive psychological advantage.

Two types of roles are particularly crucial in a multicultural organization:

1. *Top managers of business units in countries.* These managers are the "linking pins" of the organization. They should be able to function in two cultures: the culture of the business unit and the corporate culture, which is usually heavily affected by the nationality of origin of the corporation. They should have the confidence of both their headquarters superiors and their local subordinates.

2. *Corporate diplomats.* These managers are home country or other nationals impregnated with the corporate culture, multilingual, from various occupational backgrounds, and experienced in living and functioning in other cultures. They are essential in order to make multinational structures work; they serve as liaisons to the various head offices or as temporary managers for new ventures.

Ensuring the availability of such people represents a major challenge for multicultural personnel management. Timely recruiting of future managerial talent from different nationalities, career moves through planned transfers in view of acculturation in the corporate ways, and cultural awareness training for business experts who will have to operate in foreign countries can all help the organization have the proper people available when they are needed.

References

Belden, T. G., and Belden, M. R. 1962. *The Lengthening Shadow: The Life of Thomas J. Watson.* Boston: Little, Brown & Co.

Goffman, E. 1961. *Asylums: Essays on the Social Situation of Mental Patients and Other Inmates.* Garden City, N.Y.: Doubleday Anchor Books.

Hofstede, G. 1980. *Culture's Consequences: International Differences in Work-Related Values.* Beverly Hills, Calif.: Sage Publications.

Hofstede, G. 1986. "Cultural Differences in Teaching and Learning." *International Journal of Intercultural Relations* 10: 301–20.

Hofstede, G. 1991. *Cultures and Organizations: Software of the Mind.* London: McGraw Hill.

Hofstede, G., and Bond, M. H. 1984. "Hofstede's Culture Dimensions: An Independent Validation Using Rokeach's Value Survey." *Journal of Cross-Cultural Psychology* 15(4): 417–33.

Hofstede, G., and Bond, M. H. 1988. "The Confucius Connection: From Cultural Roots to Economic Growth." *Organizational Dynamics* 16(4).

Hofstede, G., Neuijen, B., Ohayv, D. D., and Sanders, G. 1990. "Measuring Organizational Cultures." *Administrative Science Quarterly* 35(2): 286–316.

Kapp, R. A., ed., 1983. *Communicating with China.* Chicago: Intercultural Press.

King, A. Y. C., and Bond, M. H. 1985. "The Confucian Paradigm of Man: A Sociological

View." In W. Tseng and D. Wu, eds., *Chinese Culture and Mental Health: An Overview*. New York: Academic Press, 29–45.

Litwin, G. H., and Stringer, R. A. 1968. *Motivation and Organizational Climate*. Boston: Harvard Business School.

Ng, S. H., Hossain, A. B. M. A., Ball, P., Bond, M. H., Hayashi, K., Lim, S. P., O'Driscoll, M. P., Sinha, D., and Yang, K. S. "Human Values in Nine Countries." In R. Rath, H. S. Asthana, D. Sinha, and J. B. P. Sinha, eds., 1982. *Diversity and Unity in Cross-Cultural Psychology*. Lisse, The Neterlands: Swets and Zeitlinger, 196–205.

Peters, T. J., and Waterman, R. H. 1982. *In Search of Excellence: Lessons from America's Best-Run Companies*. New York: Harper & Row.

Pümpin, C. 1984. "Unternehmenskultur, Unternehmensstrategie und Unter nehmenserfolg." In *GDI Impuls*, Gottlieb Duttweiler Institut 2:19–30.

Rokeach, M. 1968. *Beliefs, Attitudes and Values*, San Francisco: Jossey-Bass.

Rokeach, M. 1973. *The Nature of Human Values*, New York: Free Press.

The Chinese Culture Connection 1987. "Chinese Values and the Search for Culture-Free Dimensions of Culture." In *Journal of Cross-Cultural Psychology* 18(2): 143–164.

Tönnies, F. 1963 [1887]. *Gemeinschaft und Gesellschaft: Grundbegriffe der reinen Soziologie*. Darmstadt: Wissenschaftliche Buchgesellschaft.

8

National vs. Corporate Culture*
Implications for Human Resource Management

Susan C. Schneider**

Corporate culture has received a great deal of attention in the last five years. Popular books such as *In Search of Excellence* (Peters and Waterman 1982) and *Corporate Cultures* (Deal and Kennedy 1982), have sold millions of copies to eager executives in many countries. Although the academic community has taken a more cautious approach, it too is interested (Schein 1985; Smircich 1983; see also *ASQ*, September 1983). While the popular press has implied that excellent companies have strong corporate cultures, the link between strong culture and performance can be challenged. Different environments require different strategies; the corporate culture needs to fit that strategy (Schwartz and Davis 1981). In the case of the MNC, there is the need to address the fit of corporate culture with the different national cultures of their subsidiaries to assure strategy implementation, particularly HRM strategy.

Corporate culture has been discussed as a means of control for headquarters over their subsidiaries (see special issue of *JIBS* 1984; in particular, Baliga and Jaeger; Doz and Prahalad). In this view, corporate culture serves

Human Resource Management, Vol. 27, Number 1, pp. 133–148, Peter Lorange, copyright © 1986 by John Wiley & Sons, Inc., reprinted by permission of John Wiley & Sons, Inc.

**The author would like to thank Paul Evans, Andre Laurent, Randall Schuler, and the anonymous reviewers for their helpful suggestions.

as a behavioral control, instilling norms and values that result in following "the way things are done around here." The methods by which this is accomplished are: recruiting "like-minded" individuals, i.e., those that share the values of the company; socialization through training and personal interaction; and developing strong organizational commitment through various other HR policies such as lifetime employment, stock option plans, recreational and housing facilities, and expatriate rotation. These methods are frequently used by Japanese firms but also the so-called excellent companies such as IBM, Hewlett-Packard, Digital Equipment, all known for their strong corporate cultures (Pascale 1984).

Corporate culture is in part managed through the HRM practices (Evans 1986). Some of these practices, however, may not be appropriate given the beliefs, values, and norms of the local environment, i.e., the national culture wherein the subsidiary is embedded. Problems arise in transferring corporate culture through these practices in an effort to achieve globalization. More attention needs to be paid to the possible clash of assumptions underlying national and corporate cultures (Laurent 1986; Alder and Jelinek 1986).

The purpose of this chapter is to explore the potential clash of the corporate culture of a multinational organization and the national culture of the local subsidiary, paying particular attention to human resource practices. First, the construct of culture will be reviewed. Then the assumptions underlying human resource management practices will be discussed, questioning their fit within different national cultures. Specific attention will be paid to the implications for human resource management practices such as career planning, performance appraisal and reward systems, selection and socialization, and expatriate assignments. Case examples are used to illustrate the problem. Finally, the chapter will raise an issue often expressed by multinational companies—what does it mean to be a truly international company? What does "global" really look like? It will also question the use of corporate culture as a homogenizing force and as a mechanism of control.

Culture

The construct of culture has caused much confusion. While there are multiple definitions, they tend to be vague and overly general. This confusion is added to by the multiple disciplines interested in this topic, which while increasing richness, does not necessarily increase clarity. Anthropologists, sociologists, psychologists, and others bring with them their specific paradigms and research methodologies. This creates difficulties in reaching consensus on construct definitions as well as their measurement or operationalization.

The model developed by Schein (1985) helps to organize the pieces of the culture puzzle. According to this model, culture is represented at three levels: (1) behaviors and artifacts, (2) beliefs and values, and (3) underlying assumptions. These levels are arranged according to their visibility such that behavior and artifacts are the easiest to observe, while the underlying assumptions need to be inferred. To understand what the behaviors or beliefs actually mean to the participants, the underlying assumptions have to be surfaced. This is most difficult as assumptions are considered to be taken for granted and out of awareness.

This model can be applied to both corporate and national cultures. Laurent (1986) argues, however, that corporate culture may modify the first two levels but will have little impact on the underlying assumptions that are embedded in the national culture. This raises the issue as to whether the behaviors, values, and belief prescribed by corporate culture are merely complied with or truly incorporated (Sathe 1983). This is particularly relevant to concerns regarding motivation, commitment, and the possibility of employees sharing a common "worldview," i.e., the very reasons for promoting a strong corporate culture. Although it can be argued that changes in behavior may result in changes in underlying assumptions over time, the unconscious nature of these assumptions makes this unlikely (Schein 1985).

The underlying assumptions prescribe ways of perceiving, thinking, and evaluating the world, self, and others. These assumptions include views of the relationship with nature and of human relationships (Schein 1985; Kluckholn and Strodtbeck 1961; Wallin 1972; Hall 1960; Hofstede 1980; Laurent 1983). The relationship with nature reflects several dimensions: (1) control over the environment, (2) activity vs. passivity or doing vs. being, (3) attitudes towards uncertainty, (4) notions of time, (5) attitudes towards change, and (6) what determines "truth." Views about the nature of human relationships include: (1) task vs. social orientation, (2) the importance of hierarchy, (3) the importance of individual vs. group. For example, some cultures, often Western, view man as the master of nature, which can be harnessed and exploited to suit man's needs; time, change, and uncertainty can be actively managed. "Truth" is determined by facts and measurement. Other cultures, often Eastern, view man as subservient to or in harmony with nature. Time, change, and uncertainty are accepted as given. "Truth" is determined by spiritual and philosophical principles. This attitude is often referred to as "fatalistic" or "adaptive."

Assumptions regarding the nature of human relationships are also different. The importance of social concerns over task, of the hierarchy, and of the individual vs. the group are clearly different not only between the East and West, but also within Western cultures. In Eastern cultures, for example, importance is placed on social vs. task concerns, on the hierarchy, and on the group or collective (Hofstede 1980). By contrast, in Western cultures, the focus is more on task and on the individual, and the hierarchy is considered to be of less importance. However, research by Hofstede (1980) and Laurent (1983) demonstrate that along these dimensions there is variance between the U.S. and Europe as well as within Europe.

Human Resource Practices in MNCs

The differences described above have implications for human resource policies that are developed at headquarters and that reflect not only the corporate culture but the national culture of the MNC. Problems may arise when these policies are to be implemented abroad. According to Schuler (1987), MNCs can choose from a menu of human resource practices that concern: planning and staffing, appraising and compensating, and selection and socialization. Within this menu there are several options which need to be in line with the overall corporate strategy and culture. They also need to take into account the differences in the national cultures of the subsidiaries where they are to be implemented. This section will describe how national culture may affect these choices. In many cases, the description and examples of both corporate and national culture are exaggerated and/or oversimplified. As this is done for purposes of demonstration, it must be remembered that there remains variance within as well as between national and corporate cultures.

Planning and Staffing

Planning can be considered along several dimensions such as formal/informal, and short term/long term. Career management systems represent formal, long-term human resource planning. These systems may be inappropriate in cultures where man's control over nature or the future is considered minimal if not sacrilege, e.g., as in the Islamic belief, "Inshallah" (if God wills). Derr (1987) found that national culture was a key determinant of the type of career management systems found within Europe.

Some career management systems assume that people can be evaluated, that their abilities, skills, and traits (i.e., their *net worth* to the company) can be quantified, measured, and fed into a computer. As one British HR manager said, "A lot of that material is highly sensitive; you just don't put it into a computer." On the other hand, Derr (1987) found that the French used highly complex and sophisticated computerized systems. This may reflect a humanistic vs. engineering approach (social vs. task orientation).

Secondly, it may assume that evaluation reflects past performance and predicts future performance, which means that evaluation is based on DOING rather than BEING (active vs. passive). In other words, evaluation is based on *what* you achieve and *what* you know (achievement), and *not* on *who* you are (a person of character and integrity) and *who* you know (ascription). In the U.S., concrete results are the criteria for selection and promotion (Derr 1987). An American general manager of the U.K. region complained that people around there got promoted because of the schools they went to and their family background, not on what they accomplished. This is also common in France, where ties with the "grandes écoles" and the "grands corps" are important for career advancement.

Third, it may assume that data banks can be created of "skills" that can then be matched to "jobs," that jobs can be clearly defined and that specific skills exist to fit them. One Dutch HR manager said that the major problems of long-term planning in high technology industries is that the nature of the job in three to five years is unpredictable. IBM says it hires for careers, not jobs; Olivetti says "potential," not "skills" is most important. These differences may reflect underlying assumptions regarding uncertainty and the relationship between the individual and the group (here, organization), e.g., career vs. jobs. For example, in Japan job descriptions are left vague and flexible to fit uncertainty and to strengthen the bond between the individual and the company. In the U.S. and France, the job descriptions tend to be more specific, which may reduce uncertainty but which permits more job mobility between organizations.

Also, the nature of the skills acquired is a function of the national educational system. In many European countries, particularly France, mathematics and science diplomas have status and engineering is the preferred program of further study. This system encourages highly technical, narrowly focused specialists which may make functional mobility more difficult. In the U.S. and the U.K., psychology and human relations is valued and more generalists are welcomed. Derr (1987) found that in identifying high potentials, the French valued technical and engineering expertise whereas the British preferred "the classical generalist" with a "broad humanistic perspective." Knife and fork tests, assessment of table manners and conversation skills, as well as personal appearance were considered to be important criteria for selection in the U.K.

Many career management systems also assume geographic mobility of the work force. Geographic mobility may reflect assumptions regarding the task vs. social orientation, and the group vs. the individual. Europeans are considered more internationally oriented than Americans, as they tend to stay longer in each country and move to another country assignment rather than return home (Tung 1987). Yet, one Belgian general manager stated that the biggest problem in developing leadership was getting people to move; "Belgians would rather commute 2 hours a day to Brussels than to leave their roots. How can you get them to go abroad?" "In a survey done in one MNC, the British were most likely to be willing to relocate, while the Spanish were less so, perhaps reflecting economic considerations in Britain and importance of family in Spain. Derr (1987) found 70 percent of Swedish sample reporting it difficult to relocate geographically due to wives' careers. This is similar to Hofstede's (1980) findings that Sweden has the least differentiation between male and female roles, increasing the likelihood that women would have careers.

Finally, these systems may assume that people want to be promoted. While self-actualization needs are supposedly the same in all countries (Haire et al. 1966), it is not clear that self-actualization means promotion. Nor is it certain that Maslow's hierarchy of needs is universal, as McClelland (1961) found different levels of need for achievement in different societies. In collective societies, wherein the emphasis is on the group over the individual, need for affiliation may be much more important (Hofstede 1980). In Sweden, egalitarianism as well as the desire to keep a low profile to avoid "royal Swedish envy" (i.e., others coveting your position) may make promotion less desirable. Also, promotion may mean more time must be devoted to work, which means less time for quality of life. If promotion includes a raise, this may not be desirable due to the Swedish tax structure.

Overall, the notion of career management systems in which people are evaluated in terms of skills, abilities, and traits that will be tested, scored, and computerized may appear impersonal, cold, and objective. These systems may be seen as treating human beings as things, instrumental towards achieving company goals, with no concern for their welfare or for their "soul." Employees should be like family and friends; you don't evaluate them, and they are to be unconditionally loved. Even seeing them as "human resources" may be considered questionable.

Appraisal and Compensation

Performance appraisal and compensation systems are also examples of cultural artifacts that are built upon underlying assumptions. As mentioned before, performance appraisal implies that "performance," i.e., what is "done" or "achieved," is important and that it can be "appraised," i.e., measured objectively. What is appraised is thus behavior and not traits. In Japanese firms, however, there is more concern with judging a person's integrity, morality, loyalty, and cooperative spirit than on getting high sales volume. Furthermore, for the Japanese, the notion of "objective" truth is usually neither important nor useful; "objectivity" refers to the foreigners' point of view while "subjectivity" refers to the host's viewpoint (Maruyama 1984).

Giving direct feedback does not take into account "saving face" so crucial to many Eastern cultures where confronting an employee with "failure" in an open, direct manner would be considered to be "very tactless." The intervention of a third party may be necessary. Appraisal also assumes that the feedback given will be used to correct or improve upon past performance. This requires that individuals receiving the feedback are willing to evaluate themselves instead of blaming others or external conditions for their performance (or lack thereof). This assumes a view of man as having control over the environment and able to change the course of events. It also assumes that what will happen in the future is of importance, that the present provides opportunity, and/or that the past can be used as a guide for future behavior.

Appraisal and compensation systems are often considered to be linked in Western management thinking, as in the case of management by objectives (MBO). Here it is espoused that people should be rewarded based on their performance, what they do or achieve, or for their abilities and skills and not on their traits or personal characteristics. Management by objective (MBO) assumes the following:

1. Goals can be set (man has control over the environment);

2. With 3, 6, 12, or 18-month objectives (time can be managed);

3. Their attainment can be measured (reality is objective);

4. The boss and the subordinate can engage in a two-way dialogue to agree on what is to be done, when, and how (hierarchy is minimized);

5. The subordinate assumes responsibility to meet the agreed upon goals (control and activity); and

6. The reward is set contingent upon this evaluation (doing vs. being).

Problems with the transfer of MBO to other cultures have been discussed before (Hofstede 1980; Laurent 1983; Trepo 1973). In Germany, MBO was favorably received because of preference for decentralization, less emphasis on the hierarchy (allowing two-way dialogue), and formalization (clear goals, time frames, measurement and contingent rewards). In France, however, this technique was less successfully transferred (Trepo 1973). Due to the ambivalent views towards authority, MBO was viewed suspiciously as an exercise of arbitrary power and a manipulative ploy of management. Given that power is concentrated in the hands of the boss (importance of hierarchy), subordinates would be held responsible without having the power to accomplish goals. Within this perspective, the notion of the boss and subordinate participating in reaching a decision together is quite foreign. Also, although the French have a preference for formalization, e.g., bureaucratic systems, things tend to get accomplished outside the system rather than through it—"systeme D" or management by circumvention (Trepo 1973). Other European managers complain that use of MBO is particularly American as it encourages a short-term focus and, as it is tied to rewards, encourages setting lower, more easily attainable goals than necessarily desirable ones.

Tying performance to rewards is also suspect. It would be difficult for most Western managers to consider implementing a system at home whereby the amount that family members are given to eat is related to their contribution to the family income. Yet in the workplace the notion of pay for performance seems quite logical. In African societies, which tend to be more collective, the principles applied to family members apply to employees as well; nepotism is a natural outcome of this logic. One multinational, in an effort to improve the productivity of the work force by providing nutritious lunches, met with resistance and the demand that the cost of the meal be paid directly to the workers so that they could feed their families. The attitude was one of "How can we eat while our families go hungry?"

Preferences for compensation systems and bonuses are clearly linked to cultural attitudes. In one MNC's Danish subsidiary, a proposal for incentives for salespeople was turned down because it favored specific groups, i.e., ran counter to their egalitarian spirit. Furthermore, it was felt that everyone should get the same amount of bonus, not 5 percent of salary; in fact, there should be no differences in pay. In Africa, savings are managed or bonuses conferred by the group in a "tontine" system wherein everyone gives part of their weekly salary to one group member. Although each member would get the same if they saved themselves, it is preferred that the group perform this function.

The relative importance of status, money, or vacation time varies across countries and affects the motivating potential of these systems. One compensation and benefits manager explained that for the Germans, the big Mercedes wasn't enough; a chauffeur was also needed (status concerns). In Sweden, monetary rewards were less motivating than providing vacation villages (quality of life vs. task orientation). Also, there were different expectations regarding pensions, in part a function of the government and inflation. In Southern European countries the pension expected was 40 percent of salary, while in the Nordic countries up to 85 percent, which may reflect different roles of government in society as embedded in the "civic culture" (Almond and Verba 1963).

Selection and Socialization

One of the major concerns of many multinational companies is the training and development of their human resources. This includes concern for the level of skills at the operating levels, the development of indigenous managerial capability, and the identification and nurturing of "high potentials," i.e., those who will play major future leadership roles. At every level, this requires not only acquiring specific skills, e.g., technical, interpersonal, or conceptual (Katz 1974), but also acquiring the "way things are done around here"—the behaviors, values, beliefs, and underlying assumptions of that company, i.e., the corporate culture.

Selection is one of the major tools for developing and promoting corporate culture (Schein 1985). Candidates are carefully screened to "fit in" to the existing corporate culture, assessed for their behavioral styles, beliefs, and values. IBM, for example, may be less concerned with hiring the "typical

Italian" than hiring an Italian who fits within the IBM way of doing things. For example, IBM attempts to avoid power accumulation of managers by moving them every two years (it's said that IBM stands for "I've Been Moved"), which may not suit the Italian culture wherein organizations are seen as more "political" than "instrumental" (Laurent 1983).

One HR manager from Olivetti said that those Italians who want more autonomy go to Olivetti instead of IBM. He described the culture of Olivetti as being informal and non-structured, and as having more freedom, fewer constraints, and low discipline. Recruitment is based on personality and not "too good grades" (taken to reflect not being in touch with the environment). This encouraged hiring of strong personalities, i.e., impatient, more risk-taking and innovative people, making confrontation more likely and managing more difficult.

Socialization is another powerful mechanism of promoting corporate culture. In-house company programs and intense interaction during off-site training can create an "esprit de corps," a shared experience, an interpersonal or informal network, a company language or jargon, as well as develop technical competencies. These training events often include songs, picnics, and sporting events that provide feelings of togetherness. These rites of integration may also be accompanied by initiation rites wherein personal culture is stripped, company uniforms are donned (t-shirts), and humiliation tactics employed, e.g., "pie-in-the-face" and "tie-clipping" (Trice and Beyer 1984). This is supposed to strengthen the identification with the company (reinforce the group vs. the individual).

Other examples are to be found in Japanese management development "Hell Camps" wherein "ribbons of shame" must be worn and instruction must be taken from "young females" (*International Management*, January 1985). IBM management training programs often involve demanding, tension-filled, strictly prescribed presentations to "probing" senior managers (Pascale 1984). These "boot camp" tactics are designed to create professional armies of corporate soldiers. These military metaphors may not be well accepted, particularly in Europe or other politically sensitive regions.

Artifacts of corporate culture campaigns (stickers, posters, cards, and pins) remind members of the visions, values, and corporate goals, e.g., "Smile" campaigns at SAS, Phillips "1 Billion" goal buttons, and G.M. corporate culture cards carried by managers in their breast pockets. Many Europeans view this "hoopla" cynically. It is seen as terribly "American" in its naïveté, enthusiasm, and childishness. It is also seen as controlling and as an intrusion into the private or personal realm of the individual. Statements of company principles on the walls are often referred to skeptically. One HR manager thought that it was "pretty pathetic to have to refer to them." Others feel that it is very American in its exaggeration and lack of subtlety.

Expatriate transfers are also used for socialization and development of

an international "cadre" (Edstrom and Galbraith 1977). The rotation of expatriates from headquarters through subsidiaries and the shipping of local
nationals from the subsidiaries to headquarters occur for different reasons,
such as staffing, management development, and organization development.
These reasons tend to reflect different orientations of headquarters towards
their subsidiaries: ethnocentric, polycentric, and geocentric (Ondrack 1985;
Edstrom and Galbraith 1977; Heenan and Perlmutter 1979; Evans 1986).

Differences between American, European, and Japanese firms have been
found in the use of transfers for purposes of socialization or as a system of
control. U.S. firms rely more on local managers using more formal, impersonal
numbers controls, while the European firms rely on the use of the international cadre of managers using more informal, personal control (La Palombara
and Blank 1977; Ondrack 1985). The Japanese rely heavily on frequent visits
of home and host country managers between headquarters and subsidiaries,
using both socialization and formalization (Ghoshal and Bartlett 1987).

Some external conditions affect the use of expatriates, such as local regulations requiring indigenous management and increasingly limited mobility
due to the rise of dual career and family constraints. Also, willingness to make
work vs. family trade-offs differ between countries, the Europeans less likely
to do so than the Americans (Schmidt and Posner 1983). It is also reported
that the young Japanese managers are less willing to make the same sacrifices
to work than their parents were. Therefore, there may be convergence in
these trends but for different reasons, e.g., task vs. social orientation or individual vs. group orientation.

This section discussed the assumptions underlying various HRM practices
and explored their possible clash with the assumptions of the national cultures
of subsidiaries. This clash can cause problems in implementing HRM practices
designed at headquarters. The differences in underlying assumptions, however, may provide only the excuse. The extent to which these practices are
seen as flowing in one direction, down from headquarters to subsidiaries, may
influence the extent to which these practices are adopted and to what extent
the behavior, beliefs, and values of the corporate culture are incorporated or
even complied with. Ethnocentric vs. geocentric attitudes determine whether
there is hope for going global and whether "truly international" is really
possible. The next section will discuss some important concerns regarding the
use of corporate culture in realizing this global vision.

Going Global

Many American multinationals are moving from having international divisions
to embracing a "global" or "worldwide" perspective, i.e., stage II to stage
III development (Scott 1973). Even European multinationals having longer

histories of international business due to smaller domestic markets, a colonial heritage, and greater proximity of "foreign" countries, are asking, "How can we become more international?"

What does international or global really look like? Do they mean the same thing? Some companies point to the reduced number of expatriates in local subsidiaries, the use of third country nationals, and multinational composition of their top management team as evidence of their "internationalization" (Berenbeim 1982). Many are clamoring for "corporate culture" to provide the coordination and coherence sought. In one American MNC, the European regional headquarters president saw himself vis-à-vis the national affiliates as "a shepherd that needs to let the flock wander and eat grass but get them all going in one direction—to the barn. You don't want to end up alone in the barn at the end of the day." Is corporate culture necessary for global integration? Will socialization work as a control strategy? Several issues are raised that need careful consideration: need for differentiation vs. integration; autonomy vs control; and national vs. corporate boundaries.

Differentiation vs. Integration

To what extent can corporate culture override national culture differences to create a global company? It that desirable or even possible? This raises the issue of the extent to which global vs. local HRM practices are needed to integrate a global company. In the case of global practices, care must be taken so that "geocentric" looks different from "ethnocentric" while remaining sensitive to needs for differentiation. In the case of local, it means determining what needs to be done differently in the context of requirements for integration.

Marketing and HRM have traditionally been functions left decentralized in multinational—subsidiary relationships. Yet, global marketing has been proclaimed the wave of the future (Levitt 1983) despite obvious local market and customer differences. Global HRM runs along similar logic with similar risks. Is HRM necessarily culture-bound? Does competitive advantage derive from global HRM? Homogenized HRM may weaken competitive advantage by trying to ignore or minimize cultural differences instead of trying to utilize them (Adler 1986).

Contingency arguments abound. Doz and Prahalad (1984) argue that the simultaneous need for global integration and local responsiveness must be managed. Evans (1986) argues for the product/market logic to determine the socio-cultural strategy for adaptation. Ghoshal and Nohria (1987) argue that the level of environmental complexity and the level of local resources should determine the levels of centralization, formalization, or socialization used for control in headquarters—subsidiary relationships. These prescriptions are all quite rational but may overlook important resistances arising from the following issues regarding autonomy and boundaries.

Control vs. Autonomy

Visions of going global with corporate culture as a strategy for control may have some unforseen consequences. While Schein (1968) has likened social-ization to brainwashing, Pascale (1984) says the maligned "organization man" of the 1960s is now "in." At what point will the push to conform be met with an equal if not stronger push to preserve uniqueness? Dostoyevsky (1960) said that man would even behave self-destructively to reaffirm his autonomy. What reactance may be provoked by socialization efforts? Those managers selected out or who "drop out" may be valuable not only by providing their expertise but also by providing an alternative perspective. Certain cultures, both national and corporate, that value conformity over individuality may be better able to use corporate culture as a mechanism for control but may lose the advantage of individual initiative.

Hofstede's (1980) research demonstrates that even within a large multi-national, famous for its strong culture and socialization efforts, national cul-ture continues to play a major role in differentiating work values. Laurent (1983) has demonstrated that there is greater evidence for national differences regarding beliefs about organizations in samples of single MNCs than in mul-ticompany samples. These findings may point to a paradox that national cul-ture may play a stronger role in the face of a strong corporate culture. The pressures to conform may create the need to reassert autonomy and identity, creating a cultural mosaic rather than a melting pot.

The convergence/divergence argument (Webber 1969) states that eco-nomic development, technology, and eduction would make possible globali-zation whereas differential levels of available resources and national cultures would work against this. A simple comparison of U.S. and Japanese devel-opment, industrialization, or education is not going to bring about conver-gency. According to Fujisawa, founder of Honda, "Japanese and U.S. man-agement is 95% alike and differs in all important aspects."

Equal and opposing forces for unification and fragmentation coexist (Fay-erweather 1975) as seen within and between countries. The ongoing case of trade policies between Canada and the U.S. (Holsti 1980) and the hopes for the future of the EEC trade agreements in 1992 rest precariously on this tension. Issues of asymmetry and interdependence between multinationals and host country governments (Gladwin 1982) and between multinational head-quarters and their subsidiaries (Ghoshal and Nohria 1987) make globalization efforts precarious. Therefore, attempts by headquarters to control subsidiaries through more "subtle" methods, such as corporate culture, should take into account the dependency concerns and autonomy needs of the subsidiary and anticipate their resistance.

For example, efforts to educate Western managers to "understand" Japan met with local resistance (Pucik, personal communication) as ignorance may provide the autonomy zone desired by the local managers. Socialization as a power equalizer as argued by Ghoshal and Nohria (1987) is suspect and will be rejected for precisely this reason. As one general manager of a national subsidiary said regarding the European regional headquarters of a U.S.-based MNC, "As long as we give them the numbers they leave us alone." And U.S. headquarters? "They don't have the foggiest idea about what's going on really. They get the numbers. They get 100 million dollars a year in profit and that's probably about as much as they want to know about." Perhaps formal reporting preserves autonomy and will thus be preferred regardless of the logic of globalization.

Boundaries: National vs. Corporate

In the 1960s, multinationals threatened to take over the world; host country governments' sovereignty was at risk (Vernon 1971, 1977). However, through the transfer of technology and managerial capacity, the power became more symmetrical, even tipping the scale in the other direction as seen at one point in the rash of nationalizations that occurred in the 1970s (Kobrin 1982). While the balance has subsequently restabilized, larger forces, such as the rise of religious fundamentalism in some areas, threaten this stability.

National boundaries are again threatened. Economic victory in lieu of military victory seems to have created "occupational douce." This is reflected in the anxieties of Americans as they see their country becoming owned by "foreigners" and the Japanese invasion of Wall Street. Mitterand, President of France, said recently that in the future the French might become the museum keepers, relying on tips from Japanese tourists.

The vision of developing an international cadre of executives through frequent and multiple transfers designed to encourage the loss of identification with their country of origin and its transfer to the corporation (Edstrom and Galbraith 1977) is frightening. In these global "clans," corporate identification may come to override community and even family identification (Ouchi and Jaeger 1978). These citizens of the world, men and women without countries, only companies, become corporate mercenaries. One story has it that a French IBM executive arriving at JFK airport in New York while searching for his entry visa pulled out his IBM identification card. The customs official, seeing is said, "Oh, it's O.K., you're IBM, you can go ahead." Business schools train these corporate soldiers, dispatching them to multinationals to control the world through finance and management consulting. Perhaps now is the time for academics and practitioners to sit back and reflect about the implications.

References

Adler, N. J. *International Dimensions of Organizational Behavior.* Belmont, Calif.: Kent Publishing Company, 1986.

Adler, N. J., and Jelinek, M. Is "Organizational Culture" Culture Bound? *Human Resource Management*, 1986, 25 (1), 73–90.

Administrative Science Quarterly, 1983, 28 (3).

Almond, G.A., and Verba, S. *The Civic Culture: Political Attitudes and Democracy in Five Nations*. Princeton, N.J.: Princeton University Press, 1963.

Baliga, B. R., and Jaeger, A. M. Multinational Corporations: Control Systems and Delegation Issues. *Journal of International Business Studies*, 1984, 15 (2), 25–40.

Berenbeim, R. *Managing the International Company: Building a Global Perspective*, New York: The Conference Board, Inc., Report no. 814, 1982.

Deal, T., and Kennedy, A. *Corporate Cultures: The Rites and Rituals of Corporate Life*. Reading, Mass.: Addison-Wesley Publishing Co., Inc., 1982.

Derr, C. Managing High Potentials in Europe. *European Management Journal*, 1987, 5 (2), 72–80.

Dostoyevsky, F. *Notes from the Underground*, New York: Dell Publishing Company, Inc., 1960.

Doz, Y., and Prahalad, C. Patterns of Strategic Control within Multinational Corporations. *Journal of International Business Studies*, 1984, 15 (2), 55–72.

Edstrom, A., and Galbraith J. Transfer of Managers as a Coordination and Control Strategy in Multinational Organizations. *Administrative Science Quarterly*, 1977, 22, 248–263.

Evans, P. The Context of Strategic Human Resource Management Policy in Complex Firms. *Management Forum*, 1986, 6, 105–17.

Fayerweather, J. A. Conceptual Scheme of the Interaction of the Multinational Firm and Nationalism. *Journal of Business Administration*, 1975, 7, 67–89.

Ghoshal, S., and Bartlett A. Organizing for Innovations: Case of the Multinational Corporation. WP INSEAD No. 87/04, 1987.

Gladwin, T. Environmental Interdependence and Organizational Design: The Case of the Multinational Corporation. WP NYU No. 82–13, 1982.

Haire, M., Ghiselli, E., and Porter, L. *Managerial Thinking—An International Study*. New York: John Wiley & Sons, Inc., 1966.

Hall, E. T. The Silent Language of Overseas Business. *Harvard Business Review*, 1960, 38 (3), 87–95.

Heenan, D. A., and Perlmutter, H. V. *Multinational Organization Development: A Social Architectural Perspective*. Philippines: Addison-Wesley Publishing Company, Inc., 1979.

Hofstede, G. *Culture's Consequences*. Beverly Hills, Calif.: Sage Publications, 1980.

Holsti, J. Change in the International System: Integration and Fragmentation. In R. Holsti, R. Siverson, and A. George, eds., *Change in the International System*. Boulder: Westview Press, 1980, 23–53.

Journal of International Business Studies, Fall 1984.

Katz, R. Skills of an Effective Administrator. *Harvard Business Review*, 1974, 90–102.

Kluckholn, F., and Strodtbeck, F. *Variations in Value Orientations*. Evanston, Ill.: Row, Peterson, 1961.

Kobrin, S. *Managing Political Risk Assessments: Strategic Response to Environmental Change*. Berkeley, Calif.: University of California Press, 1982.

La Palombara, J., and Blank, S. *Multinational Corporations in Comparative Perspective*. New York: The Conference Board, Report No. 725, 1977.

Laurent, A. The Cross-Cultural Puzzle of International Human Resource Management. *Human Resource Management*, 1986, 25 (1), 91–102.

Laurent, A. The Cultural Diversity of Western Conceptions of Management. *International Studies of Management and Organizations*, 1983, 13 (1–2), 75–96.

Levitt, T. The Globalization of Markets. *Harvard Business Review*, 1983, (May–June), 92–102.

McClelland, D. *The Achieving Society*. New York: D. Van Nostrand Company, Inc., 1961.

Maruyama, M. Alternative Concepts of Management: Insights from Asia and Africa. *Asia Pacific Journal of Management*, 1984, 100–10.

Ondrack, D. International Transfers of Managers in North American and European MNE's. *Journal of International Business Studies*, 1985, 16 (3), 1–19.

Ouchi, W. G., and Jaeger, A. M. Type Z Organization: Stability in the Midst of Mobility. *Academy of Management Review*, 1978, 3 (2), 305–41.

Pascale, R. The Paradox of "Corporate Culture": Reconciling Ourselves to Socialization. *California Management Review*, 1984, 27 (2), 26–41.

Peters, T., and Waterman, R. *In Search of Excellence*. New York: Harper & Row, 1982.

Sathe, V. Implications of Corporate Culture: A Manager's Guide to Action. *Organizational Dynamics*, 1983 (Autumn), 5–23.

Schein, E. H. *Organizational Culture and Leadership*. San Francisco: Jossey-Bass Publishers, 1985.

Schmidt, W., and Posner, B. *Management Values in Perspective*. New York: AMA Publications, 1983.

Scott, B. The Industrial State: Old Myths and New Realities. *Harvard Business Review*, 1973 (Mar.–Apr.), 133–48.

Schuler, R. Human Resource Management Practice Choices. In R. Schuler and S. Youngblood, eds., *Readings in Personnel and Human Resource Management*, 3rd edition. St. Paul: West Publishing, 1987.

Schwartz, H., and Davis, S. Matching Corporate Culture and Business Strategy. *Organizational Dynamics*, 1981, (Summer), 30–48.

Smircich, L. Studying Organizations as Cultures. In G. Morgan, ed., *Beyond Method: Strategies for Social Research*. Beverly Hills, Calif.: Sage Publications, Inc., 1983.

Trepo, G. Management Style à la Francaise. *European Business*, 1973 (Autumn) 71–79.

Trice, H. M., and Beyer, J. M. Studying Organizational Culture through Rites and Ceremonials. *Academy of Management Review*, 1984, 9 (4), 653–69.

Tung, R. Expatriate Assignments: Enhancing Success and Minimizing Failure. *Academy of Management Executive*, 1987, 1 (2), 117–26.

Vernon, R. *Sovereignty at Bay*. New York: Basic Books, 1971.

Vernon, R. *Storm Over the Multinationals*. Cambridge, Mass.: Harvard University Press, 1977.

Wallin, T. The International Executive Baggage: Cultural Values of the American Frontier. *MSU Business Topics*, 1972 (Spring), 49–58.

Webber, R. Convergence or Divergence? *Columbia Journal of Business*, 1969, 4 (3).

9

The Cross-Cultural Puzzle of Global Human Resource Management*

André Laurent

Global Human Resource Management: A Field in Infancy

If the field of Human Resource Management (HRM) is still in a stage of adolescence, the emerging field of International or Global HRM cannot claim more than a status of infancy. While the need is pressing for organizations to develop global strategies for the management of their human resources, the knowledge base that could inspire new approaches is extremely limited.

Yet the globalization of markets poses new challenges to organizations by raising the international nature of their operations. In Europe alone, the 1992 horizon has contributed to motivate an increasing number of mergers, acquisitions, joint-ventures and other forms of partnership across national borders. These developments give rise to new organizations that bring together individuals and groups from different national and organizational cultures. In the process, unprecedented cross-cultural puzzles get created that may result in the most confusing disasters or develop highly creative synergies.

International HRM represents a new and largely unexplored domain that lies at the heart of such cross-cultural puzzles. The intent of this chapter is to contribute to the framing of this new domain in building upon the author's inquiry into the cultural diversity of management conceptions across nations.

Human Resource Management, Vol. 25, Number 1, pp. 133–148, Peter Lorange, copyright © 1986 by John Wiley & Sons, Inc., reprinted by permission of John Wiley & Sons, Inc.

174

HRM Practices as Institutionalized Preferences for the Management of People

Managers in organizations hold particular sets of assumptions, ideas, beliefs, preferences, and values on how to manage people toward the attainment of some organizational goals. Over time these various ideas get translated into particular policies, systems, and practices which in turn may reinforce or alter the original ideas. Furthermore, organizational members have sets of expectations related to those practices which may again reinforce or alter the existing policies. Through this complex process of mutual interaction between various actors' ideas and actions, certain preferred ways of managing people tend to emerge in some organized fashion which we may then call human resource management.

As different organizations have developed different ways of managing their human resources that seem to have been more or less successful, this observation has reinforced the intuition that more strategic thinking was required in this area and that some competitive advantage could be acquired through some form of excellence. Future historians of work organizations may well have a hard time understanding why it took so long to realize the strategic importance of the management of human resources.

If HRM policies and practices reflect managers' assumptions about how to manage people, it becomes very critical to understand such assumptions in order to correctly interpret the meaning of particular policies and practices.

National Differences in Management Assumptions: A Research Inquiry

In the past few years, we have been interested in systematically exploring management assumptions in an attempt to enrich our understanding of management and organizational processes. The initial research objective was not to explore national differences but to bring into focus some of the implicit management and organizational theories that managers carry in their heads (Laurent 1981).

As it is very difficult to inquire into beliefs that individuals take for granted, our research strategy has consisted in writing up a large number of possible assumptions about the management of organizations which we inferred from discussing organizational issues with managers. These assumptions were expressed in the form of statements within a standard questionnaire that would seek from respondents their degree of agreement/disagreement with such statements.

Typical survey statements read as follows:

- The main reason for having a hierarchical structure is so that everyone knows who has authority over whom.

- Most managers seem to be more motivated by obtaining power than by achieving objectives.

- It is important for a manager to have at hand precise answers to most of the questions that his subordinates may raise about their work.

- In order to have efficient work relationships, it is often necessary to bypass the hierarchical line.

- Most managers would achieve better results if their roles were less precisely defined.

- An organizational structure in which certain subordinates have two direct bosses should be avoided at all costs.

Successive groups of managers participating in executive development programs at INSEAD (The European Institute of Business Administration) were surveyed. These managers came from many different companies and many different countries.

When their responses were analyzed, it appeared that the most powerful determinant of their assumptions was by far their nationality. Overall and across 56 different items of inquiry, it was found that nationality had three times more influence on the shaping of managerial assumptions than any of the respondents' other characteristics such as age, education, function, type of company . . . etc.

One of the most illustrative examples of national differences in management assumptions was reflected in the respondents' reaction to the following statement: It is important for a manager to have at hand precise answers to most of the questions that his subordinates may raise about their work.

As indicated in Figure 9.1, while only a minority of Northern American and Northern European managers agreed with this statement, a majority of Southern Europeans and South-East Asians did. The research results indicated that managers from different national cultures vary widely as to their basic conception of what management is all about (Laurent 1983).

Conceptions of organizations were shown to vary as widely across national cultures as conceptions of their management did. Across a sample of 10 Western national cultures, managers from Latin cultures (French and Italians) consistently perceived organizations as social systems of relationships monitored by power, authority, and hierarchy to a much greater extent than their Northern counterparts did.

American managers held an "instrumental" view of the organization as a set of tasks to be achieved through a problem-solving hierarchy where positions are defined in terms of tasks and functions and where authority is functionally based. French managers held a "social" view of the organization as a collective of people to be managed through a formal hierarchy, where positions are defined in terms of levels of authority and status and where

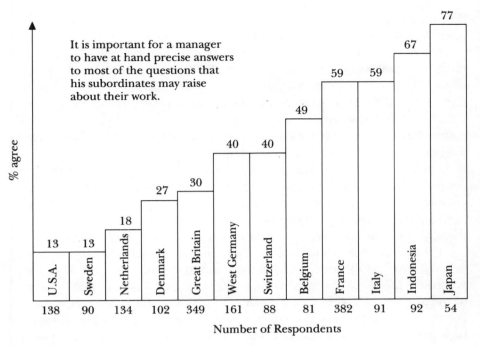

It is important for a manager to have at hand precise answers to most of the questions that his subordinates may raise about their work.

% agree

U.S.A.	Sweden	Netherlands	Denmark	Great Britain	West Germany	Switzerland	Belgium	France	Italy	Indonesia	Japan
13	13	18	27	30	40	40	49	59	59	67	77
138	90	134	102	349	161	88	81	382	91	92	54

Number of Respondents

Figure 9.1

authority is more attached to individuals than it is to their offices or functions (Inzerilli and Laurent 1983). Once these results were obtained, the question arose as to whether the corporate culture of multinational organizations would reduce some of the observed national differences and therefore bring more homogeneity into the picture.*

A new research study was designed to test this hypothesis. Carefully matched national groups of managers working in the affiliated companies of a large U.S. multinational firm were surveyed with the same standard questionnaire. The overall results gave no indication of convergence between national groups. Their cultural differences in management assumptions were not reduced as a result of working for the same multinational firm. If anything, there was slightly more divergence between the national groups within this multinational company than originally found in the INSEAD multicompany study. These findings were later replicated with smaller matched national samples of managers in several American and European multinational corporations (Laurent 1983).

The overall research findings led to the conclusions that deep-seated man-

---

*Issues of interface between national and corporate cultures are further analyzed by Susan Schneider in Chapter 8 of this book.

agerial assumptions are strongly shaped by national cultures and appear quite insensitive to the more transient culture of organizations.

Further exploration was conducted with different methods of inquiry in order to better assess the validity of the findings. In one research study, a large U.S.–based multinational corporation was approached because of its high professional reputation in human resource management. This corporation has implemented for years a standardized worldwide system for the multiple assessment of managerial potential and performance. Open-ended interviews were conducted across a number of affiliated companies in an attempt to identify what managers perceived as being important to be successful in their career. This led to a list of 60 criteria mentioned by managers as being most important for career success. Matched national groups of managers were later asked, in a systematic survey, to select among these 60 criteria those they saw as most important for career success within the firm.

For the American managers, the single most important criterion in order to have a successful career with the company was "Ambition and Drive"—a pragmatic, individualistic, achievement-oriented, and "instrumental" reading of the assessment system. The French managers saw things quite differently. For them the single most important criterion was "Being labelled as having high potential," a more "social" and political reading of the same system. The degree of consensus on what it takes to be successful was significantly higher within the American Affiliates—culturally closer to the designers of the HRM system—than it was in the British, Dutch, German, and French Affiliates.

In spite of the convergence effects that could be expected from a similar and global administrative system of assessment and reward, managed by the U.S. headquarters on a worldwide basis, a remarkable degree of cultural diversity was observed again across countries in managers' perceptions of the determinants of career success. In a later part of the study, the same national groups of managers were asked to list what they thought were the features of a well-functioning organization, the attributes of effective managers, and the most important things that effective managers should be doing.

The analysis of some of the results can be summarized as follows:

German managers, more than others, believed that creativity is essential for career success. In their mind, the successful manager is the one who has the right individual characteristics. Their outlook is rational: they view the organization as a coordinated network of individuals who make appropriate decisions based on their professional competence and knowledge.

British managers hold a more interpersonal and subjective view of the organizational world. According to them, the ability to create the right image and to get noticed for what they do is essential for career success. They view the organization primarily as a network of relationships between individuals who get things done by influencing each other through communicating and negotiating.

French managers look at the organization as an authority network where the power to organize and control the actors stems from their positioning in the hierarchy. They focus on the organization as a pyramid of differentiated levels of power to be acquired or dealt with. French managers perceive the ability to manage power relationships effectively and to "work the system" as particularly critical to their success.

From the perspective of these various results, international human resource management may only be international in the eyes of the designers.

Management Practices as Cultural Artifacts

Naive parochialism has plagued the field of management and organization studies for a long time. The societal and cultural context of theories and practices has long been ignored or overlooked by both researchers and practitioners (Hofstede 1980). Management approaches developed in one particular culture have been deemed valid for any other culture. Models of excellence (Peters and Waterman 1982) are still being presented with virtues of universality.

A comparative analysis across national cultures brings the startling evidence that there is no such thing as Management with a capital M. The art of managing and organizing has no homeland.

Every culture has developed through its own history some specific and unique insight into the managing of organizations and of their human resources. At the same time, any single cultural model may become pathological when pushed to its extreme, an illustration of the fact that every culture has also developed specific and unique blindspots in the art of managing and organizing. There lie the still largely undiscovered opportunities and threats of international management.

The emerging field of human resource management is not compelled to fall into the trap of universalism. It has the opportunity and the challenge to integrate cultural relativity in its premises. In fact, given the global context of international business, this field has no choice but to take into full consideration the international dimension of the organizational world.

Comparative research shows that managers from different national cultures hold different assumptions as to the nature of management and organization. These different sets of assumptions shape different value systems and get translated into different management and organizational practices which in turn reinforce the original assumptions. Among such practices, human resource management practices are likely to be most sensitive to cultural diversity as they are designed by culture bearers in order to handle other culture bearers. Thus the assumptions and values of the local designers are likely to be amplified by the expectations of the natives to create a cultural product that may be highly meaningful and potentially effective for the home country but possibly meaningless, confusing, and ineffective for another country.

If we accept the view that HRM approaches are cultural artifacts reflecting the basic assumptions and values of the national culture in which organizations are embedded, international HRM becomes one of the most challenging corporate tasks in multinational organizations.

With varying degrees of awareness, such organizations are confronted all the time with strategic choices that need to be made in order to optimize the quality and effectiveness of their very diverse human resources around the world. In order to build, maintain, and develop their corporate identity, multinational organizations need to strive for consistency in their ways of managing people on a worldwide basis. Yet, in order to be effective locally, they also need to adapt those ways to the specific cultural requirements of different societies. While the global nature of the business may call for increased consistency, the variety of cultural environments may be calling for differentiation.

The Dream of Corporate Culture as a Melting Pot

Faced with such a high degree of strategic complexity in managing human resources internationally, corporations have become increasingly seduced by a new and highly attractive dream called corporate culture, that would encapsulate on a worldwide basis their own genuine and unique ways of managing people. What if our corporate culture could act as a "supra-culture" and be expected to supersede some of the annoying specificities of the different national cultures in which we operate?

Indeed different organizations from the same country develop different organizational cultures over time and there is no doubt that the recent recognition of the importance and reality of organizational cultures represents a step forward in our understanding of organizations and of their management. However, and in spite of the interest of the concept, it would probably be illusionary to expect that the recent and short history of modern corporations could shape the basic assumptions of their members to an extent that would even approximate the age-long shaping of civilizations and nations. Indeed, the comparative research reported above indicates that the corporate culture of long established large multinationals does not seem to reduce national differences in basic management assumptions across their subsidiaries.

Our tentative interpretation of this finding is that a conceptualization of organizational cultures in terms of basic assumptions (Schein 1985) may be searching for the reality of organizational culture at a deeper level than it really is. To a certain extent, it may be useful to interpret the current appropriation of the concept of culture in the field of organization studies as a modern attempt at increasing the legitimacy of management in business firms by calling upon a higher order concept of almost indisputable essence. Who can deny the existence of an IBM culture?

Instead of locating the roots of organizational culture at the deepest level of basic assumptions, an alternative and possibly more realistic view would be to restrict the concept of organizational culture to the more superficial layers of implicit and explicit systems of norms, expectations, and historically based preferences, constantly reinforced by their behavioral manifestations and their assigned meanings. Under this view, organizational members would be seen as adjusting to the behavioral requirements of organizational cultures without necessarily being so deeply immersed into their ideological textures.

Consistent with the previous arguments on the deep impact of national cultures upon organizational theories and practices, our proposed interpretation of the concept of organizational culture probably reflects the Frenchness of the author through his eagerness to differentiate "actors and systems" (Crozier and Friedberg 1977).

Thus on the international scene, a French manager working in the French subsidiary of an American corporation that insists on an open-door policy may very well leave his office door open—thus adjusting to the behavioral requirements of the corporate culture—without any modification whatsoever of his basic conception of managerial authority. In the French subsidiary of a Swedish firm, whose corporate values include an almost religious reliance upon informality, French shop-floor employees were recently observed as addressing their managers by their first names and using the intimate "tu" form within the boundaries of the firm. The same individuals immediately reverted to "Monsieur le Directeur" and the more formal "vous" form whenever meeting outside the firm.

Similarly, the degree of ingeniosity and creativity that can be observed in order to recreate private space and status out of open space offices probably expresses some of the same dynamics whereby organizational members may very well play the expected game without abdicating their own personal values.

Deep-rooted assumptions could then be better understood as the historical result of broader cultural contexts like civilizations and nations. Organizations would only select from the available repertory of their larger cultural context a limited set of ideas that best fit their own history and modes of implementation. This would be called their organizational culture and would strongly reflect national characteristics of the founders and dominant elite of the organization (Hofstede 1985).

Steps Toward the International Management of Human Resources

In dealing with cultures other than their home-based culture, international organizations need to recognize more explicitly that they are dealing with different "fabrics of meaning" (Geertz 1973). Therefore, whatever can be the strength, cohesiveness, or articulated nature of their corporate cultures, the same HRM policy or practice is likely to be attributed quite different meanings by different cultural groups. Behavioral adjustment may occur at a superficial level and provide the designer from headquarters with an illusory feeling of satisfaction in front of apparent homogeneity across subsidiaries. The dances will appear similar while their actual meaning may be quite different and thus lead to very different outcomes than anticipated. Fortunately, in many other cases, the dances will also be different enough across subsidiaries so as to effectively remind headquarters that the rest of the world is different from "home."

In the Italian subsidiary, the introduction of a Management by Objectives system may be experienced as follows: "We used to be rewarded for our accomplishments and punished for our failures. Why should we now sign our own punishment even before trying?" For the Indonesian affiliate company, the inclusion of negative feedback in performance appraisal interviews may mean "an unhealthy pollution of harmonious hierarchical relationships." The introduction of a matrix-type multiple reporting relationship system may be experienced as a horrible case of divided loyalty in the Mexican subsidiary. Unlike many others, the subsidiaries of Swedish multinational corporations may complain that they do not receive enough "help" from headquarters. Participative management may mean very different things to Scandinavians and North Americans.

To a large extent, human resource managers who operate internationally know these things and multinational organizations have accumulated wisdom from experience and developed skills to handle cultural diversity. Yet, more often than not, such organizations must have learned by accident or out of necessity how to cope with cultural differences. Only on rare occasions have they explicitly and consciously set out to develop a truly multinational identity by building upon cultural differences in their human resources. How many headquarters genuinely believe that they can learn from their foreign subsidiaries? How many implement such a rare belief by internationalizing headquarters' staff and top management? It may be that recent trends toward multinational cooperative ventures and networks (Lorange 1985), characterized by a lesser degree of centralized power, will accelerate such development processes.

A truly international conception of human resource management would require a number of critical and painful steps that have not occurred yet in most instances:

- An explicit recognition by the headquarter organization that its own peculiar ways of managing human resources reflect some assumptions and values of its home culture.

- That as such these peculiar ways are neither universally better or worse than others, they are different and they are likely to exhibit strengths and weaknesses particularly when traveling abroad.

- An explicit recognition by the headquarter organization that its foreign subsidiaries may have other preferred ways of managing people that are neither intrinsically better nor worse but that could possibly be more effective locally.

- A willingness from headquarters to not only acknowledge cultural differences but also to take active steps in order to make them discussable and therefore usable.

- The building of a genuine belief by all parties involved that more creative and effective ways of managing people could be developed as a result of cross-cultural learning.

Obviously such steps cannot be dictated or easily engineered. They have more to do with states of mind and mind-sets than with behaviors. As such, these processes can only be facilitated and this may represent a primary mission for executives in charge of international human resource management. They may also represent some of the prerequisites and foundations for the development of forward-looking international corporate cultures.

Such cultures could then provide the impetus and the proper framing to address important strategic issues in the area of international HRM such as: how much consistency and which similarity in policies and practices should be developed? How much variety and differentiation and what adaptation should be encouraged? Which policies should be universal and global? Which ones should be local? Which HRM practices should be designed at the center? Locally? By international teams? Which processes can be invented to reach agreement on objectives and allow variable paths to achieve them? Which passports should key managers have in the headquarter organization and in the main subsidiaries? Home office nationals? Country nationals? Third nationals? How much and which expatriation should occur? How to manage the whole expatriation process? How to properly assess management potential when judgment criteria differ from country to country? How to orchestrate the management of careers internationally? All of these issues require strategic choices that cannot be left to an obscure function as they need to be fully integrated in a global vision of the firm and as they feed and shape that vision.

The challenge faced by the infant field of international human resource management is to solve a multidimensional puzzle located at the crossroad of national and organizational cultures. Research is needed on the various strategies that international firms are using as their own attempts at solving the puzzle.

References

Crozier, M., and Friedberg, E. *L'Acteur et le Systeme: Les Contraintes de L'Action Collective.* Paris: Editions du Seuil, 1977.

Geertz, C. *The Interpretation of Cultures: Selected Essays.* New York: Basic Books, 1973.

Hofstede, G. Motivation, Leadership and Organization: Do American Theories Apply Abroad? *Organizational Dynamics*, Summer 1980, 42–63.

Hofstede, G. The Interaction between National and Organizational Values Systems. *Journal of Management Studies*, 1985, 22(4), 347–57.

Inzerilli, G., and Laurent, A. Managerial Views of Organization Structure in France and the USA. *International Studies of Management and Organization*, 1983, 13(1/2), 97–118.

Laurent, A. Matrix Organizations and Latin Cultures. A Note on the Use of Comparative Research Data in Management Education. *International Studies of Management and Organization*, 1981, 10(4), 101–14.

Laurent, A. The Cultural Diversity of Western Conceptions of Management. *International Studies of Management and Organization*, 1983, 13(1/2), 75–96.

Lorange, P. Human Resource Management in Multinational Cooperative Ventures and Networks. Paper presented at the International Human Resource Management Symposium, Fontainebleau, August 20–23, 1985.

Peters T. J., and Waterman, R. H. *In Search of Excellence.* New York: Harper & Row, 1982.

Schein, E. H. *Organizational Culture and Leadership.* San Francisco: Jossey-Bass Publishers, 1985.

FOUR

The Developmental Context

10

The Development of the Global Leader Within the Multinational Corporation

Manfred F. R. Kets de Vries
Christine Mead

No man really knows about other human beings. The best he can do is suppose that they are like himself.
JOHN STEINBECK,
The Winter of Our Discontent

Introduction

The globalization of business is increasing at a phenomenal rate, accelerated by a breakdown of some of the barriers to international trade; for example, Europe 1992, the opening of Eastern Europe, the development of commerce with China, or the Canada–U.S. trade agreements. This raises the question of whether a new kind of leader, a "global" one, will not be needed—a person who can play the role of catalyst, who is sensitive to and adept at managing cultural diversity, and who functions effectively in different cultural environments.

As companies seek to internationalize their operations, they run into a number of blockages. Many of these blockages have their roots in cultural differences—the way in which people have chosen to work and live over time.

What should leaders be prepared for when operating in different cultures? What are the key factors that have to be taken into consideration?

In studying the question of global leadership, we touch upon the problematic area of the interaction between corporate and national cultures (Schneider 1988) and, inevitably, upon the issue of cultural adaptiveness. A number of companies have tried to cope with these challenges. For example, Schlumberger is a successful international organization in the oilfield-service industry operating in 92 countries. What is salient about Schlumberger is the emphasis placed on research and technology. This aspect is very much a part of the Schlumberger corporate culture, and people who want to work for this quiet giant are expected to subscribe to its orientation. But, although the company is very technology-driven, there are other values that have to be taken into consideration. The late Jean Riboud, former CEO of Schlumberger, touched upon these values when describing the company's "spirit" during his reign:

1. We are an exceptional crucible of many nations, of many cultures, of many visions

2. We are a totally decentralized organization . . .

3. We are a service company, at the service of our customers, having a faster response than anybody else

4. We believe in the profit process as a challenge, as a game, as a sport

5. We believe in a certain arrogance; the certainty that we are going to win because we are the best—arrogance only tolerable because it is coupled with a great sense of intellectual humility, the fear of being wrong, the fear of not working hard enough (Auletta 1984, 160)

Life at Schlumberger is different from that at many organizations. A supervisor of a rig in Ireland can receive a phone call at noon on Friday saying to close down operations there by 5 o'clock and report for work in Northern Thailand at 8 o'clock Sunday morning. Upon arrival at the airport in Bangkok, he will find a jeep and the name of a place a day's drive away he is to go to; no map, no instructions. It is very much up to him to make it happen, to make his assignment a success.

Although when describing his company Jean Riboud did not explicitly talk about the making of a global leader, certain subtle mechanisms having to do with selection and the creation of the right organizational *ambiance* are at work at Schlumberger to make its people so successful. Not only does Schlumberger choose people who fit a certain profile, but there are other factors that also play an important role. Headquarters at Schlumberger is very small. Although strategic direction is largely determined there, the company has a strong regional structure, and career progression does not depend on time spent at the head office. A great deal of operational autonomy is given to the people in the field. "Space" is provided for each national culture. At each location, the management team is made up of people from five or six different nationalities; there is not one dominant national culture but rather a group of people from different cultures who have internalized a common set of values. And this corporate culture becomes a major lever in assuring coordination among the many different units of the organization.

Schlumberger is only one among many companies that are dealing successfully with the increasing internationalization of business. We propose that leaders who are able to foster this process will make a difference. The extent to which leadership must be culturally adaptive if an organization operates in multiple cultures is not yet completely clear. However, we assume that such a quality must be an asset. Having made this assumption, it is the objective of this chapter to take a closer look at the question of what factors foster global leadership and to what extent culture plays a role. Four questions will be addressed:

1. How do companies choose people to be future global leaders?

2. What kind of management development and training enhances cultural empathy and adaptability?

3. In what organizational context does global leadership thrive?

4. And, finally, what can be said about career path management in the global corporation?

These questions will form the basis not only for a model to analyze the making of the global leader but also for a number of propositions about such leaders. This model and the accompanying propositions may be useful in assisting multinational corporations to plan for future leadership.

1. The Selection Process

For many companies, the primary criterion for choosing someone to work abroad is *technical* competence (Harvey 1985; Zeira and Banai 1984; Mendenhall and Oddou 1985, 1986; Mendenhall, Dunbar, and Oddou 1987; Tung 1981, 1982, 1987, 1988). If a manager in the home country has done a good job, the assumption is that he or she will automatically be able to repeat the successful performance in another country. This happens particularly in cases where people are being sent to oversee the setting up of a plant, the establishment of an oil rig, or the expansion of a factory—tasks considered to be basically technical. There may be very little preparation for variations in cultural approaches. After all, a manager is supposed to be someone who has the confidence to sort out any problems that deviate from usual working procedures—if something goes wrong, he or she should be able to "fix" it.

For such assignments, it cannot be denied that technical skills are necessary, but they are not sufficient. However, it is much more difficult to assess the *interpersonal* qualities and attitudes that can make an assignment a success or a failure. Although rates of success or failure vary, for U.S. companies failure rates of 23 percent have been recorded (Tung 1984). For a company, the cost of failure can be very high. Estimates range between $50,000 and $250,000 (Mendenhall, Dunbar, and Oddou 1987), not to mention the loss of business and prestige due to poor management. In addition, there are the psychological costs of failure for the individual and family involved. It is clear that other, nontechnical qualities are required to make expatriation a success, particularly when one reaches higher-level management positions.

Leadership Qualities

Recent research on leadership (Kets de Vries and Miller 1988; Kets de Vries 1989), building and complementing the work of others (MacGregor Burns 1977; Levinson and Rosenthal 1984; Bennis and Nanus 1985; Tichy and Devannah 1986; Leavitt 1986; Kotter 1988; Zaleznik 1989), shows that a number of qualities recur consistently and are likely to be applicable to the global leader.

To begin with, one essential quality must be the capacity for envisioning, that is, possessing the ability to draw up road maps to indicate future direction in an increasingly complex environment. The capacity to do so frequently depends on a strong operational code (Leites 1953; George 1969) in the person's interior world that can drive such a vision. Visions can range from more prosaic preoccupations, such as a belief in the feasibility of a new product or the entry into a new market, to wider concerns, such as ethical issues or environmental consciousness.

The nature of our relationships with significant others (i.e., parents, siblings, other family members, teachers, doctors) during childhood will very much determine the kind of cognitive and affective "maps" that we will internalize and that will form the basis for our operational codes. These personal operational codes have to be balanced with specific societal concerns. The vision can diverge from the existing preoccupations of the group to which it is applicable, but not to too great an extent. And in order to match personal agenda with "historical moment" (Erikson 1975), to create this catalyst for change, a talent in environmental sense-making is necessary. The leader's responsiveness to what is happening around him or her will be essential. Moreover, given the great diversity of sensory inputs, the global leader has a responsibility to give meaning to his or her vision through articulation and conviction. The challenge is to get others to align themselves with this vision.

The ability to instill values and inspire others leads to another important quality, that of empowerment. By communicating high performance expectations, leaders can enhance the self-esteem of their followers, the result of which is that the followers may very well meet the challenge.

Another important related skill concerns the ability to build and maintain organizational networks, which necessitates a considerable sensitivity to the dynamics of power and dependency. Interpersonal skills, in particular, adeptness in negotiation and coaching, are essential in order to provide a "holding environment" for followers. These human resource management skills will be even more important in the global corporation (Korn/Ferry International and Columbia University Graduate School of Business 1989). One key reason these skills are so essential is that the management of alliances has taken on an increasingly critical role.

A cognitive skill called "pattern recognition" is another quality required in our fast-changing world. Global leaders especially need to manage cognitive complexity to quickly sort out relevant from irrelevant information and recognize the major themes. The have to be masters in sense making, in bringing order out of the chaos that surrounds them. They need to know how to prevent themselves from being swamped by sensory and informational overloads. Without this skill, fast and accurate decision making is hampered.

Finally, a characteristic from stress literature called "hardiness" should not be forgotten (Kobassa 1979). The global company in the information age puts an incredible amount of stress on its leaders: regular travel through different time zones, massive exposure to information, long hours, and so on. Hardy people—the ones who are more able to cope with these strains—are those who possess a sense of internality, a belief that they can control and influence the events in their lives. They are of the opinion that they can make a difference, as opposed to thinking that whatever happens to them is dependent on fate or luck. Hardy people tend to be deeply committed to whatever activities they are engaged in and anticipate change as an exciting challenge to further development.

Selection Criteria for Cultural Adaptability

In addition, there are a number of values or assumptions that indicate cultural adaptability. The most obvious, perhaps, is the understanding that every culture has developed its own way of managing and that one (my) country's way is not necessarily superior (Laurent 1986). Another is that cross-cultural learning is enriching. Yet another may be the feeling that home is where I am, rather than where I come from. The understanding of where one's roots are, whether in oneself, one's family, or the country of birth, can greatly affect how easily people move from culture to culture.

Unfortunately, recommendations made by researchers interested in the question of what qualities are likely to be found among people who are culturally adaptive may be excessively broad. Among the characteristics most often listed we can find such factors as open-mindedness, self-confidence, ability to deal with ambiguity, ability to relate to people, and curiosity. In looking at top management potential, an international company such as Shell narrowed 28 qualities down to the following: helicopter view, imagination, power of analysis, and sense of reality (Muller 1970). However, many of the qualities listed by Shell and others do not seem to be that much different from those generally required from effective managers.

Interestingly enough, Gunnar Hedland (1986), taking the Jesuit order as an ideal model for an international organization, is more specific. He suggests that there are six essential qualities needed for effective functioning in an international context: an aptitude for searching and combining things in new ways; the ability to communicate ideas and turn them into action; the command of several languages, as well as knowledge of and sympathy for several cultures, in order to provide " . . . 'a stereo quality' to perception and interpretation" (31); honesty and integrity; the willingness to take risks and experiment; and faith in the organization and its activities.

Some researchers have developed lists of criteria considered important in the selection of international managers. Among them, Michael Harvey (1985) has made probably one of the more heroic efforts. He suggests 30 characteristics including mental flexibility, stability of marriage, social and cross-cultural exposure, and physical and emotional stamina, each weighted according to country and type of job.

That the search for selection criteria is a matter warranting attention is supported by a number of surveys proving that the greater the consideration paid during the selection process to adaptability and ability to communicate, the higher the success rate in the assignment (Tung 1981). However, we can question once again if these selection criteria are specifically applicable to managers on international assignments. Some of the factors (for example, interpersonal skills) probably increase effectiveness whatever the context may be. Obviously much more research is needed to refine these selection criteria.

Zeira and Banai (1984) argue that criteria for selection are often developed in a vacuum. The ideas of the host country nationals, the people who are to work with the expatriate manager, are rarely sought at the selection stage. Zeira and Banai suggest that the better the fit between the stakeholders' expectations and the expatriate manager's behavior, the less the inter-role conflict. The question becomes how to narrow the gap between expectations and reality. Research in this area indicates that early exposure to other cultures and management development for international assignments will be critical factors.

Early Socialization

With the coming of the "global village"—the increased movement of people due to greater ease in travel and communications—there is an ever-growing number of individuals that are rooted in more than one culture. Children with parents of different nationalities, who may also have changed countries several times when young, have a very different sense of belonging than those who are born and grow up in the same place (McGoldrick, Pearce, and Giordano 1982). Given the impact of childhood socialization on adult development, it is to be expected that early exposure is a determining factor in how successful the individual will be in dealing with cultural adaptability later in life. Growing up bilingual results in a sense of perception that is likely to be much wider than the single language norm. Exposure to different languages at an early age adds another layer to perception and cultural sensitivity.

"As If" Qualities

There is a paradoxical quality about being a global leader. On the one hand, it appears that the personality should have "as if" characteristics (Deutsch 1942). We are referring to those people able to conduct themselves in a chameleonlike way, individuals who have a plastic readiness to pick up signals from the external world and mold themselves and their behavior accordingly. These are the people who easily adapt to whatever culture they find themselves in. Unfortunately, in the case of the true "as if" personality, the advantage of adaptability is usually counterbalanced by a shallowness in relationships, an absence of genuine feelings, and a lack of a strong sense of identity, making for transient identifications and kaleidoscopic shifts in behavior.

On the other hand, truly global leaders need a set of core values—a part of this inner script—that will guide them and provide support in whatever environment they may find themselves. These core values should be compatible with those of the corporate culture. The challenge becomes to combine qualities of resiliency with those of plasticity. This does not necessarily have to be a contradiction. To "go native" is not the answer. Staying aloof from the host culture is not a solution either. A middle range position must be found.

Only those who lack a strong set of inner values may feel endangered and act defensively, resisting the benefits of cultural exposure. Individuals with a cohesive sense of self and a set of core values can allow themselves to "regress in the service of the ego," reworking and building on earlier experiences without becoming anxious about being swept away into the unknown if they adopt aspects of another culture. These individuals will recognize the potential for creative synergy in doing so. They are the ones who will successfully populate the organization of the future, going beyond narrow ethnocentric concerns and making the world truly a "global village."

Narcissistic Development

An essential element of the foundations of leadership, one that underlies the cohesive sense of self mentioned earlier, is the development of a person's narcissistic predispositions (Kets de Vries 1989). Narcissism is the matrix from which derive ambition, achievement, and self-confidence. The development of narcissism, however, is a question of balance. Some self-love is required for survival, yet too great a preoccupation with the self can become self-destructive. The intensity of a person's narcissistic experience is very much determined by the nature of parental interventions during childhood. If parents deal with their children's frustrations and disappointments in an age-appropriate way, mental images are retained that have a generative and restorative function and serve as a source of sustenance in dealing with life's adversities. Such an internal world—these cognitive and affective maps—makes for a cohesive sense of self and a set of core values that constitute the underpinnings of healthy functioning at work and in private life. Difficulties may arise if the child experiences prolonged disappointments due to parental understimulation, overstimulation, or nonintegrative, inconsistent interventions during this vulnerable early period of development. The legacy may be problems in self-esteem regulation. Such a state of affairs may be reflected in a lifelong search for an admiring audience to support a need for grandiosity and to combat feelings of helplessness.

The evolution of narcissistic development determines the capacity for empathy—the ability to put oneself in the psychological frame of reference of another so that the other person's thinking, feeling, and acting are understood. Extreme narcissists lack this capacity because they are too preoccupied with themselves.

It is rare for a company to have access to the ideal candidate at the time an international position becomes available. Management training to further develop cultural empathy—given the existence of a certain base—therefore becomes useful.

2. Management Development

Surprisingly little is done in the form of management education to prepare people for international assignments. In international business schools such as INSEAD or IMD, process skills applicable to working in a multinational environment are furthered through joint problem solving in multicultural groups. As far as company training is concerned, according to Tung (1988), only 32 percent of U.S. multinational enterprises provide training for international assignments. The European and Japanese companies surveyed along the same lines reported higher rates of training: 69 percent among the European companies and 57 percent among the Japanese.

One reason given by many U.S. companies for not providing training was the use of host country nationals to fill management positions. Another argument worth mentioning was that, given the temporary nature of the assignment and the short-term orientation in human resource management practices in the U.S. in light of the transcience of executives, investment in training would be too costly. Other factors were doubts as to the effectiveness of training and lack of time (Tung 1988).

Most of the training that is carried out seems to be based on cognitive approaches: language training and information about the country, culture, and style of living. In some cases, affective training is also undertaken to prepare people for situations they may encounter using case studies, simulation, Outward Bound–type situations, and role playing. However, most training programs seem to focus on the development of analytical skills and neglect the less quantifiable intuitive processes, such as stimulating a sense of cultural empathy. The enhancement of right-hemisphere capabilities (e.g., judgment, intuition, "gut feeling") has not fit smoothly into the traditional left-hemisphere, more logical business environment.

Experiential Training

The difficulty with training in the attitudes and relational qualities that indicate cultural empathy is that they are properties acquired primarily through experience. Experiential learning tends to have a much greater impact than resorting to the more traditional learning methods. A combination of on-the-job and off-the-job training tends to be most effective.

Organizational development specialists following Lewin's (1935) ideas on change have argued that learning requires a period of "unfreezing:" the loosening of habitual structures of thought and behavior and the opening up of new ones. Off-the-job training, particularly in another country, provides an occasion for such loosening up. At the end of the learning process, the opposite procedure is required—"refreezing," or building of the new structure and linking it to behavior already internalized. This process takes place best in on-the-job training. What is suggested here in terms of how international managers are trained is that the training occurs *during* the international assignment. Whatever training is done prior to departure is most effective when it is geared toward making an individual open to change and to learning in a new environment.

Nevertheless, we can question this way of looking at the process of change as overly simplistic or even mechanistic. As clinical work has shown, basic values, beliefs, and attitudes do not change overnight. On the contrary, change requires a lengthy process of "working through," of overcoming resistances and changing one's inner cognitive and affected maps (Kets de Vries and Miller 1984). It can be argued, however, that some training programs—if the right parameters are used—can be instrumental in setting a process of change

in motion. The subsequent success in reshaping a person's inner represen-
tational world and acceptance of a new reality greatly depends on a further,
sustained effort put forth by the individual.

Certain international companies follow a policy of several years abroad
followed by several years at headquarters for their international managers
(e.g., Philips, Shell, IBM, Proctor & Gamble, Rhone-Poulenc). This pattern
serves various purposes: it creates a more consistent corporate culture than
when people remain in only one country or one region, and it provides headquarters with international experience.

Zeira and Pazy (1983, 1989) report on an approach to managerial development that they found successful in providing a high level of professional
development as well as cross-cultural exposure. Their study involved groups
of aircraft engineers who were sent by their parent organizations to work for
12 to 18 months for a host country organization. Zeira and Pazy believe that
this type of training is more effective because it takes place within another
culture, as well as within a practical work environment. The host organization
also benefits from the cross-cultural experience, as its managers learn to work
with people from other cultures.

The Reaction of the Family

A critical element in the success of expatriate managers is the experience of
their spouses and children. The most frequent reason for a manager's failing
to complete an assignment in another country is the negative reaction of his
or her spouse (Hays 1974; Bartolomé and Evans 1980; Tung 1988). Research
done by Harvey (1985) and Mendenhall, Dunbar, and Oddou (1987) supports
the finding that family circumstances account for expatriate failure in the
majority of cases. Despite this, only 50 percent of American companies interview spouses during the selection procedure, and a far smaller percentage
include spouses in training programs (Tung 1988). Although we realize that
the role of the spouse is only one factor among many others, the failure to
recognize it can be a costly omission for both the company and the family.

Particularly in a situation where the executive risks finding himself or
herself cut off from other relationships, a supportive spouse and family may
be the essential factor in enabling him or her to make the necessary cultural
adjustments. And, of course, marrying into another culture provides a person
with intensive long-term experiential "training" in cultural empathy and diversity.

3. Forms of International Organization

Management training is only one factor that can influence the success of an
international assignment. Another variable that eventually affects success or

failure concerns specific structural arrangements that enhance cultural empathy and adaptability and contribute to the making of the global leader. Obviously, it would be foolish to suggest that there is an ideal structure, suitable for all organizations and cultures. Different types of organizational structures have developed from very different beginnings, and there are numerous kinds of multinational enterprises, international joint ventures, parent-subsidiary relationships across national borders, and other forms of alliances. However, there are certain structural factors that can enable an organization to make use of its international advantages.

Concepts of Multinationalism

Building on the work of Perlmutter and Heenan (1969, 1979), Gunnar Hedlund (1986) develops the conceptual evolution from ethnocentrism via polycentrism to geocentrism.[1] Hedlund mentions that relevant aspects of geocentricity are the use of third-country nationals in management, reliance on global profitability goals, and increased rotation of personnel. Interdependence is reciprocal; products, know-how, money, and people flow in complex patterns, not from the core to the periphery as in the ethnocentric firm. This kind of geocentrism makes for what Hedlund calls the "heterarchical" MNC.

Fundamental to such an MNC, is the idea that structure determines strategy, in the sense that the MNC first identifies its structural properties and then looks for strategic options following from these properties. Several points distinguish its human resource management. First of all, as a consequence of breaking up a large hierarchy into multiple organizational structures, it is no longer possible to promote people by giving them jobs higher up. Movement among centers is more common, especially as it builds up the "nervous system" of the MNC.

Next, the core of this "new" MNC consists of people with long experience in it. The employees constitute the communication network of the firm, and as such they are a strategic resource. More all-encompassing and long-term contracts are to be expected, as is participation in the ownership of the company. There is probably duality in the career system: a limited core of lifetime employees and a much larger number of people with briefer associations with the firm, combining both stability and flexibility. In its ideal form, the core provides the memory and information structure, and the looser links help to prevent rigidity by establishing channels for new ideas. Different reward and punishment systems are necessary to deal with negative feedback and to encourage the long-term investment of individuals in the company.

A great deal of personnel rotation and international travel are necessary in order for the internalization of norms to take place. Employees recruited to the core should be willing to travel and to change function in the company.

A broad range of people in the firm must develop the capacity for strategic thinking and action. This can be done by open communicating strategies and plans, decentralizing strategic tasks, actively using task forces on strategic issues, and providing early opportunities for developing management capabilities.

The Organization of Tomorrow

This whole discussion of such an MNC is obviously based on an abstract ideal, although elements of all the relevant points can be found working in organizations today. A close observer of organizational forms will notice a current trend toward "flatter" structures with less emphasis on hierarchy, greater lateral communication, complex networking systems, and loosely coupled, interdependent organizational units with innovative human resource management practices. We can also observe the increasing number of companies where there is a strategic culture—where strategic thinking is a permanent activity and permeates all levels of the organization.

The deeply internalized, commonly shared core values of the corporate culture become the new control device (Edström and Galbraith 1977). Careful management of the corporate culture becomes essential. The challenge is to retain one's corporate identity within the global environment. One key factor in this process is the way in which symbols signifying the corporate culture are managed. As Ohmae (1989, 138) argues, "Maintaining a vital corporate identity in a global environment is no trivial exercise. Formal systems and organizational structures can help, but only to the extent that they nurture and support intangible ties."

A good example of a development in this direction is Proctor & Gamble's Eurobrand teams (Bartlett and Ghoshal 1986, 1987a, 1987b). Different national subsidiaries are given the role of developing product-market strategies for specific products for the region based on the work of a cooperative team of managers across these subsidiaries.

Many global companies are beginning to think along the lines of culture-task compatibility. Some organizations have established "centers of excellence" for such functions as R&D and manufacturing, according to the cultures most favorable to these functions. For example, Philips moved its center for long-range technology development from the United States to the Far East, a regional area where they felt there would be less of a short-term orientation to problem solving (Evans, Lank, and Farquhar 1989).

Most international organizations use some form of periodic assignment to headquarters for international managers, as well as rotation of assignments within regions. In addition, most organizations seem to have several levels of managers: those who operate only within their own countries, those who are assignable within their regions, and those who are assignable globally. The more ethnocentric a company is, however, the more this last category tends to be made up of parent-country nationals.

A key trend in the new MNC is getting away from a "headquarters mentality," that is, the urge to intervene and give directions. More and more frequently, the corporate center is split into a number of relatively autonomous regional headquarters. Most important of all, the company is increasingly denationalized with a set of shared values as common denominator. The last barrier that remains, however, is the placement of non–parent country nationals on the board of directors.

4. Career Path Management

This brings us to the issue of career path management and the concurrent problem of repatriation. Research on expatriation and career advancement at the present time is not very conclusive (Mendenhall, Dunbar, and Oddou 1987). In most cases, however, we can say that an international assignment is initially seen as a step up a career ladder. The key issue in continuing this perception is how re-entry is dealt with.

An obvious method is the establishment of a human resource data bank for the purpose of making an "inventory" of an organization's human resources. This should be followed by the creation of a special monitoring unit (e.g., as at Philips, IBM, Unilever, or Shell) to take responsibility for the key people, and in particular, the expatriate executives. The unit plays a major role in career path management by assisting in succession planning with the expatriate executive prior to departure, a process that should consider length of stay, projected responsibilities when abroad, systematic management reviews, and subsequent job position on repatriation.

If such a monitoring unit is set in place, it should report to a sufficiently high level in the organization to make sure that the visibility of the expatriate is maintained. After all, most expatriate executives fear that they will lose touch with the center of action and will be forgotten for promotion at the corporate center. To minimize such fears, it has to be made very clear in word and deed that an international assignment to key markets is a major factor for eventual selection to top management.

Such a monitoring unit must also engage in regular reviews of positions to be vacated because of retirement or resignation and changes of assignment for development reasons. The need to recruit outside candidates must be assessed periodically. Much attention should be paid to succession planning. To engage in such evaluation practices of high potentials, ranking systems are often utilized to enable identification.

It is essential for headquarters to be kept informed of the expatriates' successes while they are away, otherwise their work may go unrecognized and they may lose opportunities for promotion. Given the state of international communication systems, extreme degrees of isolation probably exist only in theory. However, a feeling of isolation is very real for people returning to an organization after a gap of some years. With increasing executive mobility, they may no longer know the top level of management personally. The environment at headquarters will probably have evolved. As individuals, they have been changed by their experiences in another culture (Adler 1981, 1986). All told, the "fit" may be quite different. The "re-entry shock" of return may not be that easy to overcome.

Facilitating Return

A kind of "social contract," however, may facilitate return. For example, companies such as IBM have "on loan from the home country" policies that guarantee a position upon coming back at least at the same level as the position vacated when taking on the assignment. Numerous firms also organize support networks, involving communication through travel and company newsletters. Some companies (e.g., many Japanese ones) have institutionalized a mentoring relationship. The mentors, who often have gone through the same experiences, coach their charges and serve as an additional source of support. Other companies may have internal consultants who take on the mentoring role. Smooth repatriation and reabsorption into the corporate hierarchy are essential. One casualty can be a major setback for the corporation by giving a bad example.

A Framework for Analyzing the Development of the Global Leader

We have now come full circle in describing the various factors that contribute to the making of the global leader. Figure 10.1 shows in an oversimplified way the contributing factors that work toward global leadership. We postulate that there are three spheres of influence on the development of the global leader. The strongest influences on both leadership qualities and the ability to adapt culturally stem from childhood background and psychological development. These attributes can be further enhanced by early managerial responsibilities, international work, and educational experiences. Finally, the organizational structure provides a framework for using the global leadership qualities that exist and encouraging their further development.

Following our framework, it can be said that, in the development of a global leader, ideally it helps to have a childhood background characterized by cultural diversity, one aspect being early international experience. Such a combination may enhance the possession of language skills and also an attitude of cultural empathy. At the base of it all, however, is how one's sense of self is experienced, which is determined by the nature and quality of the person's narcissistic development.

Within the organization, exposure early in one's career to leadership

CHILDHOOD DEVELOPMENT

ADAPTABILITY FACTORS

- Narcissistic development
- Cultural diversity in family
- Early international experience
- Bilingualism
- Multiple roots
- Some "as if" qualities

LEADERSHIP FACTORS

- Self-confidence
- Responsibility
- Curiosity
- Imagination
- Hardiness
- Decision-making skills
- Envisioning
- Communication skills
- "Core values"
- Career goals and expectations

PERSONALITY SCREEN

PROFESSIONAL DEVELOPMENT

TRAINING AND EDUCATION

- Analytical skills
- Professional skills
- Study in another culture
- Study in international environment
- Languages

MANAGEMENT DEVELOPMENT

- Early responsibility
- Variety of tasks
- Early international experience
- Corporate values

PERSONAL DEVELOPMENT

- Supportive spouse
- Adaptable spouse
- "Movable" children
- Variety of interests

ORGANIZATIONAL SCREEN

ORGANIZATIONAL DEVELOPMENT

ORGANIZATIONAL STRUCTURE

- Geocentric
- Use of third-country nationals
- Flat
- Heterarchic
- Multicultural

INTERNATIONAL HUMAN RESOURCE MANAGEMENT

- Career pathing
- Re-entry management
- Selection criteria
- Succession planning
- Seriation ratings
- Communications

Figure 10.1   Factors contributing to the development of the global leader.

experiences (meaning some kind of measurable project responsibility) is important. This will hone a person's capacity to cope with difficult leadership challenges later in the career cycle. These early obstacles have to be combined with a human resource system and an organizational structure conducive to the management of international careers.

In the personal sphere, an essential aspect is the attitude of the spouse, a reaction dependent on the spouse's own exposure to other cultures and the kind of options she or he will have available. Finally, the match between the life cycle and the career cycle plays a critical role: at some stages in life the individual will be more movable than others because of children or other factors.

Keeping this diagram and the previous discussion of the factors that promote the development of the global leader in mind, the following general propositions can be made:

1. Cultural empathy and adaptability are key factors for effective functioning in different foreign environments.

2. Cultural empathy and adaptability are strongly influenced by the degree of cultural diversity within the family and early cultural exposure.

3. The existence of leadership qualities depends very much on such factors as narcissistic development and early career challenges.

4. Given the presence of leadership potential, cultural empathy, and adaptability, developing global leadership qualities necessitates challenging foreign assignments from the early career stages onward.

5. A favorable organizational environment—that is, the existence of a corporate culture conducive to foreign assignments and the inclusion of certain human resource management practices (i.e., career path management, mentoring, re-entry management)—will enhance global leadership development.

6. An organizational culture that can be described as multicultural, because it is different in each country and because each location, including headquarters, has a variety of nationalities and cultures represented, creates a learning environment for global leadership.

7. The ability of a spouse and children to be both culturally empathic and supportive of global lifestyles influences the development of additional global leadership qualities.

Concluding Remarks

Apart from the predisposition to become a global leader (which, as has been indicated, is strongly influenced by the nature of childhood development, socialization, and early exposure to different cultural contexts), the evolution of the global leader at a later stage in life is, ironically enough, very much determined by *being* a global leader. As we have said, the earlier the experience through assignments with specific project responsibility in different cultures, the greater the ability to adapt to and empathize with new cultures and the more the person is going to be prepared for global leadership. If such assignments early in the person's employment are followed up later in the career cycle with the successful completion of a very difficult task such as a turn-around problem, a merger and acquisition challenge, or a new business venture, the individual will be ready to take on a top position in the organization.

In creating leaders for tomorrow, preparing managers and their families for life in a different environment is invaluable in giving them the chance to make the necessary changes in their attitudes. And, given previous socialization practices, some personalities are more suited than others to working internationally.

Organizations that are aware of cultural differences and seek to exploit them through various forms of interchange are likely to evolve in the direction of a network of loosely coupled units. In contrast, organizations with a dominant parent-country style of operating are unlikely to be able to use the full potential of their international personnel, a serious handicap in the increasingly global world in which we live.

Notes

1. In the ethnocentric orientation, key positions are occupied by home country nationals. Foreign subsidiaries take on a subservient position. In polycentric companies, foreign subsidiaries are run by local nationals and have a great amount of autonomy as long as there are results. The head office takes a more "hands-off" position. The regiocentric orientation differs in that the action takes place in various regional headquarters. Finally, in the case of the geocentric mentation, a complex network of interdependencies exist between headquarters and subsidiaries. Organizational identity is determined both by local and more universal factors. Management development can take place anywhere in the world.

References

Adler, N. 1981. "Re-entry: Managing Cross-Cultural Transition." *Group and Organization Studies* 6(3):341–56.

Adler, N. 1986. *International Dimensions of Organizational Behavior*. Boston: Kent.

Auletta, K. 1984. *The Art of Corporate Success*. New York: Putnam.

Bartlett, C., and S. Ghoshal. 1986. "Tap your Subsidiaries for Global Reach." *Harvard Business Review* 64(6):87–94.

Bartlett, C., and S. Ghoshal. 1987b. "Managing Across Borders: New Strategic Requirements." *Sloan Management Review* 28(4):7–17.

Bartlett, C., and S. Ghoshal. 1987b. "Managing Across Borders: New Organizational Responses." *Sloan Management Review* 29(1):43–53.

Bartolomé, F., and P. Evans. 1980. *Must Success Cost So Much?* New York: Grant McIntyre.

Bass, B. 1981. *Stogdill's Handbook of Leadership*. New York: Free Press.

Bass, B. 1985. *Leadership and Performance Beyond Expectations*. New York: Free Press.

Bennis, W., and B. Nanus. 1985. *Leaders*. New York: Harper & Row.

Devanna, M., and N. Tichy. 1986. *The Transformational Leader*. New York: John Wiley & Sons.

Deutsch, H. (1942). "Some Forms of Emotional Disturbances and their Relationship to Schizophrenia," in *Neuroses and Character Types*. New York: International Universities Press, 1965, 262–81.

Edström, A., and J. Galbraith. 1977. "Transfer of Managers as a Coordination and

Control Strategy in Multinational Organizations." *Administrative Science Quarterly* 22:298–63.

Erikson, E. H. 1975. *Life History and Historical Moment*. New York: Norton.

Evans, P., E. Lank, and A. Farquhar. 1989. "Managing Human Resources in the International Firm: Lessons from Practice," in *Human Resource Management in International Firms*, P. Evans, Y. Doz, and A. Laurent, eds. London: Macmillan.

George, A. L. 1969. "The Operational Code." *International Studies Quarterly* 13:190–222.

Harvey, M. 1985. "The Executive Family: An Overlooked Variable in International Assignments." *Columbia Journal of World Business* 20(1):84–92.

Hays, R. D. 1974. "Expatriate Selection: Insuring Success and Avoiding Failure." *Journal of International Business Studies* 5(1):25–37.

Heenan, D. A., and H. V. Perlmutter. 1979. *Multinational Organizational Development* Reading, Mass.: Addison Wesley.

Hedlund, G. 1986. "The Hypermodern MNC—A Heterarchy?" *Human Resource Management* 25(1):9–35.

Kets de Vries, M. F. R., and D. Miller. 1984. *The Neurotic Organization*. San Francisco: Jossey-Bass.

Kets de Vries, M. F. R. 1989. *Prisoners of Leadership*. New York: John Wiley & Sons.

Kets de Vries, M. F. R., and D. Miller. 1987. *Unstable at the Top*. New York: New American Library.

Kobassa, S. R. 1979. "Stress Life Events, Personality and Health: An Inquiry into Hardiness." *Journal of Personality and Social Psychology* 37:1–11.

Korn/Ferry International and Columbia University Graduate School of Business. 1984. *Reinventing the CEO: 21st Century Report*.

Kotter, J. 1988. *The Leadership Factor*. New York: Free Press.

Laurent, A. 1986. "The Cross-Cultural Puzzle of International Human Resource Management." *Human Resource Management* 25(1):91–102.

Leavitt, H. J. 1986. *Corporate Pathfinders*. Homewood, Ill.: Dow Jones-Irwin.

Leites, N. 1953. *A Study of Bolshevism*. Glencoe, Ill.: Free Press.

Levinson, H., and S. Rosenthal. 1984. *CEO*. New York: Basic Books.

Lewin, K. A. 1935. *Dynamic Theory of Personality*. New York: McGraw-Hill.

McGoldrick, M., J. K. Pearce, and J. Giordano. 1982. *Ethnicity and Family Therapy*. New York: Guilford Press.

MacGregor Burns, J. 1977. *Leadership*. New York: Harper and Row.

Mendenhall, M., E. Dunbar, and G. Oddou. 1987. "Expatriate Selection & Training & Career Pathing, A Review & Critique." *Human Resource Management* 26(3):331–45.

Mendenhall, M., and G. Oddou. 1985. "The Dimensions of Expatriate Acculturation: A Review." *The Academy of Management Review* 10(1):39–47.

Mendenhall, M.. and G. Oddou. 1986. "Acculturation Profiles of Expatriate Managers: Implications for Cross-Cultural Training Programs." *Columbia Journal of World Business* 21(4):73–79.

Muller, H. 1970. *The Search for the Qualities Essential to Advancement in a Large Industrial Group*. The Hague: Shell Publication.

Ohmae, K. 1989. "Planting for a Global Harvest." *Harvard Business Review* (July–August):136–45.

Perlmutter, H. V. 1969. "National or Corporate Culture: Implication for Human Resource Management." *Human Resource Management* 27(2)231–46.

Tung, R. 1981. "Selection and Training of Personnel for Overseas Assignments." *Columbia Journal of World Business* (Spring):68–78.

Tung, R. 1982. "Selection and Training Procedures of U.S., European and Japanese Multinationals." *California Management Review* 25(1):57–71.

Tung, R. 1984. "Strategic Management of Human Resources in the Multinational Enterprise." *Human Resource Management* 23:129–44.

Tung, R. 1987. "Expatriate Assignments: Enhancing Success and Minimizing Failure." *The Academy of Management Executive* 1(2):117–26.

Tung, R. 1988. *The New Expatriates: Managing Human Resources Abroad.* Cambridge, Mass.: Ballinger.

Zaleznik, A. 1989. *The Managerial Mystique.* New York: Harper & Row.

Zeira, Y., and A. Pazy. 1983. "Training Parent Country Professionals in Host Country Organizations." *Academy of Management Review* 8(2):262–72.

Zeira, Y., and M. Banai. 1984. "Present and Desired Methods of Selecting Expatriate Managers for International Assignments." *Personnel Review* 13(3):29–35.

11

Global Development

Noel M. Tichy

A Framework for Global Development

If organizations and their leadership are required to play at intense "Olympian" levels, then traditional training and development cannot be the vehicle to prepare for quantum human system change. In a world where time-based competitiveness calls for very deep, multidimensional, people development approaches, the core concept for effective global development is "compressed action learning."

Compressed Action Learning

Human resource professionals face the same challenges as the companies they are serving. Cycle times must come down on everything—developing products, responsiveness, customer service—at the same time that higher quality and greater-impact services and products are provided. Compressed action learning is a vehicle for people development. It occurs with much shorter cycle times than traditional approaches to learning, while simultaneously having higher-impact and higher-quality developmental interventions. It is frame-breaking. Development in the new era must be seen simultaneously as an individual transformation lever and as an organizational transformation lever. This requires a new framework: blending management development with organization development.

Organization development has traditionally focused on cultural change at the group and systems levels, whereas management development has given attention (primarily cognitive) to skill development. One of the major problems with management development has been the difficulty of transferring learning when individuals go off-site, acquire new mind-sets and skills, and then return to the same social system where the new ideas have little or no impact. The problem with organization development has been one of scale.

206

Customized workshops and processes have been able to create some powerful social technology for change, but in large organizations they have had little impact. Thus, there are deep challenges in combining economies of scale and development impact. These are only heightened by the need for faster and faster cycle times. How can individual and organizational transformation be managed effectively in such circumstances?

Figure 11.1 lays out the Tichy Development Matrix. It shows the core dimensions necessary for reframing the development challenges in the 1990s. This figure deals with the depth of the intervention. As interventions become deeper, they move from a focus on developing (1) awareness and (2) cognitive and conceptual understanding to (3) actual skills, (4) new problem-solving approaches, and ultimately to (5) fundamental change. The level of risk goes up at each stage. More time is required to make the deeper intervention happen. A simple analogy helps to clarify the process.

The development of musical ability is a useful metaphor. To train someone in music, a reasonable first step might be to develop awareness and appreciation, for example, a music appreciation course. The second step, cognitive understanding, would involve learning how to read music. The third step, developing skills, would involve using concepts to synthesize knowledge and motor activity—to actually play an instrument. The fourth step, new problem-

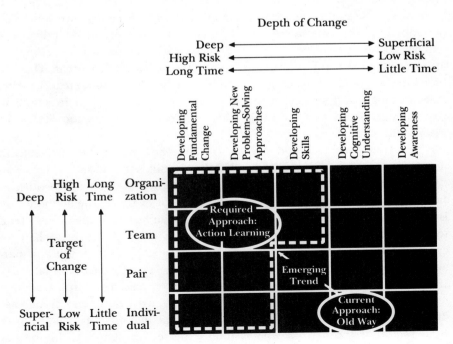

Figure 11.1   The Tichy Development Matrix.

solving approaches, would require adding skills: transposing music to change the score and then altering the repertoire of skills. The fifth step, at the deepest level, is fundamental change: performing as a composer. It is helpful to apply these five steps to specific management functional skills, for example, finance, and work through the same logic from awareness to fundamental change.

The other dimension in Figure 11.1 is the focus (or target) of the intervention, with one end of the spectrum being anchored at the individual level and the other at the organizational level. Traditional programs commonly send individuals either to internal management development programs or to external business school programs. Occasionally, boss/subordinate pairs or two colleagues attend programs. Less rare, but still part of the repertoire of traditional development programs, is to send teams and, finally, the target is sometimes the total organization. In contrast, the Tichy Development Matrix asserts that the challenge is to move development toward the upper left portion of the matrix "Fundamental Change of the Organization."

Traditional Management Development

The dominant paradigm in management development has been emerging since World War II (See Figure 11.1, lower right hand portion of the Tichy Development Matrix). In business schools, a multifunctional curriculum in such areas as finance, marketing, accounting, and organization behavior is taught. Managers and executives attend as "individuals," and most of their development is focused on cognitive awareness and understanding with some skill development. The case method is essentially a cognitive understanding tool and has become a preferred teaching tool. There is minimal skill development in terms of participants actually practicing the art of management. They interact in classrooms, discussing hypotheses instead of playing on teams, taking risks, making decisions, and living with the consequences of their actions in real settings. Simulations and role plays are very inadequate substitutes for real "clinical practice."

The same approach and curriculum have dominated the management development programs whether at IBM's Armonk facility or Philips's Eindehaven Training Center or Hitachi's Management Development Institute in Japan. There are a number of reasons for this. For example, the methodology is well developed, and the faculty who teach in the business schools also tend to dominate the senior management programs in corporations. When we examine the global development experiences available in the traditional paradigms, there are those at INSEAD, Harvard, Wharton, Columbia, IMI/IMEDE, to name a few of the more esteemed programs. These run from one to six weeks or more, involve a multifunctional curriculum, and entail case discussions, group work, and projects. Yet it is the *individual* manager (lower right sector of the matrix) who is then expected to return to his or her organization transformed in some major (preferably global) way.

It has become necessary for us to shift the mind-set from "training" to "giant workshop." If we reframe the development challenge in the upper left quadrant of the matrix, a new set of steps, tools, and approaches emerges.

Linking Development with Reality

When management development programs are reconceptualized as action workshops, real "live" problems, not case studies, command attention. People in the action experience are at real risk, and there are tangible organizational goals for transformation that are linked to the development activities. Add globalization to the agenda, and the model for successful compressed action learning becomes clear: intense cross-cultural problem solving which requires multicultural teams, a faculty that is transcultural as well as multilingual, and breaking free of the classroom into real cross-cultural settings. Only when these cross-cultural teams of executives are *required to deliver* with *real* stakes and *real* risks involved, can there be a quantum development breakthrough.

The Outward Bound Metaphor

The core of compressed action learning is a lesson learned years ago by the Outward Bound school. This school grew up in World War II as a way to train seamen in England to survive when the U-boats sank their ships. The amazing finding in World War II was that the older seamen were out-surviving the more fit and healthy younger ones. The conclusion was that survival had more to do with mind-set, self-esteem, and teamwork than brute physical strength. Thus, the Outward Bound schools focused from day one on enhancement of self-esteem and team work. It has since become a vehicle for vastly diverse populations working these agendas.

Outward Bound provides a good example of compressed action learning. Breakthroughs occur because people are put at their boundaries—both individually and as teams. They perceive real risk, whether it be in a rock climbing exercise or a sailing activity off the coast of Maine with strong winds blowing and the rocky shore nearby. In order to successfully accomplish what Outward Bound calls an "initiative," usually a team task, teams must work effectively together and individuals must exhibit personal leadership and self-confidence.

A core attribute of Outward Bound is that it creates the illusion of great risk. It is more illusion than reality. The illusion is due to careful stage-setting and putting people in a context in which they are at their boundaries—emotionally, physically and intellectually. For example, taking a desk-bound executive, training him for 45 minutes in rock-climbing techniques, putting him on a sheer, 100 foot granite cliff for his first rappel down, and then having him climb back up the cliff is an absolute emotional breakthrough experience. The executive is quickly caught up in the experience and does not perceive that there is a great deal of safety built into the situation. Instead, he pushes at his boundaries and half-way up the cliff confronts his own sense of risk taking. Logically, he has not perceived the existence of the safety rope that is attached to him and the helmet he is wearing. The perception is that if I slip, I could go all the way down to the bottom of this cliff. The same illusion is created after teaching executives for 30 minutes how to sail a 30 foot pulling boat. They are given the challenge of sailing to a harbor five miles away along the rocky coast of Maine with no experienced sailors. They quickly lose the perception that there is a trained Outward Bound instructor sitting there on the boat ready to intervene if they face true life-threatening danger.

By having this kind of pressure put on them, the teams confront their own abilities to plan, make decisions, lead, and resolve conflict. The compressed, rapid cycle of these team activities gives the teams an opportunity to push their boundaries far beyond anything that happens sitting in a case breakout room discussing the international business case of Corporation X, Y, or Z.

In global development, instead of simple physical Outward Bound activities, we replace the team activities with such complex challenges as doing a country business opportunity assessment that will actually have an impact on the company's investment strategy and that will be reviewed by the CEO. In other global development programs, teams work on global strategic issues necessary for the business to achieve long-term global success. The team's ability to solve these issues will not only have an impact on the business, but the participants also perceive that it will impact their careers. The compressed action learning calls into play cognitive understanding, multiple business leadership skills, and new approaches and sets the stage for fundamentally changing the way people work on both the "hard" business issues and the "soft" people issues.

Blending the "Hard" and "Soft" Issues

Compressed action learning deals with another paradox, namely that of impacting both the "hard" and "soft" developmental issues.

Figure 11.2 captures the challenge particularly for U.S. corporations, as they face the decade of the nineties. "Hard" issues refer to budget, manufacturing, marketing, distribution, head count, finances, and so on; whereas "soft" issues refer to values, culture, vision, leadership style, innovative behavior. Figure 11.2 implies that for large portions of the U.S. economy, companies were weak on both the "hard" and "soft" issues from World War II up until 1980. Examples include the auto industry which was dominated oligopolistically by three competitors who had no global competition to speak of, consumer electronics which was dominated by domestic players like GE and RCA, and the steel industry. It wasn't until 1980 that most of these industries began to wake up to the fact that there were real international competitors out there who were more quickly producing cheaper, better quality products. Thus, we saw the decade of the eighties as getting strong on the

Paradox of Top Line/Bottom Line Growth

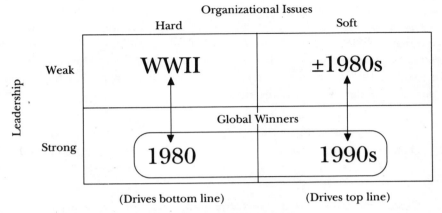

Figure 11.2   1990s Global Transformational Leadership.

"hard" issues. Companies such as GE moved out very early in the game, downsizing by over 120,000 employees, trimming its portfolio, restructuring, and dramatically improving productivity. This scenario was followed in company after company as entire industries moved to restructure in the 1980s: automotive, steel, and toward the end of the decade, the computer industry.

The long-term challenge, however, is to become strong on the "soft" issues, because it is the "soft" issues (cultures of innovation, risk-taking, and so on) that create the conditions for new products and innovation. The global winners will paradoxically manage the "hard" and "soft"—the "hard" helping to drive the lowest cost producer, the "soft" driving the most innovative. Thus, in the automotive industry Honda sets the standard. It is used by most auto companies as the bench mark because it tends to be the lowest-cost producer and the most innovative simultaneously. The Honda culture embraces the "hard/soft paradox."

Global development requires simultaneously working on real "hard" business issues and the "soft" issues. Traditional training often runs "soft" courses on cross-cultural awareness, interpersonal skills, and team activities, but it is devoid of "hard" issues. Whereas with compressed action learning, people are working on real strategic business problems and simultaneously improving their team skills cross-culturally. It is this layering of multiple training and development agendas into a highly compressed environment that is the guts of the global development challenge for the 1990s. The remainder of this chapter lays out specific examples of what is possible by taking this approach. It ends with a set of prescriptions for both the CEO and the human resource organization to drive global development into the twenty-first century.

GE's Global Development Strategy: Crotonville

General Electric's management development operation headquartered at Crotonville, New York, provides formal development experiences for GE professionals and managers worldwide. Approximately 5,000 per year come to Crotonville's 53-acre campus which has a 145-bed residential education center. In the mid-1980s, Crotonville changed its mission to focus on global development. The new objective became:

> To leverage GE's global competitiveness as an instrument of cultural change, by improving the business acumen, leadership abilities and organizational effectiveness of General Electric professionals.

Crotonville is used as a transformational level for GE, as well as an individual leadership development tool. Therefore, many of the premises that guided CEO John F. Welch's actions in the 1980s have generalized applicability to transnational companies around the world. The GE case illustrates how the training and development infrastructure of many large companies can be used to bring about much more compressed, higher impact change than currently experienced. Such global change will require that CEOs have a new mind-set, similar to the one which Jack Welch has developed. He sees that winning globally requires continuous employee development at all levels so that GE has a culture where the need for speed, continuous experimentation, and action is met.

One of the fundamental premises guiding the transformation of Crotonville during the 1980s was that revolutionaries do not rely solely on the chain of command to bring about quantum change. They carefully develop multi-channel, two-way, interactive networks throughout the organization:

1. The chain of command with its vested interest is where much of the resistance to change resides. Therefore, there is a need to stir up the populace of the organization, to begin developing new leaders for the new regime.

2. There's a need for a new set of values and templates in the organization.

3. There's a need for mechanisms to implement all these changes. Therefore, new socialization and new development processes are required.

Jack Welch perceives himself to be the leader of a major cultural revolution at GE. He has been looking for ways to best utilize GE's Crotonville resources.

The Crotonville Transformation

As is true of most university business schools, the primary focus at Crotonville has historically been on the individual participant's cognitive understanding. The shift in the Crotonville mind-set has been from a training mentality to a workshop mentality which ultimately leads to totally new program designs. It has resulted in an increasing number of teams attending sessions whenever possible. Also, participants increasingly bring real business problems and leave with action plans.

Leadership behaviors are rated by participants' direct reports, peers, and bosses before going to Crotonville. The aim is for changes in leadership behavior to be linked back to the work setting. Other action learning tools include having executives consult real GE businesses on unresolved strategic issues. Teams spend up to a week in the field consulting with these businesses. In addition, members of the CEO and officers come to Crotonville to conduct workshops on key GE strategic challenges.

Along the way, participants find the development experiences increasingly unsettling and emotionally charged. They feel uncomfortable with the feedback from their back-home organization. They wrestle with very difficult, unresolved, real-life problems. They make presentations to senior executives, argue among themselves, and work through intensive team-building experiences that include a good deal of Outward Bound–type activity. The measure of program success shifts from participants' evaluation of how good they felt about the learning experience to how the experience has impacted their organizations and their own leadership behavior over time.

In order for the Crotonville program to deliver on its new global mission in the 1980s, the total curriculum was revamped to provide a targeted "core development" experience at key career transition points for people at all levels—from new professional hires up through the top officers. Figure 11.3 shows the Crotonville core development sequence.

A Corporate Model for In-House Global Transformation and Development

GE provides many examples of what can be done through a large-scale corporate development effort. This section will highlight some specific examples to illustrate what large transnational companies with significant development infrastructures such as GE, IBM, AT&T, Shell, Unilever, CIBA GEIGY, Hitachi, Matsushista and Nomura Securities can do with "compressed action learning."

Transformational Workshops

Beginning in the early part of 1987, a series of five-day workshops was held for teams of managers from different GE businesses to work on global trans-

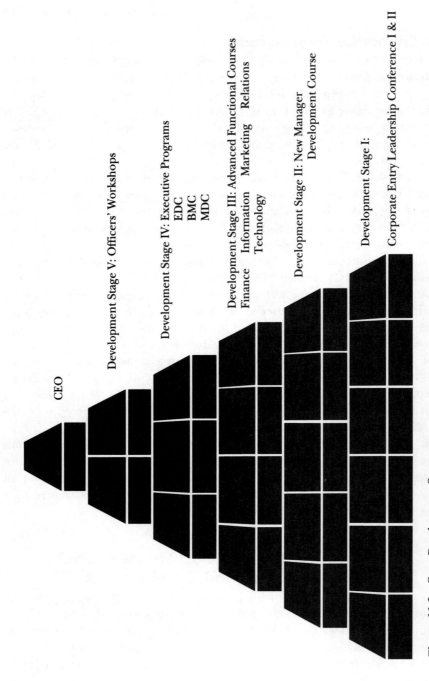

CEO

Development Stage V: Officers' Workshops

Development Stage IV: Executive Programs
EDC
BMC
MDC

Development Stage III: Advanced Functional Courses
Finance   Information   Marketing   Relations
          Technology

Development Stage II: New Manager
                     Development Course

Development Stage I:
Corporate Entry Leadership Conference I & II

Figure 11.3   Core Development Sequence

214

formational problems. The first of these workshops was held at Gotenba at the foot of Mt. Fuji in Japan. It was a five-day workshop for teams to work on specific transformational agendas as they simultaneously worked on their own global development. At this workshop were teams from GE's CALMA business, Consumer Electronics, Power Systems, GE Medical Systems, and Plastics. The majority of the participants were Japanese. There were also managers from Korea, China and the United States. Similar workshops were run in the United States in the following years, coordinated and sponsored by Crotonville. The teams were sponsored by their CEO or Senior Executive with a specific change problem to accomplish. The goals of the workshop were the following:

1. Develop a transformation strategy.

2. Develop a high-performing team.

3. Acquire a state-of-the-art input on business strategy, management technology, and implementation planning.

4. Work on transformational leadership capacity.

5. Deliver an actionable transformation product to their sponsors.

Some examples of the types of problems worked on in these transformational workshops are:

1. Integrating and leading a new process for a U.S./Japanese joint venture in the high-tech field.

2. Resolving major inventory control problems, saving millions of dollars a year.

3. Sourcing strategic alliance issues with partners in the United States and Korea.

4. Initiating the movement from a traditional work system to a innovative work design strategy for a multiplan firm.

5. Globalization strategy and market service for a domestically focused service company.

6. Downsizing encompassing the closing of three plants to streamline for global competition.

7. Acquisition strategy worked out for a manufacturing business.

8. Formulating a strategy and implementation process for a new product start-up and roll-out.

Table 11.1 lays out the contrast between the transformational workshops and traditional training. Again, the aim is to get higher-impact, multiple agendas worked out in these five-day experiences.

Global Business Management Course

One of the Senior Executive Programs at GE, the Business Manager Course (BMC), has evolved since 1986 into a four-week action learning experience, the core of which is creating five- to seven-person teams that spend over a week in the field consulting and working on real, unresolved GE strategic problems. These teams have been involved in working on such problems as the transfer of artificial intelligence capability from GE's Research and Development area to the financial services organization to joint venture considerations between construction equipment business and Fuji Electric, in Japan to NBC's global strategy in Europe.

By 1989 the focus had shifted to an even greater global challenge. The action learning focused on sending teams to China, the former Soviet Union, and India. In each case, the teams had specific GE problems to work on in these regions but were also collecting intelligence and information on GE's best and worst practices in the global arena. The teams immersed themselves in these regions' economies, dealing with geopolitical realities and ultimately pulling their intelligence together in reports that were presented to top officers (e.g., Paul VanOrden, a member of GE's CEO team and Paulo Fresco, the Senior Vice President in charge of International at GE and his team of country managers). Such an experience results in payoff to the GE operations in China, the Soviet Union, and India. New knowledge has been transferred throughout the company via the international organization. Finally, there is a tremendous impact on the teams and their individual members in developing their global capabilities.

Globalizing the Executive Development Course

The top level program for GE, the month-long Executive Development Course (EDC), has also shifted to an increasingly global set of experiences. By the end of the 1980s, the program was run partly in the United States and partly in Europe. It focused on studying "Europe 1992" and the transformations occurring in GE, both worldwide and in that region. The five-day transformational workshops, the globalized BMC, and the EDC are illustrative of development experiences that are possible through a corporate-level effort such as GE has made.

Table 11.1   How the Transformational Leadership Workshop
Process Operates:

TRANSFORMATIONAL LEADERSHIP WORKSHOP	TRADITIONAL TRAINING
Prework	
Our faculty works with you and your selected team prior to the workshop. The critical business problem or issue is identified and impactful desired outcomes set.	Participants come as individuals with little or no preparation or link with other participants.
Natural Work Groups	
Your executives come as a natural work group with the specific task of solving a critical problem or setting a new business direction. Faculty input is leading-edge global thinking and is designed to facilitate this work.	The participants are individuals from companies with widely diverse problems and cultures. Problem solving usually focuses on smaller issues. There is a low level of synergy.
Work Team Process	
The faculty and team work together to link workshop presentations and concepts to your evolving transformational action plan. Ample time is built in for this facilitation process.	Building an action plan is largely left to the individual. There is minimal interaction or work with faculty. Motivation to solve a major puzzle at the workshop is low.
Action Planning	
A plan for transformation is worked on and completed during the workshop There is a high degree of team building during this problem-solving process. Individuals and the team deal with the gut-wrenching issues involved in transformation.	Most workshops do not focus on developing implementable action plans or new business directions. They rely on the motivation and willingness of the participant. Often the tough issues of change are not surfaced or dealt with.

Table 11.1   *(Continued)*

Transformational Leadership Workshop	Traditional Training

Accountability

Because of the strategic nature of the workshop process, all participants are accountable as actors in the transformational drama. There exists the healthy pressure to arrive at a plan, by the end of the workshop, that can be presented to the team's sponsor (CEO or key executive).

Because the workshop is not adequately focused, the participants are left to formulate their action plans after returning to their business or workplace. Colleagues critical to transformation are not up to speed.

Result

The CEO or sponsoring executive joins the workshop team on day five to work with the team on plans for implementation and on commitment of resources to transform the organization.

The participants return to work and simply prepare a report to the boss and some colleagues. Where there is an action result, it is transactional rather than making sweeping global changes required by the business or organization.

Follow Through

A transformational team has been built. It will stay intact to ensure implementation of the action plan. The team members have, through new exposures and commitment development, improved their personal and professional capabilities.

Participants develop a new network, but often the contacts are passive. The participant is involved in social and professional interactions, but any groups formed during the workshop are temporary. Follow through is usually low.

The Global Leadership Program Consortium

This is the most exciting time I've ever been through in my career—more challenge, more possibility of failure . . . but more rewards.

—GLP PARTICIPANT, 1989

The Global Leadership Program (GLP) is a consortium representing leading corporations (Figure 11.4 lists the companies) in Japan, Europe, and the United States along with a global faculty and participating host countries.

The companies are part of an ongoing partnership started in 1988 jointly committed to research and development on issues of globalization. The program design, facilities, and support staff are directed by core faculty from universities in the United States, Europe, and Japan. The members of the consortium participate in a research partnership and in an intensive 5-week Global Leadership Program designed for senior executives with CEO potential. The Global Leadership Program Consortium is an ongoing partnership with the following elements:

1.   The five-week Global Leadership Program.

GLP COMPANIES

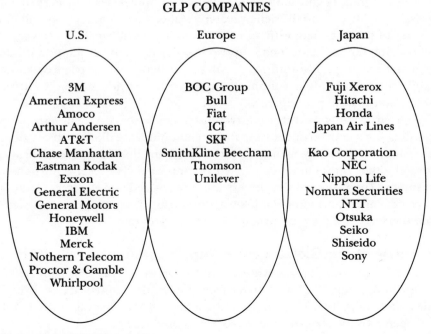

U.S.	Europe	Japan
3M	BOC Group	Fuji Xerox
American Express	Bull	Hitachi
Amoco	Fiat	Honda
Arthur Andersen	ICI	Japan Air Lines
AT&T	SKF	
Chase Manhattan	SmithKline Beecham	Kao Corporation
Eastman Kodak	Thomson	NEC
Exxon	Unilever	Nippon Life
General Electric		Nomura Securities
General Motors		NTT
Honeywell		Otsuka
IBM		Seiko
Merck		Shiseido
Nothern Telecom		Sony
Proctor & Gamble		
Whirlpool		

Figure 11.4   GLP Companies.

2. An ongoing globalization research and development program.

3. A global network of companies and individuals sharing best-management practices.

4. Synergy with the MBA program.

5. The only triad (Japan, U.S., Europe) consortium for high-level executives representing leading global companies to share and develop ideas and applications together.

The program is an intensive, multinational experience designed to expand the global mind-set, cross-cultural competency, and global networking capability of senior executives. It uses action learning to provide an intellectual, interpersonal, and physical international experience. It creates a dynamic, cross-cultural, problem-solving environment that pushes executives to their ultimate boundaries, thus providing breakthrough leadership experiences.

Cross-Cultural Compressed Action Learning

The Global Leadership Program is built around a country business opportunity assessment in which participant teams travel to different regions in the world to investigate long-term business prospects. At the same time, the teams work on their own cross-cultural understanding and team building.

The program begins long before the actual 5-week session. Participants receive specially prepared briefing materials about the country they will visit in order to provide them with an in-depth background for their assessment. The briefing books are divided into two major parts: core readings and supplemental readings. The information is researched and compiled by known experts in the field. It is continually updated to provide the most current information for the participants.

The participants also receive survey instruments to assess their perceptions regarding the characteristics of a global organization, the dimensions of global leadership, and the way managers carry out their global responsibilities. In addition, other representatives of their organization also receive portions of the survey. The results of the surveys are summarized and the information is discussed during and after the Global Leadership Program. Insights gained from the surveys are an important part of the program.

Overview of the Global Leadership Program

Figure 11.5 provides an overview of the program. It was first launched in 1989 with a group of 21 executives from Japan, the United States, Britain, Brazil, and India. In 1990, the second running of the program included 31 participants from Europe, the United States, and Japan.

The core of the program is the two-week, on-site country assessment

Week 1	Week 2	Week 3	Week 4	Week 5
University of Michigan		On–Site Country Visit		Univ. of MI
Team Building		Country Business		Preparation and
Country Business Assessment Preparation		Interviews with Government Representatives		Presentation of Final Reports
Outward Bound		Business Visits		
Washington D.C. Visit		Regional Visit and Assessment		

Global Leadership Program Mission:
"To develop global business leaders who have the mind-set, leadership, and team-building skills to both lead their institutions and contribute to world economic growth."

Program Objectives:
• Provide a deeper understanding of global geopolitical forces and their relationship to business
• Provide cross-cultural understanding and skill development
• Provide tools and techniques for carrying out overseas business opportunity assessments
• Provide exposure to the political, social, cultural, and economic environment in the host country
• Provide new global business strategies for joint ventures and alliances
• Provide global network building among business leaders, host countries, and business academic leaders

Figure 11.5 Overview of Global Leadership Program.

carried out by cross-cultural teams in China, India, and Brazil. Each executive team produces investment opportunity and entry strategy recommendations as well as video documentaries as part of their country assessment.

As impressive as the products of the teams' work and the real learning is the cross-cultural teamwork. Each team spends two weeks preparing for the country assessment by working on its personal global leadership capabilities and its global mind-set and team skills. Preparation also includes a weekend at the Outward Bound School at Hurricane Island, Maine, and a two-day assessment in Washington, D.C. Learning to create a high-performing team with senior executives from multiple cultures is one of the keys to leading world-class operations in the 1990s and the twenty-first century.

The program carefully blends rigorous intellectual development of global leaders, starting with each individuals' map of their own personal global mind-set; that is, the way they analyze the world politically, economically, and culturally. These global mind-sets are then shared and discussed intensively in each team. The team is then charged with coming up with one analytic framework to guide its assessment of a major geopolitical region of the world. They're assisted in this process by working with area experts in economics, political science, and business. In addition, they are given intensive briefings through written materials, videos, and several days of work with world experts on the region they will be visiting. While this is going on, there is intensive team-building activity so that each team becomes a high-performing, cross-cultural team. And finally, each individual's own leadership behaviors are examined through surveys filled out by their colleagues and themselves before they attended the program, as well as through ongoing feedback from their team members throughout the program.

By the second week of the program, the teams have been built and they start on their country assessments. The first step in that process is a one-day, intensive set of interviews and discussions in Washington, D.C., with the State Department, International Monetary Fund, embassies, and so on. They then return to the University of Michigan at Ann Arbor and spend the remainder of the week getting prepared for their country assessment.

The Country Business Opportunity Assessment

During the third and fourth weeks of the program, the participant teams split up and travel to three different countries. The 1989 program visited Brazil, India, and China while the 1990 program visited the USSR, China, India, and Brazil to investigate long-term business prospects as well as to continue work on cross-cultural understanding and team building. The primary task of the program is the creation of the high-performance, international team which must work across cultural boundaries to carry out a real business task under pressure of time and in an unfamiliar context. The program assigns working teams of five or six participants to a large, diverse, developing country with which the members are unfamiliar. They are required to work together for two weeks as a team to assess the long-term business prospects of the country in question. The assessment focuses on five issues:

1. What role will the host country play in the global economy over the next decade?

2. What kinds of business opportunities are best for that economy (e.g., production, sourcing, direct sales of heavy equipment, heavy or light industrial goods, consumer goods)? What regions in the host country are best for which kinds of foreign business?

3. What are the best entry strategies for that economy (e.g., joint ventures, co-production, direct sales, equity joint ventures, licensing, counter trade)?

4. What is the opinion the host country holds of the nationality of the participant? What prejudice might exist, good and bad, for large multinational corporations? How does the host government view the particular corporation doing business? That is, what is the corporate image abroad?

5. What is the global citizenship role regarding physical and human ecology in the country? What role should be played regarding such problems as air and water pollution, toxic waste, education, health care, and poverty?

The Process: Compressed Learning

In each country, one or two teams travel first to the national capital, focusing on national policy and relations between multinational corporations and the government. The participants then travel to different regions to assess business conditions and opportunities there. In India, the teams traveled to New Delhi, Bombay, Puri, Bangalore, and Madras. In Brazil, they visited São Paulo, Caxias do Sul, San Jose, Brasilia, and Rio de Janeiro. The participants return to Ann Arbor to write their reports, edit their videos, and make their presentations during the last week of the program.

During the last week of the program, the participants write their reports and make their video documentaries and presentations. This process forces them to synthesize and analyze their experiences and information. For the participants, the experience of dealing with real problems and adverse conditions provides a real test of their cross-cultural skills, both as a team and as individuals. Strong networks have been created between the team members as well as across teams.

Starting in 1990, the program began to actively involve MBA students as staff assistants to the teams. This added value to the program and also began the journey of integrating multiple layers of learners in the Global Leadership Program. Over time, a series of global leadership action learning programs will be designed for MBA students, early professionals, and mid-level managers on up to the current Senior Global Leadership Program. The aim will be to create a portfolio of action learning experiences all of which include international cross-cultural team building and utilize on-site project work in cultures that are unfamiliar to a significant number of the team members.

The Program Impact

The self-evaluations of the participants were extremely positive. It was a frame-breaking and peak life experience for many. The real measure will unfold over time, and will be tracked through research and the ongoing network which has been created. The alumni group will meet regularly and will play a role in preparing next year's participants. In addition, the program has already generated some business relationships among participants and will help build global networks among many of the participating companies. In addition, the host countries and host organizations such as Confederation of Engineering Industries (CEI), the U.S. equivalent of the National Association of Manufacturers, are building relationships with companies by helping to develop and coordinate the agenda for participants. CEI has sponsored a delegation of top CEOs from India to visit many of the sponsoring companies in the U.S.

The program is spawning business research projects and will be a catalyst to a global research program including university based research laboratories in Michigan, Tokyo, and Brussels. The Global Leadership Program will be building a worldwide research network of business schools working in close cooperation with firms and industries to meet the challenges of the new global playing field.

Conclusion

This chapter has laid out the challenges for global leadership development. It started with an assumption that the geopolitical and competitive landscape of the 1990s is requiring a new breed of leadership at all levels of the organization. We have argued that traditional classroom-type training will be insufficient for transforming both organizations and leaders. The Tichy Development Matrix can be used as a strategic concept to shift from individual training to higher-impact organizational and team change. The illustrations have included internal corporate level development such as has been carried out at GE's Crotonville and a consortium of 35 U.S., Japanese, and European companies working to develop their senior leaders.

The future provides a host of new opportunities for globalization at multiple levels. Programs within companies will multiply, but business schools and other academic institutions must undertake alternative, new ways of partnering with corporations to rapidly develop the global leaders needed to pilot our institutions into the twenty-first century.

The Collaborative Context

12

Human Resource Management in Multinational Cooperative Ventures*

Peter Lorange

Introduction

Human resource management has increasingly been recognized as a critical dimension of strategic management (Tichy 1983; Beer et al. 1984; Fombrun et al. 1984; Chakravarthy 1985). Above all, it is becoming clearer that the human resource is a strategic resource that should be managed in a more explicit, proactive manner. Even though it cannot be allocated and generated in a way entirely analogous to the financial resources of a corporation, it is still an integral part of strategic management. A strategic resource is defined as a resource that can be shifted from one business strategy application to another (Lorange 1980), not only financial funds or technological knowhow, but also human resources. Without the growth of human resources as a strategic resource within a corporation, it will be difficult to secure the long-term strategic future of the corporation, even though financial resources might be adequate.

We are currently witnessing an increase of cooperative ventures as vehicles for implementing strategy, particularly in multinational contexts where joint ventures, licensing agreements, project cooperation, and other methods of

*Human Resource Management, Vol. 25, Number 1, pp. 133–148, Peter Lorange, copyright © 1986 by John Wiley & Sons, Inc., reprinted by permission of John Wiley & Sons, Inc.

cooperation are becoming commonplace. The reasons for the growth of co-operative ventures are manifold: they may make scarce strategic resources last longer by utilizing complementary resources from several partners; they may allow faster market penetration; they may be a political necessity, and so on (Lorange 1986a). The human resource function is particularly critical to successful implementation of such cooperative ventures. Several strategic human resource issues surrounding these cooperative ventures are not well understood; therefore, the purpose of the present chapter is to raise and discuss a number of them.

First, a conceptual scheme for classifying cooperative ventures proposed elsewhere (Lorange 1986b) will be delineated briefly in the next section. Six human resource management issues as they relate to the four types of cooperative modes identified in the conceptual scheme will then be considered. Finally, the conclusion will entail a synthesis of the strategic human resource management function within each of the four cooperative venture archetypes.

The present paper is preliminary and the arguments are normative. The research is part of a broader effort to study strategic management of cooperative multinational ventures based on clinical experience in a number of cooperative ventures.

Conceptual Framework for Cooperative Ventures

It can be argued that the choice of a cooperative venture should satisfy several requirements of each participating partner. The cooperative venture must create a value-added chain by bringing together synergistic factors for a combined output greater than the sum of the outputs of each participating partner. The combined output must result in a competitive product or service, in comparison with alternative sources of supply.

The cooperative venture must also be useful for the pursuance of each partner's own individual strategy. The venture may still, of course, be of a different strategic importance to the various partners. For some partners, the cooperative venture may be an integral factor in the implementation of its overall strategy. For other partners, however, it may play a relatively minimal strategic role in this sense. Of course, this does not imply that the cooperative venture would be of little value; the dividend streams from the joint venture might still be tangible.

A partner in a joint venture may wish to keep a certain degree of discretionary control over its unique resources. Some strategic resources, such as unique technological skills or relevant marketing know-how, may not as readily be made available to the other partners as other, more common know-hows. The protection of exclusive know-hows may be particularly necessary in cases in which the joint venture is pertinent to the implementation of a parent's strategy.

Figure 12.1 portrays a two-dimensional conceptual framework for cooperative ventures, based on the relative degree of strategic importance of the venture to each partner, and the relative degree of retained discretionary control over its own resources desired by each partner. The overall rationale for the framework of this exhibit suggests an interplay among the two types of dimensions that are postulated to be important determinants of the cooperative venture's strategic context: the importance of the joint venture to the parent organizations and the degree of desired control over strategic resources retained by the parents.

Figure 12.1 also suggests several organizational forms that may be ap-

		Strategic importance of cooperative venture for the parent organizations	
		Relatively high for all	Relatively higher for some; relatively lower for others
	Cooperative venture's business adaptability capability / Cooperative venture's business organization	Relatively lower	Relatively higher
Degree of desired retained strategic control over own resources by each parent	Relatively higher	Skeleton	*Type A* Project-based cooperative networks	*Type B* Licensing and/or royalty agreements
	Relatively lower (at least for some)	Full blown	*Type C* Cooperative ventures with permanently complimentary roles by the parents	*Type D* Jointly owned business ventures/ongoing business concept

Figure 12.1   A conceptual framework for cooperative ventures.

propriate for the cooperative venture. At one extreme, the cooperative venture may be a full-blown business organization in its own right, in many ways analogous to an independent business organization. This organizational design would be implemented under circumstances in which one or more of the parent organizations have become comfortable with relinquishing exceedingly tight strategic controls over their critical resources. On the other hand, if one or more of the parents feel that they must maintain tight control over critical strategic resources, the organizational form of the cooperative venture might be more skeletal or temporary, with a number of organizational functions carried out by the partners on behalf of the cooperative venture.

The conceptual scheme also offers implications for a cooperative venture organization's capacity to be adaptable to new environmental opportunities. One might expect that a full-blown organization would be able to adapt relatively easily to new business opportunities, as would a freestanding business organization. On the other hand, there will typically be considerable adaptive constraints due to a lack of immediately available strategic resources within a less full-blown organization, due to agreements among the parents on behalf of the cooperative venture.

Figure 12.1 illustrates four types of cooperative ventures which may result from this conceptual framework. Somewhat arbitrarily they can be labeled *cooperative ventures with permanently complementary roles by the parents* (such as franchising), *licensing and/or royalty agreements, project-based cooperative networks,* and *jointly owned ventures based on ongoing business concepts.*

In the following sections, human resource management functions as they apply to the four types of cooperative ventures will be considered. We shall claim that critical human resource management issues must be addressed differently for each of the four archetypes. It will become apparent that a unidimensional approach to human resource management, without recognizing the uniqueness of each type of cooperative venture, may result in suboptimal human resource management.

Six Critical Human Resource Management Issues

Based on preliminary clinical studies, six issues appear to be among the particularly crucial ones for human resource management within cooperative ventures in multinational settings. In the following paragraphs, the manner in which each of these issues can be approached in the context of the four cooperative venture archetypes will be discussed. The six issues are as follows:

1. Assignment of managers to cooperative ventures: who should be assigned where?

2.   The human resource transferability issue: who "controls" a particular manager?

3.   The trade-off in time-spending between operating and strategic tasks among various managers involved in the cooperative venture.

4.   Judgment calls regarding the performance of the human resource in the established cooperative venture: how to avoid biases?

5.   Human resource loyalty issues: the cooperative venture vs. the parent.

6.   Individual managers' career planning issues: how can they achieve career progression through cooperative venture assignments?

A. Assignment of Human Resources to Cooperative Ventures

A difficult issue in the assignment of managers to a cooperative venture is the identification of the best persons for each job. A cooperative venture must be created in such a way that it possesses relevant complimentarities and synergies, so as to allow the cooperative venture to generate a satisfactory output through a meaningful value-added process. Managers will usually be assigned by the partners, and often they will have worked for one of them beforehand. Various partners' perceptions of the types of human skills and talents needed may differ. Some partners may have unrealistic biases regarding the quality of the managerial capabilities being assigned, and some may not wish to assign their best people because they want to keep them in their own organizations. The assigned managers may be competent as individuals but unable to work together in a cooperative organizational context due to cultural differences, communication problems, and so on. These are only a few of the issues that may impact upon the staffing of a cooperative venture.

In a project-based cooperative network, there will not be one common organization in the classical sense to be staffed jointly, but separately staffed organizational "modules" to be provided by each of the partners under their largely individual jurisdictions. Appropriate staffing is still important because there must be compatibility between managers from the different organizations. Managers being allocated to this project-based organization must be able to understand one another and develop a meaningful communication pattern. The representatives from each parent organization must, above all, be able to communicate the key concepts of their package to be contributed to the project. Equally important, each member must be able to understand the unique features of the other members' packages so as to "translate" it to integrated, project-based opportunities. As such, the creation of compatible organizational entities is of major importance to this kind of project-based network.

As to the assignment of managers to cooperative ventures based on licensing and/or royalty agreements, there will also be two separate complementary organizational entities which must interact. The licensor must assign staff capable of providing sufficient training and organizational assistance for adequate transfer of know-how. Sufficiently competent managers must also be assigned to the venture from the licensee, to promote the transfer of know-how. Due to the relative difference in the strategic importance of the cooperative venture for the parents, it is a danger that one of the partners might be tempted to assign "second-stringers," thereby creating another potential source of friction.

For cooperative networks with permanently complementary roles by the parents in which a new, temporary organization must be created, assigning human resources to the project should be accomplished according to at least the following three criteria. First, assigned human resources must reflect the necessary specialized skills that each partner has agreed to contribute to the joint venture. These skills must be of adequate quality; thus, second or third stringers should normally not be assigned to the project. Second, the managers assigned must be sufficiently compatible in style to communicate and work together in effecting the cooperative venture. This requires teamwork and cooperation across functions, not isolation within each specialized camp. Third, the assigned managers must have the ability to provide adequate feedback to their respective parent organizations, giving continuous ad hoc support for unforseen backup activities within a reasonable amount of time.

The assignment of critical management resources to jointly owned ongoing business ventures also requires that management commitments be made for longer periods of time. Usually, the joint venture organization will also attract human resources within time from sources other than the parent organization. The assigned managerial resources must have relevant capabilities and must be of adequate quality. The overall blend of these human resources must have a cultural dimension to allow the development of an effective ongoing concern. The difference in importance of the cooperative venture to each of the partners makes it possible that a partner assigns relatively weak management resources to the venture.

In summary, the assignment of relevant management resources to various cooperative ventures is critical, but in different ways. For instance, for cooperative networks with permanently cooperative roles by the parents, the development of a workable common culture will be the challenge. On the other hand, with less formalized cooperative venture organizations, such as for project-based cooperative networks and licensing, the critical management assignment issue is to employ people who can communicate and interact with one another effectively in such settings. In the more formal, full-blown, jointly owned ongoing venture, the parents' role in the assignment of human resources may become less of an issue over time, because the jointly owned organization may have to gradually bring in necessary human resources on its own, as in an independent business.

B. Transferability of Human Resources

By definition, a resource is strategic only if it can be freely transferred from one application to another, i.e., divested from an established, hopefully successful strategy to an emerging strategy to be built for the future. Financial resources have traditionally been those most frequently considered for strategic reallocation (Henderson 1979). However, the same principle applies to other strategic resources, such as unique technological know-how and human resources. But human resources can, of course, not be considered a "commodity" to be allocated in the mechanistic way; in this respect, they are different from financial resources. An adequate ethical and human rights foundation must be established for human resources to be strategically transferable from one work application to another. In the present context this implies that parents must be able to transfer human resources to and/or from the cooperative venture, and they might also be transferred within the cooperative venture from old to new job applications. In the latter case, the human resource has direct strategic value to the cooperative venture organization itself. The transferred human resource has strategic value to the parent organization due to its discretionary "power" to transfer it back. It must thus be ascertained whether the cooperative venture and/or a particular parent has discretionary decision-making powers in managerial reassignments, and within which strategic context these decisions are made. This is applicable to all of the four archetypal settings. An issue to be dealt with in a later section concerns the degree of influence decision-makers actually have over a given manager so that reassignment considerations do not lead to discontent or resignation.

The partners in a project-based cooperative network will typically maintain their own organizational capabilities within the cooperative franchising network. In such an organization, the human resource transfer issues may center on how each partner provides human resources "on loan" to the project, such as that of technical specialists being temporarily assigned to a project. The transfer of human resources tends to be temporary and is controlled by the parents. The parent in question also controls which type of assignment the manager in question will go to after the project-based venture is completed. Of course, the human resources which do not have sufficient alternative applications may be dismissed after the project is terminated. It often seems to be the case, in fact, that too many human resources are let go when a particular strategic project is over, thereby creating a "stop-go" human resource management approach which might deprive parent organizations of important strategic human assets. It should be noted that a parent organization will keep its own benefits in mind when consenting to reassign some of its key people on loan. Therefore, it may at times be difficult for the parent to justify such an arrangement, even though the competitive network as a whole might clearly benefit. Any overall half-heartedness or paranoia regarding this type of human resource assignment may, in the long run, hamper the successful development of a project-based cooperative network approach.

A similar situation might typically exist for a licensing type of cooperative arrangement. A licensor may transfer human resources temporarily to a licensee for training and technical assistance, provided that he has sufficient human resources available and that he can retrieve this resource.

As to the transfer of key human resources in a cooperative network with permanently complementary roles by the parents, the parent organizations will in principle be obligated to make available the relevant managerial resources. Each partner must, however, also have available sufficient additional human resources to cover its own independent needs. Given the nature of this type of cooperative venture, each parent organization should put particular emphasis on developing the capability to "take back" human resources, as these human skills may have significant strategic value in future organizational contexts. Some transfer of human resources among partners may at times also be necessary. For instance, a franchisor may provide human resources "on loan" to a franchisee, such as technical specialists being temporarily assigned to a franchisee. A franchisee may also "loan" human resources to a franchisor, say, to strengthen the franchisor's market understanding and ensure that the franchising package remains relevant and adapted to market realities.

In jointly owned, ongoing business ventures, the issue is whether or not a parent organization is willing to transfer critical human resources to the new business venture. These strategic human resources would normally be assigned to the joint venture for a long period of time, perhaps for the entire remaining working career of the managers in question. The parents may thus have to transfer strategic human resources on a net basis during the initial phase and will not necessarily get them returned. Human resource management decisions will gradually be handled by the joint venture organization. Within the joint venture, human resources will have to be regenerated and developed and reallocated to new jobs therein, as in an independent business organization. Given the opportunity, however, the parent organizations should attempt to "welcome back" relevant human resources from the joint venture, and not automatically release them so that they might "accidentally" end up with competing organizations.

C. Managers' Time-Spending Patterns: On Operating vs. Strategic Task Trade-Offs?

Regarding the implementation of the strategies of a cooperative venture, it is worthwhile to keep in mind that this requires expenditure of efforts at the present time in order to develop a position with future prospective payoffs. This typically might result in an immediate lessening of operation results due to the diversion of resources for strategic use. In settings with full-blown cooperative venture organizations, these managers may execute independent judgment regarding how much resources to spend on the implementation of business strategies on their own. In this case, the cooperative organization has to carry out a set of operating duties simultaneously with its development of new strategies; as such, sufficient human resources will have to be earmarked for strategic development as well as for operating tasks. In the less fully developed skeleton organization, these strategic tasks will mainly be carried out by the partners on behalf of the cooperative venture. It is therefore key in the latter type of setting that the parent organizations are willing to spend resources in a coordinated fashion to facilitate this strategic development.

Thus, it must be ascertained *where* in a cooperative network do the human resources reside which have the responsibilities, capabilities, and capacity to carry out the development of further strategic moves. In other words, how does the cooperative network, on its own or together with the parent partners, meet the challenge of tackling *both* operating *and* strategic tasks on a parallel, ongoing basis? This leads to different considerations regarding the role of human resources in these trade-offs between operating and strategic challenges in each of the four archetypes.

In a project-based cooperative network organization, a common understanding and a clear division of labor between the managers of the participating organizations must be apparent, with respect to time allotted to strategic tasks such as further development of the technical base for the project cooperation and additional marketing efforts. The premise behind this is that future projects might result as a consequence of such coordinated strategy developments—if no future potential cooperation is contemplated then the issues discussed in this section will be largely irrelevant. Usually, these activities will involve specific hands-on cooperation between the various participant organizations, sometimes in the form of task forces. The managers assigned to such committees must have the time, energy, and motivation to actively contribute to such strategic development work, using some of the time normally spent in their own organizations for strategy development or on operating tasks.

In a licensing cooperative organization, strategic development tends to take place independently within the licensor and the licensee organizations. Thus, each organization must provide the relevant human resource capacity for strategic self-renewal. Here, too, some of this will involve joint cooperation, as in project-based cooperative ventures.

Relatively few free-standing strategic development tasks will be typically carried out within the cooperative venture with permanently complementary roles by the parents, because it is created to take advantage of a strategic opportunity based on a pooling of the partner organizations' strategic capabilities. Thus, to some extent there will be independent adaptation and strategic self-renewal by each parent, to ensure that they set aside sufficient human resources to maintain unique capabilities. This splitting up of the responsibilities to adapt by strategic developments carried out by the partners alone may not be enough, however. Common strategic adaptive efforts may have to be carried out by the cooperative venture itself. In a franchising organization, for instance, a common understanding and a clear division of labor between the managers of the franchisor and franchisee organizations must be had as to time allotted to common strategic tasks, such as further development of the franchising package and additional marketing adaptability moves.

The joint, ongoing business cooperative venture organization faces a situation that is in many ways parallel to any independent business organization, in that it must be able to draw sufficient human resources from the operating mode to further develop its own strategy. If the joint venture is too thinly staffed, strategic development will suffer, and an eventual lack of self-renewal and decreasing strategic focus will result. The challenge, similar to that of any type of business organization, is to allot sufficient organizational energy and time for the pursuit of business self-renewal and further strategic development. This must always be done in parallel with the other operating tasks. Parent organizations must not exercise so much near-term pressure for operating results that the cooperative venture is left with insufficient resources for its staffing for strategic self-renewal.

D. Human Resource Competency Issues: Avoidance of Judgment Biases

Human resources assigned to cooperative ventures must be able to satisfy the skill requirements of the value-added chain in carrying out the functional activities for which each partner is responsible. The importance of choosing appropriate persons for assignment for specific tasks has been emphasized previously in Section A. In this section, human competency and skill assessment issues within the various types of cooperative ventures once in operation will be discussed. Thus, the challenge is how to judge managers in terms of how well they are able to carry out their assignments, once the assignment of executives has been made.

In project-based cooperative ventures, the bulk of the judgments regarding managerial competencies in carrying out their jobs will have to largely be executed by each partner on his own. The partners must be able to exercise human resource competency and performance judgments to develop a relevant way to execute their team roles. Although the partners will have to make human resource performance and competency judgments largely on their own, in some instances it may not be uncommon that the partners also make joint human resource judgments regarding team effectiveness and contributions towards making the cooperative project work, based on their experience regarding desirable human characteristics in this respect.

In licensing cooperative ventures, each partner will also have to make human resource performance judgments and considerations largely on their own, as in project-based cooperative networks. In addition, the licensor and the licensee must jointly assess the issue of the cooperative licensing ventures' ability to be trained, i.e., executives' performance and its abilities to give and absorb information as part of a fairly standardized learning and communication process.

Judgments in human resource performance and competency issues are also critical in cooperative networks with permanently complementary roles by the parents. The partners must cooperate in assessing their performance of one another's functional specialists. Given that each partner may feel that he will be solely responsible for making the human performance judgments that fall within his given sphere of competence, this may lead to biases, such as looking too favorably upon the performance of managers from one's own organization. This may result in the inadvertent buildup of second-string functional specialists who cannot perform as effectively within the cooperative network as is desirable. For this reason, human resource performance and competency judgment issues should be dealt with by all of the partners in cooperation. In these situations, it may be appropriate to use joint performance review committees to make judgments and give feedback that is as free as possible from individual partner culture biases.

Judgments in human resource performance and competency must also be kept strictly in mind in the going concern cooperative venture. Several joint ventures have failed because they have been inappropriately staffed, due in part to lack of cooperation between myopic, biased parent organizations. In some instances, a partner may, for instance, have intended to get rid of some managers by unloading them on the cooperative venture. Whatever the case, it is imperative that the jointly owned cooperative venture establishes a thorough human resource performance review, so that ameliorating actions can be taken with regard to less than adequate performance within the jointly owned organizational setting.

E. Management Loyalty Issues:
To the Cooperative Venture or to the Parent?

A manager may at times find himself in conflict between loyalty to his parent organization vs. loyalty to the cooperative venture organization to which he is presently assigned. These loyalty conflicts may be difficult and the management of them must be considered an integral part of the human resource management of cooperative ventures. The nature of these divided loyalty issues in the context of each of the four archetypes will now be described.

Divided loyalty issues are usually minimal in project-based cooperative networks, because the partner's employees will, of course, naturally tend to be loyal to their respective organizations. There may be "raiding" of good managers within such cooperative networks, however. A partner may easily notice outstanding human talents, given the typically close cooperation within such transparent arrangements. Thus, some managers may transfer between various partners. This may cause stress in the cooperative mode of the network, and the partners usually do well not to overdo such raiding of one another's talents.

For licensing types of cooperative arrangements, loyalty division similarly does not tend to be a major issue. Technical advisors "on loan" from the licensor will usually remain loyal to the licensor. If a technical advisor remains in an assigned advisory capacity for too long, however, loyalty may diminish. Therefore, to avoid "defections," it may make sense to rotate key technical advisors on a regular, scheduled basis.

Loyalty issues may become problematic in joint cooperative projects with permanently complementary roles by the parents. Employees are ordinarily "on loan" from the parent organization and usually expect to return to the parent after some time. At the same time they must be "loyal" to their temporary assignment if it is to succeed. This may involve having to take positions which may go against the original parent organization's wishes. Professional integrity and judgment are key in implementing such assignments. Problem areas that may create such conflicts most typically come up regarding transfer pricing and other pricing issues. In this context, the employees must be loyal to the project organization, as a practice of professional management conduct. The parent organization must have enough maturity and cultural tolerance to understand that this type of conflict is inevitable. They must not "punish" former employees who have been involved in such divided loyalty conflicts. A mature approach on the part of the parents is necessary to prevent the development of a feeling of paranoia among key employees.

Assigned executives tend to be loyal to the cooperative venture organization in the going concern cooperative context. Most employees can expect to stay with the cooperative venture for a long period of time in this instance. They may rarely return to their old parent organization at all; in fact, if a conflict arises, they would be expected to side with the cooperative venture. In global settings, there can be a problem when a national from a parent moves to a cooperative venture in another country. Despite this reassignment, he may often be perceived as still being associated with the parent organization. The loyalty issue can then become difficult and stressful for the executives involved. A similar situation can arise when national loyalty conflicts with loyalty to the cooperative ventures business which pursues global strategies that may be at odds with strict national interests.

F. Individual Managers' Career and Benefits Planning

Individual executives must be motivated to perform their assigned strategic tasks within the cooperative venture. To achieve this, one must above all create the appearance of future career relevance and a sense of job security. Assignment to a joint venture may make one's future career appear uncertain. An employee may wonder what types of jobs will be waiting, if any, after the joint venture assignment is over, and if others who remain in the parent organization will be assigned to the interesting new jobs on a "fast-track" basis, while he is "forgotten" in the joint venture assignment. Steps must be taken to ameliorate employees' feelings of "being forgotten" by the parent while assigned to the cooperative venture. A fast-track, up-and-coming executive may feel that the joint venture assignment is a side-track, that he is "out of sight and out of mind," and that this assignment will actually impair the further development of his career. Parent organizations must offer career planning to inform up-and-coming talents of potential assignments that might be available after the joint venture. However, there must be a certain degree of formality in the career-planning system to make it credible. A clear-cut career planning approach can counter the ambiguity and riskiness associated with a cooperative venture assignment.

Joint venture assignments may require relocation, which can impact on quality of living in general. This is often expensive, may be potentially disturbing for the family, may require a change of housing, and so on. Individual managers' economic and emotional discomforts must be minimized in this respect. In a cooperative venture setting, the split decision-making roles among the parents must take this issue into consideration. An executive must be able to maintain the employee benefits he would have accrued in the parent organization. Thus, the individual manager should not feel he is losing salary, retirement benefits, bonus eligibility, fringe benefits, and so on; he should be able to draw on these benefits after he temporarily leaves for the joint venture. How these career planning and benefits issues apply to each of the four archetypes will be considered next.

Within the project-based type of cooperative venture, the individual executive's career outlook and incentives will have to be closely aligned with the administrative procedures of each parent organization. The temporary nature of the project-based organization may present a problem for the individual who desires to grow, unless his parent organization provides a sensitivity to offering stimulating opportunities for further individual growth by giving the executive the opportunity to transfer to a meaningful new job within the partner's organizations or to another project-based venture assignment. The compartmentalization of jobs into free-standing temporary organization assignments should not engender a lack of willingness to implement career planning within the overall system. This overall view must override the somewhat narrower temporary organizational focus.

For a licensing type of cooperative venture, the licensee must motivate its employees to support the implementation of the license agreement. This can be facilitated by implementing a career development plan within the licenses organizations. The licensor must similarly ensure that it motivates the advisors working with the licensees to approach these jobs without fearing that they are being exploited or side-tracked. This group of executives must not feel that they are "out in the cold" and have reached an organizational dead end. Systematic job rotation schemes must be utilized for these advisors.

In the cooperative ventures with permanently complementary roles by the parents, the executive must, above all, have a strong feeling of job security. These strategic projects often involve temporary assignments, which might engender uncertainty and anxiety in the employees, as to what type of jobs they will go to next. Many of them will have to find entirely new jobs outside the present cooperative organizational network. The temporary nature of these assignments must not cause so much anxiety and perceived loss of job security that the employees become dysfunctional. Career planning seems essential here so that the employee knows what he is coming back to.

The career planning of the employees in the jointly owned business organization should be tied in with the joint venture organization itself. Here too, an employee should be given the opportunity to return to the parent organization if he so wishes, to avoid the fear of stagnating within the joint venture organization or of being deprived of promotional opportunities elsewhere in one of the parents. However, he must decide quickly whether he wants to stake out his career in the parent or the joint venture. It is important to be explicit regarding preference and expectation for the broader or narrower career tracks.

Concluding Comments

In conclusion, the human resource management function will at times differ quite dramatically in cooperative venture contexts compared to that of the better known, wholly owned corporate settings. Further, the human resource function may differ dramatically among different types of cooperative ventures, such as between the four types of cooperative ventures which have been identified.

In a project-based type of cooperative venture, the human resource management function will largely be carried out by each partner in a "compartmentalized" manner and largely on behalf of their own organizational entities. However, the strategic human resource management functions must be coordinated to some degree, particularly in the attempt to develop a relatively homogenous type of value system in approaching central dimensions of the cooperative project business, when it comes to attitude towards such as quality, competitiveness in securing follow-on projects, and so on. Also, the establishment of a common communication style can be a major determinant to success. This can be enhanced by allowing for consultation among the parents regarding such issues as dealing with biases in human resource assessments, allowing for broader career opportunities, and so on.

A similar type of quite separate human resource management arrangements among the partners will have to be made in licensing-type cooperative agreement settings. However, the human resource management groups of the licensor and licensee must find ways to cooperate to a certain extent, above all, in the assignment of advisors to the licensee.

The human resource function will probably also to some extent be dealt with independently by each parent in the cooperative venture with permanently complementary roles by the parents. In this setting there must, however, be solid coordination between the various human resource management functions of the parents, so that a common organizational approach can be established, which is functioning with the necessary compatibility among members' styles. A separate parallel human resource management function may have to be established within the cooperative venture itself, complementing the parents' human resource management capabilities.

Finally, regarding the jointly owned ongoing cooperative venture business, a strong, full-fledged human resource management function will have to be established within the joint venture itself. This function will have to find ways to work closely with that of each parent, however, particularly during the first years. The human resource function within the joint venture must gradually encourage the development of new human resource capabilities which can enhance the strategic progress of the joint venture.

Overall, the human resource management function within all types of cooperative ventures will have to attempt to undertake two types of tasks. First, it will attempt to assign and motivate people in appropriate ways, so that the value creation within the cooperative venture will proceed as well as possible. To create such an arrangement requires particular attention to job skills, compatibility of styles, communication compatibility, and so on. Second, human resources will have to be managed strategically. This means that human resources will not only have to be allocated with a view towards the needs of the cooperative venture activity, but also with a view towards potential repatriation to a parent, to be used later in other contexts for other strategic purposes. As such, the cooperative venture must be seen as a vehicle to produce not only financial rewards, but also managerial capabilities, which can be used later in other strategic settings.

References

Beer, Michael, Spector, Bert, Lawrence, Paul R., Mills, D. Quinn, and Walton, Richard E. *Managing Human Assets*, New York: The Free Press, 1984.

Chakravarthy, Balaji S., "Human Resource Management and Strategic Change: Challenges in Two Deregulated Industries," *Wharton School Working Paper*, Philadelphia, 1985.

Fombrun, Charles, Tichy, Noel M., and Devanna, Mary Anne. *Strategic Human Resource Management*, New York: John Wiley & Sons, 1984.

Henderson, Bruce C. *Henderson on Corporate Strategy*, Cambridge: Abt Books, 1979.

Lorange, Peter. *Corporate Planning: An Executive Viewpoint*, Englewood Cliffs: Prentice-Hall, 1980.

Lorange, Peter. "Cooperative Strategies: Planning and Control Considerations," to appear in Hood, Neil, and Walne, Jan-Erik, *Strategies in Global Competition*, Chichester: Wiley, 1986a.

Lorange, Peter. "Cooperative Ventures in Multinational Settings: A Framework," to appear in Johanson, Jan, and Hallen, Lars, *International Markets as Networks*, Sweden: Uppsala, 1986b.

Tichy, Noel M. *Managing Strategic Change*, New York: John Wiley & Sons, 1983.

13

Strategic Alliances, Organizational Learning, and Competitive Advantage*
The HRM Agenda

Vladimir Pucik

Strategic Alliances and Competitive Collaboration

Partnerships and alliances between two or more multinational firms are becoming increasingly common. Recent examples include AT&T's cooperation with Olivetti and IBM's links with Matsushita in office automation equipment; a tripartite venture of Honeywell, Bull, and NEC in computer mainframes; Philips and AT&T's alliance in telecommunications; Toyota and General Motors' joint manufacturing at NUMMI; or General Electric and Fanuc's worldwide collaborative network in robotics. New strategic alliances are not limited to the manufacturing sector, they are increasingly frequent in the financial sector (e.g., the joint venture of Credit Suisse and First Boston Corporation or the tie-up of Nippon Life and Shearson Lehman) and other service industries as well.

Some of the new alliances are clearly short-term in nature (e.g., General Motors and Toyota); others aim for a long-term strategic synergy between

Human Resource Management, Vladimir Pucik, copyright © Spring 1988, Vol. 27, Number 1, pp. 77–93, by John Wiley & Sons, Inc., reprinted by permission of John Wiley & Sons, Inc.

such alliances with increasing frequency (Harrigan 1985; Perlmutter and Heenan 1986). The rationale and the scope of international alliances are becoming increasingly complex (Contractor and Lorange 1988; Root 1988).

In the past, alliances were seen primarily as a means to reduce capital investment and lower the risks associated with entry into new markets. Ties between firms were also formed in order to secure fast and reliable access to previously closed markets, or to respond to a government's preference (formal or informal) for local participation in the business (Leontiades 1985). Today, the rationale behind the formation of new alliances in most cases is related to the increasing speed of technological change and the rapidly growing competitiveness in global markets. Partners join in order to diversify risks inherent in developing new technologies or to take advantage of the complementarity of each partner's developmental skills (Hergert and Morris 1988). The new partnerships can also provide essential economies of scale and market power to withstand a dominant competitor whom neither partner can challenge individually (e.g., international alliances in the computer industry targeted at IBM).

Strategic alliances can take many forms: technical exchange and cross-licensing, co-production and OEM agreements, sale and distribution ties, joint product development programs, or creation of joint venture firms with equity distributed among the partners. Such a functional classification of alliances, however, does not say much about their competitive context. To understand the strategic logic of the new partnerships and the implications for human resource management, it is essential to consider the changing patterns of global competition. In contrast to traditional single-market joint ventures between large multinational firms and much smaller local firms, the new alliances are often formed by partners of comparable strength whose activities are often global and who are or may become direct competitors (Contractor and Lorange 1988).

The rapid increase in international partnerships among competitors does not necessarily imply the heralded dawn of a new cooperative era in the global economy (Ohmae 1985; Perlmutter and Heenan 1986). The change from competitive to collaborative strategies is often merely a tactical adjustment aimed at specific market conditions. Many of these new partnerships should be viewed as a hidden substitute of market competition, not its dissipation. The objective is similar: attaining the position of global market leadership through internalization of key value-added competencies. The potential competitive relationship between partners distinguishes strategic alliances that involve *competitive collaboration* from more traditional complementary ventures (Doz et al. 1986).

The strategic and managerial implications of the two types of alliances are fundamentally different. In a truly cooperative relationship the underlying assumption is the feasibility (and desirability) of long-term win/win outcomes.

In the partnerships that involve competitive collaboration, the strategic intent of achieving dominance makes the long-term win/win outcome highly unlikely. This does not imply that all partnerships between multinational firms are always competitive in nature. However, many of them are, especially when seen in a long-term dynamic context. Partnerships that involve competitive collaboration are dynamic in nature. The relative endowment of resources, skills, and competencies and the sources of bargaining power can change over time. For one firm to be able to sustain its long-term competitive advantage, the organization and control of the partnership has to reflect its competitive context.

Another way to look at strategic partnerships is to examine the source of leverage exercised by the individual partners. In this sense, strategic alliances may be classified into those leveraging *resources* and those leveraging *competencies*. The cross-licensing, technical agreements, joint development programs (pooling of resources), and co-production or co-distribution (resource economies of scale) are examples of alliances that focus primarily on resource leverage. The resources contributed to a partnership usually have a specific market value, be it land, equipment, labor, money, or patents. Both the contribution and withdrawal of resources are explicit and thus relatively simple to control.

In contrast, competencies are fundamentally information-based invisible assets (Itami 1987) that cannot be readily purchased and their market value is difficult to ascertain. Examples are management and organizational skills, knowledge of the market, or technological capability. Invisible assets are embodied in people within the organization. These assets represent a tacit knowledge that is difficult to understand and that only can be appropriated over time, if at all (Teece 1987). Accumulation of invisible assets is seen as the foundation for a sustainable competitive advantage (Itami 1987).

Invisible assets are closely linked to information, its stock as well as its flow. To increase invisible assets is to increase the amount of information available in the firm as well as its capacity to handle the information. Invisible assets can be accumulated through an explicit action, such as training, or implicitly as a by-product of daily operations (Itami 1987). Alliances that leverage competencies usually take the form of an OEM supply agreement or a joint venture aimed at a specific market. Superior competencies in different parts of a value chain are combined to achieve a distinct competitive advantage in the market, or at least to protect market position against a superior joint competitor.

Table 13.1 summarizes a classification of international partnerships that considers the competitive context and the source of leverage. While the issue of strategic control as related to the distribution of benefits from the alliances is important in all four quadrants of the strategic alliance matrix, it is especially critical in quadrants III and IV that represent conditions of competitive col-

Table 13.1 Strategic alliances, strategic context, and source of leverage

| | | | SOURCE OF LEVERAGE | |
			RESOURCES	COMPETENCIES
S				
T	C	COMPLEMENTARITY	I.	II.
R	O			
A	N			
T	T			
E	E	COMPETITION	III.	IV.
G	X			
I	T			
C				

laboration. Implicit in a competitive collaboration is the risk that benefits from the alliance may be accrued asymmetrically by the respective partners. The process of appropriation is influenced by the characteristics of organizational assets leveraged in the partnership.

Obviously, in most cases, strategic alliances involve the contribution and leverage of both visible and invisible assets. The type of contribution can be different for each partner. Nevertheless, the traditional management focus is concentrated on the control of visible assets. In complementary partnerships, lack of attention to the accumulation of invisible assets may erode the competitive advantage derived from the venture. However, in the context of competitive collaboration, where competencies provide the critical leverage (quadrant IV), lack of attention to invisible assets may result in a loss of control over the direction of the alliance. It is for this reason that management processes that support accumulation and control of invisible assets are of such critical importance.

The distribution of benefits related to visible assets, such as new products or profits, is relatively easy to monitor. Protection against asymmetry can be instituted through administrative protocols and rules regarding the implementation of the partnership agreement. However, the asymmetric appropriation of invisible benefits—such as the acquisition of product or market know-how for use outside of the partnership framework, or even to support a competitive strategy targeted at the partner—cannot be easily protected. The asymmetry results from the internal dynamics of the strategic alliance. Benefits are appropriated asymmetrically due to differences in the *organizational learning capacity* of the partners. The shifts in relative power in a competitive partnership are related to the speed at which the partners can learn from each other. Not providing a firm strategy for the control of invisible assets in the partnership, and delegating responsibility for them to operating managers concerned with short-term results, is a sure formula for failure.

A good illustration of such a process is the reversal in the competitive relationship between Japanese and Western firms in many industries over the last several decades. The asymmetrical distribution of benefits from these alliances often was the fundamental cause of such a reversal. Japanese firms used access to technology through licensing or joint ventures to master new competencies, and then used the newly acquired knowledge to gain sole control of the market in Japan and even penetrate markets previously dominated by the Western partners with their own superior products. The list of firms (e.g., Allied/Bendix, General Electric, General Foods, International Harvester, Philips, Renault, USX, Westinghouse) that gave up more than they gained is long and is not limited to a single country or industry.

While other factors contributed to the high failure rate of Western joint ventures in Japan (Wright 1979; Zimmerman 1985)—such as policies of the Japanese government that at least until the mid-1970s made it difficult for Western partners to achieve bargaining power parity—much of the imbalance in the appropriation of benefits was caused by disparities in learning between Japanese and Western partners. Many Japanese firms have developed a systematic approach to organizational learning (Cole 1985; Nonaka and Johansson 1985). This approach involved more than an explicit rejection of the parochial "not-invented-here" syndrome. Japanese firms put in place managerial systems that encourage extensive horizontal and vertical information flow and support the transfer of know-how from the partnership to the rest of the organization. The policies guiding the management of human resources at all levels and functions constituted a vital part of such a learning infrastructure (Pucik 1983).

The organizational capability to learn is the key to protect competitive advantage in competitive collaboration and to control the strategic direction of the cooperative venture. An organization has many tools to manage the process of learning (Hedberg 1981), but in principle, the learning ability of an organization depends on its ability to accumulate invisible assets. As invisible assets are embodied in people, policies regarding human resources are critical to organizational learning. The objective of the HRM activities is to complement line management in providing a supporting climate and appropriate systems to guide the process of learning. Organizational learning results from a combination of hard and soft organizational practices anchored in specific HRM techniques.

Human Resource Management and Obstacles to Organizational Learning

Organizational learning is not a random process. Preventing an asymmetry (or creating an asymmetry in one's favor) in organizational learning must be the key strategic priority for human resources executives in multinational firms engaged in strategic alliances. Removing the organizational obstacles to learning is closely linked to the strategic priorities of the human resource function and its involvement in the design and management of the strategic partnership. However, this strategic priority is often buried under the pressure of daily operational concerns. The key obstacles to organizational learning identified from research on Western joint ventures in Japan (Pucik 1988) are listed in Table 13.2.

The obstacles to organizational learning reviewed in greater detail below are not limited to a specific organizational climate that can easily be changed.

Table 13.2   Obstacles to organizational learning in international strategic alliances

HR FUNCTION	KEY OBSTACLES
HR PLANNING	• Strategic intent not communicated • Short-term and static planning horizons • Low priority of learning activities • Lack of involvement by the HR function
STAFFING	• Insufficient lead time for staffing decisions • Resource-poor staffing strategy • Low quality of staff assigned to the alliance • Staffing dependence on the partner
TRAINING AND DEVELOPMENT	• Lack of cross-cultural competence • Unidirectional training programs • Career structure not conducive to learning • Poor climate for transfer of learning
APPRAISAL AND REWARDS	• Appraisal focused on short-term goals • No encouragement of learning • Limited incentives for transfer of know-how • Rewards not tied to global strategy
ORGANIZATIONAL DESIGN AND CONTROL	• Responsibility for learning not clear • Fragmentation of the learning process • Control over the HR function given away • No insight into partner's HR strategy

Rather, they result from a complex set of HR practices and policies that, while often rational in the short term, may ultimately lead to a loss of control over the destiny of the partnership, if not to the loss of the entire business. Understanding the obstacles to learning is the first step in the process of restoring competitive balance.

Human Resource Planning

Strategic intent not communicated throughout the firm. Most alliances take place in a highly complex competitive environment. The desirability of cooperation may easily be perceived differently among various parts of the organization, depending on their level of involvement in the creation of the alliance and their responsibility in executing the strategy. Top management often emphasizes the cooperative nature of the new alliance, partly to set the right tone for the partnership, partly to break down any resistance from those opposed to the cooperative strategy. What is often not made clear are the boundaries of cooperation and the specific nature of the missing competencies that led to the alliance in the first place.

Short-term and static planning horizon. Planning of the alliance is often driven by short-term contingencies, such as an improvement of profitability by cutting production costs through an OEM arrangement, without considering long-term effects on the sustainability of the firm's competitive advantage. General Electric's recent withdrawal from the consumer electronics field was forced by a series of "correct" short-term decisions during the previous two decades that led to a transfer of critical product and process competencies from GE to its competitors. The logic behind many short-term decisions assumes that the existing balance of competencies in the alliance will not change with time.

Low priority given to learning activities. The traditional focus of business plans is on the utilization of and the return on tangible assets. The projected outcomes from the partnership are scrutinized in terms of returns on equity invested, savings from pooled research and development, cost reductions from outsourcing components and products, and/or increases in sales from added distribution channels. However, the accumulation of invisible assets, such as experience regarding the production process, intimate knowledge of the market or relationship with customers, is not evaluated, as traditional planning systems cannot assign a financial value to these outcomes. Activities that cannot be evaluated in financial terms are generally not funded. Organizational learning is left with no support.

Lack of involvement by the human resource function. In the rush to launch the alliance, insufficient attention is given to a critical evaluation of the learning capacity of the organization and to the steps necessary to upgrade the learning skills and learning climate appropriate for the new venture. Often, the human resource function does not play any role in the negotiation process or becomes involved only at a very late stage. The compatibility of philosophies regarding the management of human resources between the partners and its implications for organizational learning are seldom a factor in the decision-making process.

Insufficient lead time for staffing decisions. When the alliance involves a creation of a new organization, staffing decisions regarding the key representatives should be made well in advance of the conclusion of the agreement; all relevant future players can thus be involved in the negotiation process. Institutional memory breaks down when negotiators are replaced by implementors without continuity. Insufficient lead time also forces shortcuts in training for the managers to be assigned to the partnership. In general, everyone agrees with the idea of training, but many firms are reluctant to invest in the preparation of managers for the new venture until the outcome of the business negotiations is clear; yet after the deal is signed, there is no time to train. As a result, what is won laboriously at the front end through long, arduous bargaining is often lost through the inability to control implementation of the partnership agreement.

Resource-poor staffing strategy. As the motivation for the alliance is often driven by cost consideration, firms cut expenses by limiting the size of managerial staff assigned to the partnership. In particular, this can be observed in alliances that have the major location of their activities overseas, where the cost of expatriates seem prohibitive. Yet, while the expense of staffing a position in an overseas venture can be substantial, such economizing does not consider two substantial benefits derived from expatriate posts: improved control over the management process in the venture and ability to transfer skills from the venture into the home organization. Organizational learning often requires at least some slack resources. When an overextended management team just keeps on dousing fires, the last thing on a manager's mind is the transfer of know-how.

Low-quality of staff assigned to manage the alliance. It is often the case that after the initial period of high visibility for the new alliance, management positions in the partnership become a dumping ground for sidetracked executives. The emphasis is on "making the deal," not on its implementation. The dispatched managers don't have the necessary learning skills; they are expected to "watch the books" only. Even if they gain new knowledge, they may lack the credibility to effectively transfer the know-how to the parent firm, especially if this involves challenging existing "sacred cows." The partners in the alliance are generally well aware of the low skill and credibility level of these mangers and do not hesitate to freeze them out of the important decisions.

Staffing dependence on the partner. When staffing is considered a cost rather than an investment, it is very tempting to go along with the offer by the partner to assume the responsibility for staffing the new venture. Naturally, there is always a greater concern over the composition of the top management team. However, very little learning ever occurs in the boardroom: learning takes place in the laboratories, on the production floor, and in interactions with the customers. The partner who controls positions critical to the accumulation of invisible assets gains substantial leverage over the direction of the alliance. Short-term excursions will not do; long-term participation is essential. As GM learned at NUMMI, a videotape of new work practices is a far less efficient learning tool than hands-on experience.

Training and Development

Lack of cross-cultural competence. Many managers and staff involved in international partnerships do not have sufficient intercultural skills (language competence, familiarity with partner's culture, etc.). Expatriates are dispatched abroad with no or limited training at best, with the assumption that knowledge of the business should compensate for the lack of cultural understanding. While the partner's perfect fluency may not be essential, the ability to understand the basic flow of a business conversation and to interact informally with the customers and employees should be the minimum prerequisite for an international assignment. This is important for an expatriate's effectiveness, even in a wholly owned foreign affiliate (Tung 1984); the price to pay for the lack of cross-cultural skills in an alliance may be higher: both inability to learn and inability to control.

Unidirectional transfer of know-how. One of the most effective means of learning is through temporary personnel exchange between the partners. However, this exchange is often asymmetrical, especially when the partnership takes the form of a joint venture. While the flow of personnel from the Western joint ventures in Japan often includes staff temporarily seconded from the Japanese parent, the training assignments in the opposite direction are infrequent (Pucik 1988). Even when transfer of personnel into the joint venture occurs on a regular basis, it is seldom for the purpose of skill acquisition. Rather, staff is transferred either to control or manage the joint venture or to serve as a conduit for transferring know-how into the venture. It is often felt that there is no need to learn (and thus expend resources) on knowledge already possessed in the joint venture. Yet, by gaining independent know-how, a firm can avoid becoming hostage to the uncertain future of the partnership.

Career structure not conducive to learning. Personnel exchange can have a positive impact on the amount of accumulated knowledge only if administered in a consistent and planned fashion over a period of time. Unless the firm posts the returnees from the partnership ventures into positions where the acquired know-how can be effectively used and disseminated, the invisible asset accumulation will not be possible. The amount of time spent learning and transferring know-how is the critical constraint. An effective transfer of know-how requires a long-term commitment of qualified personnel, which clashes with expectations of fast mobility among the most promising executives. While many managers (on a personal basis) may benefit even from a relatively short assignment abroad, a single short-term assignment—especially when it comes relatively late in an executive's career—will not do much for the accumulation of invisible assets in the rest of the organization.

Poor climate for transfer of learning. A large amount of critical invisible assets is embedded in the staff involved in the partnership. To what degree these assets are shared with the parent depends largely on the parent's receptivity to new ideas and on the quality of the interaction between the cooperative venture and the parent firm. When learning from the outside, in particular from abroad, is seen as an admission of weakness, the receptivity will be poor (Westney 1988). The ossification of the learning infrastructure reflects the low priority given to the accumulation of invisible assets in the execution of a company's strategy. Low receptivity to inputs from the partnership will naturally encourage a passive attitude towards the transfer of knowledge among the partnership staff. This tendency is further reinforced if the socialization activities in the partnership are controlled by the local parent, as is often the case in Western joint ventures in Japan.

Appraisal and Rewards

Appraisal focused on short-term goals. Organizational learning is fundamentally a long-term activity, stretching far beyond a typical one-year appraisal time frame. Also, the costs associated with learning are immediate, while the benefits (most of them difficult to quantify under standard accounting procedures) are accrued over time. Support for organizational learning thus may have a negative impact on the short-term measurements used to evaluate a manager's performance. The expectation of short tenure in a given job is another critical constraint. The pressure to get immediate results forces managers to economize on expenditures with long-term payoffs, no matter how attractive such payoffs may be. The issue is not sacrificing profits for abstract learning, but forfeiting a long-term superior performance in order to inflate short-term results.

No encouragement of learning. With little or no rewards given for contributions to the accumulation of invisible assets, learning becomes a "hobby," not a prerequisite of the job. In many leading Japanese and Korean firms, the cross-fertilization of skills across functional areas is actively encouraged, and both foreign language ability (tested by the company) and familiarity with principal foreign markets are considered before promotion to an executive position. In contrast, the skill base of typical Western managers is rather narrow, as are their intercultural skills. Even in firms with decades of experience in the Far East, only a handful of managers speak any of the local languages and have a first-hand knowledge of local conditions. In a joint venture, asymmetry in the distribution of skills will result in an erosion of competitive advantage and the loss of leverage.

Limited incentives for transfer of know-how. The reward systems in many multinational firms encourage hoarding of critical information, not sharing it. Information is treated as a source of power, not as a resource. Smart managers assigned to an international joint venture, who otherwise may expect few opportunities for upward mobility, can make themselves indispensable by blocking the flow of information. Such a behavior is not only tolerated, but these "valuable experts" are often rewarded in terms of superior compensation and considerable operational autonomy. Any increase in information concerning the activities of the partnership outside of their own domain is seen by these managers as a threat to their power. In an alliance that involves competitive collaboration, the other parent and some of the company's own managers may share an interest in limiting the transfer of know-how.

Rewards not tied to global strategy. Performance of executives assigned to manage a partnership venture is often appraised solely on the basis of results in a limited business area or market. There is very little incentive for the "core" partnership staff to worry about the competitive conditions facing other businesses of the distant parent. These managers have nothing to gain from allocating scarce resources to organizational learning benefiting an organization in which they have no tangible interest. This tendency is especially pronounced if these managers are actually dispatched from the other "competing" parent. In such a case, their attitude towards transfer of competencies can easily turn from conservative to downright hostile.

Organizational Design and Control

Responsibility for learning not clear. Who gains and who loses from a strategic alliance often depends on the vantage point. A "win-win" partnership strategy on a corporate level often entails a "win/lose" scenario at the business unit or business function level. For example, a shift from captive manufacturing to an OEM partnership may contribute to immediate cost reduction and thus enhance the product's position in the market while the production competence is eroded. Under such conditions, incentives and responsibility for learning may become unfocused. When competencies are lost, operation managers blame faulty strategy while the corporate staff cites incompetent implementation.

Fragmentation of the learning process. In diversified, complex firms, the stakes in organizational learning may differ by business unit and function. Each subunit has only a partial view of the exchange of competencies involved in the partnership. The perceptions of the potential value of the relationship may therefore differ, as will the commitment to support competencies needed to defend the long-term competitive advantage. In firms with decentralized business units (e.g., SBUs), organization-wide learning activities have low priority in comparison to a business unit's immediate needs.

Control of the HR function is given away. The HR function is seen as a cost burden, not as a powerful tool of control over the strategic direction of the partnership. In particular, when the alliance involves a venture inside the new partner's territory, responsibility for the Human Resource function is often delegated to the partner. In fact, the very possibility of utilization of the partner's know-how concerning the local labor market conditions is often a factor leading to the creation of the alliance in the first place. However, what is gained in lowering the cost of entry may be lost over time, as control over human resource deployment enables the partner to control the patterns of organizational learning, thus the distribution of benefits from the partnership.

No insight into partner's HR strategy. The learning strategies of the partner can be monitored through the control of personnel exchange between the joint operations and the parent. The objective is not to stop learning, but to gain understanding about the direction of the partner's learning strategies and its long-term impact on the balance of power in the collaborative relationship. However, when personnel control is abdicated in favor of the partner, the logic of the learning process is obscured. The boundary between the partner's organization and the partnership operation becomes fuzzy and impossible to control. Valuable competence may leak without notice and without reciprocity. A learning asymmetry is again likely to occur.

HRM Agenda in
Competitive Collaboration

The challenge of competitive collaboration creates a new agenda and new priorities for the management of human resources. This challenge can't be avoided by staying away from strategic alliances. The economic forces in the environment will continue to push firms into more complex sets of global relationships. Those who learn from these relationships will survive; the others will perish. The organization's ability to learn (or the lack of it) will influence the shape of the global markets for many years to come.

Experience shows that the competitive balance in strategic alliances, and in joint ventures in particular, cannot be controlled through structural solutions. The successes and failures of the alliances are often embedded in the same organizational context (Killing 1983). Neither can symmetry in the appropriation of benefits from a partnership be protected through legal clauses. The complexity of international commercial law and rapid technological change make legal protection impractical. In fact, the reliance on legal means to safeguard the company interests can be counterproductive as it encourages "we-are-safe" attitudes and thus decreases the stimuli to learn.

The accumulation of invisible assets, be it manufacturing competence, market know-how, or global coordination capability, should be explicitly recognized as a value-enhancing activity. It is dangerous to act as if the existence of a partnership permits lowering commitment to the maintenance and expansion of core competencies. Such a strategy assumes that the partner is unwilling or unable to learn and thus unable to alter the long-term bargaining power regarding the appropriation of benefits. In the context of competitive collaboration, such an assumption is unsupportable. It also does not make sense to set up barriers to learning. Artificial constraints imposed on information flow in the partnership may hinder its ability to sustain its competitive advantage and thus erode the competitive position of both parents. The only sustainable response is a proactive policy encouraging organizational learning that, at minimum, matches, if not surpasses the learning ability of the partner. Everything else is an inferior solution.

A number of specific agenda points for the HR function in firms engaged in international strategic alliances can be drawn from the experience of firms that continuously incorporate organizational learning into their competitive strategy:

1. *Get involved early.* The human resource function should be involved in the formation of the strategic alliance from the early planning stages. In a dialogue with the appropriate line functions, HR staff should assume responsibility for the development of a thorough organizational learning strategy. It is essential to precisely identify the critical value-added learning activities in a given business and the means to control them. The objective is to support and expand core competencies essential to sustain the long-term competitive advantage of the firm.

2. *Build learning into the partnership agreement.* In order to maintain a long-term symmetry in the distribution of benefits from the partnership, both parties have to learn simultaneously. The process of parallel learning can and should be made explicit. An attempt to prevent the partner from learning is most likely fruitless, as organizational learning is impossible to police. Instead, provisions should be made in the agreement to safeguard the reciprocity in the transfer of competencies (e.g., personnel exchange).

3. *Communicate strategic intent.* As a part of its responsibility for corporate communications, HR should cooperate with operational managers to assure that the strategic intent with respect to the partnership is adequately communicated to the employees. Training programs should be developed to prepare managers to deal effectively with the am-

biguity and complexity of strategic alliances. The competitive context has to be made explicit: hushing it up does not fool anybody but your own employees.

4. *Maintain HR input into the partnership.* The control of the HR function in partnership operations, such as joint ventures, should not be bargained away, as it is within the boundaries of such an entity that much of the learning occurs. Once the partnership agreement is concluded, the HR function should continuously monitor the congruence between the learning strategy and the operational HR activities related to the launching and the implementation of the agreement. Periodic reviews of the learning process should be set up with the participation of top management.

5. *Staff to learn.* The accumulation of invisible assets should be the key principal guiding the staffing strategy. Staffing and development plans should be established to cover the existing blind spots. Such an approach may require a considerable investment in the development of core competencies within the parent firm through a carefully calibrated transfer policy. Some attrition must be considered inevitable. In joint ventures, this also means the development of a local staff that is fundamentally loyal to the joint venture entity and has no vested interest in blocking the transfer of critical information. While the immediate costs of the "staff to learn" program may be high, they are far smaller than the long-term negative consequences of lost competence.

6. *Set up learning-driven career plans.* From an individual perspective, effective learning and transfer of competencies span the entire career. While cross-cultural learning is most effective during the early career stages, functional learning and its effective application may require considerable business experience. In the context of international partnerships, this may imply a necessity for multiple assignments, which is seldom done at the present time. A greater use should be made of reciprocal trainee programs. The notion that all expatriates should be managers is obsolete.

7. *Use training to stimulate the learning process.* Three kinds of training activities can create a better climate for learning. First, in internal training, managers should be made aware of the subtleties involved in managing collaboration and competition at the same time. Second, open communication and trust within the partnership is essential for the smooth transfer of know-how. Team-building and cross-cultural

communication training should be offered regularly at all management levels. Finally, any training program geared to the acquisition of a specific competence should be, in principle, reciprocal. This diminishes the incentives for opportunistic behavior.

8.   *Responsibility for learning should be specified.* In order to create a climate receptive to learning, a specific responsibility for learning should be written into business plans for managers transferred into the partnership operations as well as those in the receiving units. It should be made clear who is responsible that the information actually flows as intended, in necessary quality and speed, and what supporting mechanisms are needed to be put in place. Where appropriate, support for mutual learning should be made explicit in the partnership agreement.

9.   *Reward learning activities.* Management behavior that encourages organizational learning, such as sharing and diffusion of critical information, should be explicitly recognized and rewarded. Long-term incentives (e.g., career opportunities) should be provided to managers actively seeking to acquire new skills. The framework of expatriate transfers into critical locations must be restructured to make them more attractive without incurring prohibitive compensation costs. Dead-end assignments are costly to the organization.

10.   *Monitor the HR practices of your partner.* Throughout the duration of the relationship, attention should be given to the partner's HR activities. Beginning with an HR audit prior to the establishment of the partnership, much insight can be gained from the continuous monitoring of the partner's staffing and training. In joint ventures, the career records of staff transferred from the partner's organization should be carefully scrutinized, including their assignments after returning to the partner. It must be assumed that the partner is doing the same, as much of the necessary information is actually in the public domain.

In summary, the strategic agenda for the HRM function in firms involved in international alliances must be centered around the process of learning. In the context of competitive collaboration, the competitive advantage of a firm can be protected only through the organization's capability to accumulate invisible assets by a carefully planned and executed process of organizational learning. As this process is embedded in people, many of the necessary capabilities are closely linked to HRM strategies and practice. The transformation of the HR system to support the process of organizational learning is clearly the key strategic task facing the HR function in many multinational firms today.

References

Cole, R. E. "The Macropolitics of Organizational Change: A Comparative Analysis of the Spread of Small-Group Activities." *Administrative Science Quarterly*, 1985, 30, 560–85.

Contractor, F., and Lorange, P. "Why Should Firms Cooperate? The Strategy and Economics Basis for Cooperative Ventures, in F. Contractor and P. Lorange, eds., *Cooperative Strategies in International Business.* Lexington, Mass.: Lexington Books, 1988.

Doz, Y., Hamel, G., and Prahalad, C. K. "Strategic Partnerships: Success or surrender?," paper presented at the Conference on Cooperative Strategies in International Business, The Wharton School and Rutgers University, October 1986.

Harrigan, K. R. *Strategies for Joint Ventures.* Lexington, Mass.: Lexington Books, 1985.

Hedberg, B. "How Organizations Learn and Unlearn," in P. C. Nystrom and W. H. Starbuck, eds., *Handbook of Organizational Design.* New York: Oxford University Press, 1981.

Hergert, M., and D. Morris. "Trends in International Collaborative Agreements," in F. Contractor and P. Lorange, eds., *Cooperative Strategies in International Business.* Lexington, Mass.: Lexington Books, 1988.

Itami, H. *Mobilizing Invisible Assets.* Cambridge, Mass.: Harvard University Press, 1987.

Killing, J. P. *Strategies for Joint Venture Success.* New York: Praeger Publishers, 1983.

Leontiades, J. C. *Multinational Corporate Strategy: Planning for World Markets.* Lexington, Mass.: Lexington Books, 1985.

Nonaka, I., and Johansson, J. K. "Organizational Learning in Japanese Companies," in R. B. Lamb, ed., *Advances in Strategic Management.* Greenwich, Conn.: JAI Press, 1985, 3, 277–96.

Ohmae, K. *Triad Power: The Coming Shape of Global Competition.* New York: Free Press, 1985.

Perlmutter, H. V., and Heenan, D. A. "Cooperate to Compete Globally." *Harvard Business Review*, 1986, 64 (2), 136–52.

Pucik, V. "Management Practices in Japan and Their Impact on Business Strategy," in R. B. Lamb, ed., *Advances in Strategic Management.* Greenwich, Conn.: JAI Pres, 1983, 1, 103–31.

Pucik, V. "Joint Ventures with the Japanese: Implications for Human Resource Management," in F. Contractor and P. Lorange, eds., *Cooperative Strategies in International Business.* Lexington, Mass.: Lexington Books, 1988.

Root, F., "Some Taxonomies of International Cooperative Agreements," in F. Contractor and P. Lorange, eds., *Cooperative Strategies in International Business.* Lexington, Mass.: Lexington Books, 1988.

Teece, D. J., "Profiting from Technological Innovation: Implications for Integration, Collaboration, Licensing and Public Policy," in D. J. Teece, ed., *The Competitive Challenge: Strategies for Industrial Innovation and Renewal.* Cambridge, Mass.: Ballinger Publishing Company, 1987.

Tung, R. *Key to Japan's Economic Strength: Human Power.* Lexington, Mass.: Lexington Books, D.C. Heath, 1984.

Westney, D. E. "Domestic and Foreign Learning Curves in Managing International Cooperative Strategies," in F. Contractor and P. Lorange, eds., *Cooperative Strategies in International Business.* Lexington, Mass.: Lexington Books, 1988.

Wright, R. W. "Joint Venture Problems in Japan." *Columbia Journal of World Business.* 1979, 20 (1), 25–31.

Zimmerman, M. *How to Do Business with the Japanese.* New York: Random House, 1985.

The Comparative Context

14

Expatriate Reduction and Strategic Control in American Multinational Corporations*

Stephen J. Kobrin

Twenty years ago a visitor to an overseas subsidiary of an American firm was likely to find U.S. expatriates in most significant managerial positions. The chief executive and financial officers, as well as the heads of marketing and manufacturing, were typically Americans and it was not unusual to find expatriates in the second and third levels of management. A return to the same subsidiary today would find the situation radically changed. The visitor would have to look long and hard to find an American expatriate, and when (s)he did, the employee might well be on a very short-term assignment. There has been a dramatic and significant replacement of American expatriates abroad by local (or third country) nationals. Both managers and academics note a number of good business reasons for the replacement of expatriates by local nationals, including environmental competence and cost reduction. The sharp decrease in their number is taken positively as one more indication of the internationalization or globalization of American firms. In this chapter I dissent, arguing that the replacement of expatriates has gone too far, much further in fact than in European and Japanese competitors. Although all of

Human Resource Management, Vol. 27, Number 1, pp. 63–75, Stephen J. Kobrin, copyright © 1988 by John Wiley & Sons, Inc., reprinted by permission of John Wiley & Sons, Inc.

the reasons given for the phasing out of expatriates are valid, I suggest one that is not discussed actually dominates: the difficulty many Americans have had adapting to overseas assignments and the abysmally high failure rates they have experienced. Put simply, Americans have not been able to handle working and living in other cultures and U.S. MNCs have found it easier to replace them with foreign nationals than to make an effort to solve the underlying problem. I conclude that the cutback of expatriates has important implications for the strategic management of American multinational firms. First, if most employees are local then there are precious few who either have an encompassing knowledge of the worldwide organization or identify with it and its objectives. Second, in many diversified MNCs, personnel are a critical instrument of headquarters' strategic control and the virtual elimination of expatriates affects control adversely. Last, at least in American firms, managers have gained their international expertise on the job through overseas assignments in one or more countries. The significant reduction in these opportunities raises important questions about future sources of such expertise, and indeed whether Americans who spend their careers at home will be competent to run their own worldwide corporations.

The Replacement of American Expatriates

The evidence indicates a marked reduction in the assignment of American expatriates abroad. In a 1984 study of larger U.S.–based international firms (industrials and banks), I found that half of the companies surveyed indicated a significant reduction in expatriates in the past decade, 26 percent reported no change, and only 23 percent an increase. When asked about trends over the next ten years, 41 percent projected a continued reduction, 40 percent no change, and 18 percent an increase (Kobrin 1984, 43).

Interviews confirmed the survey results; many respondents who said that their firms used expatriates heavily in the past could count those currently abroad on the fingers of one hand and noted that most were there shortterm, to fill a specific need. (Banks, and to a lesser extent petroleum and construction firms, are exceptions as they still tend to use significant numbers of expatriates abroad.)

Tung (1982) found that well under half of the senior management positions in U.S. subsidiaries were staffed by Americans and that the Middle and Far East aside, less than 10 percent of middle management positions were held by home country nationals. A Conference Board Study (Berenbeim 1983:v) reported that 80 percent of U.S. firms surveyed employed a local national as head of a majority of country operations. In the main, expatriates have been replaced with local nationals, although there are significant numbers of third country (neither home nor host) nationals in the managerial ranks of many MNCs.

It should be absolutely clear that past over-reliance on American expatriates was neither effective nor efficient; there are a number of good reasons for their wholesale replacement with local nationals. As managerial and technical competence in many countries (developing as well as industrialized) increased, a large number of proficient managers became available. All things equal, a local national who speaks the language, understands the culture and the political system, and is often a member of the local elite should be more effective than an expatriate alien.

The cost of maintaining an American (and an American family) abroad is often prohibitive. U.S. salary levels—and often incentives—must be paid in countries where local pay scales may be considerably lower. Furthermore, other costs such as private schooling, trips home, benefits, living allowances, club memberships, and the like can become excessive very quickly. One estimate of the direct costs of expatriates is three times the domestic salary plus relocation expense (Harvey 1983).

In many countries there is pressure (explicit or implicit) to "nationalize" management. There may be regulatory limits on the numbers of expatriates that can be employed, difficulties in obtaining visas or work permits, or more subtle government pressures to train and promote local nationals. Last, over-reliance on expatriates can cause severe morale problems in subsidiaries due to home country managers' inability to deal with culturally different employees or simply because local managers feel that they are discriminated against when it comes to promotion.

On the whole, the replacement of expatriates with local nationals has been seen as a positive trend: lowering costs; increasing managerial effectiveness; minimizing conflict with both employees and environmental groups; and contributing to host country managerial and technical development. Berenbeim concludes that ". . . there is a near unanimity of opinion as to the desirability of using local nationals to manage local operations," (1983, 24). It is seen as a reflection of the maturation of American multinationals; indeed the number of foreign employees is often taken as an index of internationalization. A firm that has operations in a large number of countries and competes globally should reflect its geographical composition in its employees. In summary, the reduction in expatriates can be seen as an appropriate response to changed environmental conditions.

The Failure of Americans Abroad

There is another, less appealing explanation for the drastic reduction in U.S. expatriates: corporate experience with overseas assignments has been disastrous. Zeira and Banai (1985) summarize eight studies of failure rates of expatriates abroad that range from 30–70 percent, with higher failure rates in developing countries or relatively distant cultures such as Japan. Harvey (1983, 72) notes that "depending on the source, from 33 to 80 percent of expatriated families return to the United States before their contract expires." Although it is difficult to define failure precisely and the estimates should not be taken as hard data, it is very clear that the overseas assignment of Americans has been a difficult and costly process and one that cannot be deemed successful.

There is a large literature on expatriate selection and performance that deals with reasons for the failure of American managers abroad (see Edwards 1978; Harvey 1983; Mendenhall and Oddou 1985; Tung 1982, 1987; and Zeira and Banai 1985). Although it is not my purpose to discuss reasons for failure here, it is attributed to selection procedures—typically domestic performance (Miller 1973), inadequate preparation, and the general difficulty that individuals from an isolated environment have in adapting to different cultures.

The costs of expatriate failure are enormous in terms of direct expenses, management time, and most important, human misery. Although it is certainly a hypothesis rather than a conclusion, I argue that the high failure rate and its attendant costs have played a major role in the decision of many multinationals to reduce drastically the number of Americans assigned abroad. In the short run, it is easier to train and promote host and third country nationals than it is to select high potential candidates and expend the resources necessary to give them the attitudes and cultural skills they need to function effectively abroad. It must be noted that the problem is exacerbated by the scandalously low levels of international awareness and language competence found in graduates of American universities and business schools.

The European and Japanese Experience

Tung's extensive studies of European and Japanese multinationals provide data on both expatriate usage and failure rates that are at least consistent with the hypothesis I suggest above. In Western Europe, U.S. deployment of expatriates in senior management slots is only marginally below that of European firms: 33 vs. 38 percent. Both are well below the Japanese average of 77 percent. Once one moves to the developing countries—where there generally are lower levels of managerial and technical competence and where the cross-cultural adjustments are more difficult for Americans—the differences are considerably more striking.

In Latin America, 44 percent of senior management positions in U.S. subsidiaries were filled by home country nationals, compared to 79 percent in European firms and 83 percent for the Japanese. In the Mideast the numbers are 42, 86, and 67 percent; in the Far East 55, 85, and 65 percent; and in Africa 36, 75, and 50 percent (see Tung 1982, 61; the data are for the early 1980s).

Two points must be made. First, the comparison must take differences in managerial systems into account, particularly when comparing U.S. and European firms with Japanese. Second, I am not arguing that the levels of expatriate staffing found in European or Japanese firms are correct; rather, that the U.S. reduction may be excessive and a response to difficulty in cross-cultural adjustment rather than changed business conditions.

In a later paper (based on the same data) Tung (1987) compares American, European, and Japanese failure rates. More than half of her American respondents had failure rates of 10 to 20 percent and for an additional seven percent of the sample, a failure rate of 30 percent was reported. (She concludes that "these statistics are consistent with the findings of others that approximately 30 percent of overseas assignments within U.S. multinationals are mistakes;" Tung 1987, 117). In contrast, she found that 59 percent of the European MNCs had failure rates of under five percent, an additional 38 percent of 6–10 percent, and 3 percent of 11–15 percent. Seventy-six percent of the Japanese firms had failure rates of under 5 percent, 10 percent of the sample 6–10 percent, and 14 percent of 11–19 percent.

Tung attributes the lower failure rates among European and Japanese firms to a combination of: selection procedures; career planning; better preparation for overseas assignments; expatriate support; and in the European case, a more developed international orientation and language capability (Tung 1987). Summarizing the study, U.S. MNCs appear to have reduced use of home country expatriates to a much greater extent than their European and Japanese competitors (especially outside of Western Europe) and have had significantly greater "failure rates" in the past.

Although the evidence is much too limited to draw any general conclusions, it is consistent with my—admittedly speculative—argument. U.S. MNCs may have gone too far in substituting local (and third country) nationals for expatriates and they may have done so in response to the difficulties that Americans have had in adjusting to other cultural environments rather than for the usual reasons of effectiveness and efficiency cited above. Put directly, Americans may not have been able to handle international assignments and many U.S. firms may have "solved" the problem by virtually getting out of the expatriate business.

Replacing expatriates with local nationals certainly has a number of important benefits to both the firm and the host country. The overuse of expatriates is dysfunctional from the firm's point of view and stunts the development of local nationals as managers and of the host country economy. On the other hand, a multinational firm comprised primarily of employees who identify with the local subsidiary rather than the worldwide organization raises some major issues for strategic management and control. I now turn to those questions.

Consequences for the Global Firm

In the past few years there has been a good deal of academic and managerial attention given to the global firm and global competition (see Porter 1986 for a summary). As Porter notes, "Competing internationally is a necessity rather than a matter of discretion for many firms" (1986, 1). The pressures for international integration of strategy and operations flow from the increases in the scale of production and technology and from the need to exploit new sources of competitive advantage.

In many industries (automobiles are an example) the minimal scale of production has increased to the point where few national markets are large enough to support efficient operations. In others (such as computers) technological demands are so great that returns from even the largest domestic markets are insufficient to support adequate research and development efforts. In both instances firms must integrate transnationally to compete; they must link operations in a number of national markets to achieve the minimal scale required to produce efficiently or to remain in the race technologically. Put another way, the geographic territory required for efficient business operations is larger than that of most nation states.

Even in industries where most national markets are large enough to support efficient operations—consumer products and processed food are prime examples—there are competitive pressures for some degree of international coordination or integration; to exploit knowledge gained in one market in others and save time and lower costs (Porter 1986). Thus, many multinationals face competitive pressures to coordinate and integrate operations transnationally: they face global competition.

The world, however, is not multinational and firms must compete in an environment comprised of over 160 sovereign, territorially defined, independent nation states with very different objectives, political systems, cultures, languages, and modes of social organization. That, in turn, puts pressure on all MNCs to respond to political and sociocultural differences between markets by fragmenting strategy and operations.

The critical challenge facing managers of multinational firms is trading off pressures for integration and fragmentation: responding to what Prahalad and Doz (1981a) call the economic and political imperatives of global business. An appropriate balance must be struck between reaping the benefits of integration and responding to local conditions and objectives. I agree with Bartlett (1986) that forces for both integration and fragmentation are likely to increase in strength in the future and that firms must be able to respond to both simultaneously. That requires accurate and up-to-date knowledge of a large number of local environments, an understanding of how local conditions affect the worldwide system, and centralized integration and coordination of strategy and operations. It requires the ability to develop a global strategy, strong local management operating in a global context, and the exercise of sufficient control to insure the strategy is implemented.

A MNC is a paradox in that even the most integrated strategy must be executed by national subunits. Effective management of a diversified MNC entails exploiting the strengths and knowledge of the subsidiary within the context of the global system. Furthermore, optimization at the system level is more complex than a simple sum of local optima; the subsidiary's role is to maximize its contribution to worldwide objectives rather than local returns. Given the complex environment of the MNC, there may well be a conflict between achieving local and systemwide objectives.

That implies that at least a core of managers simultaneously understand and identify with the global organization and are knowledgeable about, and sensitive to, local differences. It also implies some means of exerting control over geographic and (often) culturally diverse subsidiaries.

The reduction in expatriate assignments by U.S. MNCs means that most employees of the firm are part of, and identify with, a single local unit. The exceptions are headquarters managers who, at least in theory, identify with the corporation as a whole. However, to the extent that they are home country nationals with limited international experience, their outlook is likely to be ethnocentric and narrow. That may be the case in many U.S. MNCs, as data from the early 1980s indicates that only about one-third have even one foreigner who is a top manager and that the median percentage of top executives with foreign experience is only 15 percent (Berenbeim 1983, 16, 19).

The sharp reduction in expatriate assignments in U.S. MNCs raises four issues for strategic management and control: (1) identification with firm-wide rather than local objectives; (2) knowledge of, and identification with, the global organization; (3) corporate control of local subsidiaries; and (4) acquisition of international expertise by home country nationals.

Identification with Firm-Wide Strategic Issues

To a local national who works in a subsidiary the corporation as a whole is an abstraction. The manager's task environment is immediate and it is local performance that matters. As noted above, corporate–subsidiary strategic conflict is not exceptional in an MNC, particularly one that is integrated transnationally. A subsidiary, for example, may want to export but be prohibited from doing so by headquarters because of potential intra-organizational conflict, underutilization of other facilities, or the like. Sourcing decisions may be systemwide, even though they conflict with established relationships with local suppliers or involve a higher cost to a given local unit. Manufacturing may be rationalized, limiting a subsidiary to component production, or it may even be shifted entirely to meet the more important demands of another host country.

Corporate–subsidiary conflict can be exacerbated by local government demands for control and autonomy; it may well object to shifts in the locale of manufacturing or from final product to component assembly. Although the conflicts are unavoidable, and any manager—regardless of his or her experience—has some tendency to identify with the immediate task environment, it is critical that some core of managers in the MNC, who influence subsidiaries' strategic decisions, identify with the global task environment: with the corporation as a whole.

It is obvious that home country expatriates are only one means of accomplishing this end. Furthermore, I am not suggesting that U.S. MNCs return to the practice of staffing all of the important managerial posts in subsidiaries with Americans. Rather, I am trying to point out some of the costs of the sharp reduction in use of expatriates by U.S. firms. I will deal with these points in more detail in the following section.

Identification with the Worldwide Organization

The replacement of expatriates with local nationals increases the difficulties MNCs face in creating informal organizational links across subunits. Although any diversified corporation serving a large geographic area faces problems of this sort, the MNCs are exacerbated by larger geographic distances, time changes that make direct social communication via telephone more difficult, and especially cultural and linguistic differences.

To the extent managers are hired by, and spend most—if not all—of their careers in the local subsidiary, there is a greater tendency to see managers from other subsidiaries or headquarters as alien, as "they." Although many American expatriates were not well integrated into subsidiaries and were perceived as alien, they formed a core of international managers who had personal links worldwide. While that network tended to exclude local employees, it did serve as a corporate-wide informal organization. Its function—without its discrimination against local nationals—is essential in a MNC.

This problem takes on particular importance as MNCs attempt to organize in ways that facilitate formulation and implementation of global strategies. Bartlett (1982) argues that the complex strategic problem facing MNCs—the need to be simultaneously globally competitive and national responsive—makes a single structural solution problematic. Rather, he views organization of the MNC ". . . as an adaptive evolutionary process rather than as a series of powerful, and sometimes traumatic, reorganizations" (1982, 26).

He argues for open and flexible cooperative arrangements that are difficult to achieve through formal organization. "The subtlety and complexity of a flexible multidimensional decision-making process appears difficult to achieve solely (or even primarily) through formal organizational change" (1982, 32). Rather, by focusing on transfers, assignments, careers, and meetings, senior management shifts its means of influence from the formal to the informal structure.

Several points are relevant. First, MNCs have had a great deal more difficulty with global organization than with global strategy. Second, one does not have to go as far as Bartlett to accept that informal organizational links are critical in MNCs and that there are very significant barriers to establishing them. Extensive direct social contact is required to overcome organizational conflicts and cultural/linguistic differences.

Personnel moves and assignments within the firm, including temporary assignment of host country nationals to other units and short-term transfers or significant and repeated travel, are critical. Managers within the MNC must get to know and trust one another, despite the very real barriers to doing so. However, it is also critically important that home country nationals—who for better or worse are more likely to rise to the senior corporate ranks—develop informal linkages throughout the corporation. Again, assignment of home country expatriates abroad *alone* is not a sufficient, effective, or fair solution to this problem. However, by drastically reducing expatriates—to the point where they are rare in many firms—management has given up an important instrument of policy and control.

Control

The control problems faced by any large diversified organization are exacerbated in the MNC. First, as noted above, the geographic and cultural distances between subunits are significantly greater in the international firm. Second, differences in political and legal jurisdictions may well place limits on subsidiary responsiveness. Third, subsidiaries tend towards autonomy: many MNCs built up international organizations through acquisition of previously independent firms, and even where subsidiaries have always been owned by the parent there was typically a polycentric period with little headquarters control exercised.

Prahalad and Doz (1981a) address control problems in MNCs, arguing that as subsidiaries mature, resources such as capital, technology, and access to markets no longer provide an adequate basis for headquarters control. Rather, MNCs must create an organizational context that blends structure, information systems, measurement and reward systems, career planning, and a common organizational culture.

As do others, they argue that managers in a global firm must balance conflicting pressures for integration and fragmentation (in their terms, economic and political imperatives). They suggest three organizational mechanisms that substitute for resource-based control: data management, managers' management, and conflict resolution (1981b). The second concerns managerial selection, career paths, development, and socialization. The third concerns mechanisms for integration and coordination mechanisms. In short, strategic control in a mature multinational depends on control over personnel and the informal organization.

It is difficult for any manager in a MNC to strike an appropriate balance between integration and national responsiveness. Headquarters managers may well underestimate the importance of local social and political factors and place too much emphasis on standardization and rationalization. On the other hand, local nationals may well feel caught between conflicting corporate and local interests. It may be hard for them to transcend their cultural and political background and strike an appropriate balance between integration and national responsiveness. They may find themselves allied with local policy makers against corporate headquarters.

There are mechanisms other than home country expatriates that allow headquarters to gain control: career planning, development, and assignment of local nationals can certainly play a role as can other socialization mechanisms. However, a core of international employees—third as well as home country nationals—simplifies problems of strategic control through personnel and facilitates the socialization needed to build a common organizational culture worldwide. Expatriates will not (and should not) automatically identify with home vs. host country; rather at their best, they should be able to assess local interests in the context of global strategy and identify with the worldwide organization. One can not deny, however, that they are more likely to be responsive to the objectives of headquarters management than host country nationals who spend their entire careers in a subsidiary. They are clearly a more effective vehicle to exercise control through personnel.

Acquiring International Expertise

Most American managers who become internationalized do so on the job; they acquire cross-cultural expertise, language skills, and knowledge about other countries' social, political, and cultural systems as a result of travel and overseas assignment. A mailed survey and interviews of managers in large, U.S.-based international firms (Kobrin 1984) indicates that very few managers with international responsibilities began their careers as internationalists. When asked to evaluate sources of their international expertise, less than 16 percent said that Peace Corps, government, military, or religious service abroad was an important factor, and less than 15 percent felt that education—graduate or undergraduate—was important.

The vast majority of managers said that they acquired their international expertise from either business travel or assignment abroad. Many, if not most, of the managers I spoke with who were committed internationalists had served tours of duty abroad. It is important to note that over half were not "volunteers"; they went abroad at the request of the company. A surprising number recalled how their first expatriate assignment had changed their lives; how living and working abroad had enlarged their horizons and generated excitement about other cultures and languages.

In summary, very few managers in American MNCs were internationalists as a result of pre-career experience. The vast majority gained their commitment and knowledge on the job, particularly through assignment abroad.

American managers can gain international expertise through university and mid-career education, travel that involves serious intercultural interaction and a systematic attempt to learn, or in a number of others ways. To this point, however, the primary vehicle for doing so has been assignment abroad. As the decline in expatriate assignments has resulted in a significant reduction in opportunities for medium- or long-term tours abroad, the typical manager (in all but a few industries) will not have that opportunity during his or her career.

Conclusions

In this chapter I have argued that: (1) there has been a sharp reduction in use of expatriates by American MNCs; (2) the abysmally high failure rate among Americans assigned abroad—reflecting the difficulties of many managers in making cultural adjustments—is as, if not more, important an explanation than the positive reasons usually cited; (3) the cutback has gone further than in European and Japanese firms; and (4) the reduction in expatriates has resulted in costs in terms of identification with the global strategy and organization, control, and the internationalization of managers.

The multinational firm is a paradox; regardless of how globally integrated the strategy, it must be executed by local units that are inherent parts of a given social, cultural, political, and economic system. A core of expatriate managers can offset this centrifugal tendency, as their primary identification is corporate rather than local. Furthermore, they can have a "multiplier" effect as they can help internationalize local management, develop knowledge of and identification with the corporation as a whole, and help spread and institutionalize the corporate culture.

In theory, there is no reason that home country nationals have to participate in this process. As the firm's sales and profits become increasingly international, one would expect employees from an increasingly large group of nations to play an important managerial role. The core of expatriates could be comprised of third country nationals assigned to headquarters often enough to assimilate corporate culture and objectives and develop the contacts necessary for the informal organization to develop.

In practice, I wonder if American MNCs and the U.S. economy would be willing to tolerate the logical results of that strategy. To the extent that international expertise is a requisite for top managerial jobs—and it is far from clear that all managers agree that it is—fewer and fewer Americans would qualify. U.S. MNCs would face the choice of having top management dominated by foreign nationals or promoting unqualified individuals on the basis of citizenship.

I would hope that as U.S. firms become global competitors that managerial selection would take place on the basis of qualifications regardless of nationality; that any individual joining the company in any country in the world would have the same chance of becoming CEO. However, unless the expertise obtained from overseas assignments is gained in other ways, Americans may simply become unqualified for top management roles in the future.

I am not recommending that the old model of quasi-permanent corps of long-term U.S. expatriates be resurrected. Rather, that the corps of expatriates served a number of important functions and their placement on the endangered species list leaves a vacuum that must be filled. I do feel that there is increasing value to expatriate assignment as firms become global competitors and that a means must be found to provide this experience to as many managers as possible. That would probably involve shorter-term expatriate assignments whose purpose is avowedly developmental—for both the individual and the organization.

References

Bartlett, C.A. "Building and managing the Transnational: The New Organizational Challenge," in Michael E. Porter, ed., *Competition in Global Industries*, 367–404, 1986.

Bartlett, C.A. "How Multinational Organizations Evolve." *Journal of Business Strategy,"* Summer 1982, 20–32.

Berenbeim, R.E. *Managing the International Company: Building a Global Perspective*. New York: The Conference Board, 1983.

Edwards, L. "Present Shock and How to Avoid it Abroad." *Across the Board*, February 1978, 36–43.

Harvey, M. G. "The Multinational Corporation's Expatriate Problem: An Application of Murphy's Law." *Business Horizons*, January-February 1983, 71–78.

Kobrin, S.J. *International Expertise in American Business*. New York: Institute of International Education, 1984.

Mendenhall, M., and Oddou, G. The dimensions of expatriate acculturation: A review. *Academy of Management Review*, 1985, 39–47.

Miller, E.L. "The International Selection Decision: A Study of Some Dimensions of Managerial Behavior in the Selection Decision Process." *Academy of Management Journal*, 1973, 239–252.

Porter, M.E. "Competition in Global Industries: A Conceptual Framework," in Michael E. Porter, ed., *Competition in Global Industries*. Boston: Harvard Business School Press, 1–60, 1986.

Prahalad, C.K., and Doz, Y.L. "An Approach to Strategic Control in MNCs." *Sloan Management Review*, Summer 1981a, 5–13.

Prahalad, C.K., and Doz, Y.L. "Headquarters Influence and Strategic Control in MNCs." *Sloan Management Review*, Fall 1981b, 15–29.

Tung, R.L. "Selection and Training Procedures of U.S., European, and Japanese Multinationals." *California Management Review*, Fall 1982, 57–71.

Tung, R.L. "Expatriate Assignments: Enhancing Success and Minimizing Failure." *Academy of Management Executive*, Summer 1987, 117–26.

Zeira, Y., and Banai, M. "Selection of Expatriate Managers in MNCs: The Host Country Point of View." *International Studies of Management and Organization*, 1985, 33–51.

15

New Challenges for Japanese Multinationals*
Is Organization Adaptation Their Achilles Heel?

Christopher A. Bartlett**

Hideki Yoshihara

The doubling of the stock of Japanese foreign direct investment between 1980 and 1986 provides clear evidence that Japanese multinational companies (MNCs) are at a critical juncture in their development. Spurred on by mounting political pressures, fast-developing competitive forces, and a plunging dollar, many of the best known of these companies are in the process of radically and rapidly altering their global posture.

Over the past decade, most have made some important transitions: from export-based strategies to ones based more on substantial foreign investment; from a concentration on less-developed and newly industrialized countries towards a major presence in the industrialized developed nations; and

Human Resource Management, Vol. 27, Number 1, pp. 19–43, Christopher A. Bartlett and Hideki Yoshihara, copyright © 1988 by John Wiley & Sons, Inc., reprinted by permission of John Wiley & Sons, Inc.

**We would like to acknowledge the helpful comments of Sumantra Ghoshal, Kichiro Hayashi, Nitin Nohria, M. Y. Yoshino, and an anonymous reviewer.

from a centralized management philosophy to one emphasizing more localization and delegation. Suddenly, their international organizations have been transformed from a tight Japanese core with a scattering of assembly plants in developing countries, to a much larger worldwide network of complex, integrated, self-sufficient national companies.

Yet, even in companies that were at the vanguard of the Japanese export invasion of overseas markets, there often seems to be a remarkable lack of understanding about the international operating environment and little sophistication in the management of the newly evolving worldwide organization. In many ways, their current problems are similar to those of their American counterparts when they were building their international organizations in the immediate postwar decades. But in addition to the limitations of an ethnocentric perspective, the Japanese manager must also overcome the huge obstacle presented by an organizational system that is strongly rooted in Japanese culture, and in many ways is ill-suited to the newly imposed internationalization task.[1]

In the process of undertaking a broader study comparing the organizational structures, processes, and capabilities of European, American, and Japanese MNCs, we were asked by some Japanese managers to describe the nature of the challenge they faced, to draw some general conclusions, and to make broad recommendations for action. Drawing on data obtained from our sample of Japanese companies—some of the country's largest and most successful MNCs—we have tried to define the nature and sources of some of their common problems, and outline some approaches to resolving them.

Although the analysis and recommendations directly concern Japanese companies, the findings also have relevance for managers of American and European companies. In recent years, much has been written about the Japanese organizational forms and management processes as the source of their outstanding success.[2] Our study of some of their leading MNCs, however, indicates that their organization may represent a major impediment to the global restructuring of their operations. This is important for Western managers to understand since it is creating a strategic window of opportunity for them in the battle for global market share. In some sense, the battle has shifted to one of organizational capability, and those companies first able to overcome the challenges of managing a globally integrated organization while retaining their market sensitivity and innovative flexibility will have a major advantage.[3]

The chapter starts with a brief assessment of the traditional approaches and existing capabilities of Japanese companies, and evaluates them against the emerging challenges in the international environment. After identifying some constraints and barriers to effective response to these new demands, we propose some actions to overcome the problems, drawing on the experiences of some of the companies we studied.

Japanese MNCs:
Traditional Approaches

All multinational companies (MNCs) are partial captives of their historical development and their national origin, but until recent years most Japanese companies have been pretty comfortable prisoners. The pattern and timing of their international development and the influence of their national culture have been important contributors to their outstanding success in the international environment in the postwar era.

For many reasons—for example, the country's geographic and political isolation and the late arrival of the industrial revolution—Japanese companies expanded internationally somewhat later than their European and American counterparts, although many had engaged in some earlier efforts to capture incremented export sales to neighboring Asian markets. It was only when the postwar domestic boom slowed that most Japanese companies began to regard overseas expansion as an important element in their strategy.[4]

When internationalization finally gained momentum within these companies, some unique Japan-bound institutional and cultural factors encouraged most of them to expand primarily through export rather than through foreign investment, as the Europeans and Americans had done in an earlier era. First, the drive for international expansion was motivated in large part by companies' need to ensure the continued advancement of employees in their domestic organization. In a system of lifetime employment, growth was the engine that fueled organizational vitality and self-renewal, and export orders became an important element of that growth. Second, the Japanese management system was so culture-dependent that it tended to impede the development of international investments. Even beyond the obvious language barriers, the basic decision processes were built on an assumption that participants with shared values could engage in intensive face-to-face discussions and negotiations—conditions difficult to achieve where managers were continents apart.[5] Finally, through historical good fortune, trading companies were well-established Japanese institutions that had far more overseas knowledge and contacts than almost any manufacturer. Their existence facilitated the development of exports, and reduced the need for companies to establish strong foreign operations of their own.[6]

While these various internal factors were shaping the decision of most Japanese companies to build their international operations primarily through export, external forces were reinforcing this approach. Most basically, Japan's Ministry of Finance (MOF) had to approve all overseas investment, and at least until the late 1960s, were strongly biased towards upstream natural resource projects and downstream trade-related operations rather than offshore manufacturing investments.[7]

But such policies were not too damaging to most companies since an export strategy based on assets, expertise, and strategic control concentrated in Japan fit perfectly with the international environment of the time. GATT negotiations had brought tariffs to their lowest levels in half a century. Revolutions in air travel, telecommunications, and shipping caused transport and communications barriers to crumble in the 1960s and 1970s. At the same time, new product and process technologies, the rising cost of R&D, and shortening product life cycles were all reinforcing the need for global scale economies.[8]

As a result, in consumer electronics, automobiles, office equipment, electronic components, industrial machinery, and many other industries, Japanese companies with strategies based on standardized products, global scale operations, and central control were able to take market share from European and American MNCs. Having expanded abroad in an earlier era of high tariffs and logistical barriers, these more mature international companies had built their operations on a foundation of independent national companies offering products developed and manufactured for their local market. To respond to the new environmental conditions, these well established Western MNCs had to scramble to redesign their products, rationalize their manufacturing facilities, and establish control over their various national operations. Unburdened by such diverse and independent worldwide organizations, most Japanese companies found their centralized Japanese organization configurations to be a source of great strategic advantage.

International Trends: Emerging Challenges

The various globalizing forces that emerged in the immediate postwar decades and dominated the competitive environment of the 1960s and 1970s, continued to exert their influence into the 1980s. In recent years, however, these forces have been joined and to some extent counter-balanced by some other trends that have emerged, at least in part in reaction to the powerful impact of the globalizing forces of the previous era. These new trends present a challenge to the strategy and management processes of those companies that followed centrally driven global strategies.

In contrast to the earlier influences that favored larger global scale manufacturing operations, such as those developed in Japanese companies like Toyota, Komatsu, and Canon, the recent trend towards flexible manufacturing processes employing robotics, computer-aided design and manufacturing, and other emerging technologies, has had the effect of reducing minimum efficient scale in many industry segments. In the words of Mr. C. J. van der Klugt, President and Chairman of the Board of Management of Dutch electronics giant, Philips, "The debate about global products will be short-lived when flexible automation becomes the dominant production technology."[9]

Perhaps as important as their impact on manufacturing scale has been the way in which these new technologies have allowed a broadening of the range of product variations that can be produced efficiently. As Mr. van der Klugt points out, "Basic models . . . will easily be able to be translated into more individualized models." This reinforces a market trend that is also emerging in the 1980s. Perhaps reacting to an overdose of homogenized and standardized global products, consumers have begun to demand products more tailored to their specific needs. A Matsushita manager explained that in response to this shift away from standardized items, his company was being forced to produce more models in smaller runs. In tape recorders, for example, the company had doubled the number of offered models since 1976, but sales per model had declined 60% in the same period. "Increasingly, we are having to grasp the consumers not en masse, but as target groups—even down to the individual," he said.

The trend towards more locally differentiated products is reinforced by the growing importance of software in a large number of industries—from telecommunications to computer to consumer electronics. This trend is requiring companies to adapt standard hardware-oriented products into hardware plus software systems and services that need to be much more sensitive and responsive to local market differences.

Coupled with a continually accelerating product life cycle, the need for more flexible and differentiated products and systems gives an important competitive edge to companies that are closest to their markets. Those with sensitive, flexible, and responsive product development and manufacturing capabilities close to the consumer, often have an advantage over those relying on globally standardized products from distant and inflexible global scale plants. It is through following such an approach, for example, that the upstart British company, Amstrad, has been able to build a major market position against established global competitors, right at the time when the low-cost Japanese companies were trying to establish positions in the U.K. as their beachhead for a broader European attack.

But the most important countertrend of the late 1970s and 1980s has been the reactions of many national governments to the dramatic success of the global companies, and particularly to the Japanese. In the 1960s, large MNCs may have held "sovereignty at bay," to quote Vernon's classic phrase, but by the late 1970s, national interests were certainly striking back.[10] Faced with the rapid penetration of their markets by foreign-source products shipped by efficient global companies, many countries began to bend, sidestep, and even ignore trade agreements in their attempt to stem the import flood. The trend spread from developing to industrialized countries, and even the United States, long the champion of free trade, began negotiating orderly marketing agreements and voluntary trade restraints with Japan.

Well into the 1980s, the political stakes kept rising. Those companies that responded to mounting protectionist pressures by increasing the number of local assembly plants found themselves facing still tougher host government demands. Through increasingly sophisticated industrial policies, governments began to intervene more in companies' foreign investment strategies. So-called "screwdriver plants," set up to assemble knock-down kits, have become an unacceptable way to circumvent the trade barriers. Local content laws, technology transfer requirements, and a host of other national legislation is designed to force global companies to move an increasing part of their value-added operations into the host country, and establish themselves as truly local national entities.[11]

The combined impact of these emerging forces has been dramatic. Under pressure to adapt their export-based, centrally controlled operations, Japanese companies have made major commitments to expanding their overseas operations. The rapid rise in the value of the yen in recent years (going from a dollar exchange rate of 239 yen in the fourth quarter of 1985 to 159 a year later) has only made the need to change their dependence on a Japan-centered sourcing strategy more urgent.

As their overseas operations become larger, more diverse, and increasingly complex, many Japanese companies will begin feeling the need to modify old organizational structures and management processes to allow them to manage the new reality. The managers we talked to recognized that the key success factor in this massive reorientation of their international strategy was their ability to surmount the substantial barriers that lay in the way of the required organizational adaptation.

Barriers to Response

Like the European and American companies that met the same challenges in an earlier era, the Japanese companies that are becoming true multinational companies in the 1980s are facing barriers to the adaptation of their strategy and structure. In the sample of companies we studied, we were conscious of three major impediments that seemed common to all of them—the constraints of the Japanese organization processes, the limitations of the traditional strategic assumptions, and the barriers due to management mentality.

Japanese Organization System

We described earlier why the discussion-intensive, group-oriented characteristics of the Japanese management system fit well with the requirements of a centralized export-based strategy. The classic process of *nemawashi* (consensus building) and *ringi* (shared decision making) required close physical proximity and shared cultural values.[12] As an increasingly important part of the company's asset base and task responsibilities were shifted offshore, however, strains began to appear. Unlike the more systems-oriented approach in American-based companies, this people-dependent and communication-intensive management process is not easily stretched over barriers of distance, time, language, and culture.

In the companies we studied, there were two key ingredients that allowed their management processes to operate internationally—a group of Japanese managers who knew the company, its strategies, and processes, and were willing to go abroad as the linkages in the worldwide organizational process; and a travel budget and logistical arrangement that allowed these widely dispersed managers to engage in the intensive discussions and negotiations that were at the center of the management system of each of these companies.[13]

Kao, the leading Japanese branded package goods company, provides a good illustration of this dependence on the use of individuals to link the organization. Despite the modest size of its overseas operations—small soap and detergent companies in seven southeast Asian countries and a couple of larger industrial operations in Spain and Mexico—this company has a cadre of sixty expatriate Japanese managers and technicians running overseas operations with only 2000 employees. This is more than double the number of American expatriates its U.S.-based competitor Procter and Gamble has in an international business with total sales over twenty times larger. More significantly, all of the top management positions in Kao's overseas companies and most of the level below that are Japanese nationals; in P&G only five of the 44 subsidiary general managers are American. A similar contrast can be made between Matsushita and 3M. The former has over 800 expatriates in an international business with 40,000 employees; the American company has less than 100 expatriates to manage its 38,000 foreign employees.

As the size and complexity of foreign operations has grown, the need for expatriate managers has increased. But, for many companies, demand is outstripping supply. Takeda, the chemical and pharmaceuticals company which had deliberately created and nurtured a large pool of employees for overseas postings, now finds many of them are uninterested in future international assignments. The contributing causes are numerous. Overseas allowances to compensate for differences in foreign salary levels have shrunk, numerous examples of managers losing career opportunities due to being out of touch with headquarters have surfaced, and the strain on families has become clear, particularly when wives stay at home to ensure children receive a good Japanese education. The problem has become so widespread that the expression "escaping from overseas banishment" has achieved currency in the business jargon common among Japanese managers today.

The operation of the Japanese management system internationally has also become strained by pure logistics. The need for detailed information sharing and intensive face-to-face consultations and negotiations has led Japanese companies to spend huge amounts on travel and communications. In 1984, for example, NEC Japan personnel made over 10,000 overseas trips. Companies are becoming increasingly aware of the substantial financial and human cost that such intensive travel is placing on their organizations. Indeed, many feel that managers are already stretched beyond reasonable limits, but without any other means of coordinating their worldwide operations, they are obliged to expand this system of "jet age *nemawashi*," as one manager called it.

But there is another side to the limitation of the Japanese management system in the international environment. To participate in the system one needs a thorough understanding of the complex culturally based decision processes, an established internal network of contacts, and an ability to communicate intensively in Japanese. The very nature of the system makes it virtually impenetrable to non-Japanese except at the periphery, and even then, in the most superficial way.[14] In almost all Japanese MNCs, the core of the decision-making process remains purely Japanese. Because of this, many foreigners recognize that not only is their career advancement limited to the national organization, but even there, they must operate in an environment in which their influence and power is often constrained. The lower starting salaries and slower promotion process prescribed by the Japanese system also serve as major barriers to entry for most individuals considering joining foreign affiliates of Japanese companies. In the words of one disillusioned American manager in the U.S. subsidiary of a large Japanese company, "It is ironic that the very factors that have made this company's management of its production workers abroad so successful (participation in decision making, job security and advancement opportunities, and an egalitarian attitude) all seem to be missing from their treatment of management. I am becoming very doubtful that I can look forward to a satisfying career here."

As a consequence, several of the Japanese companies we studied had experienced difficulty recruiting and keeping the most talented individuals for their foreign operations. This, in turn, reinforced the Japanese managers' inclination to keep parent company expatriates at the center of all key decisions, and a vicious cycle was established.

Institutionalized Strategic Roles

The classic Japanese company's pattern of international expansion from Asian countries to other developing nations, and finally to industrialized markets, influenced the perception of the appropriate strategic role and organizational responsibilities that could be assigned to overseas units. By concentrating first in developing markets, companies found it relatively easy to meet local demands with the more basic and mature products that had succeeded in the Japanese market. Sony's international business was built on the base established by its ubiquitous transistor radio; Komatsu found ready acceptance for its all purpose bulldozer; Kao could sell its basic soap and detergent lines. Although all of these companies tried to be sensitive to local market needs and to modify their products where necessary, there was little need to challenge the established product technologies and marketing approaches, and local sales companies became the delivery pipelines for products and strategies developed at the center.

Similarly, when manufacturing began to move offshore, the first plants were simple assembly operations built in response to the demands of host governments in the developing countries that had provided the first export markets. Matsushita's approach was typical: it set up plants with equipment it either built or specified, trained local workers in manufacturing techniques it developed, and supplied the operations with components and subassemblers it manufactured in Japan. The limited supply of skilled managers in many of these companies meant that expatriates took most key positions, and the company found it easy to direct, support, and control such operations from the center.

This proved to be such a successful means of managing that some of the strong strategic assumptions that emerged in this phase of development became institutionalized.[15] Among the most powerful was the conviction that the center's role was to direct, support, and control the activities of foreign operations. Under this assumption and practice, overseas companies became dependent units whose role was to implement corporate directions.

As these companies expanded into more developed countries, the situation changed dramatically. There was an ample supply of sophisticated managers and technical people, the markets were at least as advanced as Japan's and sometimes more so, and the feasibility of supporting, directing, and controlling a larger number of more diverse, more sophisticated national operations became questionable. Yet, in many companies, the institutionalized assumptions and practices were hard to break. Many of the companies we studied tried to sense and respond to the market, technological, and competitive environment of the developed country from the center, just as they had done so successfully for less developed markets. But the new situation was infinitely more complex, more diverse, and more dynamic than before, and the center's capacity and capability to perform the task were soon overloaded.

NEC is one company that has successfully emerged from these constraining assumptions, as later examples illustrate, but only after it's learned from the problems they caused in the early years of its U.S. telecommunications operations. While the company's central product development group was concentrating on an electronic switch based on an analog system, a strong preference was emerging in the U.S. for digital technology. Although NEC management in New York tried to communicate their perception of the developing "digital fever," it was only after the enormously successful market penetration by its Canadian competitor, Northern Telecom, that the central group finally began work on a digital switch.

Even after developing hardware that was more responsive to the more advanced U.S. market, the fact that NEC had concentrated its major software capability in Tokyo to serve worldwide market needs continued to constrain its viability. The telecommunications systems and market needs in North America were so different that there were almost continuous requests on headquarters for major software changes. But the Tokyo group resisted such demands and even when they did agree, it took a long time to communicate, interpret, and negotiate every change between the U.S. and Japan. As a result, NEC's early reputation in the North American market was a company with excellent hardware but unadapted software.

However, the problems associated with the strategic dependence of subsidiaries on the center were not limited to the decreased efficiency of centralized direction and control and the limited capacity of headquarters to support more complex and demanding overseas activities. We also saw evidence of motivational problems as managers in overseas companies became increasingly frustrated by their constrained roles and limited responsibilities. Yet, as indicated in our earlier argument, the Japanese organizational systems locked them out of headquarters management processes and prevented them from working to change the assumptions, even when the capabilities of the foreign operation seemed to indicate that a different role and relationship would be appropriate.[16]

For example, when Matsushita acquired Motorola's TV operations in the U.S., the operation had a strong R&D capability. Within the first year after acquisition this group had developed a synthesizer tuner that was adopted by the parent company for worldwide models. However, the U.S. group became frustrated when ten Japanese engineers arrived to provide direction and coordination with Matsushita's main development departments in Japan. They soon recognized they were out of the mainstream of development, and felt they had lost much of their freedom. Within a short period of time half the group had left, including most of the best engineers, and the flow of innovations from Motorola stopped. The group took on a local design and production engineering role. The assumption that only central groups could provide innovation and leadership became a self-fulfilling prophesy.

Even in many developing countries, subsidiary company managers felt they had matured to a stage where they could assume substantially more responsibility, and the headquarters assumption of their strategic dependency became increasingly frustrating. Some managers in Matsushita's Asian operations told us they resented the fact that the Japanese domestic plants would retain the production of the newest products and guard the latest technologies. By collaborating with three other local companies, Matsushita's Taiwan joint venture even went as far as to develop independently its own picture-in-a-picture TV, not only to ensure it has the technology, but also to prove that it had the capability to do so.

The constrained strategic role of overseas subsidiaries has also had unfortunate political repercussions for many Japanese MNCs. Widespread perceptions of corporate imperialism led to anti-Japanese riots in southeast Asia in the early 1970s.[17] The lingering presence of such perceptions presents a continuing risk for Japanese companies operating in developing countries, where some have regarded dependency as being synonymous with exploitation.[18] One manager in a South American subsidiary complained that new products and new programs came down from Japan so fast that they had no time to think or question them. Besides, they had no significant spare resources to make changes, and little opportunity to influence central strategy: "We feel a bit like the peasant woman whose husband ensures her loyalty and fidelity by keeping her barefoot and pregnant," he said.

Despite these numerous operational, motivational, and even political problems and pressures, the persistence of this headquarters-dominated strategic posture is still a widespread phenomenon in Japanese MNCs. It is embodied in their culturally bounded centralized decision processes; it is reinforced by the accumulation and concentration of assets, resources, and skills in the home country; and it is defended by the many vested organizational interests whose power base rested on their ability to support and control overseas operations.

Constrained Management Mentality

The third barrier we saw impeding the adaptation of some Japanese companies to the new international forces was one that had also represented an important problem for their European and American counterparts. It related to a management mentality that resisted the need to change Japanese products, strategies, or organization approaches to accommodate the diverse and changing international demands. Even in some of the most globally oriented companies in Japan, we were surprised to find managers whose attitudes reflected a view of the emerging international changes not as sources of new opportunity or even as normal environmental developments to which the company had to adjust. Rather they seemed to be viewed as destructive forces to be resisted, since they were forcing the company to compromise its existing efficient operations and its effective organizational processes.[19] Such narrow views and ethnocentric biases have developed as a result of a long history of management isolation from international business. They were reinforced by the insulating effects of the strong cultural aspect of their management systems, and for some, became justified by the initial success of their companies using such an approach in international markets.

As a result, the localization programs introduced by many large Japanese companies were often undertaken under sufferance, primarily in response to government pressure for greater local content or increased local employment. Rarely at the middle management level did we see a recognition that such changes could actually offer major strategic benefits for their companies. In Toray, the large Japanese textile company, the international managing director fought a long hard battle to convince management to build a new polypropolene film plant in the U.S. He is now engaged in an even more difficult struggle with corporate technical staff, who insist that the new plant must be operated strictly on Japanese lines. Yet increasingly their European and American competitors were recognizing that by dispersing their assets and resources they could capitalize on some important yet underutilized potential assets. Perhaps the most important was an exposure to a wider range of stimuli (consumer needs, technological changes, competitive actions) that could trigger innovative responses. Equally important was the improved access such operations provided to a worldwide pool of management talent and technological skills—some of the scarcest of all management resources.[20] In many Japanese companies, parochial management attitudes impede the full exploitation of such potential benefits.

For example, as Kao expanded aggressively in East Asian markets during the 1970s, top management emphasized the importance of contributing to the national economies in which it operated. But while the company made every effort to employ locals, build local plants, and even transfer its mature technology, the strong tradition of competing through technologically superior products and highly efficient operations led most managers to regard these companies as little more than foreign appendages that gave the company local market access. Thus while the localization of assets, responsibilities, and resources continued to build capabilities in the overseas operations, such newly developed capability went underutilized. In contrast, Unilever's management had long regarded its overseas companies in even the least developed countries as important sources, both of new ideas and management personnel. Its Turkish subsidiary developed a vegetable oil equivalent of the middle eastern clarified butter product, *ghee*; its Indian company adapted advanced detergent technology to local stream-washing practices by developing a process to make detergent bars to replace the dominant bar soap product. In such an entrepreneurial subsidiary environment, local management was developed into a valuable corporate resource, who were transferred throughout the company and promoted to the most senior corporate positions.

In recent years, however, many of these narrower traditional management views began to broaden and the ethnocentric biases began to break down. Unfortunately, they have been replaced, at least in some quarters, by a more disturbing trend in management attitudes—a growing management chauvinism, or even in some cases, arrogance. Fed by the phenomenal success of many Japanese companies abroad, some managers we interviewed questioned the need to change either the existing management processes or the strategic posture of their companies' international operations. Younger managers, in particular, seemed convinced that the Japanese way of managing was superior and should not be compromised. Many whose management experience was concentrated in the last decade appeared to have taken to heart the popular slogan "Japan as number one," and developed an attitude that a winning team should not change its approach.[21]

Whether due to limited international exposure or a chauvinistic inflexibility, such mentalities in the managers of Japanese multinationals represent important barriers to their companies' adaptation. As we will discuss in the next section, they are barriers that are difficult to break down.

Prescriptions and Recommendations

As the foreign direct investment statistics so dramatically indicate, the transformation of Japanese multinational enterprise is already in full swing. As foreign subsidiaries become larger, more sophisticated, and more strategically important, the question facing most companies is not whether to, but how to manage the emerging reconfiguration of assets and redistribution of responsibilities. High on the list of priorities for most managers in Japanese MNCs are questions relating to the three important barriers to internationalization we identified. Drawing heavily on the lessons and experiences of the companies we observed, but also adding our own normative suggestions where we observed gaps in current practice, we have drawn up a brief list of recommendations and prescriptions for Japanese managers as they attempt to meet these challenges.

Open the Organizational System

The first and most basic barrier we identified was one that is culturally built into the Japanese management system. We do not suggest that companies abandon their consensus-building values and their group-oriented processes. We do, however, suggest that these processes be made a little less impenetrable by "outsiders." Such changes will not be made quickly or easily, but unless companies begin to make some effort, they will remain culture-bound captives of their ethnocentric biases.

There are two important thrusts to this approach: one is to educate the non-Japanese and provide them with knowledge, contacts, and opportunity to enter the company's management processes; the second is to create the conditions within the company to allow foreign managers to become legitimate participants in the on-going processes.[22]

The task of educating foreign managers in ways that will help them gain access to their Japanese company's systems should begin at the point of their employment—in the company's overseas operations. The most basic step is to provide employees with some form of formal education on the norms, practices, and values of the company. Matsushita represents a good example of a company that has taken steps to ensure that all new employees worldwide are exposed to an education program to inform them of the company's philosophies, beliefs, and practices. All foreign employees are exposed to training built around a series of video tapes that have been prepared in Japanese, English, Spanish, and Chinese. Topics include the company's overall philosophy, manufacturing practices, personnel management, and marketing approaches.

If the acculturation process stops there, however, there is a risk that many employees may be left with some knowledge of a new system that is greatly different from anything they have had experience with before, and a vague feeling that they will never be able to penetrate it. More than theoretical knowledge, the non-Japanese needs the tools to help enter the systems and the experience of operating in it. Ideally, he or she should become proficient in Japanese, but the reality is that the language is difficult and few develop the proficiency to participate in the complex and subtle discussions that lead to decisions in the Japanese system.

But while none of the companies we studied was successful in developing any kind of Japanese language fluency in their overseas operations, they found that just offering regular language and culture classes had two important side benefits. First, it gave non-Japanese managers a basic communication skill that led to a greater sense of social ease with their Japanese colleagues.[23] Perhaps more importantly, by offering such programs to their management, they sent a signal of their willingness to break down barriers and include them in the mainstream of the decision processes.

The language barrier is only the first that must be overcome, however, and the next important step in opening the management system to non-Japanese is to ensure that the tight internal social systems do not routinely exclude them from the daily business processes. In most Japanese companies, there are formal and informal mechanisms that have tended to institutionalize the exclusion of non-Japanese from the decision process. "Contact positions" staffed by Japanese whose main task is to communicate back to headquarters can short circuit linkages between local managers and the parent company; after-hours meetings of expatriate Japanese managers to discuss the day's activities can become the real decision-making forum; and the practice of having expatriate Japanese make most visits to headquarters alone or perhaps with foreigners tagging along in token roles can reinforce the image of local managers being the periphery. To different degrees, in every company we studied, the non-Japanese were very aware of—and highly frustrated by—such exclusion from the management mainstream. Many had become cynical and viewed those discussions and decisions in which they were involved as charades, designed to reach conclusions already agreed by their Japanese colleagues over late night drinks or received in a telex from Tokyo. Unfortunately, there were many occasions in which such assumptions were correct.

Because of the larger number of expatriates typically used by Japanese companies, the temptation to develop a two-tiered management system and parallel communication channels will always be great. However, working around local management rather than with them is not only extremely demotivating, it is also highly inefficient. As the local nationals become more familiar with the system's processes and norms, and as they develop more contacts and relationships, it is important to leverage their knowledge and expertise by bringing them into discussions and negotiations on key issues early, and by ensuring that their involvement is real and not token. Companies serious about doing so can help ensure it occurs by making their expatriate managers understand that their success in doing so is regarded as important as their achievement in the marketplace.

But foreigners will never be integrated into the Japanese system until they have contacts and credibility in the parent company headquarters. Building such relationships takes time and persistence, as managers at Sony have discovered. Twelve years after it first established regular quarterly meetings between top managers in its Japanese and American companies, the company feels it is only now beginning to achieve good communications. For this reason, it is important that key foreign managers are brought to Japan frequently not just for brief visits, but also for extended stays of several months, and when possible, for even longer term assignments. They must be given the opportunity not only to meet but also to work with their Japanese counterparts. Although they may never build up the network of personal relationships that a Japanese manager would have, they can at least penetrate the ranks and overcome the perceptions of being an "outsider."[24]

Ajinomoto, the Japanese giant, is one company that has tried to achieve this objective as part of its training program. The company brings most foreign technicians and some managers to Japan for a three- to six-month training program in which they not only work and train with their Japanese counterparts, they live and eat together in the same company facilities. The foreigners are given sufficient language training to develop a 300 word vocabulary—enough to communicate with and get to know their colleagues. NEC has gone even further. Through the efforts of its international personnel division, it has established a program by which non-Japanese managers from its overseas operations are rotated through two year parent company assignments. At the end of their time in Japan, these individuals not only have a good understanding of the company's strategies and technologies, they also appreciate much better the values, norms, and practices of their Japanese parent company, and they have begun to develop the contacts and channels to communicate more effectively to headquarters.

Mr. Tabuchi, president of Nomura Securities, also recognized this need. He said: "Without true internationalization a company cannot be prosperous in the future. It may be very advantageous to have blue-eyed executives at the corporate head office. By changing the form of our processes and thinking, we can change the content."

But there is no point in preparing foreign managers for participation in the corporate system if the headquarters group remains unreceptive. In NEC's experience, the most effective way of opening their organizational system has been to internationalize a larger proportion of its management group to make them more conscious of the importance of foreign operations and more open to their ideas. By giving a broad group of key managers the experience of living and working abroad, the company has greatly improved understanding of the differences in national environments and their sensitivity to the difficulties of operating at long distances from the corporate headquarters. Furthermore, by giving parent company expatriates the opportunity to develop relationships with foreign managers while simultaneously improving their language abilities, NEC's top management believes it has been able to significantly increase the openness and enhance the quality of the overall management process.

Develop the Foreign Operation Role

The second barrier to an effective response to the new demands for national responsiveness lies in the historical attitude of Japanese companies toward their foreign operations as dependent children, and several companies are now trying to break out of the constraints of a parent-subsidiary relationship based on dependency by the subsidiary company and direction, support, and control by the parent.

The overall objective can be thought of as developing the worldwide national organizations into an interconnected network of competence centers, capable not only of implementing the company's strategy, but also of making important contributions to it.[25] While this means removing the constraints that often limit the role of local operations, it does not imply reducing the important role that the central groups play in determining the company's strategic direction by scanning the global environment, analyzing trends, and developing responses. It only suggests that there will be a diminishing ability to sense and respond to the growing diversity of demands and the increasing rate of change from headquarters. By creating multiple groups with the responsibility and resources to develop innovative responses to emerging national opportunities and threats, the company not only increases the total capacity and scope of its innovative capability, it also creates an internally competitive environment that tends to sharpen managers' entrepreneurial edge.

The challenge is a substantial one. It involves redefining the basic role and responsibilities of the company's foreign operations, and restructuring their relationship with the parent company. This is not a task that can be quickly achieved. Its successful implementation depends on the sequential development of the national organization in three stages—resources should be transferred, local knowledge, skills, and expertise must be developed, and finally, responsibilities can be expanded.[26]

The first task of transferring resources may be a painful decision for the company, but it is not difficult to implement. In responding to protectionist pressures or to host governments' legislation for higher local content or increased technology transfer, many companies have managed to build plants, expand capacity, or establish development laboratories in their overseas subsidiaries. The mistake has been that many have stopped there, expecting that this injection of capital will make the foreign operation more productive or innovative. The problem is that while the physical assets may be expanded, the local entity is still operating with its limited internal skills and capabilities, and is being managed under the old dependency/control management relationship.

In 1985, ten years after its establishment, Matsushita's plant in Cardiff, Wales, was still highly dependent on the parent company for direction and support. In an unusual step for a Japanese chief executive, company president Mr. Toshihiko Yamashita used an interview with the *Financial Times* to express his unhappiness with the situation, suggesting that the plant needed to be more creative and innovative and rely less on headquarters. "They have to become self-sufficient and stand on their own two feet," he said.

To become more self-sufficient, however, top management must be willing to develop the skills and knowledge base within national companies so they can break their dependence on the parent. The first need is to build a management group with the potential to act in the new role planned for the national company. Their profile may be quite different from the good solid operating managers who succeeded in the past by implementing well.

Some companies have tried to bring in the required creativity and leadership by recruiting experienced managers into senior positions. But having gained all of their extensive experience managing in another way, these individuals are sometimes less flexible in making the adjustments necessary to fit into a different management system. Indeed, many will accept the position only on the condition they have operating freedom and autonomy. Such an arrangement represents too traumatic a break from their past for most Japanese organizations, and can end in failure.

One of the earliest and most publicized examples of this problem occurred when Sony recruited Harvey Schein, a manager with extensive senior management experience in large U.S. companies, to head up its North American company. While providing the necessary leadership, drive, and independence, he also created in the U.S. company an organization system and management process that isolated it and inhibited its relationship with Japan. After five years he resigned. However, after gradually building better communications and understanding through regular quarterly meetings, the isolation and antagonism had been broken down so effectively that the parent company even adopted the internal budgeting and planning systems developed in its American unit.

Learning from the traumatic experiences of those who tried rapid change of their local personnel and systems, more companies are attempting to upgrade the quality of their national operations gradually, by recruiting high-potential managers at the entry level, often from good business schools and by building relationships slowly, as Sony has done. Even here the challenge is to overcome the reputation of Japanese companies as offering limited responsibility, slow advancement, and poor salaries. But those willing to spend the substantial time and effort developing a positive image on selected campuses find the effort rewarding.

The next task in developing an independent local capability is to ensure the new recruits are allowed to grow to their full potential in the national company. This requires the commitment of headquarters to train and develop these managers and technical experts and provide them with the fullest understanding of existing company knowledge and expertise in their field. But the development process involves more than knowledge transfer. It requires giving these individuals the managerial freedom and organizational support to build their expertise, test their ideas, and develop their sense of independence.

An example will illustrate the effective implementation of these steps. NEC's decision to develop an advanced software capability in its U.S. telecommunications company was made in response to two problems: the difficulty of responding to U.S. market needs with only a central software capability, and the chronic shortage of software engineers in Tokyo. The company hoped not only to become more responsive to the market, but also to capitalize on its access to American engineering talent. Recruiting of software engineers began in the early 1980s, and initially they were given responsibility only for "patching" problems in software at customer sites. When this embryonic group requested funding for two personal computers for a development project, they were given the resources. Soon they had created an innovative means for patching software from a central terminal rather than having to make individual site visits (an innovation subsequently adopted by the parent company). To ensure local managers would be properly trained, the company sent to the U.S., as engineering vice president, the manager responsible for the software development for the company's latest switch. He recruited an expanded group of engineers and asked headquarters to transfer still more responsibility. When he felt they were sufficiently familiar with the company systems, he created a separate design engineering department, and obtained authorization to expand from 20 to 50 engineers in the first year. Almost immediately, the group was able to undertake major independent software development for the U.S. market.

Within a few years the U.S. group had evolved from its dependency role as deliverer of centrally developed products to become a substantially free-standing unit, able to sense market needs and opportunities and develop innovative responses. Furthermore, by tapping into valuable local technical resources, it had built itself into an important corporate resource, able to make valuable contributions such as the software patching system which could be adopted by the broader corporate system.

Thus, having developed strong innovative capabilities in its various national operations, management can evolve the role of that company from dependent subsidiary, to self-sufficient national company, to contributing corporate resource. The role of headquarters shifts from controlling and supporting the activities of dependent operations to coordinating worldwide centers of competence, monitoring their innovations and new proposals, and integrating their various capabilities into an interdependent global network of operations.

Broaden Managers' Perspectives

Our first two recommendations represent fairly radical proposals to change the company's organization processes and strategic orientation, albeit gradually. Although we have described a series of implementation steps for each of them, their successful adoption basically depends on the willingness, openness, and flexibility of management to make such drastic change. Yet, we described our third major barrier to changing the international orientation of Japanese companies as a parochial management mentality, constrained by ethnocentric biases or conservative inflexibility.

Before the first two recommendations can be achieved, management must deal with any negative or narrow perception of the required changes in organizational processes and strategic roles. Rather than viewing such changes as concessions that will compromise the company's global effectiveness, they should be embraced as important developments that provide an opportunity to build new corporate capabilities, create a more innovative environment, and tap into a new and larger pool of managerial and technical talent.

The challenge of changing an entire organizational mentality is one that requires strong and consistent top management leadership over an extended period of time. There are two important approaches that can be effective in achieving the objective: developing a clear vision of the kind of international company the organization wants to become and communicating a commitment to achieve it; and stimulating, guiding, and reinforcing the changed mentality to the point it is absorbed into the company's value system.

The backbone of any change in management perceptions and attitudes must be a clearly articulated and well-communicated alternative model and set of assumptions. Matsushita's President Yamashita uses every opportunity he can to communicate to his organization the corporate commitment to change the role and relationship of its foreign operations. Throughout the organization, employees know that the company intends to double the percentage of its offshore manufacturing to 25% by 1990, and that the company's Operation Localization commits it to localizing personnel, technology, materials, and capital in all its overseas operations. Sony has made a similar commitment to increase its overseas capacity from 20% in 1986 to 35% by the end of the decade.

But the simple communication of expected change is usually insufficient. Even after new resources are transferred and additional responsibilities are delegated, managers may find it hard to evolve out of their old ways of managing. Mr. Yamashita's frustration at the lack of initiative being taken by managers in the company's Welsh plant illustrates the problem.

Often it takes some kind of major discontinuity or crisis atmosphere to trigger an unfreezing of attitudes and subsequent reorientation of thinking. Where an external threat already exists—and for many companies the 40% appreciation of the yen against the dollar has provided such a problem—management's role is to identify it, focus the organization's attention on it, and use it to galvanize action that will force managers to reevaluate their ideas and approaches. If no such external event exists, management may be able to create internal discontinuities to shake up complacent views and conventional wisdom. Two examples illustrate the approach.

The collective mentality of NEC management was forced to change under pressure of urgent strategic demands in the U.S. The company recognized that after deregulation there would be a five-year window in which to establish a strong presence in the North American public switching market, and thus a viable position as one of the three or four key companies in the global telecommunications industry. The urgent challenge to evolve rapidly from a small, dependent subsidiary of a Japanese company to a competent, responsive company able to meet the very different and fast-changing needs of the U.S. market provided management with a rallying point. The urgency and importance of the task caused managers to become more open in their attitudes and more flexible in their approaches.

When Sony's chief executive, Akio Morita, wanted to change the mentality of his organization toward its overseas operation, he decided to make the bold and dramatic move of relocating to New York and personally taking responsibility for Sony's American operations. This sent two clear messages to his managers—that overseas operations were a vital part of the company, not just foreign appendages, and that the company was prepared to adapt its way of managing in order to accommodate these important entities.[27]

Having jolted management mentality into a state of accepting the need to change, management must then concentrate on stimulating, guiding, and reinforcing that change. This involves such operational programs as the ones suggested earlier for the increased rotation of Japanese managers through

international assignments to break down parochial views and broaden organizational contacts. Conscious efforts must also be made to publicly reward
individuals and groups whose behavior conforms to the ideal of the new
international vision.

Conclusion

Having used their highly cohesive centralized organizations as the means to
penetrate world export markets, many Japanese companies are now faced
with the challenge of dismantling the very engine that drove their success and
rebuilding it in a different form. Their continued success depends on their
ability to respond to new forces in the international environment that are
driving them to decentralize concentrated assets, disperse centralized resources and capabilities, and delegate decision-making responsibilities from
headquarters. The trick will be to overcome the strong cultural influences
that constrain such changes, without destroying the strength and cohesion
they provide. To a large degree, their success in building this new organizational capability overshadows the strategic tasks these companies face.

For western companies, the nature of the challenge and the way in which
Japanese managers are able to deal with it are of vital importance. This period
of organizational adjustment represents a breathing space in which European
and American managers can regroup and prepare for the next stage of the
global battle. The timing is fortuitous since many of them need to use the
time to establish effective strategic control over their disparate, loosely coordinated worldwide operations. Indeed, in many ways the competitive race
has turned into one for effective global organizational capability.

Notes

1. Perlmutter (1965) first distinguished between ethnocentric, polycentric, and geocentric conceptions of the MNC. This distinction rests on the differences in the
   characterization of the international business environment by the MNC: ethnocentrism reflecting a primarily home country view; polycentrism a multicountry
   view on a country by country basis; and geocentrism a global view that recognizes
   the interdependence of different national contexts.
2. See, for example, Ouchi (1982) and Pascale and Athos (1981).
3. Bartlett and Ghoshal (1987a, b) discuss the development of such organizational
   capabilities in detail.
4. For a fuller description of the internationalization of Japanese companies, see
   Yoshihara (1979).
5. Yoshino (1976) correctly predicted that the management processes he described
   so richly would present an impediment to the internationalization of Japanese
   organization systems.
6. For an excellent discussion of the role of trading companies and their relationship
   with manufacturing companies, see Yoshino and Lifson (1986).

7. A fuller account of such Japanese institutional barriers is contained in Encarnation (1986).
8. See Levitt (1983) for a fairly extreme view of the pervasiveness of such forces of globalization.
9. van der Klugt (1985) makes a persuasive case that some approaches to globalization have been simplistic.
10. For a discussion of how the MNCs kept sovereignty at bay, see Vernon (1971). The more recent trend towards a reassertion of sovereignty rights by governments is eloquently discussed by Doz (1986).
11. See Doz (1986).
12. For a more detailed description of these subtle and complex processes, see Yoshino (1976).
13. The use of personnel transfers as a means of coordinating and controlling MNCs was discussed extensively in Edstrom and Galbraith (1977).
14. For a discussion on how the Japanese use this cultural system as a form of control, see Yaeger and Baliga (1985).
15. The aphorism "success breeds failure" has been given theoretical support by the notion of "structural inertia." Thus, Freeman and Hannan (1984) and DiMaggio and Powell (1983) have asserted that organizations often find it difficult to adapt to changed circumstances, since they are afraid of losing social and normative legitimacy that exists in the successful current practices.
16. As Hedlund (1986) has suggested, the international environment has created a relationship between headquarters and subsidiary that is increasingly reciprocal in nature. That their traditional patterns of subsidiary company dependence require fundamentally different organizational structures (Thompson 1967) is something that Japanese MNCs are only slowly beginning to realize.
17. For a description of the infamous Tanaka riots, see Ozawa (1979).
18. The dependencia school of political economy has had a powerful influence, particularly in Latin American countries. For a good review of dependencia and post-dependencia perspectives of foreign direct investment, see Greico (1985).
19. The difficulty of changing cognitive frames of reference and the way in which such frames impede strategic adaptation has been discussed by Dutton and Duncan (1987).
20. The importance of viewing the MNC as a distributed pool of geographically dispersed capabilities and information that derives its distinct competitive advantage precisely by leveraging this multinationality has also been stressed by Hedlund (1986).
21. Meyer and Rowan (1977) have commented on the importance of visible myths in sustaining particular organizational forms. Thus the very visible organization practices that are seen as being the very reason for the "Japan as #1" myth are difficult to shed.
22. Van Maanen and Schein (1979) are amongst the pioneers of the view that socialization establishes particular definitions of membership as well as the acceptance of particular organizational processes as a way of life. Inasmuch as these practices are idiosyncratic and unique and rely on certain cultural preconditions (e.g., being Japanese), they present difficult and and imposing barriers to entry for the outsider.
23. Steiner (1975) for instance, stresses that being multilingual represents a qualitatively different state than being monolingual and that the former has distinct advantages in terms of adaptation to new situations.
24. This description of an alternate socialization strategy that would move foreigners from the "periphery" to the "core" is consistent with the patterns described by Van Maanen and Schein (1979) in their discussion of socialization strategies.

25. For a more detailed description of how multinational companies are integrating differentiated subsidiary roles into a global strategy, see Bartlett and Ghoshal (1986).

26. See Bartlett (1986) for a more detailed description of the organizational challenges facing MNCs, and the characteristics of the emerging "transnational" organizational form.

27. Symbols and ceremonies can act not only as sources of organizational inertia, but also as the means to precipitate quantum change. See Meyer and Rowan (1977) for a discussion of the used symbols and ceremonies and Miller and Freisen (1984) for more detail on strategies for quantum change.

References

Bartlett, C.A. "Building and Managing the Transnational: The New Organizational Challenge," in M.E. Porter, ed., *Competition in Global Industries*. Boston: Harvard Business School Press, 1986.

Bartlett, C.A., and Ghoshal, S. "Tap Your Subsidiaries for Global Reach." *Harvard Business Review* Nov.–Dec., 1986:87–94.

Bartlett, C.A., and Ghoshal, S. "Managing Across Borders: New Strategic Requirements." *Sloan Management Review* Summer 1987a:7–18.

Bartlett, C.A., and Ghoshal, S. "Managing Across Borders: New Organizational Responses." *Sloan Management Review* Fall 1987b:43–53.

DiMaggio, P., and Powell, W. (1983). "The Iron Cage Revisited: Institutional Isomorphism and Collective Rationality in Organizational Fields." *American Sociological Review* 82:929–64.

Doz, Y. "Government Policies and Global Industries," in M.E. Porter, ed., *Competition in Global Industries*, Boston: Harvard Business School Press, 1986.

Dutton, J., and Duncan R. "Strategic Issue Diagnosis and the Creation of Momentum for Change." *Strategic Management Journal* 1987 (8);179–295.

Edstrom, A., and Galbraith, S.R. "Transfers of Managers as a Coordination and Control Strategy in Multinational Organizations." *Administrative Science Quarterly* June 1977:248–63.

Encarnation, D.J. "Cross Investment: A Second Front of Economic Rivalry," in T.K. McCraw, ed., *American Versus Japan*. Boston: Harvard Business School Press, 1986.

Freeman, M., and Hannan, J. "Structural Inertia and Organizational Change." *American Sociological Review* 1984 (49):49–64.

Greico, J. "Between Dependence and Autonomy: India's Experience with the International Computer Industry," in T. Moran, ed., *Multinational Corporations: The Political Economy of Foreign Direct Investment*. Lexington, Mass.: D.C. Heath, 1985.

Hedlund, G. "The Hypermodern MNC—A Heterarchy." *Human Resource Management* Spring 1986:9–35.

Jaeger, A.M., and Baliga, B.R. "Control Systems and Strategic Adaptation: Lessons from the Japanese Experience." *Strategic Management Journal* 1985: 6(2).

Levitt, T. "The Globalization of Markets." *Harvard Business Review* May–June 1983.

Meyer, J., and Rowan, B. "Institutional Organizations: Formal Structure as Myth and Ceremony." *American Journal of Sociology* 1977 (83):340–63.

Miller, D., and Freisen, P. *Organizations: A Quantum View*. Englewood Cliffs, N.J.: Prentice-Hall, 1984.

Perlmutter, H.V. "L'enterprise Internationale—Trois Conceptions." *Revere Economique et Sociale* 1965:23.

Ouchi, W. *Theory Z*. Reading: Addison-Wesley, 1982.

Ozawa, T. *Multinationalism, Japanese Style: The Political Economy of Outward Dependency*. Princeton, N.J.: Princeton University Press, 1979.

Pascale, R., and Athos, A. *The Art of Japanese Management*. New York: Warner Books, 1981.

Steiner, G. *After Babel*. Oxford University Press, 1975.

Thompson, J.D. *Organizations in Action*. New York: McGraw Hill, 1967.

van der Klugt, C.J. "Penetrating Global Markets: High Tech Companies." Speech presented at the Going Global Conference sponsored by *The Economist* Conference Unit, London, June 17, 1985.

Van Maanen, J., and Schein, E. "Toward a Theory of Organizational Socialization," in B.M. Staw, ed., *Research in Organizational Behavior*, Vol. 1, Greenwich, Conn.: JAI Press, 1979.

Vernon, R. *Sovereignty at Bay*. New York: Basic Books, 1971.

Yoshihara, H. "Japanese Multinational Enterprises: A View from Outside." *Kobe Economic and Business Review*, 25th Annual Report, Kobe University, 1979.

Yoshino, M.Y. *Japan's Multinational Enterprises*. Cambridge, Mass.: Harvard University Press, 1976.

Yoshino, M.Y., and Lifson, T.B. *The Invisible Link: Japan's Sogo Shosha and the Organization of Trade*. Cambridge, Mass.: MIT Press, 1986.

16

Self-Renewal of the Japanese Firm and the Human Resource Strategy*

Ikujiro Nonaka

Introduction

The successful pattern of business development for typical Japanese firms has been based on a mass-production paradigm that seeks to achieve the highest level of efficiency. These companies set up mass-production plants in Japan, where a stable supply of high quality labor was readily available. Then they added incremental improvements to products, the basic concepts of which had been developed primarily by foreign firms. In this way, they have been able to achieve simultaneously unchallengeable reductions in cost and quality improvements, enabling them to dominate the international market. Fierce competition for increased domestic market share occurs when many Japanese firms establish mass-production plants at the same time due to the resultant overproduction. Such competition, however, has contributed positively toward product quality improvements and production cost reductions. This, in turn, has led to a rapid increase in international competitiveness. Intense competition between domestic firms will continue to play a positive role as long as the domestic market itself continues to grow.

But the global market today is no longer as open to Japanese firms as it was before. In the domestic market, Japanese firms are now required to develop more diversified products that will satisfy a wider range of customer needs. In addition, these firms must work harder to provide a more flexible

*_Human Resource Management,_ Vol. 27, Number 1, pp. 45–62, Ikujiro Nonaka, copyright © 1988 by John Wiley & Sons, Inc., reprinted by permission of John Wiley & Sons, Inc.

contemporary industrial society. It has come time for Japanese firms to shift away from the current mass-production paradigm. In other words, they are now required to achieve self-renewal in order to meet changes in their environment by switching their strategical paradigm from an efficiency-centered to a creativity-centered model.

A new style of human resource management has been highlighted recently as an approach to the self-renewal of the firm. It has become popular for American companies to let the personnel department take the initiative in reinforcing human resource management. These companies are establishing personnel systems that excavate human abilities and talents buried inside organizations and are encouraging entrepreneurship in employees. The personnel department has been changing its role from one of overseeing traditional "personnel administration," labor relations, payroll accounting, and employee welfare to one of initiator and coordinator, responsible for planning and executing corporate strategies (Fombrun et al. 1984). Its new mission is to develop and allocate human resources in a way that will best fit these strategies.

The same situation can be found in Japan and it has stimulated the repositioning of the personnel management function in Japanese firms. In this chapter, I will discuss the emerging trends in human resource management in Japanese firms and present key factors for creative HRM that leads to the self-renewal of the firm.

Paradigm Shift of Corporate Strategy

In its 1987 White Paper on International Trade, the ministry of International Trade and Industry (MITI) proposed that Japanese firms abandon market-share-oriented business policies. MITI points out that the fundamental cause of intense trade and economic conflict between Japan and other foreign countries is the dominant Japanese business policy that emphasizes gaining market share by cutting cost through mass production. MITI advocates more profit-oriented corporate activities of a more "appropriate" style. This is the first proposal on micro-level activities of business firms made by the Japanese government.

Since the end of World War II, Japan has been in pursuit of international competitiveness to gain the foreign currency necessary for reconstruction of the damaged national economy. Japanese firms adopted a so-called follower strategy, characterized by the active introduction of advanced technology from the U.S. and Europe, and cost reduction through mass production, including process improvement and mass marketing. By focusing on economies of scale, they succeeded in surpassing other countries in international price competitions, and then were required to invest more in production facilities in order to meet rapidly increasing demand. On the other hand, these massive investments increased fixed costs, and Japanese firms then had to reduce costs again through mass production and marketing. In this way, market share has become the most critical indicator of business development for Japanese firms. These firms have been involved repeatedly in a cycle of mass production, marketing, and investment. In many studies it has actually been proven that while the foremost priority for American firms is return on investment (ROI), for Japanese firms it is the market share increase ratio (Kagono et al. 1985).

This market-share-oriented strategical paradigm is, however, gradually losing its validity when applied to the changing environment surrounding Japanese firms today. The growth rate of GNP, which was close to 10% in the era of rapid economic growth, is now only 3 to 4%. The rise of protectionism in overseas markets is accelerating, and the trade conflict is worsening, year by year. If Japanese firms continue to sell their high-quality products in overseas markets, this will inevitably lead to terrible economic conflicts.

Creative Human Resource Management

Japanese firms are now entering a very critical phase. It is necessary for them to shift from the production-oriented paradigm to a new product- or concept-oriented one as quickly as they can. Successful self-renewal of some leading Japanese firms has been realized through the introduction of creativity-oriented or creative HRM.

There are three main pillars of creative HRM. The first pillar is creation of a strategic vision by commitment of the employees. The second pillar is the entrepreneurial middle management who should assume leadership in the self-renewal of the firm. The last is multidimensional personnel management that emphasizes more varied and individual-based career development.

1. Creation of Strategic Vision by Commitment

The best way to actuate self-renewal of the firm is to implant strategic visions or dreams corresponding to the paradigm shift into the minds of people. When a vision or dream concerning the future image of the company is formed and shared by the employees, it will energize them and help them to visualize and accomplish what they are dreaming. Since a strategic vision itself is nothing more than a concept, it is absolutely necessary to activate the vision through the involvement of other people in order to make it practical and effective. The vision is best activated when it is created by the people who will be directly responsible for its realization.

An increasing number of Japanese firms are actively enacting their strategic corporate missions or domains. The following examples of recent mission definitions indicate each company's direction toward fundamental differentiation in the future: "Keeping Information Alive"—Nippon Telephone & Telegraph; "Natural Food Corporation"—Kagome (dominant tomato products manufacturers); "Creation of Environmental Beauty"—INAX (a leading household ceramics manufacturer); "Total Communications Service"—Dentsu (the largest advertising agency in Japan). These missions are metaphors in the sense that they encourage employees to think imaginatively about the meaning of these ambiguous directions and to relate the underlying reasons to the obstacles to be overcome in the course of realizing the missions.

Strategic visions must be created in compliance with these organizational missions. Furthermore, people's active commitment is necessary in order to create such visions. With it, the process of vision creation will expand by itself to a greater movement toward establishing the "Corporate Identity." The "2001 Project" of Asahi Chemical Industry, a leading chemical company, is a typical case. The aim of this project is to create future images of the company through use of a project team composed of younger employees who will be operating the company in 2001 A.D. Key persons are middle to lower managers such as *Kacho* (section chief) and *Kakaricho* (senior staff). Another aim of this project is to exclude the elder managerial staff members from the vision creation process, as they tend to adhere to their own manner, which was effective in the past. It is highly probable that younger middle managers will work passionately to realize the visions they actually create and propose under their own name, as in the case of diversification into the electronics and biotechnology businesses.

In many companies, the top management or corporate planning office is assigned to define a general outline of the corporate vision. Those visions have been enforced in the top-down style. Japanese companies have learned this system from the U.S., long the teacher of the mass-production paradigm. U.S. companies commonly execute organizational restructuring from the top down (e.g., drastic organizational changes at General Electric and General Motors as well as mergers and acquisitions). However, no vision can be realized unless it is shared by a middle management that recognizes "We should change ourselves first." Strategic visions must be internalized by middle- and lower-level managers who are to take initiative in the self-renewal process.

2. Middle Management as a Key Strategical Node

As is explained above, creation and implementation of strategic visions cannot be expected without the active commitment of middle management. However, traditional management styles (such as top-down and bottom-up) are not effective in helping middle management to play such a critical role. I have been proposing "middle-up-down management" as the third style of management, in contrast to the two dominant styles of management (Nonaka 1988a). The middle-up-down management style puts emphasis on the importance of middle management in the process of self-renewal.

The first phase of middle-up-down management involves visions or dreams proposed by top management to generate "creative chaos" (Nonaka 1988b) in the firm. Middle management is stimulated to create and activate practical concepts to bridge the gap between the status quo and the visions or dreams. In other words, the middle managers deploy grand theories presented by the top into more empirically testable, middle-ranged theories, and take leadership initiative in executing them by involving the top management, as well as employees at the bottom. This is the most effective management style for the continuous creation of new concepts or information in a firm, a step which is indispensable to the firm's self-renewal. This is best realized through middle-up-down management because it is not a hero (e.g., a clever staff planner, a powerful top manager, etc.) but a group of mini-heroes and mini–mini-heroes that guides the self-renewing process. For this management style, middle management is particularly important as the key node that connects the top and the bottom toward the creation and realization of concepts or information. Top management holds macro-level and context-free information, and tends to deductively develop this "articulate knowledge" into grand theories. On the other hand, employees at the bottom accumulate micro-level and task-based information attained through their actual experiences and examples, and tend to inductively construct a system of "tacit knowledge" (Polanyi 1966). The knowledge of the former type is defined as "hands-off" knowledge compared with the latter, defined as "hands-on" knowledge. The middle has direct access to both, and consequently is in the most strategic position, relating both to create concepts or information.

However, being of key strategic importance, middle management tends to become exhausted if preventive measures are not taken properly. Since middle management is the connecting node between hands-off information from the top and hands-on information from the bottom, the information and decision burden flows into the middle, overloading them. From the viewpoint of organizational structure, the middle, as the "linking pin" between the top and the bottom, also serves as the node in communication channels that run vertically, horizontally, and diagonally throughout the organization. In the process of the self-renewal of the firm, middle managers are strongly required to be creators and activators of a practical corporate vision, as well as to be information nodes. Overloading is the greatest contributing factor to exhaustion, which hinders the middle's creative activities. Under an efficiency-oriented system, employees tend to pursue only those visible results that can be recognized by everyone. In other words, the system emphasizes the completion of routine operations, rather than the planning or creating of new concepts. Consequently, employees are going to be worn out from routine operations, and unable to undertake more "creative" activities.

Considering all these problems, we should immediately take every possible measure to refresh and vitalize, or in other words, to recreate the middle management. It is also absolutely necessary to develop a truly "entrepreneurial" middle management that is competent and strong enough to handle such a heavy but challenging work load.

The third pillar of creative HRM is multidimensional personnel management that includes all these practical methods and systems.

3. Multidimensional Personnel Management

Based on a kind of egalitarianism resulting from the institutional introduction of American democracy in the period shortly following World War II, unidimensional personnel management prevailed among Japanese firms as a fundamental element of lifetime employment and the seniority system. In principle, the monodimensional system uniformly deals with employees as a group. The grouping criteria for employees are age, educational background, business background, and so forth. People are treated rather anonymously in their earlier career stages, and are selectively promoted during relatively late stages, at a slow pace, so as to keep all of them motivated for as long as possible.

Although this monodimensional system has functioned very well thus far, Japanese firms now need to introduce creative HRM in order to achieve self-renewal. The creation and activation of the corporate vision owes much to the creativity of the individual, entrepreneurial middle managers. A group-based, monodimensional system should be compensated by an individual-based, multidimensional system. The characteristics of multidimensional personnel management will be described in the following section.

(1) Multidimensional Career System. Career development in most Japanese firms has generally been a single ladder. Employees are strongly oriented and motivated to climb, one step at a time, the only ladder toward line managerial positions. This tendency is reinforced especially under the efficiency-oriented system. The system requires strong line management to process routine assignments efficiently. Thus, once an employee is promoted to a managerial line position, promotion to higher positions becomes his/her foremost ambition. Performance appraisal is usually conducted primarily to measure managerial and supervisory ability, necessary for promotion to these positions. Excellent specialists are given less favorable evaluations than generalists, unless they possess good managerial ability. In this single ladder system, individual creativity tends to be crushed, and cannot be fully developed or realized.

In order to encourage employees' creative activities, it is necessary to recognize multiple career paths as equally important for the company. Major career ladders are those for R&D staff, product managers, and in-house entrepreneurs.

Even among Japanese banks that are still conservatively maintaining traditional, seniority-based personnel systems, Kansai Sogo Bank, one of Sumitomo Bank's affiliates centered in the western region of Japan, has put into place an "early selection system" of key strategic personnel. The bank evaluates the ability and aptitude of new employees recruited right after graduation through an introductory, generalist training of two years that is chiefly OJT (on-the-job training) of fundamental banking positions. Evaluation of ability is accomplished by careful discussions between each employee and his/her direct and indirect supervisors. Those who are evaluated as possessing high potential ability to work as key strategic personnel (such as management planning staff and dealers) are transferred to headquarters while the others are assigned as salesman at branch offices. The aim of the "early selection system" is to select and train from their younger stages those key strategic personnel as specialist staff to meet the cut-throat competition which is expected to occur soon in the Japanese financial market.

Different appraisal criteria should be designed so as to measure the special abilities unique to these job functions. Different education and training programs also need to be provided so as to satisfy the needs identified by these improved appraisals.

In October 1987, Kyowa Bank, one of the metropolitan banks in Japan, introduced the so-called Open Appraisal System that discloses to each employee the results of performance evaluations done by supervisors. The aim was to improve the appraisal's objectivity. The evaluation cannot be completed until both the supervisor and subordinate have agreed with the evaluation results after thorough discussions. One of the essential evaluation criteria is the achievement of half-year term goals pertaining to task and ability improvement, the evaluations being held every spring and fall. Thus, introduction of "Management by Objectives" into the performance evaluation is also becoming popular among Japanese firms.

Nippon Sanso K.K., a leading Japanese chemical company mainly producing oxygen gas for industrial use, introduced a "job qualification" system, which divides all jobs in the company into 41 job clusters. Every job in each cluster is ranked as one of four job grades according to its difficulty. The aim of this system is to determine and describe the job contents in as much detail as possible in order to analyze and evaluate objectively each employee's performance and ability. The results of the evaluation are disclosed to the employee to discuss future improvements. Promotion, bonus amounts, and training programs are also determined based on the results.

(2) Revising Compensation System. The compensation system should also be changed to a more ability-based system in accordance with the above changes. However, it is not wise to introduce into Japanese companies a completely job-based pay system as is prevalent in the U.S. The current Japanese pay system is too much a seniority-based system, generally speaking, and is fairly discouraging to highly competent middle managers. As scouting and job switching of middle and top management is steadily increasing, "higher pay-

ment for higher ability and performance" should be the corporate compensation policy in order to retain excellent personnel.

With this consideration in mind, many Japanese companies are now actually implementing a salary system based on the employee's job performance ability. The system is a mixture of the typical Japanese and American pay systems, but more strongly characterized by the latter, rather than by the mild blend advocated thus far.

Nippon Telephone & Telegraph (NTT), the telecommunications giant in Japan that was privatized in 1986 by a decision of the Diet, introduced a new compensation system in October 1987 to meet challenges from new telephone companies. The new system is an ability-related qualification system for its 270,000 employees. The main salary determinant used to be the employees' positions, the assignments of which were seniority-based. The new compensation system is composed of a seniority-based part and an ability-based part. The ability-based qualification system enables younger employees of great ability to be quickly promoted to lower- and middle-managerial positions. It also provides a dual qualification ladder system for employees with more than ten years in the company (one for planning staff and the other for sales persons). Such an ability-based, dual ladder system is expected to facilitate the early selection and training of competent young personnel.

The adoption of an incentive system will also bring about significant changes in the traditional seniority-based system.

It should be noted that Nippon Steel Corp. also adopted a new ability-based compensation system that is applicable to 11,000 middle managers. Nippon Steel Corp., now suffering severely from the decline of the Japanese steel industry that is representative of structurally depressed industries, used to be the leading company in Japan with respect to its sales, profitability, and a compensation system that was most typically Japanese, namely a seniority-based one. Even though its business situation has worsened considerably, employees who can enjoy its extraordinary vested privileges do not feel the severity of the phase they are facing. Therefore, it is very symbolic, in the light of the paradigm shift of Japanese firms, that such a typical Japanese company decided to introduce an ability-based compensation system. The new compensation system of Nippon Steel has three characteristics. The first is the introduction of a short-term incentive system that reflects individual middle manager's business performance per half-year term in his/her bonus of the term. The second is the complete removal of longevity pay from the compensation for middle managers. Entirely ability-based pay and position allowances are all part of their salary. The third characteristic is the lowered ceiling age, for from 50 years old to 45, longevity pay increases for lower managers. This means lower managers who cannot be promoted to higher positions by age 45 can no longer be given any pay increase.

(3) Multiple-Career Ladder. Toyo Soda Mfg. (Toso), a chemical company pro-

ducing industrial chemical products, clearly states in the first article of its new corporate philosophy that human resource management is the principal corporate issue. Last year, Toso transferred its Director of R&D to the Director of Personnel Administration for the purpose of establishing a multidimensional personnel system. Through a name change from Toyo Soda to Toso, it is aiming to diversify itself into high-tech areas such as fine chemicals. Establishment of a multiple-career ladder is necessary in order to develop the skills and ability of the excellent chemists and engineers, and to motivate them by providing challenging jobs and favorable work conditions. In other Japanese firms, the Directors of Personnel are being transferred to the R&D section.

Toshiba introduced a dual ladder system consisting of a managerial ladder and a specialist ladder quite early. These two ladders are parallel and completely equivalent to each other. Employees are assigned to one of these two ladders according to their ability and own choices. Research staff members generally start their career as specialist researchers, and those who have ability to make good managers will be transferred to the managerial ladder. But if they have a strong desire to continue their research as specialist researchers, they will be moved back to the original ladder.

In Kao Co. Ltd., a leading chemical firm in Japan, the career ladder for researchers is also clearly separated from that of line managers. Directors of Kao's 12 research laboratories are all promoted within the research staff ladder, and there is no difference in their salary based on individual position level. The compensation is determined exclusively by their level of skill and competence as researchers.

Honda Motor Co. Ltd. changed all Japanese position names of the Honda Technical Research Laboratory, one of its subsidiaries, to English titles such as President, Executive Chief Engineer, Assistant Chief Engineer, etc. Honda aims at preventing the Laboratory from becoming bureaucratic due to the use of Japanese position names. English names indicate the nature of the staff as specialist researchers more distinctively, and this name change manifestly transmits the company's basic policy that all researchers are equally important, regardless of their titles.

(4) Renovating "Shukko" System.   Japanese companies have frequently utilized the "temporary transfer" or "shukko" system, transferring their employees to subsidiaries for a limited period. This system has two opposite meanings. For excellent top or middle managers, this system is an "express lane of promotion." If they perform very well at the assigned position in subsidiaries, which is usually one or more steps higher than their previous one, they will surely be offered a higher position in the parent company after some period. The system provides wonderful OJT for these competent managers. However, in the case of the below-average performers found at all levels, this system means transfer without the possibility of returning. This type of shukko is

very prevalent among structurally depressed industries like steel and ship building. As a typical example, about 1000 employees of Nippon Steel will be ordered to transfer sometime during this year. Most of them are clerical workers and managers, and half of them will be transferred to "outside" companies that do not belong to the Nippon Steel Group.

Now that new business development in Japanese companies is often initiated by their newly established subsidiaries, we should examine this traditional system in a new light. As these new subsidiaries offer the best OJT to all middle managers of all career paths, especially to the entrepreneurial middle, shukko should be scheduled as an important career step in their career development.

Last year, C. Itoh & Co., Ltd., one of the five biggest trading firms in Japan, established a career-path system that requires job-transfer experience as one of the five compulsory qualifications for promotion to "*Jicho*" (assistant department manager).

Some other Japanese companies suffering from structural depression in their traditional main businesses, like Nippon Light Metal Co., Ltd., have come to send the most competent employees to their subsidiaries. These excellent staff members are expected to develop these subsidiaries so that they may become reliable customers of the parent company. The key for this long-term strategy of group-wide growth is to transfer truly competent employees who meet true needs of the subsidiaries, without imposing on or interfering with their management and personnel policies.

Toray, which was a dominant rayon manufacturer in Japan, has succeeded remarkably in transforming itself into a high-tech firm in the field of new materials and biotechnology. Its KFS (Key Factor for Success) is its drastic human resource management measures, such as recruitment of its board members from top executives of subsidiaries. Some ambitious employees of Toray are now even expecting to be sent to subsidiaries, regarding it as an express lane of promotion. Osaka Gas Co. and Showa Shell Oil Co. have started open recruitment among middle managers for the positions of president of their various new subsidiaries. Nippon Chemical Condensor Co. has ceased to use the name "shukko." The company virtually makes those employees who are to be hired by group companies first resign from the parent company, in order to motivate them more strongly to work for the new companies. They are even paid a "retirement allowance" at the time of transfer, which is deducted from the total amount of retirement allowance that they will receive from the parent company at the time of true retirement following their return to the parent company.

It is also important to establish a loser-recovery system, especially for entrepreneurs. The traditional unidimensional system is based on the production system of a plant that is designed to perfectly achieve "zero defects." In the efficiency-oriented system, noise, fluctuations, and chaos of all kinds are to be eliminated. The system permits no flexibility within, and it pursues perfectionism. Performance appraisal for such a perfection-oriented system involves counting the number of mistakes that employees make instead of the number of contributions. Career trees of the unidimensional system, therefore, offer no way of recovery to losers who fail once to step up the ladder. However hard employees have tried to clear the first step, the second, and so forth, it is all over for them if they fail at the last step for a higher managerial position. The result of such harsh competitions is that both winners and losers naturally burn out. The Japanese labor market is not fluid enough to give these losers the opportunity to move to another company for further career development, like the American labor market. In order to encourage creative challenge in entrepreneurs within the firm, a multidimensional career tree with a loser-recovery system needs to be adopted. Some innovative companies in Japan have already introduced this type of system with a specified ceiling for permissible failures. The effectiveness of such a loser-recovery system in Japanese firms is reported in a recent study by Hanada (1987). He compared career trees of traditional Japanese firms with that of an innovative firm, and found the latter to be equipped with this system.

(5) Heterogeneous Staffing. When the individual-based multidimensional career system is in place, the next step is to know who is where, and then assign them positions in compliance with these strategies. If there is no one who meets the strategic requirements, mid-career employees from outside should be recruited.

Since individual-based personnel management has been conducted primarily by line managers thus far, it is rather difficult to carry out company-wide searches for strategically required talents. The so-called "skills inventory system" is neither sophisticated nor popular in Japan, and grasping who has what skills at the practical level needs to be shared at the corporate level. NEC, taking advantage of being a computer manufacturer, has installed a computerized total personnel information system that includes a skills inventory (the most advanced system of this kind in Japan). A computerized, company-wide personnel information system is now regarded as a very powerful strategic tool for Japanese companies.

Strategic staffing needs to be carried out, based on the personnel information attained in the above manner. Some Japanese firms like Honen Oil, a dominant food oil manufacturer, have authorized department directors to obtain necessary staff from other departments. Such interdepartmental staffing is an attempt toward the best strategic staffing by realizing company-wide free allocation of human resources. Another attempt is strategic rotation from one key strategic position to another. Rotation from the personnel section to the labor relations section bears no significant meaning for the company. However, rotation between the R&D section and the marketing section is strategically meaningful indeed, because information concerning the seeds of new business and customer needs information are related to each other. Strategic rotation is conducted between key sections so that different types of information may be combined to create new perspectives or concepts. Kao and NEC are practicing typical strategic rotations as a system. In the key phases of its business development, NEC transferred many personnel from R&D to the sales and marketing sections. Asahi Glass, a leading flat glass manufacturer, has made it a general rule to relocate all clerical employees with five years of service.

In August 1987, Sanyo, a leading consumer electric/electronics company, conducted an extraordinary large-scale transfer of about 300 middle and lower managers, which amounts to about 10% of all managers. The primary aim was to realize heterogeneous staffing by transferring managers who have only one career field. Meanwhile, Matsushita Electric Industries carried out an interdepartmental rotation of about 200 employees. Through this large-scale movement of personnel, 200 personnel staff members from various personnel sections were moved to other sections, and many specialists in the field of sales, production, and R&D were transferred to the personnel section in turn. Matsushita has already introduced a multiple career ladder system, and this action aims to prevent personnel staff members from becoming too specialized in only one field (personnel management).

Hasegawa Komuten, a leading Japanese general contractor, has decided to execute quite a unique personnel plan in April 1988. The company will hire all the employees of its subsidiaries, and then transfer them to their original companies as a form of shukko. It is expected that such personnel changes will motivate and raise the work morale of employees of its subsidiaries, wipe out feelings of inequality in the minds of staff members of the parent company who are temporarily transferred to subsidiaries and their regular employees, and moreover, enable strategic optimization of company-wide human resources.

If there are not enough human resources available for strategic staffing within a company, a supply from outside is necessary. Recruitment of mid-career employees has two important implications. One is the need for procurement of the required human resources from outside. In the case of new business development, the present staff may be able to define a general outline of the strategic domain through hands-off analysis of technological and/or market synergy. What is really necessary for the company is excellent specialists who possess hands-on and tacit knowledge of the particular field of the new business. However thoroughly the company preplans the process of new business development, it is impossible to forecast technological problems that can be solved only with hands-on, task information and knowledge. The multidimensional personnel system is indispensable in attracting and obtaining specialists who possess this invaluable knowledge and expertise. The other implication of the recruitment of mid-career employees is the likelihood of the formation of a counter-culture inside of the firm. Innovative companies such as Honda, Canon, and Sony frequently recruit mid-career employees as a kind of corporate custom. Counter-culture inside the firm creates the organizational chaos that stimulates creative activities for generating a variety of information throughout the entire company.

As another form of heterogeneous staffing, globalization of personnel management (especially that of the top management and R&D staff) is of high strategic importance. Toyota Motor is planning to double its number of domestic employees of foreign nationality to about 30 employees in the coming three years. Fujitsu Ltd., one of the largest computer manufacturers in Japan, has also started to temporarily transfer foreign employees from its 40+ overseas subsidiaries to its Japanese headquarters on a shukko basis in order to train them to be middle managers of subsidiaries. Canon's French subsidiary will considerably increase its R&D staff next year by recruiting new graduates of the national university located in the neighborhood of its French headquarters.

However, there are few executives of foreign nationality in Japanese companies at present. Even among the five major trading companies, C. Itoh & Co. is the first company to make a person of foreign nationality an executive board member. This took place in July 1987. According to a recent survey, there is only one manufacturing company that has employed an executive of foreign nationality in Japan, excluding foreign affiliates (Takeuchi 1987). Although many Japanese companies are oriented toward overseas business expansion and globalization of middle and lower management, globalization of their top management is still quite slow. The globalization is truly effective in renewing top management (which tends to be very stiff in Japan because aged executives often remain at the top, maintaining strong influential power within the company and friendly relationships with stockholders). Since it is impossible for middle management to renew top management by using bottom-up approaches, a systematic introduction of diversity into the top management ranks is a must.

As for the globalization of R&D staff, it should be noted that some Japanese companies have started their globalization with global R&D activities. This new pattern of globalization is quite opposite to the traditional pattern that starts with overseas marketing, then proceeds to overseas production, and finally moves to overseas R&D activity. Kao, for example, established an R&D laboratory in West Berlin. Otsuka Pharmaceutical has three "satellite laboratories" in Frankfurt, West Germany, and two in the U.S. (Maryland and Seattle). The cross fertilization of R&D staff through globalization is expected to increase the occurrence of technological breakthroughs.

Strategic Tasks of the Personnel Department in Creative HRM

The personnel department of Japanese companies, in general, used to be a more strategic section when compared with that of typical Western companies. Personnel and financial management are relatively centralized in Japanese companies, and there are considerable numbers of top executives who have developed their careers chiefly in the personnel department. In recent years, however, the tasks of the personnel department have become limited to more routine activities (such as the recruitment of new graduates, payroll-related activities, employee benefits and welfare, and labor relations) as the corporate organization has become more bureaucratic due to expansion in size. In particular, negotiations with the labor union, which sticks to the reservation of its vested rights and gradual improvements of the present system, is a rather retrospective task. It is difficult to get ideas for creative destruction of the current system from these routine and retrospective activities. Since all of these activities are group-based, the personnel department tends to be ignored by the corporate planning office and the president's office, which need more individual-based, vivid personnel information. Personnel managers of major Japanese firms now share a strong anxiety that their departments are losing strategic importance and they are afraid that they have become the least advanced section in the company. The strategic task required of the personnel department in introducing creative HRM is to facilitate this introduction using every possible means. The three pillars of creative HRM cannot be realized without the strong leadership of the personnel department.

To begin with, the personnel department must use every possible technique to evoke creativity at all levels of the firm. In order to excavate the human talent buried within a large organization, many Japanese companies such as Sony, Mitsubishi Corp., CSK (the largest computer software company), Kyowa Bank, Asahi Glass, and Showa Shell Oil, have established an open recruitment system for challenging positions. These positions are for members of promising project teams, the top management of new subsidiaries, or the managers of foreign offices. Recently reported with wide attention was that even Mitsubishi Heavy Industries Ltd., well known as the most conservative, bureaucratic "Japanese" company (now being damaged considerably by a structural depression), assigned five employees in their 30s and 40s to form a special project team for new business/product development. All five members have been stationed in foreign countries before, and are equipped with an abundance of curiosity and wide business experience.

Even with all the supportive devices and systems described above, it is still difficult to make creative HRM truly effective. The personnel department is now required to take the initiative in human resource development and the management of corporate culture. These are essential strategic tasks for the future. As mentioned before, it is indispensable to design and facilitate career development of exceptional line managers, in-company entrepreneurs, and various specialists on an individual basis. For example, a tailor-made career development program designed through joint work by the employee, his/her supervisors, and the personnel department is an ideal system. A system that allows employees to select various education and training programs freely, which might be called "cafeteria-style," is also effective. Strategic rotation works as an important means of career development if planned properly to best fit the needs of the individual.

In the organization of typical Japanese firms, there is no section exclusively in charge of the management of corporate culture. Corporate culture is characterized by a fundamental philosophy or value system, which is shared by every person in the company. One of the approaches for the management of such a basic but ambiguous culture is to state the essential philosophy clearly in the written corporate policies. IBM, for example, states clearly in its corporate policy that the company must observe the dignity of individual employees. These policies are usually stipulated by top management. The task of the personnel department is to help it to become a shared value among all employees. In other words, implementation of such a philosophy should be accomplished through the active commitment of employees at all levels.

Paradigm Shift of HRM: Toward Humanistic HRM

In this chapter, I have pointed out the necessity of a paradigm shift in the human resource management of Japanese firms. The cases presented clearly show that Japanese companies have already become involved in and started active responses to this paradigm shift megatrend. So-called Japanese management has been strongly supported by the incremental, case-by-case improvement of personnel management. However, such an approach is no longer effective in a global era of drastic change that requires fundamental restructuring and self-renewal of Japanese firms.

It may be said that traditional "Japanese personnel management" has been quite effective in the existing production-centered paradigm, and in fact has overadapted itself to the model. Thus, in order to achieve self-renewal to overcome the existing paradigm, creative HRM needs to be realized through the active commitment of employees, especially that of the entrepreneurial middle management ranks. Moreover, self-renewal of the firm is a self-transcendental challenge which is hardly achieved solely through passive reaction against environmental pressures and changes. Inner momentum towards self-guided evolution is the critical factor. Creative HRM should elicit creativity and entrepreneurial spirit from within the employees.

Japanese firms' traditional, group-based HRM needs to be replaced by a more individual-based HRM. This movement is quite opposite to the current U.S. HRM trend that aims at introducing group-based methods into their individualistic approach to managing human resources. The task of the personnel department is to initiate and support such a fundamental paradigm shift through various personnel systems, human resource development, and the management of corporate culture. Consequently, the restructuring of the personnel department itself is required, so that it can be more strategic in coordination with both the corporate planning office and the human resource development department.

All of these arguments, however, make no sense unless they are based on strong faith in the value of the human being. No system or technique is truly effective without human commitment. Japanese-style management has been characterized thus far as providing very tender care for employees. However, under the influence of today's sluggish economy and trade conflicts, we should reexamine traditional Japanese-style management to see if it is still a good model for employees. If not, Japanese HRM should be redesigned to realize a harmonious relationship between systems both inside and outside of the firm, such as those systems within the community, society, and culture. Various personnel systems and the culture inside of the firm must be in harmony with those on the outside so that employees can function smoothly in both. The key for such a harmonious relationship is to install a manifest confidence in people in the corporate culture, emphasizing the value of the individual as its most fundamental philosophy. Today, the paradigm shift to such a human-centered or humanistic HRM is a key success factor for self-renewing Japanese firms.

References

Fombrun, C., Tichy, N.M., and Devanna, M.A., eds. *Strategic Human Resource Management*, New York: John Wiley & Sons, 1984.

Hanada, M. "A Study on the Principle of Competition in Personnel System—Personnel Strategy of Promotion Systems in Japanese Firms." *Organizational Science* 1987.

Kagono, T., Nonaka, I., Sakakibara, K., and Okumura, H. *Strategic vs. Evolutionary Management: A U.S.—Japan Comparison of Strategy and Organization*. Amsterdam: North Holland, 1985.

Nonaka, I. "Speeding Organizational Information Creation—Toward "Middle Up-Down Management." *Sloan Management Review* 1988a.

Nonaka, I. "Creating Organizational Order Out of Chaos: Self-Renewal in Japanese Firms." *California Management Review* 1988b.

Takeuchi, H. "Conquering the Isolationist Mentality in Human Resources." *Chuou Kouron* October 1987 (in Japanese).

Polanyi, M. *The Tacit Dimension*. London: Routledge & Kegan Paul, 1966.

Global Research and Teaching in the 1990s

17

The Global Agenda for Research and Teaching in the 1990s

Introduction

Either we develop effective philosophies to bring current business practices and problems into the classroom, or we recognize that we serve only the role of historians.
—ANONYMOUS FACULTY MEMBER, 1990

The U.S. industrial base is under siege. If educational institutions continue on their current path, industry will, also. It becomes an important national policy issue for the business schools to develop themselves.
—ANONYMOUS EXECUTIVE, 1990

The Need for Global Change

American business school students have received what is widely regarded as one of the best graduate educational experiences in the world—in the past. Today's competitive business context has radically altered the structural features of the corporations which, in many schools, MBAs are being insufficiently trained to lead and to manage. Thus, the need to reassess traditional models for institutional administration, research, and teaching has never been more

---

*The author wishes to acknowledge the helpful comments of Noel Tichy, Allen Spivey, and Karl Weick on earlier drafts of this chapter.

319

urgent. Yet, U.S. business schools have demonstrated a reluctance to stimulate major transformations in how they educate students for managerial practice. They are not alone.

Many U.S. organizations in government, industry, and education appear to be braced at the borderline of radical change. They struggle with interpreting the meaning of globalization for their fields. Their inertia is attributable, in part, to the fact that there are no simple questions or answers to global challenges: "Complex realities require complex approaches" (Bolman and Deal 1991, 309). Enigmatic as the situation may be, few would argue that contending with the repercussions of globalization is imperative for organizational capability in the 1990s. The acute need for new and fluid paradigms that facilitate U.S. institutions operating in frame-breaking ways has rapidly developed into the single most serious threat to national competitiveness since the turn of the century.

National Competitive Advantage

> [John] Kotter spent months observing senior managers and rarely found them making a decision. Instead of being made, decisions emerged from a fluid and sometimes confusing series of conversations, meetings, and memos. Managers often have sophisticated information systems that ensure an overload of detail about what happened last month or last year, yet fail to answer the far more important question: What is likely to happen tomorrow? . . . For such decisions, managers operate mostly on the basis of intuition, hunches, and the kind of judgment that they have derived from long-term experience in their organization. They are far too busy to spend time thinking or reading; they get most of their information orally—in meetings or over the telephone. They are hassled priests, modern muddlers, and corporate wheeler-dealers (Bolman and Deal 1991, 321) [emphasis added].

Although the complexities of production and competition have increased exponentially in the last 50 years, the fundamental organizational issues remain the same: how to manage a social system to maximize the activities of both the technical organization and the human organization—often viewed as antithetical processes. For U.S. companies hastening into the twenty-first century, revving up the human engine seems to be the more perplexing of the two. Though hypotheses abound, there is no definitive vision of the twenty-first century global enterprise and its requisite technologies nor are there adequate tools for measuring organizational effectiveness on a worldwide scale.

Business schools and corporations need a common score card by which to evaluate U.S. progress in globalization. What should that score card be? One argument is that it must be the competitiveness of U.S. business in world markets. Many U.S. business schools, companies, and in fact, industries, are just beginning to understand and interpret the meaning of today's radically transformed competitive environment—a domain which encompasses not just firms or industries, but nations.

Both micro- and macro-level forces are determining the productivity standards by which the United States' global competitiveness is evaluated. The characteristics of the American work force have undergone dramatic social and economic metamorphosis during the postindustrial period, and today corporations are enjoined to frame creative solutions to rising work force expectations. In addition, short- as well as long-term people- and technology-oriented needs are demanding unconventional thinking, planning, and action in order to perpetuate our status and role as world business leaders. Finally, globalization presents intellectual and managerial challenges that point to major changes in the quality and intensity of the relationship between business and business schools.

A Symposium on Global Research and Teaching in the 1990s

The University of Michigan Business School's "Symposium on Global Research and Teaching in the 1990s" illuminated the intellectual and managerial challenges of globalization. The purpose of the symposium was to stimulate dialogue and debate regarding the business/business school relationship as well as to mobilize energy for action. The conference helped to frame the specific research and teaching issues that can rally faculty on both departmental and school-wide levels. Working together, academic and industry participants generated team reports on today's pressing global context issues along with implications for future teaching and research.

Conference participants recognized at the outset that new approaches to learning will demand multiframe thinking and powerful innovations in current teaching methods. As a first step, they developed definitions of "globalization:"

1. What does a global organization look like?

2. What does a global business school look like?

3. What does a global curriculum in a business school that serves global corporations look like?

Industry and academic participants grappled with the challenge of articulating their concepts of "global organizations." The "definitions" and "core issues" of globalization that were generated as "pre-work" to the June meeting provided a critical, preliminary backdrop for reformulating existing concepts of the industry/academe relationship. The next section of this chapter presents the definitions of globalization that participants generated for the conference, conducted during June 1990 in Ann Arbor, Michigan.

Defining the Globalization of Business

Associate Professor Ray Reilly,
  University of Michigan, Business Administration
Brian Campbell, President, TriMas Corporation

Definition: Globalization is the integration of business activities across geographical and organizational boundaries. It is the freedom to conceive, design, buy, produce, distribute, and sell products and services in a manner which offers maximum benefit to the firm without regard to the consequences for individual geographic locations or organizational units. There is no presumption that certain activities must be located in certain places or that existing organizational boundaries are inviolable. Instead, the global firm stands ready to respond to changing market conditions and opportunities by reconsidering its options from a broad economic perspective and choosing the alternatives which are thought to be best in the long run. Globalization incorporates a willingness to consider worldwide sourcing for parts which were previously manufactured in our own at-home plant, the development of relationships for distribution and selling through otherwise unrelated firms located in other countries, and the use of joint ventures with international partners to develop and exploit a new technology. The global firm is not constrained by national boundaries as it searches for ideas, talent, capital, and other resources required for its success. In short, the global firm operates with few, if any, self-imposed geographic or organizational constraints on where or how it conducts its business operations.

Professor Noel M. Tichy, University of Michigan, OBHRM

Definition: The capacity to treat the world as one market while paradoxically dealing with it as many culturally diverse merchants. It requires a totally new human engine for corporations, one that can deal with the paradoxes of:

1. Global economies of scale and local customization

2. Transnational and domestic mind-sets

3. Speed and quality

Core issues:

1. Development of global product/service/market strategies

2. Development of worldwide coordination and integration mechanisms

3. Development of capacity for successful strategic alliances and partnering

4. Development of global staffing and career development systems

5. Development of capacity for continuous organizational transformation

Professor Karl E. Weick, University of Michigan, Organizational Behavior and Psychology

Definition: The collective capability to differentiate and integrate five components of competitive advantage—resources, information, processes, products, and markets—between two or more countries, through structures that are managerially enacted rather than geographically imposed.

Key words in this definition are understood as follows:

1. *Collective* emphasizes that this is a social rather than individual activity.

2. *Differentiate* means people need to discover and create the categories and distinctions that are important.

3. *Integrate* means categories and activities must be tied together and coordinated.

4. *Components of competitive advantage* are the substantive focus of attention in global management.

5. *Two or more countries* is minimal point at which a domestic frame of reference begins to prove inadequate in predicting outcomes.

6. *Managerial enactment* emphasizes that global structures and environments have their origins as much in deliberate strategic choices as they do in imposed national constraints.

Core Issues:

1. Is global management really different from domestic management?
   This question is crucial because it affects how much of what we know about domestic management can be generalized to global management and how much must be discarded and replaced by new concepts.

2. How can managers coordinate responsible units without destroying responsiveness?

    Globalization intensifies the need for structures that are *simultaneously* loosely coupled and tightly coupled, decentralized and centralized. These are among the most difficult structures to design, implement, and maintain.

3. How can we improve the comprehension of complex events?

    As global organizations become more complex, people will be tempted to use more abstract, less meaningful indicators and models simply to preserve the illusion that they are able to keep up with what is happening. Because of their remoteness from actual events, these indicators are likely to give increasingly inaccurate representations and to encourage either unwarranted complacence or misguided intervention.

Professor Paul Danos, University of Michigan, Accounting

Definition: Globalization is the process by which markets expand to include competitors for customers and productive inputs without regard to national boundaries. Borders do not protect global businesses from their competitors and, ideally, borders would not deter penetration of all markets by nondramatic competitors. A global business, therefore, must assemble and locate productive resources and choose markets based on economic, not nationalistic, criteria. In a sense, a truly global business is "market-centered" and not "state-centered," because, without government-imposed protection, a business's prosperity will depend purely on global market forces and the talent and resourcefulness of management.

All of the preceding assumes that the political, economic, and cultural systems in which all relevant parties operate are such that global competition is fostered. Virtually every social process, including business, can be dominated by politics; and as long as there are independent governments in each nation, there will be the possibility of politically imposed distortions of market forces. Even among those nations espousing capitalism, there are many variations in the nature of competition allowed, from that which approaches laissez-faire to highly coordinated systems where cartels and governments control business decisions and act strategically.

Business leaders, politicians, and general citizens should beware of the ideology that states: "Businesses operating independently of each other, with little or no coordination with governments, will always lead to maximum social welfare." This may have been reasonably valid at one time, but the great post–World War II economic recoveries give evidence that, at minimum, this is not a generalizable statement. In a world characterized by large-scale producers who operate in unison with financial institutions and governments for long-run market dominance, perhaps the model of fiercely independent businesses is not in keeping with current global realities.

Core Issues:

1. *Quality*: Quality of products and services is the *sine qua non* of business survival in competitive markets.

2. *Cost efficiency*: Costs must be known and acted upon if competitiveness is to be maintained.

3. *Market share*: Short-term profitability cannot be allowed to dominate expansion of market share as the criterion for management decisions.

4. *National differences*: Issues related to culture, taxes, regulation, and local politics, in all of its guises, must be thoroughly understood and taken into consideration.

5. *Management*: Choices about market strategy, location of facilities, degree of centralization, reward structures, information systems, transfer pricing, and all other important management decisions must be made with a global perspective.

Professor Gunter Dufey, University of Michigan, International Business and Finance

Definition: Managing strategic and functional aspects of business enterprise by taking systematically into consideration environmental linkages in terms of economic, cultural, and political dimensions.

Core Issues: To develop strategy and policy that is appropriate for new environmental conditions and tailor organization accordingly. This determines success or failure of corporation in global environment.

Professor Dennis G. Severance, University of Michigan, Computer and Information Systems

Definition: The operating environment in which a firm is driven to design, engineer, manufacture, purchase, assemble, market, distribute, and/or service its products on an international basis in order to achieve superior performance.

Core Issues: Both external and internal forces push firms towards globalization. Externally, customer demands for global products or service, competitor offerings of one-stop shopping, and government regulations on product features or domestic content have forced international deployment on some reluctant participants. On the other hand, the potential for significant market growth, the promise of economics of scope and scale, and the opportunity to leverage scarce resources (i.e., management, equipment, expertise) have moved other firms toward globalization of their own volition.

Richard Measelle, Chief Executive Officer, Arthur Andersen & Company

In recent years, the term "global" has increasingly been used in place of the term "multinational." In many respects the term is being used as a substitute for multinational, much in the same manner that other terms such as "Pan-European" are beginning to emerge to describe European operations in the face of 1992. To think about this evolution as simply substitution is to miss an important point as to the real difference between multinational and global.

It is my contention that in the multinational organization, which characterized the way many American companies, for example, operated in the 1950s, 1960s, and 1970s, investments are made outside of the host countries. These investments, whether they are joint ventures or majority or wholly owned subsidiaries, are managed from a central location in an essentially hierarchical manner; i.e., decision making goes in one direction from the headquarters to the overseas subsidiary. In a global organization, however, there is real decentralization of decision making and much more sharing of responsibility and much more authority. In a global organization, these initiatives go in both directions. I believe that truly global organizations are increasingly being seen as the way to recognize the fact that there are diverse cultures and business conditions. In a word, companies must become more multicultural.

Our own firm is a good case study of this. Arthur Andersen started as a Chicago-based accounting firm and did not expand outside of the United States until after World War II. The initial forays into Europe were led by Americans who were dispatched to the European capitals. Slowly, however, we began to assimilate European nationals into our operations and, by the early 1960s, a few of these Europeans were in leadership positions in their countries. The mere assignment of a national leader, however, does not mean that you are a global firm. It was only when we began to truly decentralize our organizations and empower our local partners to have a much greater voice in their operations that we began to move in the direction of being a truly global enterprise. In our own case, I believe, we are still in the beginning stages of this move from multinational to global, but the trend is irreversible.

This decentralization has numerous benefits, including the fact that when errors are made, as inevitably they are, the impact of the errors is much less because they are not replicated in every single country. Also, with additional authority goes responsibility for results and this increased level of stewardship also pays important dividends.

Today, I believe, there are only a handful of truly global enterprises, but in the future, moving about in an increasingly shrinking world in an effective manner will argue conclusively for this type of organization. This does not mean that these operations are franchise or federations and that there is no glue that holds the disparate parts together. Quite the contrary, there is glue in certain cultural and value imperatives which must be respected. The point is that these imperatives are the result of a more open environment of management which respects local differences, and the fact that each market has its own characteristics and is not part of a global network. Internal structures and styles must be created that match diverse cultures of the market.

In the May 14 issue of *Business Week*, they coin a phrase that I have not seen before about the "stateless corporation." Incidentally, the lead in that article is ABB (Asea Brown Boveri) which, in my way of thinking, may be the prototypical global company in the world today.

At Arthur Andersen, we are placing a great deal of emphasis on the notion of thinking globally and acting locally. We talk about global strategies, area plans, and local tactics.

Dean Ruwe, President and CEO, Copeland Corporation

Definition: Having the products and facilities to serve markets anywhere.

Core Issues:

1. *Engineers close to customers*: More accurate and timely product development

2. *Quality awareness*: USA buyers not as discriminating as Japanese and northern Europeans

3. *Engineering organization—centralized or local?* Standard design and local modifications

4. *Production facilities*: Ability to shift products

Professor Dennis G. Severance, University of Michigan, CIS
Jacque Passino, Andersen Consulting, Partner, Arthur Andersen & Co.

Definition: The operating environment in which a firm is driven to design, engineer, manufacture, purchase, assemble, market, distribute, and/or service its products on an international basis in order to achieve superior performance.

Core Issues:

1. Management structure

2. Communication

3. Flexibility

4. Coordination

5. Decision making

Lawrason D. Thomas, Executive Vice President, Amoco Corporation

Definition: Globalization means doing business with a worldwide focus basis rather than doing business in an international market with the focus from a U.S. viewpoint. Global integration of economic activity is driven by increasing mobility of capital and people, expanding flows of information and knowledge, advancing technology, progressively more homogeneous markets, and lowered trade barriers. A successful global business understands business conditions both locally and worldwide and conducts its activities (manufacturing, marketing, distribution, finance, human resources, R&D, and design and engineering) on a global optimized basis.

Core Issues:

1. *Management*: Cope with more complex decisions

2. *Human resource*: Accommodate cultural differences, multinational workforce; use varying expertise and know-how

3. *Political environment*: Governments sometimes regulate movement of capital, goods, and services across borders

4. *Economic environment*: Impacts trade, profitability, capital and profit repatriation

5. *Strategic alliances*: Partner can make vital contribution

6. *Technology*: Key element of competitive advantages

Paul W. Van Orden, Executive Vice President/ Corporate Executive Office, General Electric Company

Definition: A business, with significant presence in worldwide markets, utilizing effective processes and measurements for centrally rationalizing strategic resource trade-offs as well as integrating tactical programs.

Core Issues:

1. *Global strategy development*: Essential to have a game plan

2. *Processes*: Manage global complexity effectively

3. *Measurements*: Impacts all business processes

4. *Human resources development*: The engine of global business

5. *Strategic alliances*: Essential for access

6. *Social issues*: Environment, education, etc. are global issues

Dr. Deb Chatterji, Chief Executive—Technical Activities, The BOC Group

Definition: Globalization is the conscious and disciplined management process of stepping out of the intellectual and operational confines of a domestic enterprise to fully recognize and address global opportunities and threats in a strategically and operationally integrated manner. Globalization is much more than setting up plants and offices in foreign countries: it is a total approach to managing business around the world that seeks the whole to be greater than the sum of the parts. In a successful global company, each geographic entity enriches the other in more ways than providing an outlet for products or services.

Core Issues:

1. Top management mind-set and strategies

2. Understanding of and respect for the "new frontiers"—avoiding "ugly American syndrome"

3. Effectively bridging communication and cultural gaps across many organizational layers

4. Establishing strategic alliances and other types of business arrangements

5. Ability to integrate functions and projects across geographic and cultural barriers—build teams

6. Ability to think globally but act locally—and expediently!

7. Developing next generation of global managers

8. Managing strain on financial and intellectual resources

Ralph F. Hake, Corporate Vice President and Controller, Whirlpool Corporation

Definition: Globalization is a process which expands the market opportunities and basis of competition for business and institutions. The process is evolutionary and is driven by both reduction of barriers to competition and enhanced worldwide availability of capital and an educated workforce, as well as efficient communication and information flows. In the past, the typical global competitors evolved because of their requirements to source raw materials in one part of the world, with major markets in other geographic areas. In the future, global competition will be driven by the ability to organize human, technical, and capital resources to provide products or services to any attractive national or regional market.

Core Issues:

1. *Consumer and market research*: Evaluate worldwide opportunities

2. *Organizational capabilities*: Perspective to organize and manage global enterprises

3. *Strategic evaluation and direction*: There must be a clear, long-term direction to evaluate relative opportunities and allocate resources

4. *Government regulatory, environmental, and monetary risks*: Limitations on ability to pursue opportunities

Defining the Globalization of Business Schools
Professor Kim S. Cameron, University of Michigan, OBHRM

The globalized business school curriculum would be organized in a way that is different from any university-based business school currently in operation.

- *Multilingual.* All students and faculty would study at least one other language during their programs of study. Preference would be given to multilingual students in admission decisions. Some reading from current periodicals in other languages (e.g., German, Japanese) would be required in every course. For students and faculty not knowing that particular language, they would find a partner to read to them. Partnerships among students speaking other languages would be encouraged and fostered.

- *Cultural Exposure.* Part of the curriculum requirements would be significant exposure to at least one other culture. This could be accomplished through international internships, significant travel experience, or organized month-long excursions by the business school in which plant tours, management interviews, market analyses, and so on, were planned. Part of the curriculum offering would be student exchanges with other universities and businesses worldwide.

- *Comparative.* Every topic in traditional discipline-focused courses would be comparative. For example, accounting systems, personnel practices, and market strategies in the United States would be compared to those in Eastern Europe, Asia, Western Europe, South America, and so on. Special focus would be placed on the issues that arise from crossing boundaries, merging differences, and operating in multiple systems.

- *Problem-Centered.* A significant number of courses would be offered that are problem-focused rather than purely discipline-focused. Problems such as quality, improving customer service, market share expansion, downsizing and cost containment, corporate ethics, managing a mobile work force, and international government relations might be examples. In each case, the problems would be approached from a worldwide perspective rather than from a domestic or multidomestic perspective. Consciousness-raising and awareness-expansion as well as management skill development would be desired outcomes. Faculty members from multiple disciplines would form partnerships to teach these courses. Partners from business would also participate regularly. For example, professors from marketing, organizational behavior, production management, and international business might teach a course on improving customer service, and several representatives from partner businesses engaged in global customer service might be asked to deliver guest lectures.

- *Flexibility in Timing.* Much more flexibility would be permitted in terms of the kinds of experiences receiving course credit, the amount of full-time on-campus experience required of students, and the expectation that the program would last exactly four semesters. Courses would not necessarily meet for the traditional three hours a week for 16 weeks. Most students would spend part of their program in international settings, not necessarily in formal classroom work.

Students should emerge from such a program with a global mind-set, rather than a multidomestic one. They also should emerge with a broader multidisciplinary perspective. Because most issues would be analyzed using multicultural and multidiscipline approaches, students would be both more flexible and more savvy in their perspectives. An inclination toward forming partnerships with individuals from other countries and ethnic groups would result from the pedagogical structure of the program so that, whereas national patriotism would not diminish, a world-citizen mind-set would be fostered.

The Business School of the Future

Education in the 1990s and the twenty-first century will demand that business school faculty, students, and executives assume the mind-sets of pioneering cosmopolites. The educational mission of the 1990s includes discovering knowledge about the business environment and disseminating it through teaching and publishing on a new, interdisciplinary scale. Faculty need to be able to work together as nonhierarchical partners, thinking in global terms, and establishing worldwide network relationships that will free them of any monolithic limitations.

Global Action Agenda:
Building the New Paradigm for the 1990s

The business school graduates of the 1990s will require new and diverse skills to facilitate their professional roles as members of management teams operating in a virtually borderless world. What will propel the American economy in the next decade is a different version of competition than has existed in the past. The familiar tale of triumphant individuals and enterprising heroes no longer provides adequate models for the new age economic success possible only through collective entrepreneurship.

The team is the new corporate hero, and this means a new, fluid paradigm for faculty collaboration as well. The more interdisciplinary the faculty become, the higher the probability that their graduates will be able to lead competitively in global business breakthroughs and cutting-edge discoveries.

To prepare students for the new age managerial challenges means breaking frame with conventional models of business school education.

The key characteristics of a globalized business school will include:

1. Cultural exposure through international internships and student exchanges with other universities and businesses worldwide; much more flexibility in terms of experiential course credit.

2. Language programs for students and faculty.

3. Comparative courses in all disciplines (e.g., accounting systems, personnel practices, and market strategies in the U.S. compared to Eastern Europe, Asia, Western Europe, South America, etc.).

4. Teams as learning units to develop skill sets useful in global organizations; team building within culturally diverse student groups leveraging non–U.S. students (as well as faculty) as country "experts" to enliven the cultural dimension of case studies.

5. New visiting faculty recruited from foreign countries as well as the United States for collaborative research and teaching that enriches international studies.

6. Faculty development policy update: establish new exchanges between U.S. and foreign universities as well as with global corporations.

7. Problem-centered courses taught by faculty from multiple disciplines

forming partnerships in teaching; business executives participating regularly (e.g., courses on global customer service, quality, market share expansion, corporate ethics, international government relations, etc.).

8. Courses focusing on particular applications instead of generic skills (via exposure to issues such as culture, teamwork, information systems, and risk taking) for global leadership development. A curriculum designed to enhance global competence requires skill development in negotiation, initiating and managing change, coping with overload, self-management (e.g., patience, persistence), construction of processes, communication, improvisation, sense-making, persuasion, representation of complex systems. Curriculum redesign involves helping students to develop an understanding about five key bodies of knowledge: (1) the effects of overload and uncertainty on individuals and groups, (2) how knowledge is organized and modified, (3) organizational politics, (4) alternative forms of organization, and (5) the nature of interpretation systems.

9. Courses that draw on the interdisciplinary strengths of the entire university community: political science, psychology, sociology, anthropology, social work, public health, law school, engineering school, language department, and so forth.

10. Developing nontraditional teaching methods to teach the required "new knowledge" triggered by the globalization of business.

The modernistic, fluid paradigm for a globalized business school requires continuous experimentation and development as the school searches for new ways to capture and build on its existing knowledge and skill base. In the atmosphere of collective entrepreneurship, individual skills are integrated into multidisciplinary groups where the power to innovate becomes greater than the sum of its parts. The American business school needs to reinvent itself in a frame-breaking way that is different from any current day university-based school. This demands changing mind-sets, learning the subtleties of network management, and embracing more paradoxical ideas. The globalization phenomenon forces us to re-examine the process by which business schools, as institutions, can change and thereby expand the horizon for research and teaching in the twenty-first century.

The Opportunities of Globalization

All true world-class competitors are capable of rapid transformation. Thus it becomes critical for institutions of higher education to devote energies to quickly discovering what attributes foster continuous improvement and innovation in the university setting—without such learning, competitive advantage can never be achieved or sustained. Perhaps the greatest challenge of the globalization phenomenon is to develop a business school culture that can repeatedly, creatively destroy and rebuild itself; that is, a self-transforming institution.

Restructuring at a global pace requires an enabling vision of the 1990s business school to catalyze debate, choice, and action among the faculty. Now is the time. "Go slow to go fast" is an aphorism that threatens to cripple progress—by the time consensus from the slowest is gained, the fastest will have lost hope and momentum.

To become partners in the future means reconceptualizing the business school's mission and values and committing resources to participate in their redesign. We will find no argument about the swift pace of change in the global environment. As U.S. industry has learned in the last decade, now business schools must compete against time to effect requisite and radical institutional change.

Toward a New Paradigm: The Goal of MBA Education in a Global Environment

Your market is changing. If students are the product, then industry is the market. Industry is changing because of globalization and restructuring in most businesses. Hierarchical structures are breaking down—MBAs are going into a world with less structure.
—ANONYMOUS EXECUTIVE, 1990

The way to secure a company's position within its industry is to find the most demanding customers, determine their needs, and serve them better than competitors do.
—STALK AND HOUT 1990, 272

The challenge that U.S. business schools face every September is how to train hundreds of the brightest 25- to 35-year-olds in the country to be effective leaders of global corporations. The new mandate is to redesign the entire MBA experience, not just the curriculum. It is time to begin teaching MBA students to think globally, to view themselves as world citizens, to cultivate the habits of lifelong learning, and to value action.

Managing global organizations demands a brand of leadership, imagination, determination, and sense of duty that most MBAs have not been taught before. To be able to act independently, self-reliantly, and creatively has become a critical asset not only for the individual manager's success, but for the global corporation's and for society's. The MBAs of the 1990s must have a different vision and a new set of values, skills, and abilities than earlier generations of students who have been trained to take managerial roles in domestic or multidomestic companies.

Strategic Alliances: Rethinking the Academic and Industry Interface

Globalizing education in business administration challenges both industrial and academic leaders to develop new methods and technologies to overturn existing fixed constraints in the system. Such innovation requires a commitment to sustained investment in research, physical capital, and human resources. Through academic/executive partnerships in teaching, we see both the promise of an educated and trained work force as well as the capability for innovation in continuously reorganizing our entire system.

Industry/Academia Alliances. The study of organizations through faculty-dominated lectures and cases alone has become inadequate to meet the managerial needs of today's globalizing firms. First-hand observations, simulations, video reenactments, laboratory experiments, team building and team-focused learning, new practicums, and redesigned internships have been recommended by corporate executives as contemporary teaching tools to produce business school graduates who are better equipped for managing global companies. Students need to learn how to use networks and they need help in developing conceptual models and exercises for the multicultural/multinational teamwork that will be demanded of them upon entry into the corporate world. The importance of learning about coalition building cannot be overemphasized. And the required new cognitive processes and knowledge cannot be taught in the traditional ways.

Executives, faculty, and students need to become part of an ongoing laboratory experiment on globalization. Some feel that business school students tend to think as followers. To encourage leadership thinking, practicum and internship assignments with global companies working on real-time problems and projects would provide a strong learning opportunity as a follow-on to school-based simulations. Cross-cultural student teams—as a new core learning unit—would master not only the functional skills, but also the total business process including the dynamics of competitive factors through studies of industries, countries, and companies. The curriculum needs to be revised to incorporate more teaching about the integration of business, government, and industry sector exchanges. Executives are calling for MBAs who have specific skills within the global context. The best way to meet their needs is through a multinational student body and faculty team-based approach to education:

... it is possible, at least over a period of several years, for a small group of faculty members to become committed to collective inquiry into teaching and learning. It is possible to create surprisingly durable 'traditions' that channel faculty and student interactions in new ways. Faculty members can find it exciting, even liberating, to make their own teaching into a subject for mutual exploration. And when they do so, their substantive research interests are engaged.

Most important, many faculty members thirst for an intellectual community. When such a community presents itself as a real possibility, it taps a powerful source of energy for reflection-in-action in curriculum redesign.

—Schon 1987, 342

Experiential learning through student and faculty teams will contribute to shifting our focus to the entire business process without jeopardizing attention to the functional areas.

Interdisciplinary Alliances.

There are multifunctional problems in business and they need to be addressed as such.

There are really very few integrative mechanisms at the University. Only in Executive Education are faculty forced to work together and cooperate.

We know that team teaching is beneficial but we simply don't practice it.

—Anonymous faculty member, 1990

Alliances have become a common tool for extending or reinforcing the competitive advantage of global firms. Today, multidisciplinary teams within business units are beginning to replace the more traditional functional expertise on corporate staffs. Historically, universities have not taken a problem-based approach to building interdisciplinary faculty teams. Yet, in order to fulfill their service to society, business schools now must create an environment that encourages faculty to work together across disciplines. As corporate hierarchical structures are breaking down, entry-level MBAs must be educated and sensitized to the interrelatedness of the functions within the businesses they aspire to manage.

Integrated learning is the key. Business school teaching must focus on the total business process, blending functional concentrations into the framework. Experimentation with new teaching methods, faculty commitment to the process, and resources for learning are some of the operating mechanisms to produce students who are problem-driven instead of functionally driven.

Team learning units need to be employed for students to more effectively develop skill sets required in new age organizations. The MBA program must emphasize the interrelatedness of all business functions and faculty teamwork must be the driving force if we are to close the gap between academia and managerial practice.

Short-Term and Long-Term Needs: Teaching and Research

The standard American corporate questions about quality improvement are, "What do we do? (But keep it simple)" and "How long will it take? (But keep it short)".

—DOBYNS 1990

Long development times and short-run profit goals complicate the globalization balancing act both for industry and academe. But there seems to be consensus that the leading global companies at least are discovering how to simultaneously balance and blend a variety of paradoxical issues.

As the definitions of globalization indicated, a global company integrates activities across geographical and organizational boundaries. It is free to conceive, design, buy, produce, distribute, and sell products and services in a manner that offers maximum benefit to the whole without regard to the consequences for individual geographic locations or organizational units. There is no presumption that certain activities must be located in particular places or that existing organizational boundaries are inviolable. Instead, the global organization stands ready to respond to changing market conditions and opportunities by reconsidering and constantly reframing its options from a broad economic perspective for both short- and long-term success. The global firm is not constrained by national boundaries as it searches for ideas, talent, capital, and other required resources. It functions with few, if any, self-imposed constraints on where or how it conducts its operations.

Global organizations develop a collective capability to differentiate and integrate key components of competitive advantage across boundaries through structures that are managerially enacted rather than geographically imposed. Thus, global structures and environments have their origins as much in deliberate strategic choices as in imposed national constraints. Globalization intensifies the need for structures that are simultaneously loosely coupled and tightly coupled, decentralized and centralized—some of the most difficult structures to design, implement, and maintain.

A parallel process exists for academia. A globalized business school must be capable of:

1. Recruiting the best multicultural faculty and students from all regions of the world;

2. Designing the curricula for both functional and interdisciplinary relevance;

3. Teaching courses within a problem/practice-oriented, team-based framework;

4. Facilitating and supporting multidisciplinary research projects and programs on an international level; and

5. Serving a dual role as the trainer of new managers and business historian/analyst.

Some hold that business school education gives executives knowledge that helps them to make better decisions, but their businesses give them experience. Globalizing the entire business school demands consideration of the educational system's core values: Should the key role of the university be to teach people how to learn? Should the purpose and value of research be linked to society's problems or the faculty development system? Is it possible to integrate these objectives into a new set of values and standards? These represent some of the most critical issues that the business school faculty must address in the immediate future. There are no easy answers.

As a civilization, we sit completely astride the Machine Age and the Systems Age. As a result, our consciousness, our philosophy, is split right down the middle. . . . In effect, we keep on trying to solve the problems of the Systems Age with our old Machine Age mentality. Some of this is due to just plain old-fashioned denial . . . part of the difficulty involved in making the transition that any profound revolution in human affairs calls for.

. . . [not only is there] no significant change without considerable pain, but . . . unless the pain is dealt with directly . . . there is no hope of significant change either within individuals or their organizations. We kid ourselves when we think that our problems can be dealt with purely at the intellectual level.

I have no doubt whatsoever that if our society is to make the transition successfully to the Systems Age and thereby continue to be a major player in the global economy, then more and more executives [and academics] will have to learn to expand their thinking.

—(MITROFF 1988, 179–80, 181–82, 183) [bracketed material added].

An Action Agenda

The next several years are clearly transition years for most of the major U.S. business schools. Now is a time of new leadership, new vision, and an opportunity to help set the world standard. As professional schools, business schools produce students who practice the art of management and leadership. As academic researchers and teachers, the faculty's responsibility goes beyond personal research interests—what impact does any faculty want to have through teaching on the major wealth-producing institutions of the world, i.e., on business organizations? The challenge is difficult but unavoidable:

> As the world increasingly becomes a single system, if anything goes wrong, everything goes wrong. As the world becomes more like an organism and less like an ecosystem, its vulnerability increases. Organisms die, ecosystems merely get transformed in a long, continuous process. . . . Now we are faced with a world economy and a world political structure with literally nobody in charge. This may be just as well, but it is at least a little frightening.
>
> —BOULDING 1989, 191

References

Anonymous executives' comment(s). 1990. The Symposium on Global Research and Teaching in the 1990s (June 3–5) Ann Arbor, Michigan.

Anonymous faculty members [Michigan Business School] comment(s). 1990. The Symposium on Global Research and Teaching in the 1990s (June 3–5), Ann Arbor, Michigan.

Bolman, L. D., and Deal, T. E. 1991. *Reframing Organizations—Artistry, Choice, and Leadership*. San Francisco, Calif.: Jossey-Bass.

Boulding, K. E. 1989. *Three Faces of Power*. Newbury Park, Calif.: Sage Publications.

Dobyns, L. 1990. "Because Better Costs Less." *Smithsonian* 21(5):74–85.

Mitroff, I. I. 1988. *Break-Away Thinking*. New York: Wiley.

Schon, D. A. 1987. *Educating the Reflective Practitioner*. San Francisco, Calif.: Jossey-Bass.

Stalk, G. Jr., and Hout, T. M. 1990. *Competing Against Time—How Time-based Competition is Reshaping Global Markets*. New York: Free Press.

18

Globalization
*The Intellectual and Managerial Challenges**

C. K. Prahalad

Introduction

A significant characteristic of the 1980s has been the change in the locus of industrial leadership in a wide variety of industries. As shown in Table 18.1, intellectual and market leadership in several industries moved away from U.S. firms to primarily Japanese (and in some cases to European) firms. This trend has created an industrial landscape that is less skewed in favor of U.S. firms as it was during the 1950–1975 period. The changing nature of industrial leadership has had a profound impact on the *managerial agenda.*

Senior managers, in a wide variety of firms, in the United States, in Europe, and in Japan are experimenting with approaches designed to cope with new demands imposed by the emerging competitive order. We will outline some of these managerial challenges in this chapter. However, the academic community in leading business schools in the United States appears to be less willing to experiment and innovate. The paradigms used, the issues researched, and the curricula taught—the *academic agenda*—does not reflect a concerted effort to actively participate in and influence the evolution of the managerial agenda for the 1990s and beyond.

The basic thesis of this chapter is that the need for active collaboration between practitioners (managers) and researchers (academics) has never been more pronounced. If not carefully nurtured, the two groups may drift apart; and an opportunity for building a symbiotic relationship would have been

Human Resource Management, Vol. 29, Number 1, pp. 27–38, C.K. Prahalad, copyright © 1990 by John Wiley & Sons, Inc., reprinted by permission of John Wiley & Sons, Inc.

Table 18.1 Changing pattern of industrial leadership

INDUSTRY	LEADERS 1950–1975	CHALLENGERS 1980–
Automotive	GM Ford	Toyota Nissan Honda
Semiconductors	TI Motorola	NEC Toshiba Fujitsu Hitachi
Tires	Goodyear Firestone	Michelin Bridgestone
Med. systems	GE Philips Siemens	Hitachi Toshiba
Cons. electronics	GE[a] RCA[a] Philips	Matsushita Sony
Photographic	Kodak	Fuji
Xerography	Xerox	Canon
Earth moving eqpt.	Caterpillar	Komatsu

[a]Discontinued operations.

lost. The chapter is divided in four parts. In Part I we will describe the emerging world of the manager in a diversified multinational corporation (DMNC).* We will then go on to outline some of the competitive challenges faced by these firms. In Part III we will examine the mismatch between the managerial and the academic agenda using an issue set. Finally, we will outline both the need for and an approach to developing a shared agenda between practitioners and researchers.

*While global competition will impact both small and large firms, domestically oriented as well as multinational firms, in this chapter we will focus only on the impact on DMNCs. The DMNC provides the most complex managerial work environment. Many of the issues covered, therefore, may be as applicable to other settings as well.

The World of the DMNC Manager

The best way to describe the world of the DMNC manager is to start with a few examples of firms.

Let us consider ASEA Brown Boveri (ABB), a $20.0 billion company created by the merger of ASEA (Swedish base), BBC (Swiss base), and Combustion Engineering and parts of Westinghouse (U.S. base), and a whole host of other smaller acquisitions around the world. The company operates in 145 countries, is organized into 3,500 profit centers, incorporates 1,150 legal entities, and employs over 190,000 people around the world. The company is involved in so many licensing and co-production agreements that it is hard to keep track. Its portfolio of businesses consists of a very wide variety of businesses—from a $2 switch to a $1 billion power system for a country. ABB is, by the very nature of its businesses, subject to significant host governments' pressures.

Consider Nestle. Unlike ABB, Nestle's sales of $30 billion derived primarily from packaged and branded goods businesses. It operates 380 factories around the world. In most of its businesses, Nestle competes with local rivals as well as global rivals (such as Unilever) in various markets. Each country market—U.S., Germany, India, and Ivory Coast—is different in terms of the competitive dynamics as well as product needs.

Consider IBM. At $60 billion IBM operates around the world in a complex and turbulent industry. Its development and manufacturing capabilities are dispersed leading to a complex product development and logistics process. By the very nature of the industry in which it participates, it has to contend with a wide variety of rivals—large firms like Fujitsu and NEC as well as small niche players like Tulip computers in the Benelux countries.

The three foregoing examples of the nature of the DMNC suggest that managers are confronted with issues such as: integration of large international acquisitions (ABB), understanding the meaning of performance and accountability in a globally integrated system of product flows (IBM), building and managing a worldwide logistics capability (IBM), ability to develop country specific corporate strategies that takes into account the political as well as the economic imperatives (ABB) management of brand equities around the world with differing competitive dynamics in each market (Nestle), forming and benefiting from a series of collaborative arrangements (OEM contracts, licensing, alliances, joint ventures) around the world, balancing the need for global integration as well as simultaneously responding to local demands—a task that presents qualitatively different demands in all three companies, and managing in a multicultural environment. The above is not intended to be an exhaustive but an indicative list of the types of issues faced by managers.

The portfolios of these firms contain a wide variety of businesses. For example, ABB's portfolio contains electric motors and nuclear power plants. This diversity in the portfolio requires that managers recognize the differences between a strategy for a single, discrete, stand alone business, strategies that include multiple, interlinked businesses, a strategy for a key country in which several business groups may participate, and corporate strategy. Priorities in a business change with the perspective one takes. What appears to be the most critical issue from the perspective of a business unit may not appear to be so if one takes the perspective of several interlinked businesses. Priority setting for resource deployment, in such a context, can be quite onerous. In addition, considerations such as equity, fairness, engendering commitment of all employees around the world to a shared competitive agenda, and administrative ease often conflict with the need to customize and develop unique organizational solutions to reflect the characteristics of specific businesses. These conflicting demands imposed by strategies (a reflection of the turbulence and complexity in the external environment) coupled with internal administrative difficulties (the need for uniformity and equity) create the world that the DMNC manager lives in; a world where variety, complex interaction patterns among various subunits, host governments, and customers, pressures for change and stability, and the need to reassert individual identity in a complex web of organizational relationships are the norm. This world is one beset with ambiguity and stress. Facts, emotions, anxieties, power and dependence, competition and collaboration, individual and team efforts are all present. The substantive and the organizational, the logical and the intuitive, data and judgment, the analytical and the emotional coexist. Managers have to deal with these often conflicting demands simultaneously. It is hard to abstract away the complexity created by these interactions without essentially changing the very nature of the world in which the DMNC manager lives and works.

The Competitive Challenge

It is from this DMNC world that managers must develop strategies, deploy resources, and compete. The competitive landscape dramatically altered during the 1980s. For example, DMNC managers had to meet new standards for quality, cost, cycle time, responsiveness to the customers, and flexibility. Yet another emerging concern during the decade of the 1980s, was the perceived need for developing "global products." Managers appear to have accepted the twin demands on business strategies—finding the right balance between the need to be globally integrated and locally responsive. DMNCs have had varying levels of success in mastering these demands. However, as they enter the 1990s, managers are likely to be confronted with *an additional set* of demands. The task of managing a DMNC will get more complex. For example, during the 1990s, managers will have to come to terms with the impact of:

1. *Shifting patterns of trade and funds flows across the regions of the world.*

The emergence of trading blocks—the North American trading block (U.S. and Canada and eventually Mexico), European Community [originally the Western European countries—the EEC—but eventually including both the Northern European countries (EFTA) and the emerging Eastern European countries], a South East Asian or Pacific Region dominated by Japan, and potentially a Latin American Region (centered on Brazil)—will strongly influence the patterns of trade and funds flows. No longer is it adequate to think in terms of nation states; managers must take into account the impact of the emergence of trading blocks and economic regions. These considerations will impact manufacturing investments, organization of marketing and sales efforts, sensitivity to currency fluctuations, and product and funds flows within the firm. The political imperative may transcend the national (e.g., demands imposed by the French government) and incorporate the goals and aspirations of the trading block as a whole (e.g., European Commission).

2. *Competition for restructuring mature industries.* The evidence that this will be a major issue is already in. The sequence of mergers, acquisitions, and alliances in the power systems, telecommunications, chemicals, automotive, tires, computer, paper machinery, packaged goods, public accounting, management consulting, financial services, entertainment and consumer electronics, and major domestic appliances businesses around the world during the 1985–1991 period is just a start. The motivations for restructuring are many. They include global excess capacity, deregulation, new approaches to global competition, changing patterns of access to erstwhile protected and fragmented markets, and the desire on the part of aggressive competitors to enlarge the market scope of their businesses. Few firms such as ABB and Alsthom (power systems), Alcatel, AT&T, and Siemens (telecom), and Fujitsu (computers), P&G, Unilever, and Kao (packaged goods and personal care products), and Michelin and Bridgestone (tires), and Whirlpool and Electrolux (appliances) for example, have redrawn the map of these industries and the basis for competition. Not surprisingly, governments have a keen interest in both the process and the outcome of these global restructuring efforts. Often, these actions are based on the premise that large firms are trying to create an industry structure that is favorable to them, at the expense of smaller and domestically oriented firms, in the medium and long term. These restructuring initiatives involve an intense interplay of the political and the economic imperatives. They also involve questions of social cost (who pays for the redundancies and the downsizing of capacity?), national sovereignty, and the fate of industrial infrastructure in a given country. Even in the U.S., where the rhetoric is often market forces and free trade, there has been a significant public concern over these restructuring efforts as in the case of Fujitsu's attempt to buy National Semiconductor. Organizationally, this international restructuring effort demands that managers learn to integrate acquisitions with totally different cultures, product, and market philosophies, and often

overlapping market presence. It also requires a capacity to calibrate the political sensitivities and balance them against strategic benefits.

3. *Competition for structuring an emerging industry.* In many high-technology sectors and emerging industries, competition may exist even before products and services are introduced in the market place. Take, for example, businesses such as digital audio tape (DAT), High Definition TV (HDTV), UNIX, MAPS, CompactDisc Interactive (CD-I), Digital Compact Cassette (DCC), Intelligent Vehicle and Highway Systems (IVHS), and Chemical handling. In every one of these industries, firms are jockeying for a position favorable to them. Consider the case of VCRs. A coalition of firms was formed to explicitly support alternate formats and standards (VHS and Betamax). This competition to establish compatibility standards is not just for market share and profits in a given product market space—but to secure the right to define the nature of the industry. By capturing the industry standard, a coalition of firms can then influence the competitive battle for products and services yet to come. Both the vigor of this competition as well as the pervasiveness of this phenomenon in a large number of industries make this a unique development during the later part of the 1980s. Managers must recognize the need for collaboration to establish a standard and compete as a cluster (say those who favor the VHS format over Betamax) and at the same time compete among themselves for market share and profits. Both intercluster and intracluster competition is present.

4. *Competition for creating industry space.* Again traditional views of competition implicitly assume that competitive battles are aimed at gaining an advantage in today's markets. In such a framework, cost, quality, cycle time, and responsiveness to the customers are key ingredients to success. The emerging competition is not waged just in the existing industry space. The goal is to compete for competencies that allow one to create new businesses, continually. Personal fax, personal copiers, laptop computers, electronic games, microwave-oriented foods, environmentally sensitive packaging, digital key boards, and electronic diaries are just a few examples. The capacity to create these new businesses rests on a very intimate understanding of the customers' emerging and dormant needs and functionalities, coupled with a carefully developed competence portfolio that allows a firm to be able to identify, and respond both quickly and creatively to such opportunities. Competition in this sense may be moving away from primarily product—market competition toward competition for gaining and sustaining competence or the capacity to create new businesses. The capacity to nurture core competencies, and acquiring them at low cost becomes a major issue.

5. *Understanding the dynamics of collaborative arrangements.* In several industries such as automotive, communication, computing, and pharmaceuticals, the propensity to form a collaborative arrangement, often with competitors, is in evidence. This raises interesting questions. When the

alliance is based on a need to share skills across partners (as opposed to benefiting from economies of scale—an oil refinery, or accessing natural resources—bauxite or lumber from a developing country), does collaboration eliminate the intent to compete? If partners collaborate in one business, but compete in other related businesses, what is the meaning of collaboration? Can such collaborations have a long life? How do firms extract value from these collaborations? The demands of collaboration and competition between firms can create an organizational schizophrenia. How open should we be? Where do we draw the boundaries? How do we manage the flow of information in the alliance? The failure rates and the disappointments with these arrangements is only matched by the euphoria at the time of entering these relationships.

6. *Protecting intellectual property.* In a wide variety of businesses such as financial services, software, pharmaceuticals, and semiconductors, the real source of competitive advantage is in intellectual property—the concepts, design, approach—that is not captured necessarily in investments in plant and equipment as in an automobile assembly plant. The concept of "windows" in PC software or chemical composition of an active ingredient in a drug, or a new financial instrument, for example, is qualitatively a different type of intellectual property from the design of a manufacturing plant. Competitors can duplicate a new financial instrument at a very small fraction of the cost it took the pioneer, and almost instantaneously, as compared to the intellectual property captured in a manufacturing plant. In traditional manufacturing businesses, competitors often had to make comparable investments. Even legally, it is easier to protect patents of manufacturing processes and traditional products, compared to ideas and concepts that are the basis for the new industries. Intellectual property is people embedded (in contrast to capital embedded property in manufacturing plants). Capital, in this sense can be assumed "to wear shoes and ride elevators." Loss of a critical group of individuals can severely hurt the firm.

7. *The blending of hardware and software.* The distinctions that we have traditionally used to describe businesses may no longer be relevant. Hardware and software are becoming totally integrated. A VCR, a color TV, or a copier has a significant software component embedded in it. Increasingly, the functionalities and features in these products will be software driven. Similarly, all businesses have a manufacturing and a service component to it. The traditional distinctions are becoming less relevant. We need a whole new language system even to describe these businesses. Further, we need to recognize that the relationship between costs, value to customers, pattern of investments, and the ability to protect those investments are all changing. Often, manufacturing oriented firms have difficulty understanding the logic of embedded software and the skill mix needed to harmoniously blend the two.

8. *Intellectual transformation of major industries.* A large number of indus-

tries are undergoing unprecedented intellectual transformation. The basic paradigms and the disciplines behind these industries are rapidly changing. For example, imaging used to be a chemical business (photography). Imaging is increasingly incorporating electronics—electronic imaging leading to a whole host of new opportunities. The automotive business was primarily mechanical. During the last ten years, the role of electronics in engine and vehicle controls, entertainment, and information have basically transformed that business. Further, new materials such as engineered plastics, are also changing the nature of the industry. Telecommunication is moving from a staid telephone service provider to the provider of a whole host of lifestyle telecommunication products—from fax to mobile phones. We call this an intellectual transformation of the industry as it calls for a whole new set of disciplines, skills, and competencies to be creatively merged with the traditional skills. Thus, a firm like Kodak or Fuji needs to master the new electronics skills and blend them with their historical capabilities in chemical imaging. This demands educating the organization, the channels, customers, and suppliers.

The seven emerging issues will not impact all industries the same way. Neither will all firms in a given industry have the same difficulties coping with the new demands. What is clear is that no one can operate as if it is "business as usual." All firms (and managers) will be forced to reexamine their approaches to management, audit their skill base, recalibrate their performance, and learn new behaviors. Managers must:

1. Develop an ability to conceive of and execute complex strategies;

2. Cope with decreasing degrees of strategic freedom;

3. Protect and nurture invisible assets—intellectual property, commitment of people, brands, multicultural work force, longstanding relationships with host governments, etc.;

4. Cope with an increasingly complex interface between public and private policy;

5. Integrate totally new technologies—learn to operate outside their comfort zone;

6. Provide administrative and intellectual leadership; and

7. Become fast and flexible without loosing clarity and consistency to direction.

While all managers and firms are not grappling with these issues, many of the well-managed firms are. While the contours of the problems and opportunities are becoming visible and understood by managers, the issues are not well researched. In fact, many of the issues get scant research attention from the academic community in the major business schools.

Emerging Issues and the Research Agenda— A Mismatch?*

The influence of the emerging managerial agenda, a result of the inherent nature of the "world of managers" and the competitive challenges on the academic agenda of research and teaching is not yet clear. Needless to say, such a broad statement of the state of the art in research and in management is bound to attract criticism as both an inaccurate portrayal of reality and a disservice to those academics who have labored to advance some of the issues outlined above. The focus of this chapter is not to undervalue the work that is done in dealing with these complex issues by a few scholars, but to suggest that the center of gravity for most academic research in the area of management, as evidenced by publications in scholarly journals, does not reflect a sensitivity to these issues.

The problems of the manager tend to be "messy"; not susceptible to clean modelling. Since substantive issues of strategy and resource allocation are inextricably linked with the organizational processes of planning, budgeting, and rewards, and individual concerns of careers and power, delinking the interactions of the three component parts of the management task into "bite-size pieces" robs it of its richness especially when there is no accepted language system or a disaggregation-reaggregation methodology. The conceptual building blocks of this complex phenomenon have received very little research attention. As such, individual researchers have to contend with one of two unattractive options: behave as if the "bite-size piece" that one is researching is the total reality or undertake research which is "messy," not additive in terms of knowledge and often not replicable. The trap that academic research falls into is either too little effort at theory building or too little understanding of the phenomonen.

An approach that academic research has embraced is to ground itself in a theory and study the phenomenon from the perspective of that theory—be it transaction costs, population ecology, or agency theory. While this can often yield rich insight into parts of the managerial problem, it falls short of de-

---

*There have been some efforts to challenge the relevance of academic research. See, for example: Paul Shrivastava, Rigor and Practical Usefulness of Research in Strategic Management, *Strategic Management Journal*, Vol. 8, 1987, and Jack N. Behrman and Richard I. Levin, Are Business Schools doing their Job? *Harvard Business Review*, January–February 1984. Predictably, these attempts have had little impact on the direction of academic research.

veloping a comprehensive understanding of a theory of managerial action in a complex global environment. Seldom, if ever, are the following questions asked: Are the underlying assumptions of the paradigms used in research culturally neutral? Does it incorporate substance and process? Does the research explicitly recognize the informal and the formal or the relationships between the specifics and the general? Is there a particular action and the framework within which that action is initiated and carried out? What are the toxic side effects of the paradigms and managerial processes (e.g., accounting systems) used by managers?

The disconnect between the problems faced by managers trying to cope with the ever-increasing complexity of global competition and the scope of academic research is obvious. However, this need not be so. The challenge faced by managers is primarily intellectual. The need for a new intellectual anchor—a new framework and a methodology—permeates all aspects of their jobs, be it motivating an international work force or assessing the value of intellectual property.

The "nature" of this disconnect—managers eager for new insights and academics wanting to make an intellectual contribution—can be captured in a list of topics for research. The topics are derived from the emerging patterns of global competition and the world of the DMNC manager described earlier. Here is a sample.

In the area of corporate strategy research, for example, there is very little work done on issues such as:

1. Competition for establishing standards. The total estimated value of businesses where standards is a major problem (computers, telecom, consumer electronics, factory automation, . . .) is estimated to be a trillion dollars or more by the year 2000. Important as standards are to the evolution of these industries, very little research effort is focused here.

2. Participating in emerging nontraditional markets such as India, China, and the former Soviet Union. These represent bureaucratically defined, quasi-market economies. They also represent the next frontier of market opportunities.

3. Managing intellectual transformation of critical industries.

4. Managing invisible assets such as brands on a global basis; assessing their value, and understanding the nature of disciplines required within the firm to maintain a consistent brand positioning around the world.

5. Valuing intellectual property—the legal, managerial, and strategic issues associated with it.

6. Managing collaboration and competition simultaneously. Firms partner across some programs and businesses and compete in others. Often partnerships are time-bound. How do we educate the organization to be both good partners and tough competitors at the same time?

7. Ability to create new competitive space rests not on undirected entrepreneurship but managed innovation. What is the basis for new business creation in a DMNC, on an ongoing basis?

8. How do we account for "invisible assets" such as commitment of the work force, capacity to learn, global brands, core competencies, a global logistics and information network, and a well-developed global supplier network? Do our accounting systems only track physical capital? In the emerging competitive milieu, does that leave us vulnerable to not protecting and investing in critical assets?

9. How do managers create a shared mind-set and a commitment to the firm's goals given a multinational work force?

10. How do we translate concepts (such as value engineering, cycle time, flexibility) into organizational capabilities?

11. What is due process in a large DMNC environment? Can the same standards and rules apply around the world? Should it?

12. What is the process by which knowledge, management disciplines, and a sense of mutual obligations are transmitted and embedded in a large DMNC?

13. What are the differences between individual learning and collective and team learning? When does individual learning become a competency for the organization?

14. How do we manage diversity—ethnic, cultural, gender, and intellectual—in a DMNC?

15. What is the meaning of "governance" in the emerging, network-based, global organization?

The above listing is intended to be suggestive of the types of problems that are waiting to be solved. Needless to say, others can generate an equally interesting list of issues. The point that we want to make is quite simple. There is no dearth of issues that are complex and challenging. Managing is increasingly an intellectual activity. The surprise is that so little of the intellectual energy of the academic community, in business schools, is focused on them as evidenced by the scholarly output.* It is no wonder that managers do not perceive academic output as "relevant" to the task of managing. This situation also leads academics to distance themselves from the "real world" of messy problems. A concerted effort by the academic community, we believe, is needed to create a new "theory of the firm," a view of the value added of management in a complex DMNC, and an approach to understanding the human capacity to cope with complexity. Is the opportunity big enough for academics and managers to work together?

The Way Forward

If we assume that academics in business schools are the producers of knowledge intended to improve practice and managers as the consumers of this knowledge, then as academics we cannot be disconnected from our customers. While the contributions of the two groups—academics and managers—are differentiated, we need to ask ourselves: Do we need a shared agenda? What is the meaning of academic success if our ideas do not lead to managerial success? Can producers survive without customers in the long run? Do we have the courage to discard what we know to seek what will more closely bond us with our customers? Managers need this reexamination of their role in this partnership as well. The development of a new language system, a new set of tools of analysis, and a reexamination of the theory of the firm and the task of management is a collective challenge. Managers and academics, by themselves, cannot do it. We need each other. The stakes are too high to let it evolve without active debate and discussion.

Managers need a careful and honest "audit" of the dogmas that have evolved over the years with a view to fundamentally reevaluate their utility in the competitive milieu of the 1990s and beyond. Academics need to reexamine and "audit" how their research capacity is being spent. What issues are getting the attention? Why? What issues are totally ignored? What is the "relevance" check on research? It is estimated that over $200 million is spent on research in business schools. Each published paper represents an investment of more than $10–15,000. Can society continue to afford research devoid of an active academic-manager partnership, mechanisms for identifying intellectual and administrative dilemmas inherent in globalization, and seeking appropriate and relevant knowledge? This then is the managerial and intellectual challenge of globalization.

---

*A study of the evolution of strategy literature, directed by the author, using an analysis of articles published in the *Administrative Science Quarterly, Harvard Business Review, Sloan Management Review*, and *Strategic Management Journal*, during the period 1970–1990, reveals that less than 5% of the articles published related to the issues identified in this chapter. If we exclude *Harvard Business Review*, the percentage will be even lower. (The data for *Strategic Management Journal* covers the period 1980–1990.)

Index

Organization *(continued)*
  international forms of, 196–99
  of tomorrow, 198–99
Organizational Boundaries, 62
Organizational Competencies, 63–65
Organizational Cultures
  differences in, 152–56
  dimensions of, 153–56
Organizational Design, 67–68
Organizational Development by Layering, 99–101
Organizational Learning, 5, 63–64, 248–53
Outward Bound Metaphor, 209–10

Passino, Jacque, 327–28
Power Distance, 143, 144, 147, 148–49
Privatization, 33–34
Proctor & Gamble, 31

Reed, John, 40
Regionalization of Economic Activity, 16–17, 24–27, 39, 174
Reilly, Ray, 322–31
Research Agenda, 348–51
Research and Develoment (R&D)
  transfer of, 64
  competes with marketing and manufacturing, 32
  increase in, 32
  in Japan, 312
  in shared equity alliances, 42
Riboud, Jean, 188
Robotics, 21, 31
Ruwe, Dean, 327

Schopenhauer, Arthur, 15
Self-Renewal of Japanese MNCs, 300–15
Severance, Dennis G., 325–26, 327–28
"Shukko" System, 308–10
Slack, 39, 41–43
Socialization of Management, 140–42, 167–68, 193
"Soft" Issues, 210–11
Specialization, 22
Staffing, 68–70, 162–64, 310–13
Steinbeck, John, 187
Strategic Alliances
  and academic-industry interface, 335–36
  appraisal and rewards for learning in, 252–53
  and competitive collaboration, 243–47
  design and control of organizational learning in, 253–54

human resource planning in, 249–51
  interdisciplinary, 336–37
  training and development in, 251–52
Strategic Control
  centralization-decentralization, 62
  and reduction of American expatriate managers, 263–75
  and strategic variety, 120–25
Strategic Development and Layering, 98–99
Strategic Layering, 101
Strategic Thinking, 6
Strategic Vision, 9, 302–3
Sub-contracting, 37
Sumner, W. Graham, 37
Symposium on Global Research and Teaching, 321–31

Third World
  foreign indebtedness of, 26
  left out of expansion, 16, 26–27
Thomas, Lawrason D., 328
Three Mile Island, 17
Tichy, Noel M., 322–23
Tichy Development Matrix, 207–8
Training and Development in Strategic Alliances, 251–52
Transformational Leadership, 5
Transformational Workshops, 213–15
Transportation
  costs in global markets, 31
  improvements in, 19–21

Uncertainty Avoidance, 147–52
United States
  cultural exports of, 29–30
  international banking by, 24
  managers abroad decreasing in number, 9, 263–75
  regional trade of, 25
University of Michigan Business School, 321–31

Van Orden, Paul W., 328–29
Variety
  controlled in MNCs, 119–35
  strategic, 120–25
Vision, Company, 110–13

Weick, Karl E., 323–24
Welch, John F., 212–13
Wriston, Walter, 22

Patrick : 576-7794
elis : 834-6893